the photoshop elements book for digital photographers

Scott Kelby

The Photoshop Elements Book for Digital Photographers Team

CREATIVE DIRECTOR
Felix Nelson

TECHNICAL EDITOR
Chris Main

EDITOR
Richard Theriault

PROOFREADER
Barbara Thompson

PRODUCTION DIRECTOR
Kim Gabriel

PRODUCTION LAYOUT
Dave Damstra

PRODUCTION ART
Ted LoCascio
Margie Rosenstein

COVER DESIGNED BY
Felix Nelson

COVER PHOTOS COURTESY OF
Brand X Pictures (www.brandx.com)

THE NEW RIDERS TEAM

ASSOCIATE PUBLISHER
Stephanie Wall

EXECUTIVE EDITOR
Steve Weiss

PRODUCTION MANAGER
Gina Kanouse

SENIOR PROJECT EDITOR
Kristy Knoop

COMPOSITOR
Gloria Schurick

Published by
New Riders Publishing

FIRST EDITION: August 2003

International Standard Book Number: 0-7357139-2-8

Library of Congress Catalog Card Number: 2003109549

07 06 05 04 03   7 6 5 4 3 2

Interpretation of the printing code: the rightmost double-digit number is the year of the book's printing; the rightmost single-digit number is the number of the book's printing. For example, the printing code 03-1 shows that the first printing of the book occurred in 2003.

Composed in Cronos and Helvetica by New Riders Publishing

www.scottkelbybooks.com

For my wonderful wife Kalebra,
and my precious little boy Jordan.
It's amazing just how much joy and love
these two people bring into my life.

ACKNOWLEDGMENTS

First, I want to thank my amazing wife, Kalebra. As I'm writing this, she's lying on the couch across from me reading a book (not one of mine, sadly), but I have to say that just looking at her makes my heart skip a beat, and again reminds me how much I adore her, how genuinely beautiful she is, and how I couldn't live without her. She's the type of woman love songs are written for, and I am, without a doubt, the luckiest man alive to have her as my wife.

Secondly, I want to thank my 6-year-old son, Jordan, who spent many afternoons with his adorable little head resting on my lap as I wrote this book. God has blessed our family with so many wonderful gifts, and I can see them all reflected in his eyes. I'm so proud of him, so thrilled to be his dad, and I dearly love watching him grow to be such a wonderful little guy, with such a tender and loving heart. (You're the greatest, little buddy.)

I have to thank my wonderful, crazy, hilarious, and loving dad for filling me with childhood memories of nothing but fun, laughter, and love. His warmth, compassion, understanding, ethics, and sincerity have guided me my entire life, and I could never repay him for all that he's done for me. I love you, Dad.

I also want to thank my big brother, Jeffrey, for being such a positive influence in my life, for always taking the high road, for always knowing the right thing to say, and just the right time to say it, and for having so much of our dad in you. I'm honored to have you as my brother and my friend.

My heartfelt thanks go to the entire team at KW Media Group, who every day redefine what teamwork and dedication are all about. They are truly a special group of people, who come together to do some really amazing things (on really scary deadlines) and they do it with class, poise, and a can-do attitude that is truly inspiring. I'm so proud to be working with you all.

A special thanks to Dave Cross for his writing contributions, and for all his help in the development of the Elements version of this book. His ideas, input, and hard work have had a major impact and I can't thank him enough.

Thanks to my layout and production crew. In particular, I want to thank my friend and Creative Director, Felix Nelson, for his limitless talent, creativity, input, cover design, overall layout, and just for his flat-out great ideas. To Chris Main for putting every technique through rigorous testing, and catching the little things that other tech editors might've missed. To Kim Gabriel for keeping us all on track and organized, so we could face those really scary deadlines. To Margie Rosenstein for adding her special touch to the look of the book, and to Dave Damstra and Ted LoCascio for giving the book such a tight, clean layout. To Barbara Thompson for stepping in to help proof the book. Thanks to my compadre Dave Moser, whose tireless dedication to creating a quality product makes every project we do better than the last. Thanks to Jim Workman, Jean A. Kendra, and Pete Kratzenberg for their support, and for keeping a lot of plates in the air while I'm writing these books. A special thanks to my Executive Assistant, Kathy Siler, for keeping me on track and focused, and for doing such a wonderful job. Somehow she manages to keep an amazingly upbeat attitude, and puts on a brave face, while behind it all she knows all too well that when my World Champion Tampa Bay Buccaneers face her beloved Redskins later this year, the Redskins are going to take yet another loss at home, perhaps keeping them out of the playoffs. Again. (I'm going to pay for that one.)

I want to thank my longtime friend and first-class Editor, Richard Theriault. This is the ninth book Dick has worked on with us, and we're totally hooked—we couldn't do it without him, and we wouldn't want to if we could.

I owe a special debt of gratitude to my friends, Kevin Ames and Jim DiVitale, for taking the time to share their ideas, techniques, concepts, and vision for a Photoshop Elements book for digital photographers that would really make a difference. Extra special thanks to Kevin for spending hours with me sharing his retouching techniques, as well.

I want to thank all the photographers, retouchers, and Photoshop experts who've taught me so much over the years, including Jack Davis, Deke McClelland, Ben Willmore, Julieanne Kost, David Cuerdon, Robert Dennis, Helene DeLillo, Jim Patterson, Doug Gornick, Manual Obordo, Dan Margulis, Peter Bauer, Joe Glyda, and Russell Preston Brown.

Thanks to the brilliant and gifted digital photographers who graciously lent their talents to this book, including Carol Freeman, Jeannie Theriault, Jim Patterson, Jack Davis, Nancy Adamson, and Todd Morrison.

Also, my personal thanks to Jeffrey Burke at Brand X Pictures for enabling me to use some of their wonderful photography in this book.

Also thanks to my friends at Adobe Systems: Barbara Rice, Terry White, Gwyn Weisberg, Kevin Connor, Addy Roff, Tanguy Leborgne, Karen Gauthier, Julieanne, and Russell.

Thanks to my friend and Editor, Steve Weiss (who totally "gets it"), and to Nancy Ruenzel at Peachpit Publishing Group for welcoming me so warmly into their fold, and for her commitment to excellence in book publishing.

And most importantly, my deepest thanks to the Lord Jesus Christ for always hearing my prayers, for always being there when I need Him, for blessing me with a wonderful life I truly love, and such a warm loving family to share it with.

ABOUT THE AUTHOR

Scott Kelby

Scott is Editor-in-Chief and co-founder of *Photoshop User* magazine, Editor-in-chief of Nikon's *Capture User* magazine, and Editor-in-Chief of *Mac Design Magazine.* He is President of the National Association of Photoshop Professionals (NAPP), the trade association for Adobe® Photoshop® users, and he's President of KW Media Group, Inc., a Florida-based software education and publishing firm.

Scott is author of the best-selling books *Photoshop 7 Down & Dirty Tricks, Photoshop Photo-Retouching Secrets, The Photoshop Book for Digital Photographers* and co-author of *Photoshop 7 Killer Tips,* all from New Riders Publishing. He's a contributing author to the books *Photoshop Effects Magic,* also from New Riders; *Maclopedia, the Ultimate Reference on Everything Macintosh* from Hayden Books; and *Adobe Web Design and Publishing Unleashed* from Sams.net Publishing. Scott has authored two best-selling Macintosh books: *Mac OS X Jaguar Killer Tips,* and the award-winning *Macintosh: The Naked Truth,* both also from New Riders; and the new *Mac OS X Conversion Kit: 9 to 10 Side-by-Side, Jaguar Edition* from Peachpit Press.

Scott introduced his first software title in 2003 called "Kelby's Notes for Adobe Photoshop" which adds the answers to the 100 most-asked Photoshop questions, accessed from directly within Photoshop.

Scott is Training Director for the Adobe Photoshop Seminar Tour, Conference Technical Chair for the PhotoshopWorld Conference & Expo, and he is a speaker at graphics trade shows and events around the world. He is also featured in a series of Adobe Photoshop training videos and DVDs and has been training Adobe Photoshop users since 1993.

For more background info on Scott, visit www.scottkelby.com.

CONTRIBUTING AUTHOR

Dave Cross

Dave Cross is Senior Developer, Education & Curriculum for the National Association of Photoshop Professionals (NAPP), and Lead Instructor for the Photoshop Seminar Tour. He is a member of the Instructor "Dream Team" at the PhotoshopWorld Conference & Expo and teaches at the Mac Design Conference. Dave is Contributing Editor to *Mac Design Magazine,* contributing writer to *Photoshop User* magazine, and Editor of *Enhance,* the Photoshop Elements newsletter.

Dave is the co-author of two books: *Photoshop 7 & Illustrator 10: Create Great Advanced Graphics* (Friends of Ed, 2002) and *Photoshop 7 Trade Secrets* (Friends of Ed, 2002). He is featured on a series of training videos and DVDs, including *Photoshop Elements for Beginners* and *Photoshop Elements for Photographers.*

Prior to joining NAPP, Dave ran his own consulting and training business in Ottawa, Canada, training thousands of people across North America since 1989.

TABLE OF CONTENTS

CHAPTER 1 2

Start Me Up

Mastering the File Browser

Saving Your Digital Negatives 4
Creating a Contact Sheet for Your CD 6
Browser Basics 12
Browser Essentials 15
Batch Renaming Your Files 22
Editing in the Browser 26

CHAPTER 2 28

Cream of the Crop

Cropping and Resizing

Custom Sizes for Photographers 30
Cropping Photos 34
Cropping to a Specific Size 37
Cropping Without the Crop Tool 39
Using the Crop Tool to Add More Canvas Area 41
Straightening Crooked Photos 43
Using a Visible Grid for Straightening Photos 45
Resizing Digital Camera Photos 48
Resizing and How to Reach Those Hidden Free Transform Handles 51
The Cool Trick for Turning Small Photos into Poster-Sized Prints 52

CHAPTER 3 54

The Big Fixx

Digital Camera Image Problems

Compensating for "Too Much Flash" or Overexposure 56
Removing Digital Noise (AKA Color Aliasing) 58
Fixing Photos Where You Wish You Hadn't Used Flash 60

Fixing Underexposed Photos 63

When You Forget to Use Fill Flash 65

Instant Red-Eye Removal 68

Removing Red Eye and Recoloring the Eye 70

Repairing Keystoning 74

CHAPTER 4 78

Color Me Badd

Color Correction for Photographers

Before You Color Correct Anything, Do This First! 80

Color Correcting Digital Camera Images 82

Drag-and-Drop Instant Color Correction 90

Automated Color Correction (Correction for Chickens) 93

Adjusting Flesh Tones 94

Color Correcting One Problem Area Fast! 96

Getting a Better Conversion from Color to Black & White 99

CHAPTER 5 104

The Mask

Selection Techniques

Selecting Square, Rectangular, or Round Areas 106

Softening Those Harsh Edges 108

How to Select Things that Aren't Round, Square, or Rectangular 109

Selecting Areas by Their Color 111

Making Selections Using a Brush 112

Selecting Everything on a Layer at Once! 113

Saving Your Selections 114

Getting Elements to Help You Make Tricky Selections 115

CHAPTER 6 116

Head Games

Retouching Portraits

Removing Blemishes 118

Removing Dark Circles Under Eyes 122

Lessening Freckles or Facial Acne 124

Removing or Lessening Wrinkles 128

Dodging and Burning Done Right 130

Colorizing Hair 134

Whitening the Eyes 136

Making Eyes that Sparkle 138

Enhancing Eyebrows and Eyelashes 140

Whitening and Brightening Teeth 144

Removing Hot Spots 146

Glamour Skin Softening 148

Transforming a Frown into a Smile 150

Digital Nose Job 152

CHAPTER 7 154

Invasion of the Body Snatchers

Body Sculpting

Slimming and Trimming 156

Removing Love Handles 158

Slimming Buttocks, Thighs, and, Arms 160

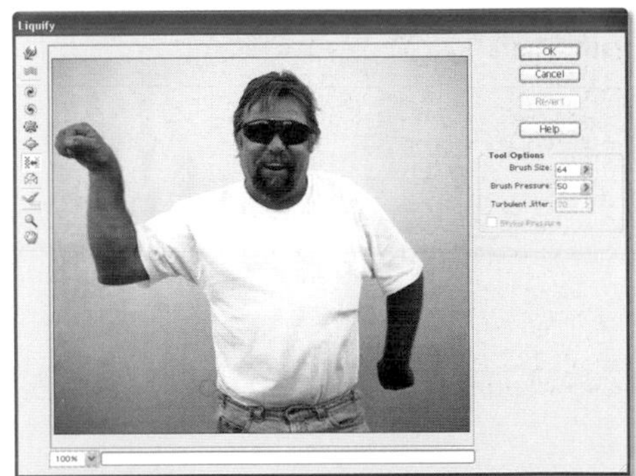

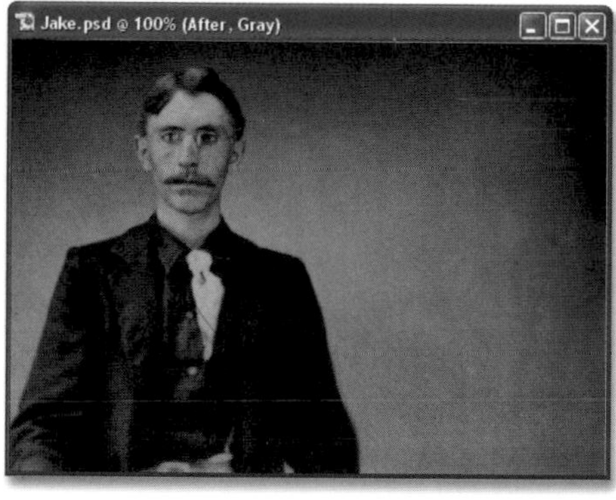

CHAPTER 8 166

38 Special

Photographic Special Effects

Blurred Lighting Vignette 168
Using Color for Emphasis 170
Adding Motion Where You Want It 172
Changing an Object's Color 174
Replacing the Sky 176
Replicating Photography Filters 178
Creating Photo Montages 180
Adding Depth of Field 182
Creating the Classic Vignette Effect 184
Sepia Tone Effect 186
Creating a Photo Backdrop 188
Turning Photos into Drawings 192
Getting the Polaroid Look 196
Photomerge 200

CHAPTER 9 206

Get Back

Photo Restoration Techniques

Repairing Washed Out Photos 208
Colorizing Black & White Photos 210
Removing Specks, Dust, and Scratches 212
Repairing Damaged or Missing Parts 214
Repairing Rips and Tears 216

CHAPTER 10 218
Sharp Dressed Man
Professional Sharpening Techniques

Basic Sharpening 220
Luminosity Sharpening 225
Edge Sharpening Technique 227
Sharpening with Layers to Avoid Color Shifts
and Noise 230

CHAPTER 11 232
The Show Must Go On
Showing It to Your Clients

Watermarking and Adding Copyright Info 234
Putting Your Photos up on the Web 238
Getting One 5″x7″, Two 2.5″ x 3.5″, and Four
Wallet Size on One Print 242
How to E-Mail Photos 246

Contributing Photographers 248
Index 250

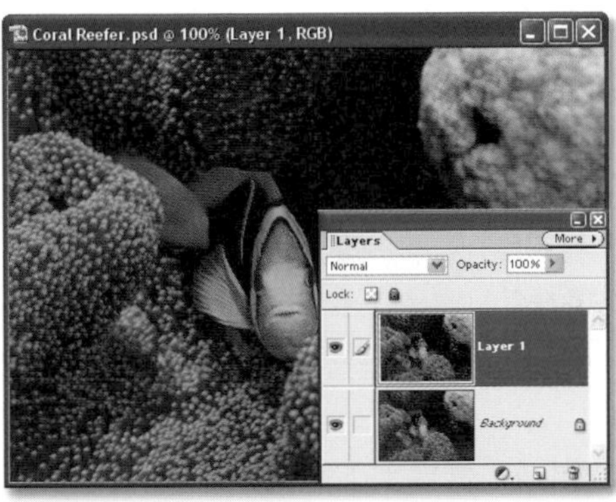

READ THIS FIRST, BEFORE SOMETHING BAD HAPPENS

I had no intentions of writing a book on Photoshop Elements

Actually, I had no intentions of writing the book that led to this book (which was on Photoshop 7.0), but it's because of that book, that you're holding this book. (Note: I intentionally made that confusing, so you'd have to read how the story of how the first book came about, which explains why it was so important for me to write this special version for Photoshop Elements). See, on some level, doesn't that make sense?

So here it was, about four weeks before I would be flying up to New York City to teach a one-day seminar to more than 1,200 professional Photoshop junkies. (Okay, it was more like 1,160 pros, 42 people who just wanted a paid day off from work, and one total freak who kept asking me if I'd ever been in prison. I told him unequivocally, "Not as far as you know.")

Anyway, the seminar was just four weeks away, and there was one session that I still didn't have an outline for. It was called "Correcting Photos from Digital Cameras" (which is dramatically better than my original working title for the class, "Die, Traditional Camera User, Die!").

I knew what I needed to cover in the session because for the past ten years I've trained thousands of traditional photographers on how to use Photoshop. Most of them either have now gone digital or are in the process of going digital, and all these digital photographers generally seem to have the same type of Photoshop questions, which I'm actually thankful for, because now I can give them the answers. If they constantly asked different questions, I'd get stumped from time to time, and then I'd have to resort to "Plan B" (providing answers that sound good, but are in reality just wild-ass guesses).

So I knew what I had to cover, but I wanted to do some research first, to see if other people in the industry were addressing these questions the same way I was, or did they have a different take on them, different techniques or ideas? So I went out and bought every single book I could find about digital photography and Photoshop. I spent nearly $1.2 million. Okay, it wasn't quite that much, but let's just say for the next few months I would have to cut out some luxuries such as running water, trash collection, heat, etc.

I started reading through all these books, and the first thing I thought I'd look up was how they dealt with digital noise (High ISO noise, Blue channel noise, color aliasing, etc.), but as I went through them, I was amazed to find out that not one single book addressed it. Not a one. Honestly, I was shocked. I get asked this question many times at every single seminar, yet not one of these books even mentioned it. So then I started looking for how they work with 16-bit photos. Nothing. Well, one book mentioned it, but they basically said "it's not for you—it's for high-end pros with $15,000 cameras." I just couldn't believe it—I was stunned. So I kept up my search for more topics I'd been asked about again and again, with the same results.

Well, I went ahead with my New York session as planned, and by all accounts it was a big hit. I had photographer after photographer coming up to tell me, "Thank you so much—those are exactly the things I was hoping to learn." That's when I realized that there's a book missing—a book for people who already know how to shoot, they even know what they want to do in Photoshop; they just need somebody to show them how to do it. Somebody to show them how to deal with the special challenges (and amazing opportunities) of using digital photos with Photoshop. I was so excited, because I knew in my heart I could write that book.

So now I had intentions

The day after the seminar I flew home and immediately called my Editor at New Riders (we'll call him "Steve" because, well…that's his name) and I said, "I know what I want my next book to be—a Photoshop book for digital photographers." There was a long uncomfortable pause. Steve's a great guy, and he really knows this industry, but I could tell he was choking a bit on this one. He politely said, "Really, a digital photography book, huh?" It was clear he wasn't nearly as excited about this concept as I was (and that's being kind). He finally said, "Ya know, there are already plenty of digital photography books out there," and I agreed with him, because I just about went broke buying them all. So now I had to convince my Editor that not only was this a good idea, but that it was such a good idea that he should put our other book projects on hold so I could write this book, of which there are (as he put it), "already plenty of digital photography books out there."

Here's what I told my Editor what would be different about my digital photography book:

(1) It's not a digital photography book; it's a Photoshop book. There'd be no discussion of film (gasp!), f-stops, lenses, or how to frame a photo. If they don't already know how to shoot, this book just won't be for them. (*Note: Editors hate it when you start listing the people the book* **won't** *be appropriate for. They want to hear, "It's perfect for everybody! From grandma right up to White House press photographers," but sadly, this book just isn't.)*

(2) I would skip the "Here's What a Digital Camera Is" section and the "Here's Which Printer to Buy" section, because they were in all those other books that I bought. Instead, I'd start the book at the moment the photo comes into Photoshop from the camera.

(3) It would work the way digital photographers really work—in the order they work—starting with sorting and categorizing photos from the shoot, dealing with common digital photography problems, color correcting the photos, selecting areas to work, retouching critical areas, adding photographic special effects, sharpening their photos, and then preparing the photo to be output to a print.

(4) It wouldn't be another Photoshop book that focuses on explaining every aspect of every dialog box. No sirree—instead, this book would do something different—it would show them how to do it! This is what makes it different. It would show photographers step-by-step how to do all those things they keep asking at my seminars, sending me e-mails about, and posting questions about in our forums—it would "show them how to do it!"

For example, I told Steve that about every Photoshop book out there includes info on the Unsharp Mask filter. They all talk about what the Amount, Radius, and Threshold sliders do, and how those settings affect the pixels. They all do that. But you know what they generally *don't* do? They don't give you any actual settings to use! Usually, not even a starting point. Some provide "numerical ranges to work within," but basically they explain how the filter works, and then leave it up to you to develop your own settings. I told him I wouldn't do that. I would flat-out give them some great Unsharp Mask filter settings—the same settings used by many professionals, even though I know some highfalutin Photoshop expert might take issue with them. I would come out and say, "Hey, use this setting when sharpening people. Use this setting to correct slightly out-of-focus photos. Use this setting on landscapes, etc." I give students in my live seminars these settings, why shouldn't I share them in my book? He agreed. I also told him that sharpening is much more than just using the Unsharp Mask filter, and it's much more important to photographers than the three or four pages every other book dedicates to it. I wanted to do an entire chapter showing all the different sharpening techniques, step-by-step, giving different solutions for different sharpening challenges.

I told him about the File Browser, and how there's so much to it, it's just about a separate program unto itself, yet nobody's really covering the things photographers are telling me they need to know—like automatically renaming their digital camera photos with names that make sense. Other books mention that you can do that in the File Browser—I want to be the guy that "shows them how to do it!" I want a whole chapter just on the File Browser.

Steve was starting to come on board with the idea. What he didn't want was the same thing I didn't want—another digital photography book that rehashes what every other digital photography and Photoshop book has already done. Well, Steve went with the idea, and thanks to him, you're holding a the second version of the book that I am so genuinely excited to be able to bring you. But the way the book was developed beyond that took it further than Steve or I had planned.

How the book was developed

When Steve gave me the final approval (it was more like, "Okay, but this better be good or we'll both be greeting people by saying, 'Would you like to try one of our Extra Value Meals today?'"), I sat down with two of the industry's top digital photographers—commercial product photographer Jim DiVitale and fashion photographer Kevin Ames—to get their input on the book. These two guys are amazing—they both split their time between shooting for some of the world's largest corporations, and teaching other professional digital photographers how to pull off Photoshop miracles at events such as PhotoshopWorld, PPA/PEI's Digital Conference, and a host of other events around the world.

We spent hours hammering out which techniques would have to be included in the book, and I can't tell you how helpful and insightful their input was, and this book is far better than it would have been thanks to their contributions.

New and improved (with the same great taste!)

When we first released *The Photoshop Book for Digital Photographers* it became a huge hit overnight. In fact, as I write this introduction today (months after its release), on Amazon.com (the world's largest bookstore) not only is it the best-selling book on digital photography, it's the number one selling book of ALL computer books on Amazon.com, and it's ranked as high as #12 of ALL books on Amazon.com. Pretty freaky!

In short—the concept worked, and that's why I knew I had to do a special version of the book for Photoshop Elements users because Elements was designed from the beginning as a tool for digital photography. In fact, Elements has features for digital photographers that not even the full-blown Photoshop 7.0 (at five times the price) still doesn't offer. That let me cover things I couldn't cover in the Photoshop 7.0 version of the book, and that's especially gratifying for me.

Best of all, I learned a lot from writing that original book, and I've learned a lot of new techniques since I wrote it; and you're getting the benefit of both in this new version of the book just for Elements users.

This version has a secret weapon

Although Elements does offer some cool digital photography features Photoshop 7.0 doesn't offer, obviously there are plenty of features that Photoshop 7.0 has, that Elements 2.0 still doesn't have (things like Layer Masking, Channel Mixer, etc.). But here's the cool part: the single thing that I'm most proud of in this Elements book is that I've been able to figure out workarounds, cheats, and some fairly ingenious ways to replicate some of those Photoshop features from right within Elements. In some cases, it may take a few more steps to get there than it does in Photoshop 7.0, but son-of-a-gun, the result looks pretty darn close, and you'll be the only one who'll know the effect was created in Elements, not in Photoshop 7.0. This will test how good you are at keeping secrets.

So what's not in this book?

There are some things I intentionally didn't put in this book. Like punctuation marks (kidding). No, seriously, I tried not to put things in this book that are already in every other Photoshop book out there. For example, I don't have a chapter on the Layers palette, or a chapter on the painting tools, or a chapter showing how each of Elements' 102 filters looks when it's applied to the same photograph. I also didn't include a chapter on printing to your color inkjet because (a) every Photoshop book does that, and (b) every printer uses different printer driver software, and if I showed an Epson color inkjet workflow, you can bet you'd have an HP or a Canon printer (or vice versa) and then you'd just get mad at me.

Is this book for you?

I can't tell you that for sure, so let's take a simple yet amazingly accurate test that will determine without a doubt if this book is for you. Please answer the following questions:

(1) Do you now, or will you soon have a digital camera?

(2) Do you now, or will you soon have Photoshop Elements?

(3) Do you now, or will you soon have $29.99 (the retail price of this book)?

Scoring: If you answered "Yes" to question #3 then yes, this book is for you. If you answered yes to questions 1, or 2, that certainly is a good indicator, too.

Is this book for Windows users, Mac users, or both?

Because Elements is identical on Windows and on the Macintosh, the book is designed for both platforms. However, the keyboard on a PC is slightly different from the keyboard on a Mac, so any time I give a keyboard shortcut in the book, I give both the PC and Mac keyboard shortcuts. See, I care.

How should you use this book?

You can treat this as a "jump-in-anywhere" book because I didn't write it as a "build-on-what-you-learned-in-Chapter-1" type of book. For example, if you just bought this book, and you want to learn how to whiten someone's teeth for a portrait you're retouching, you can just turn to page 144, and you'll be able to follow along and do it immediately. That's because I spell everything out. Don't let that throw you if you've been using Elements since version 1.0.; I had to do it because although some of the people that will buy this book are talented traditional photographers, since they're just now "going digital," they may not know anything about Elements. I didn't want to leave them out, or make it hard for them, so I really spell things out like "Go under the Image menu, under Adjust Color, and choose Levels" rather than just writing "Open Levels." However, I did put the chapters in an order that follows a typical correction, editing, and retouching process; so you might find it useful to start with Chapter 1 and move your way through the book in sequence.

The important thing is that wherever you start, have fun with it, and even more importantly, tell your friends about it so I can recoup the $1.2 million I spent on all those digital photography books.

Wait, one more thing! You can download the photos used in the book.

Another thing I wanted to do was to feature beautiful photographic images throughout the book. I was able to convince some of my very favorite photographers to lend some of their work for the book (learn more about them on pages 248–249). I also asked what I feel is the hottest up-and-coming royalty-free stock provider, Brand X Pictures (www.brandx.com), to lend some of their wonderful images for the book, and they graciously agreed. I couldn't be more delighted with their breadth of imagery and their wonderful photography that goes far beyond the standard "businessman-shaking-hands" stock photos that permeate the rest of the market. They're really doing something special in royalty-free stock and I'm indebted to them for their generosity.

Thanks to these photographers, and Brand X Pictures, most of the photos used in this book are available for you to download from the book's companion Web site at **www.scottkelbybooks.com/elementsphotos.html**. Of course, the whole idea is that you'd use these techniques on your own photos, but if you want to practice on these, I won't tell anybody. Okay, now turn the page and get to work!

Photographer | Jim Patterson

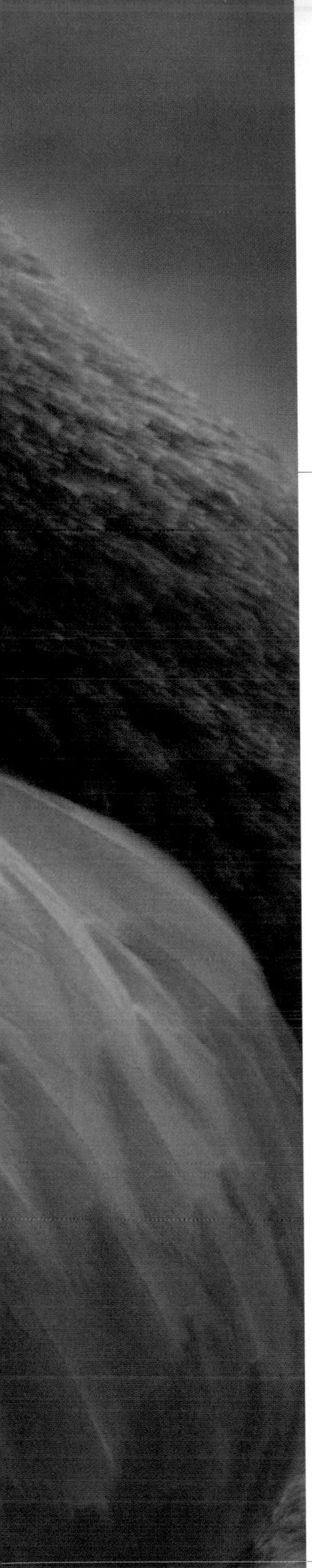

At first, you might not think that Photoshop Elements' File Browser deserves its own chapter, but when you look at all the things it's done for the community (including taking meals to other

Start Me Up
mastering the file browser

software applications that are less fortunate), you realize it probably does deserve it after all. Especially when you take into consideration the fact that the File Browser all by itself is probably more powerful than many stand-alone products, like the Whopper (that computer in the movie *War Games* with Matthew Broderick) or Microsoft Office 2000. Sure, the Whopper could simulate a Soviet First Strike, but frankly, it was pretty lame at sorting and categorizing your photos (as is Microsoft Office). In fact, I'm not sure the Whopper could sort or categorize photos at all, which is probably why no Photoshop Elements book to date has a chapter on the Whopper; but you'd think that with all the cool things the File Browser does, surely at least one Photoshop Elements book out there would dedicate a chapter to it, right? Well, not as far as I've found. So I set out to do just that—really dig into to the meat of the Browser, uncover its hidden power, and see if once and for all it was really written by a man named Professor Faulken (this is precisely why they shouldn't let me write these chapter intros after 1:00 a.m.).

Saving Your Digital Negatives

Okay, I know this is the File Browser chapter, but there are just a couple of critically important things we have to do before we actually open Photoshop Elements.

Step One:

Plug your card reader (CompactFlash card, Smartcard, etc.) into your computer and the images on the card will appear on your hard drive (as shown). Before you do anything else, before you even open Elements, you need to burn these photos to a CD. Don't open the photos, adjust them, choose your favorites, and then burn them to a CD—burn them *now*—right off the bat.

The reason this is so important is that these are your negatives—your digital negatives, which are no different than the negatives you'd get from a film lab after they process your film. By burning a CD now, before you enter Elements, you're creating a set of digital negatives that can never be accidentally erased or discarded—you'll always have these "digital negatives."

Now, what if you don't have a CD burner? That's easy—buy one. It's that critical, and such a key part of your digital setup. Luckily, burning CDs has become so fast, inexpensive (you can buy blank writable CDs for around 10¢ each), and easy-to-do that you can't afford to skip this step.

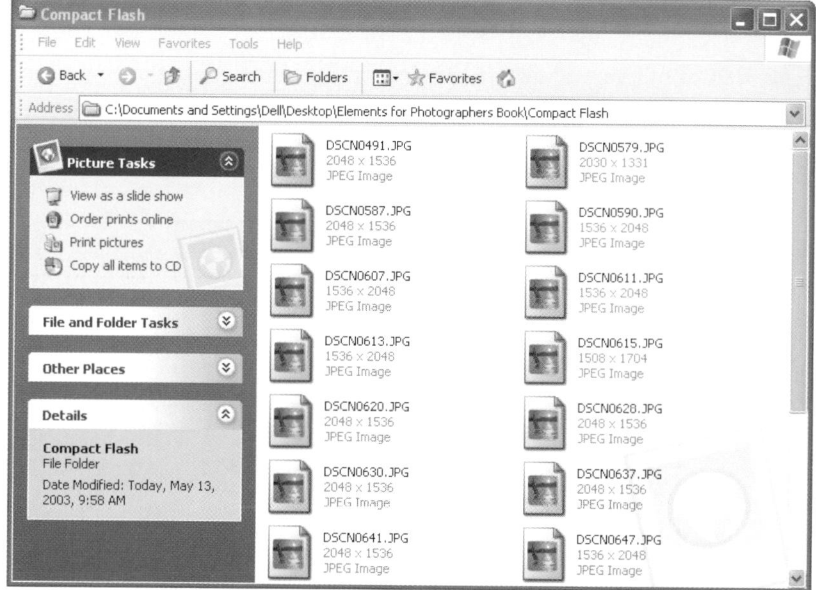

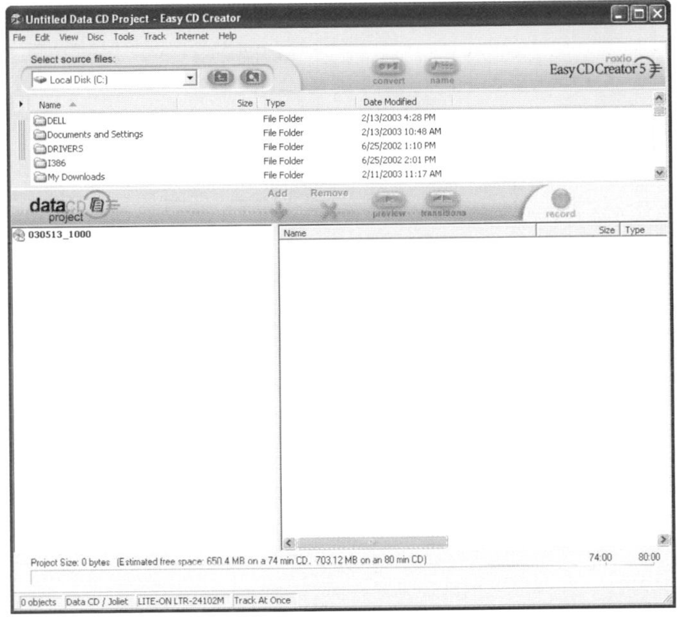

Step Two:

My personal favorite CD-burning software is Roxio Toast Titanium for the Macintosh or Easy CD Creator for Windows (its interface is shown here). It's become very popular, partially because its easy-to-use drag-and-drop interface is a real timesaver. Here's how it works: Select all the images from your card reader, then click-and-drag the whole bunch into the data window.

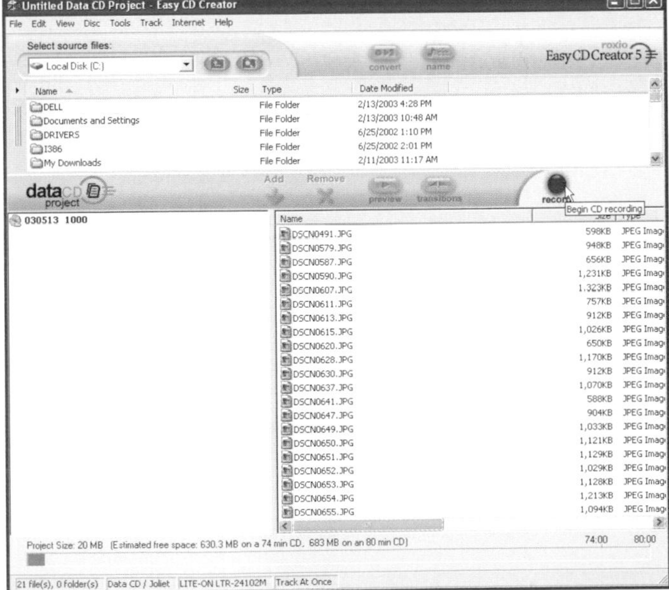

Step Three:

Once your images appear in the data window, double-click on the tiny CD icon in the window and give your disk a name. Then simply click the record button and Toast (or Easy CD Creator) does the rest, leaving you with a reliable, protected set of digital negatives. If you're the extra-careful type (read as "paranoid"), you can burn yourself another copy to keep as a second backup. There's no loss of quality, so burn as many copies as you need to feel secure (remember, just because you're paranoid, doesn't mean they're not out to get you).

Creating a Contact Sheet for Your CD

All right, your CD of "digital negatives" is burned and it's time to launch Elements, but before you go any further, you can save yourself a lot of time and frustration down the road if you create a CD-jewel-box-sized contact sheet now. That way, when you pick up the CD, you'll see exactly what's on the disc before you even insert it into your computer. Luckily, the process of creating this contact sheet is automated, and after you make a few decisions on how you want your contact sheet to look, Photoshop Elements takes it from there.

Step One:

In Photoshop Elements, go under the File menu, under Print Layouts, and choose Contact Sheet.

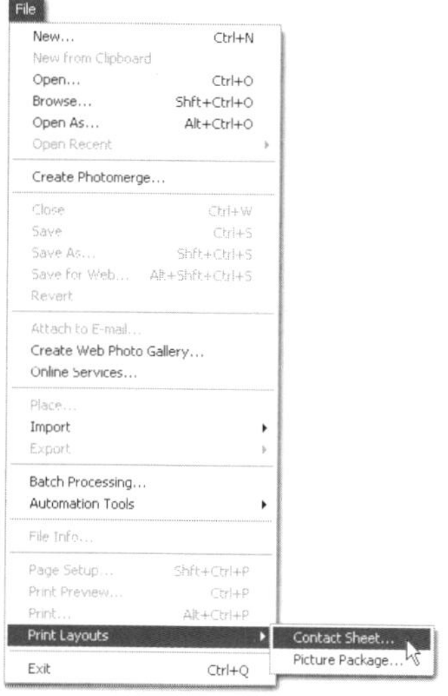

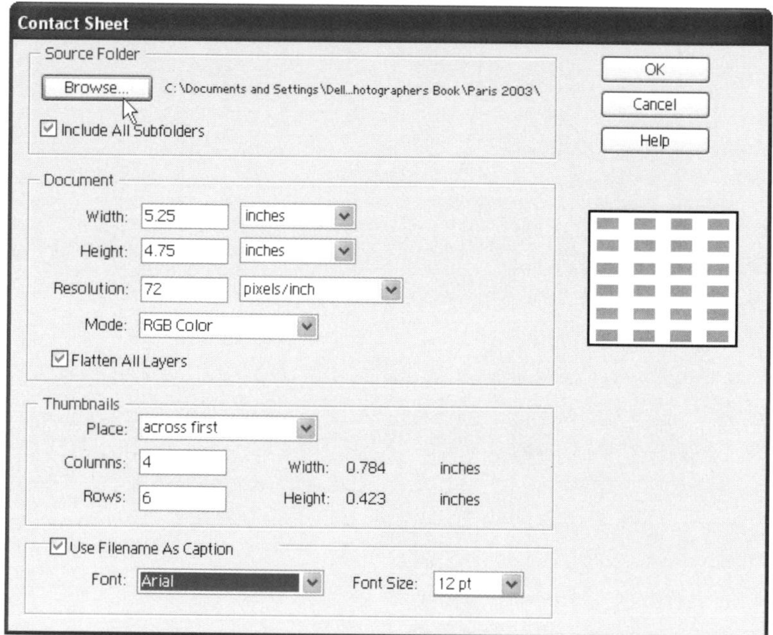

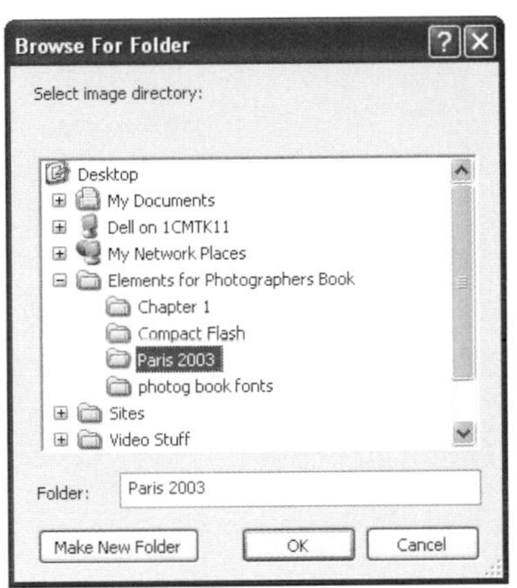

Step Two:

When the Contact Sheet dialog appears, (opposite page) under the Source Folder section, click the Browse (Mac: Choose) button and the standard Open dialog will appear (shown here). Navigate to your newly burned CD and click the OK (Mac: Choose) button in your Select dialog box. This tells Elements to make your contact sheet from the images on your CD.

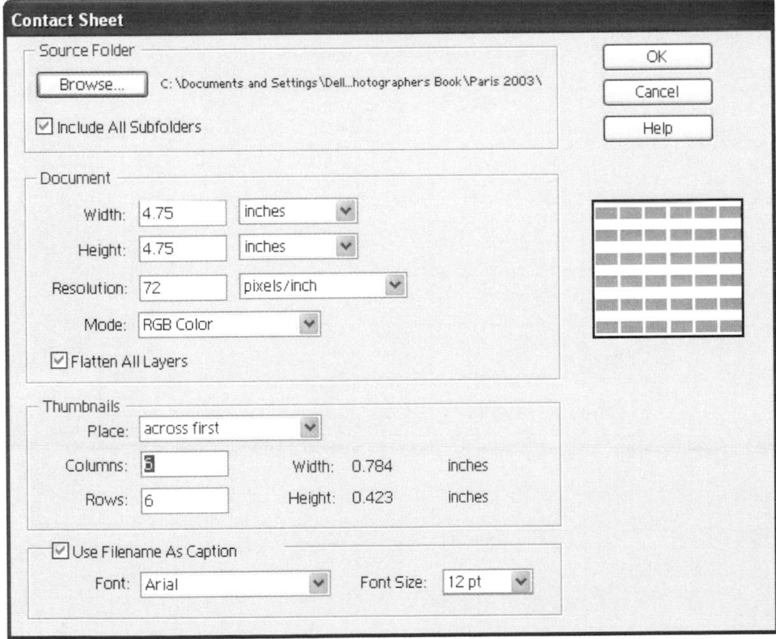

Step Three:

The rest of the dialog box is for you to pick how you want your contact sheet to look. Under the Document section of the dialog, enter the Width and Height of your jewel box cover (the standard size is 4.75" x 4.75") and the Resolution for your images. (I usually choose a low resolution of 72 ppi because the thumbnails wind up being so small they don't need to be a high resolution, and Contact Sheet runs faster with low-res images.)

I also leave the Mode as RGB (the default) and I choose to Flatten All Layers; that way I don't end up with a large multi-layered Elements document. I just want a document that I can print once and then delete.

The Thumbnails section is perhaps the most important part of this dialog, because this is where you choose the layout for your contact sheet's thumbnails (Columns and Rows). Luckily, Adobe put a preview box on the far right side of the dialog, using little gray boxes to represent

Continued

how your thumbnails will look. Change the number of Rows or Columns and this live preview will give you an idea of how your layout will look.

Lastly, at the bottom of the dialog, you can decide if you want to have Elements print the file's name below each thumbnail on your contact sheet. I strongly recommend leaving this feature turned on. Here's why:

One day you may have to go back to this CD looking for a photo. The thumbnail will let you see if the photo you're looking for is on this CD (so you've narrowed your search a bit), but if there's no name below the image, you'll have to launch Elements and use the Browser to search through every photo to locate the exact one you saw on the cover.

However, if you spot the photo on the cover, and see its name, then you just open Elements, then open that file. Believe me, it's one of those things that will keep you from ripping your hair out by the roots, one by one.

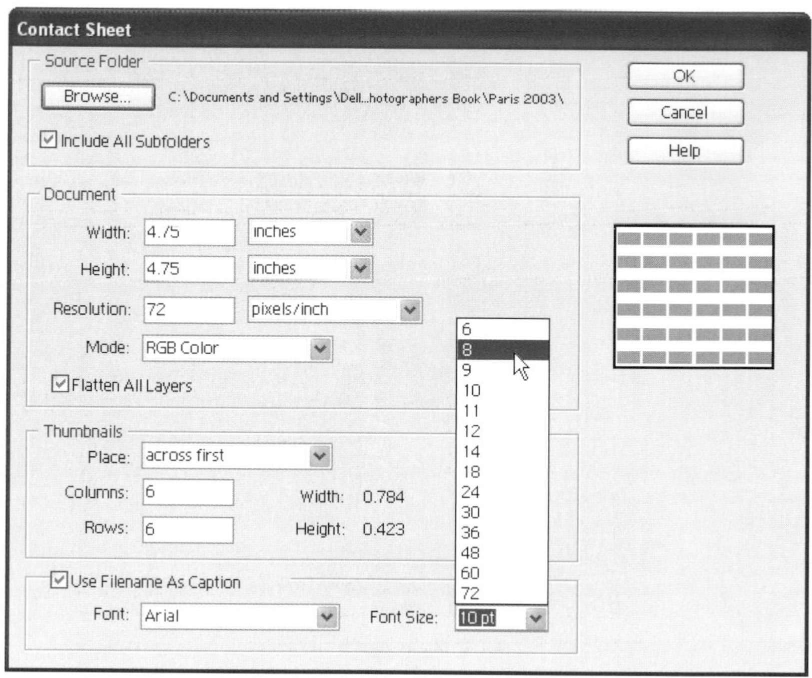

There's also a pop-up menu for choosing from a handful of fonts and font sizes for your thumbnail captions. The font choices are somewhat lame, but...well, that's all you've got!

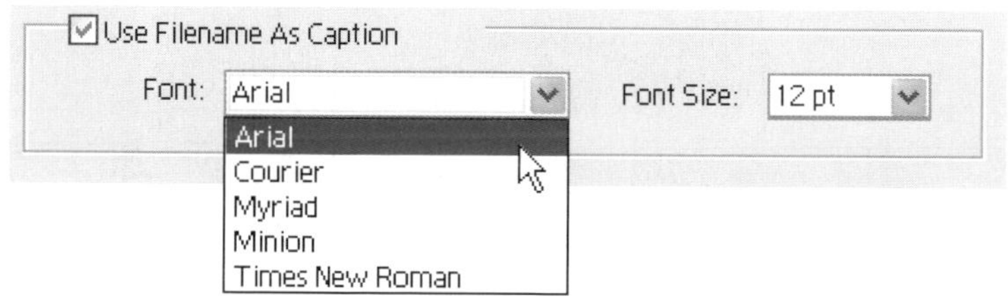

When you put a lot of thumbnails on your contact sheet, you'll need to make the font size smaller, or you'll see only the first few characters.

Here's the same contact sheet with a much smaller font size. Not only can you now read the full name but the thumbnails are larger too.

TIP: When you're choosing a font size for your thumbnail captions, make sure you decrease the default size of 12 to something significantly lower. This is because of the long file names assigned to the images from your digital camera. In this example, I had to lower the Font Size to 6 to actually be able to read the entire file name under each thumbnail. If I left the Font Size at the default of 12, you'd get the result shown at top, where you see only the first few letters of the file name, making the whole naming thing pretty much useless. So how small should you make your type? The more thumbnails you're fitting on your contact sheet, the smaller you'll need to make the Font Size. Also note that in the contact sheet above, the thumbnails themselves are actually smaller than the thumbnails in the image below because they need to make room for the larger 12-point type.

Continued

Step Four:

Now all you have to do is click OK, sit back, and let Elements do its thing. (It may take up to two and half hours to create a single contact sheet. Kidding! Had you going there, didn't I?) It only takes a minute or so, and when you're done, you're left with a contact sheet like the one shown at right, with rows of thumbnails and each photo's file name appearing as a caption below its thumbnail.

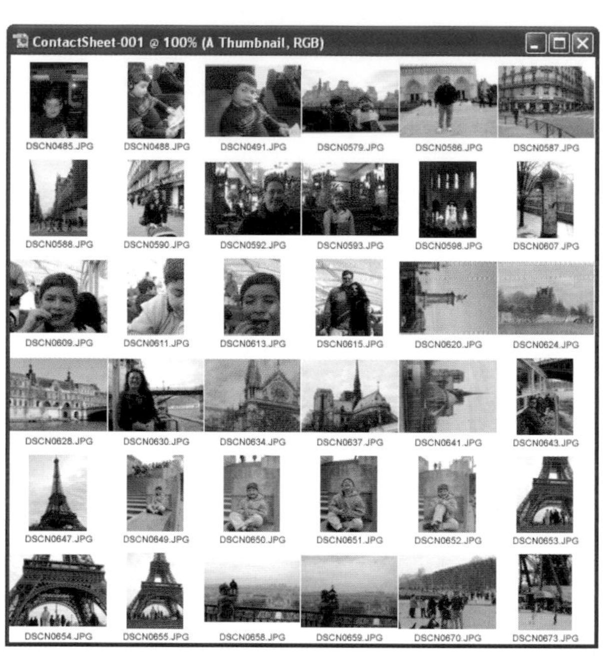

Step Five:

This is more like a tip than a step, but a number of photographers add a second contact sheet to make it even easier to track down the exact image they're looking for. It's based on the premise that in every roll (digital or otherwise) there's usually one or two key shots—two really good "keepers" that will normally be the ones you'll go searching for on this disc (after all, it's pretty rare to shoot 30 or 40 shots and each one of them is just fantastic. Usually, there's a couple of great ones, 15 or so that are "okay" and the rest shall never see the light of day, so to speak). So what they do is make an additional contact sheet that either becomes the front cover of the jewel case (with the regular contact sheet on the inside cover of the case), or vice versa (the regular contact sheet is visible on the outside of the jewel case, and this

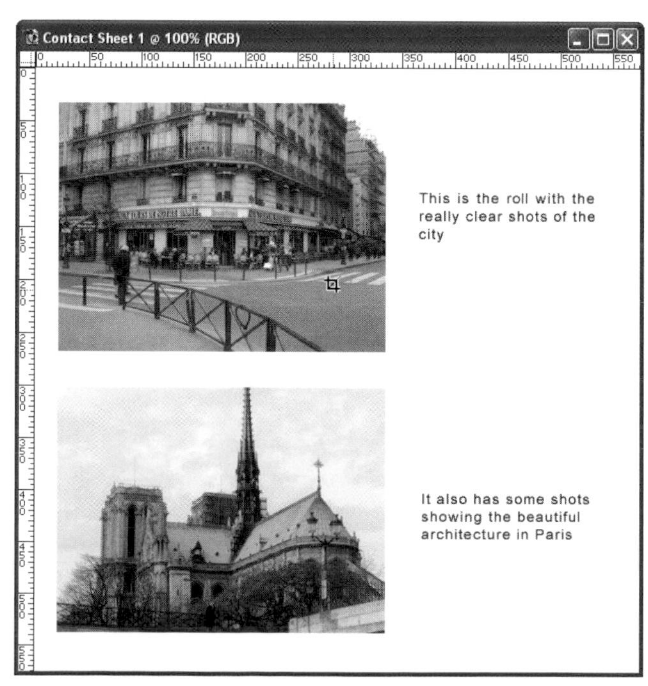

additional contact sheet is on the inside). They create this additional contact sheet manually and only include the one or two key photos from that roll, along with a description of the shots, to make finding the right image even easier. The capture shown on the previous page (bottom) shows a two-photo contact sheet for the cover of the CD jewel case.

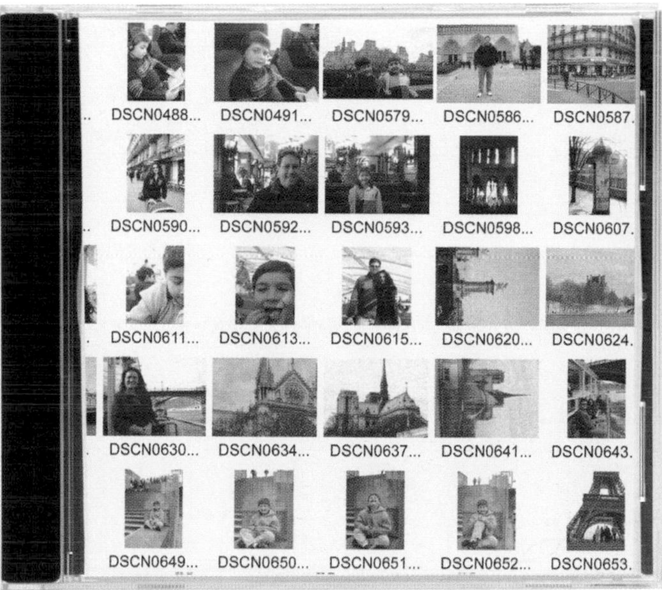

Step Six:

Here's the final result, after the contact sheet has been printed and fitted to your CD jewel case.

Browser Basics

Okay, we've burned our CD and we've created our contact sheet to keep track of all our images, so now we're going to open the images right from the CD using the File Browser (which is what we use to sort and categorize our digital camera images).

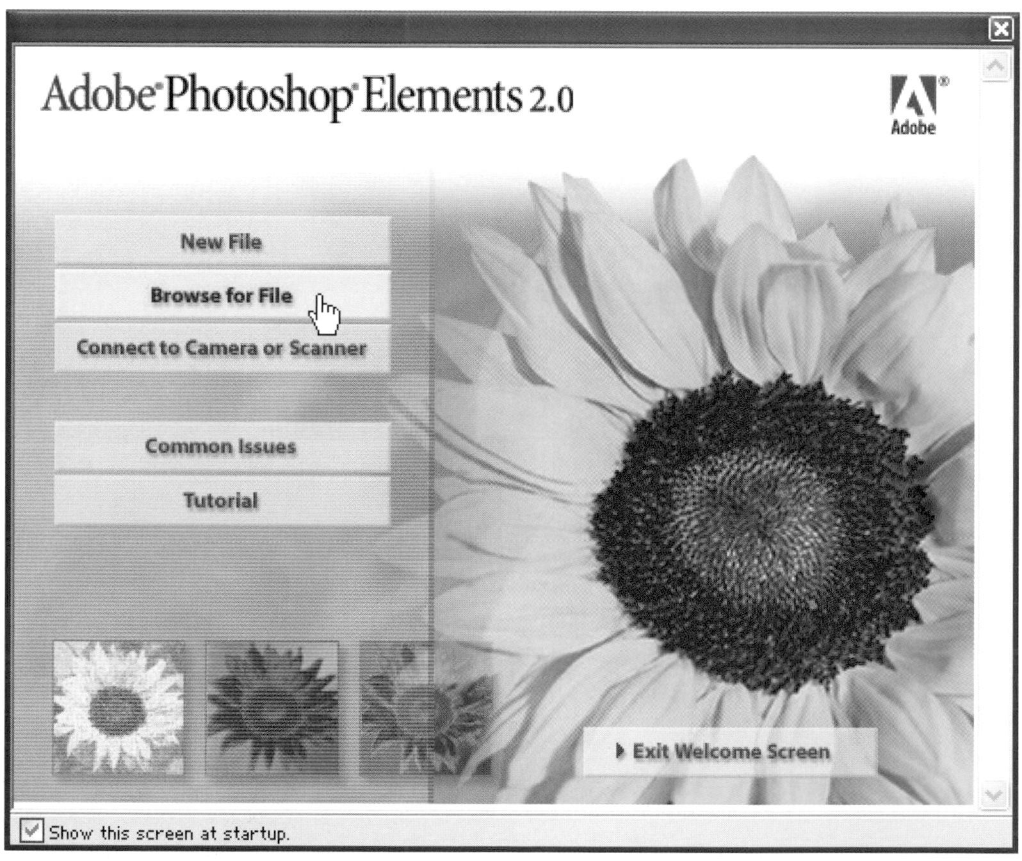

There are four different ways to access the File Browser. By default when you launch Elements, the Welcome Screen appears. Click on the "Browse for File" button to launch the File Browser. Of course, if you've taken advantage of the ability to skip this screen every time you start up (by unchecking the "Show this screen at startup" box), this option will not be available, so you'll have to use other methods to get to the File Browser.

Other Ways to Access the Browser:
If the Welcome Screen isn't an option, you can access the File Browser from Browse in the File menu. An even quicker way is to use the keyboard shortcut Shift-Control-O (Mac: Shift-Command-O), or click on the Browse button on the Shortcuts Bar. Or, you can even open it from the Window menu by choosing File Browser.

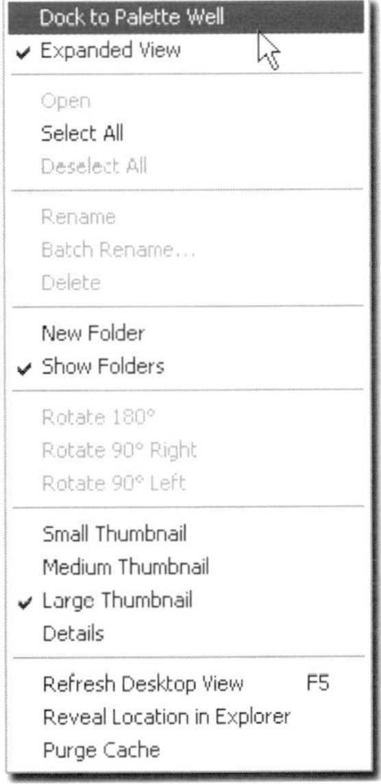

Undocking/Re-Docking the File Browser:
Here's one that gets a lot of people stuck—you've opened the Browser, and now you want to put it in the Palette Well. Here's the problem—where's the tab? Can you drag it back up there if you can't find the tab? Ahhhhh. (Gotcha!) Actually, it's pretty easy (if you know where to look). Just choose Dock to Palette Well from the Browser's pop-down menu (found by clicking on the More button at the top right of the File Browser palette).

TIP: If you can't get the Browser to appear no matter which method you use, try choosing Reset Palette Locations from the Window menu, then the Browser should be accessible using any of the methods described above.

Continued

Thumbnail Generation Extraordinaire:
One of the main features that I love about the File Browser is that it does something wonderful to digital camera images—it automatically creates full color thumbnails of any images you open within it. For example, when you open a folder, or CD of images, for just a moment you'll see the generic icons (or question marks as shown here), just as you would if you opened the memory card from your computer. As you can see, when it comes to finding an image, these generic icons are basically worthless.

However, in just a second or two, Elements automatically generates gorgeous thumbnails in their place (below). Elements is pretty quick about it too, but obviously the more images you have, the longer it will take (it could take up to three or four seconds), but believe me—it's worth the wait. Also, it builds thumbnails from the top down, so even though you see thumbnails in your main window, if you scroll down, the thumbnails further down could still be drawing. Just be patient and they'll appear (coming soon to a Browser window near you!).

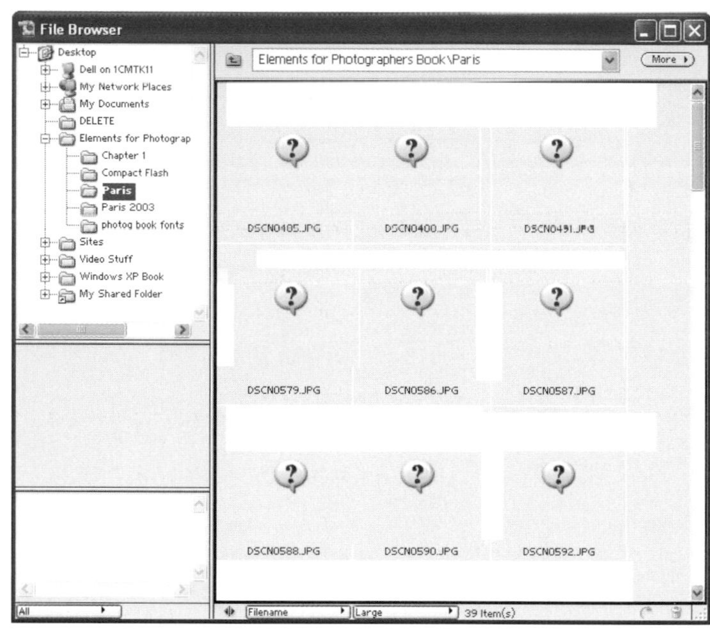

The File Browser takes the lame default icons and transforms them into...

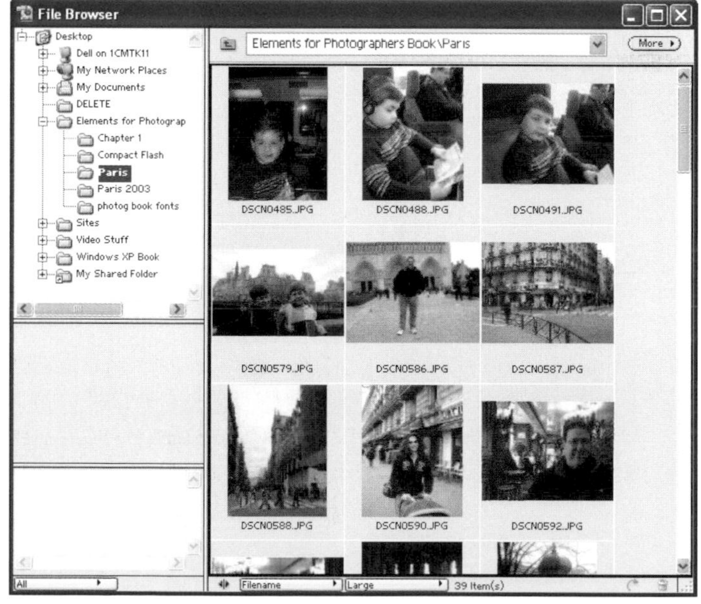

...full color thumbnails. Ahhhhh, that's better!

Browser Essentials

If you look at either picture on the opposite page, you can see that the Browser is divided into four different "panels," and each panel has its own set of features and functions. Here's a quick look at the four panels, and the essential techniques you'll need to get the most out of the Browser.

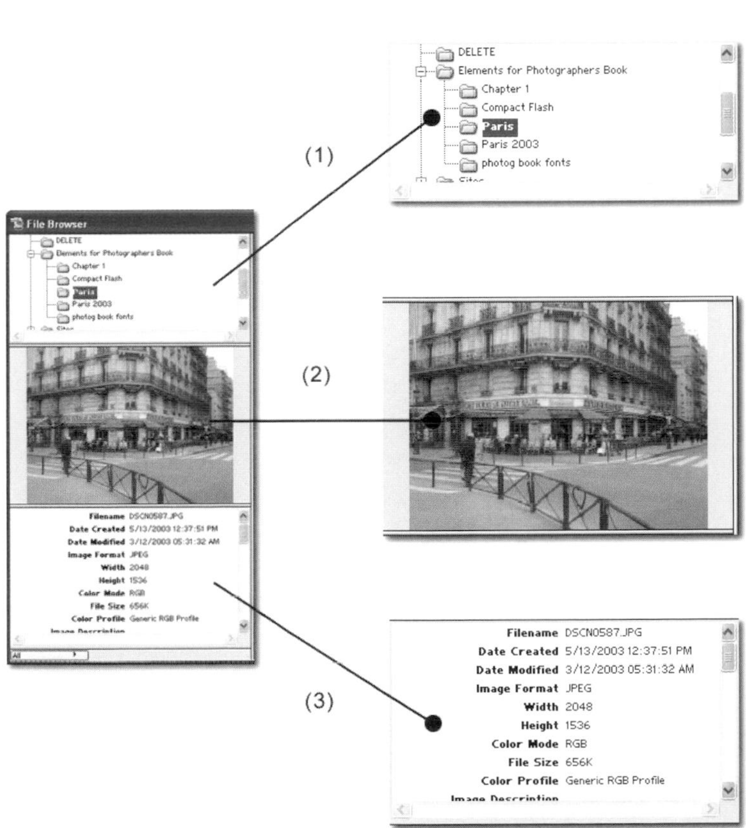

(1) NAVIGATION: The top left panel is designed to let you navigate to your digital camera's memory card, to your hard drive, a CD of images (hint, hint), a network drive—you name it. The idea behind this is simple: It gives you access to your digital camera images without having to leave Elements. You can sort images by dragging thumbnails from the Browser window directly into folders which appear in this panel.

TIP: If you hold Alt (Mac: Option) as you drag, you'll send a copy there, rather than the original.

(2) PREVIEW: The area directly below the navigation panel shows you a larger preview of your currently selected thumbnail. I've got a cool tip for using this preview, so check it out on page 18.

(3) DATA WINDOW: The bottom left panel displays the EXIF data (Exchangeable Image File data) that's automatically embedded into your photo by your digital camera. This data gives background details on your image, including size, resolution, and camera settings. Plus, Elements adds some info to this panel as well (called meta data), so you're getting the EXIF data and

Continued

Elements' embedded meta data, as well. What Elements adds is pretty minor: the file's name, the date the Elements file was created, when it was last modified, the size (in pixels), which file format it's saved in, etc. This is followed by the EXIF data, whose first entry is the Make of the camera that shot the image.

If you prefer to see just the EXIF data, and not the other info that Elements throws in, you can ask that only the EXIF data be displayed by changing the pop-up menu just below the data window from All to EXIF.

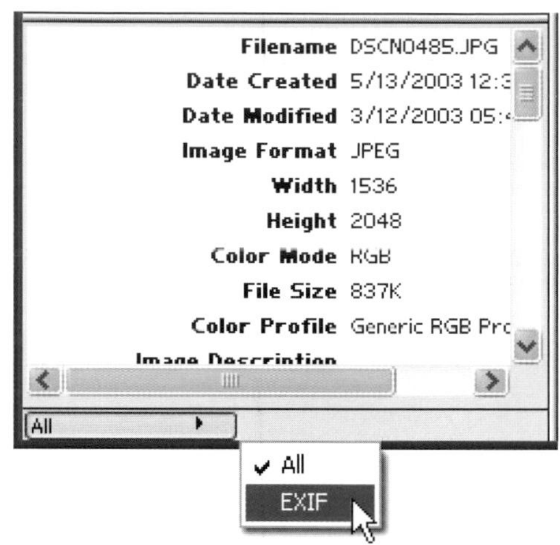

TIP: If you're not working in the File Browser but you want to view the EXIF data for the currently open image, you can—just go under the File menu and choose File Info. When the dialog appears, choose EXIF from the Section pop-up menu at the top (as shown here).

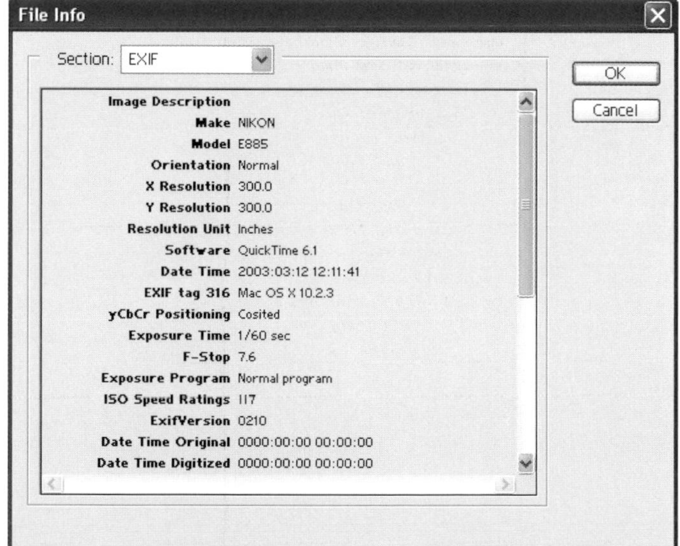

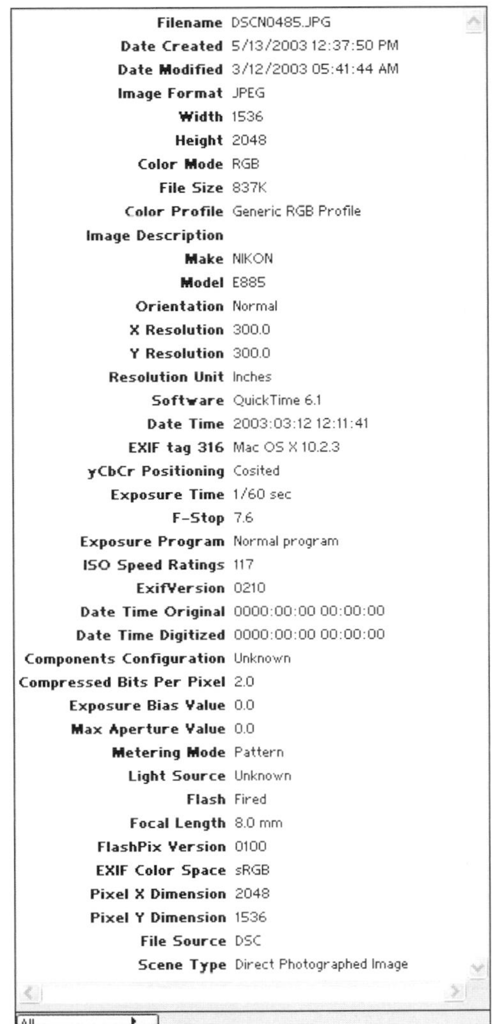

EXIF's Brain Dump:

So how much information does the EXIF data really have about your image? Probably more than you'd care to know. It knows the make and model of the camera that took the shot, the exposure setting, F-stop, whether or not your flash fired, your ISO speed, whether you've bought any dotcom IPOs, seen any UFOs, or have a 401(k). Shown here is the All setting: Elements' meta data and the EXIF data.

Continued

TIP: Before we leave the "left-column" panels, I wanted to give you one more quick tip: When you click on any thumbnail image (in the main window, which we'll cover next), a larger preview of that thumbnail appears in the center of the left column. The problem is that this preview, while larger than the thumbnails, just doesn't seem large enough. But the cool thing is, you can increase its size. If you look at the captures here, you'll see a divider bar between each of the four panels. These bars are moveable, and if you drag them upward, downward, or to the right of the preview area, the preview itself will grow to fill in the space, giving you a much larger and more useful preview.

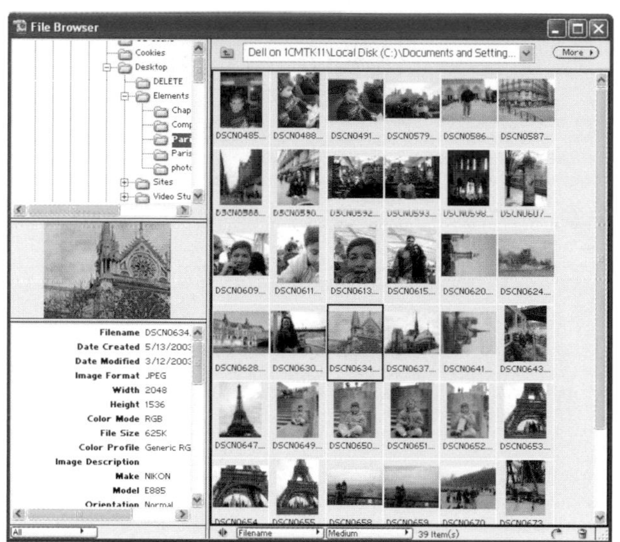

The default preview is pretty small (left column, center).

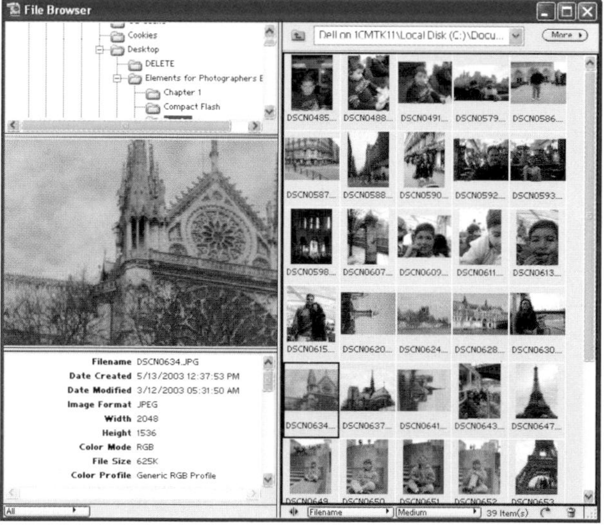

But it doesn't have to stay like that! Slide the divider bars above and below the preview and the preview grows to fill the space. Drag the divider to the right of the Preview panel, and it grows to fill that space as well.

(4) THUMBNAIL VIEW PANEL (sometimes called Desktop View Window): The fourth panel (and the one you'll work with most) is the thumbnail window (it's the entire right side of the Browser), which displays thumbnail views of your photos.

If you click on a thumbnail within this panel, a black line appears around the thumbnail (as shown here), letting you know it's selected, and its preview is displayed in the Preview panel in the left column of the Browser. If you want to open the full-size image in Elements, just double-click on it.

You can select multiple photos to open at the same time by clicking on the first photo you want to open, holding the Control key (Mac: Command key), and then clicking on any other photos. You can select entire rows by clicking on the first thumbnail in a row, holding the Shift key, and clicking on the last photo in that row.

You can navigate from thumbnail to thumbnail by using the Arrow keys on your keyboard.

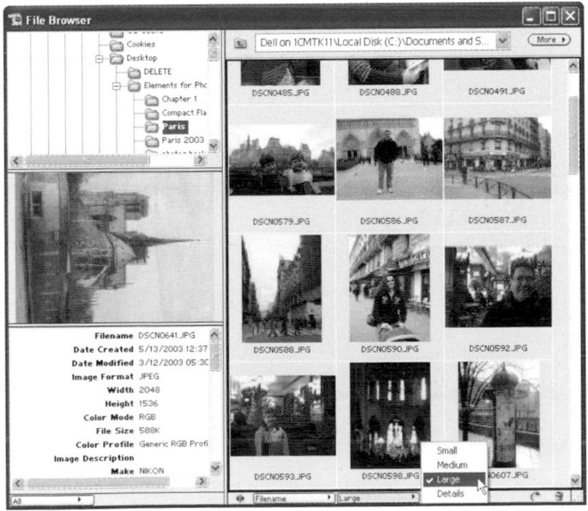

Thumbnail View Options:

There's a View By pop-up menu at the bottom of this panel that lets you decide how large you want your thumbnails displayed. In the captures we've shown thus far, I've had the view set to Medium. In the capture shown here, I switched the thumbnail view to Large, and you can see what a big difference that makes.

Continued

Viewing Things Your Way:
Back to the panels in File Browser. The default setup for your Browser isn't the only option for how your Browser looks and displays its data. One of the most popular views hides the Navigation panel, the Preview panel, and the EXIF Data panel, leaving just the thumbnails in view. This is particularly effective if you've set your thumbnail view size to Large, because at this larger size, the Preview panel becomes much less important. To view just the thumbnails, either:

(a) choose Expanded View from the More pop-down menu to "uncheck" (turn off) this feature (it's on by default), or

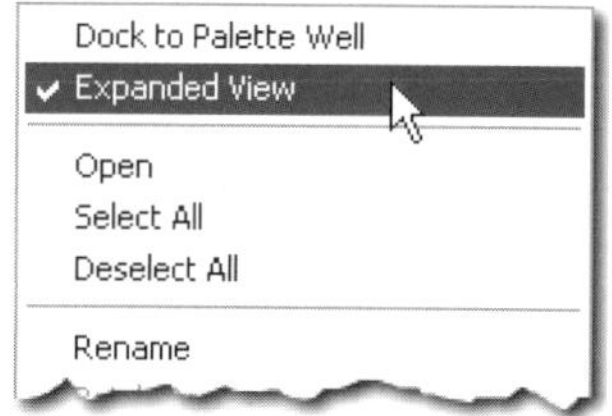

(b) click the two-headed arrow at the bottom of the thumbnails, to the immediate left of the Sort By pop-up menu (as shown below).

(4)

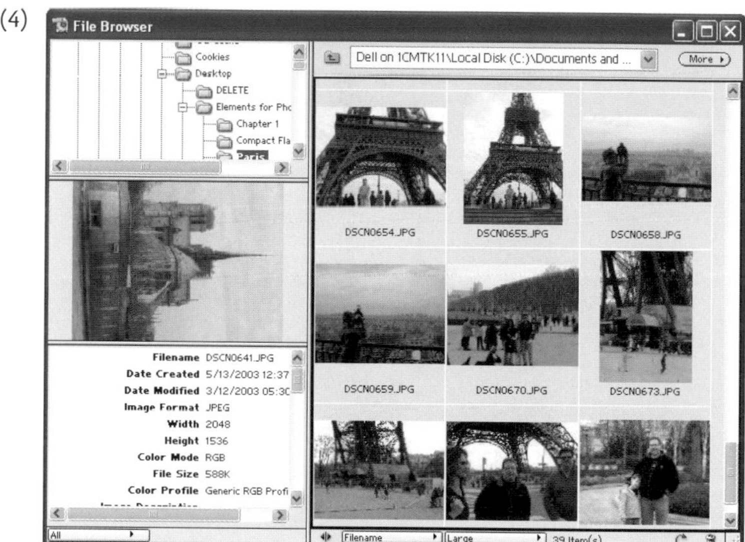

Here's the standard default layout (notice that only three thumbnails across are visible).

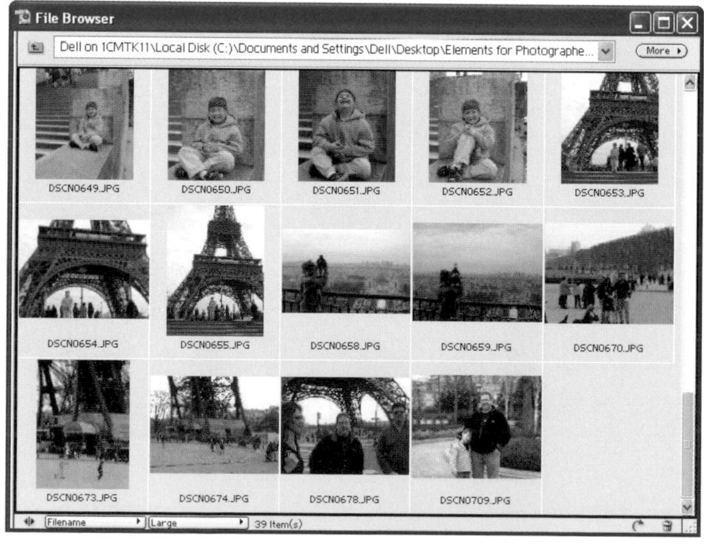

By turning off Expanded View you now get five rows across in the exact same amount of space.

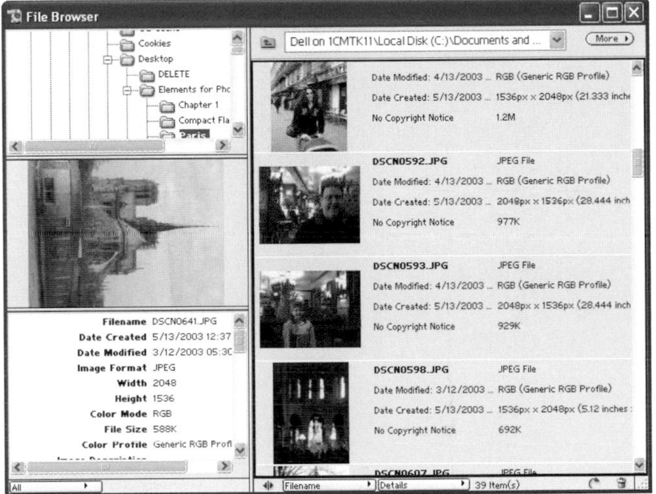

Getting the Details:

There's another layout view for your Browser window, and this particular view is very popular with professional photographers because not only does it display the thumbnail at a large size but to the right of the thumbnail it also displays pertinent information about the photo.

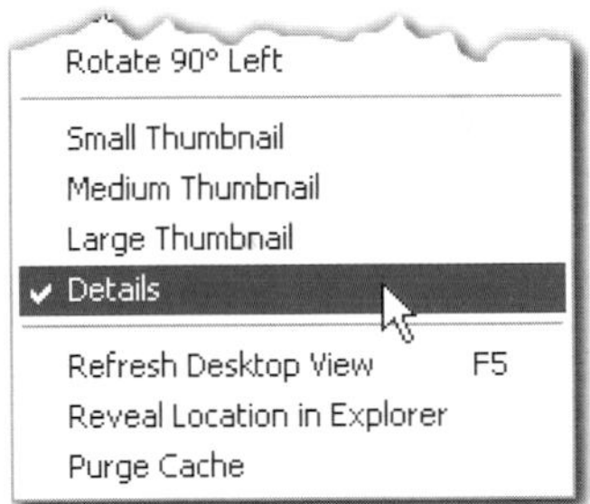

To switch to the Details view, simply choose Details from the Browser's pop-down menu (as shown above).

Batch Renaming Your Files

The File Browser will actually let you change the name of an entire folder (or disc) full of images so your digital camera photo names are no longer the cryptic DSC01181.JPG, DSC01182.JPG, DSC01183.JPG variety, but names you choose that will be more recognizable, such as Concert Shot 1, Concert Shot 2, Concert Shot 3, etc.; and best of all, the whole process is automated. (Incidentally, this is particularly helpful when you're working off your CD, because you can have it create a duplicate folder of these photos on your hard drive with the new names). Here's a step-by-step:

Step One:

You can hold the Control key (Mac: Command key) and click on only the photos you want to rename, but a more likely scenario is that you'll want to rename all the photos displayed in your Browser, so go under the Browser's pop-down menu and choose Select All (as shown here).

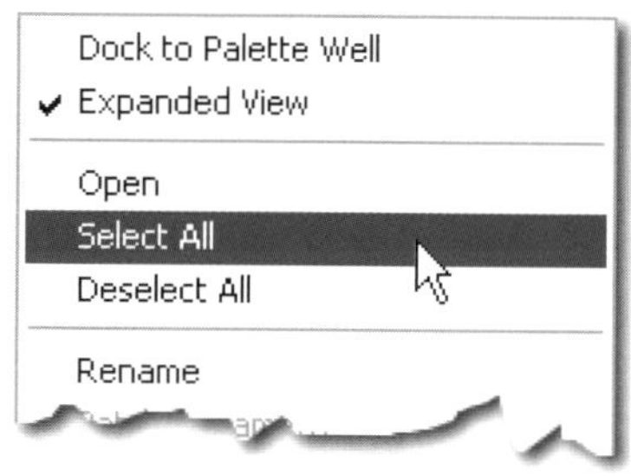

Step Two:

Once you have selected all the photos that you want to rename, go under the Browser's pop-down menu again, but this time choose Batch Rename.

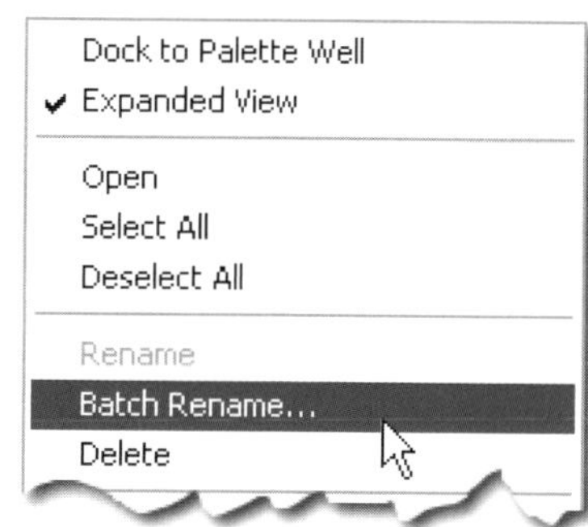

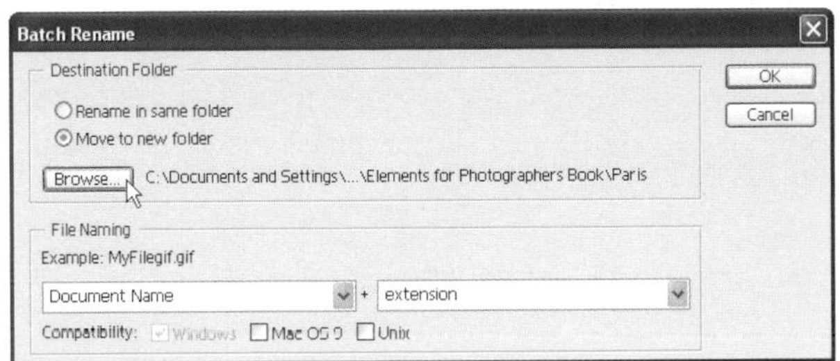

Step Three:

When the Batch Rename dialog appears, you first need to choose a destination for these renamed photos. Your choices for the Destination Folder are limited to either renaming the photos in the same folder where they reside (if you're working off a CD of saved originals, this really isn't a choice), or Move to new folder (which is what you'll probably choose). If you choose Move to new folder, you'll need to click the Browse (Mac: Choose) button (as shown here), and in the resulting dialog box, navigate to the folder you want your photos moved into once they're renamed. One limitation of Batch Renaming is that it either renames your originals or moves them to a new folder. I wish there was an option where Elements would make copies (leaving the originals untouched) and rename only the copies; but at this point, there's not.

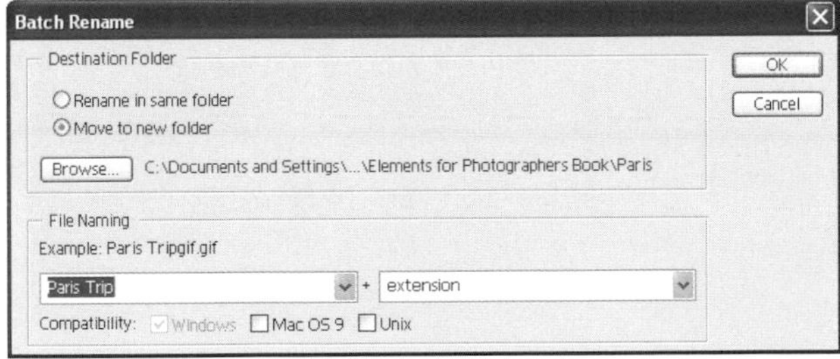

Step Four:

Under the File Naming section of the dialog box, the first field on the top left is where you type in the name you've chosen (in the example shown here, I'm renaming the files "Paris Trip," which is where our family went on vacation shown in the photos). Just click your cursor in this field, and type in the name.

Continued

Step Five:
The next field to the right is where you tell Elements the numbering scheme you'd like to use following the name you assigned (after all, you can't have more than one file in the same folder named "Paris Trip." Instead, you'd need them named "Paris Trip1," Paris Trip2," etc.). To use Elements' built-in auto-numbering, click-and-hold on the arrow to the immediate right of the field and the pop-up menu shown here will appear. Here you can choose to number your photos with a 1- to 4-digit serial number, letters, or by date. In our example, we'll choose 1 Digit Serial Number to have Elements automatically add a sequential number after the name, starting with "1."

Note: If you're concerned about making a mistake when you rename your files, don't be, because directly below the File Naming section header is a live Example of what your file name will look like. **Freak Out Warning:** Don't let it freak you out that it always shows .gif as the file extension even though your file is a JPEG—it's just using .gif to let you know that you chose an extension to be added. The real extension it adds will be based on the file format of the files you chose to rename. So if your files are in JPEG format, Elements will add the .jpg extension, not .gif as the live example shows. This FOW (Freak Out Warning) is based on actual real-world testing and evaluation (meaning the first time it happened to me, I freaked out).

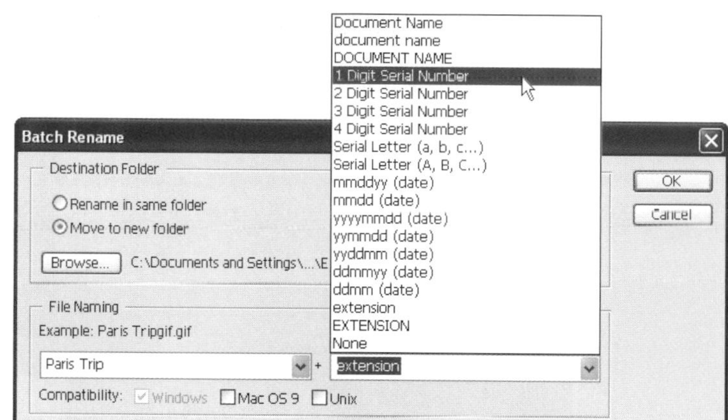

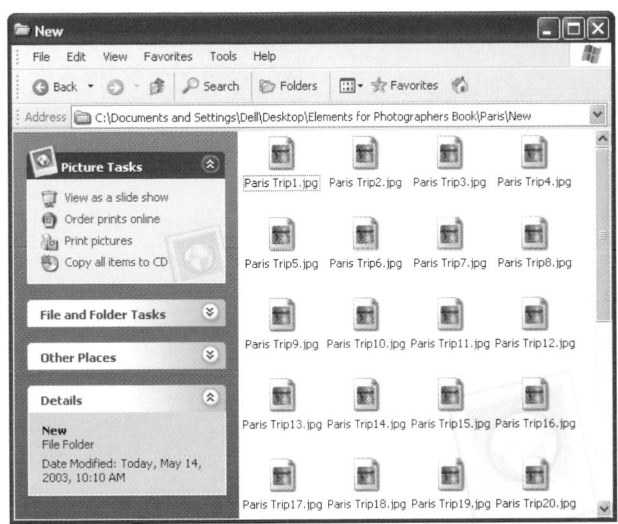

Step Six:

When you click OK, Elements does its thing, and in just a few seconds, your photos will appear in the new folder sporting their brand-new names. Now, when you view those images in the File Browser, they'll have more meaningful names (shown below).

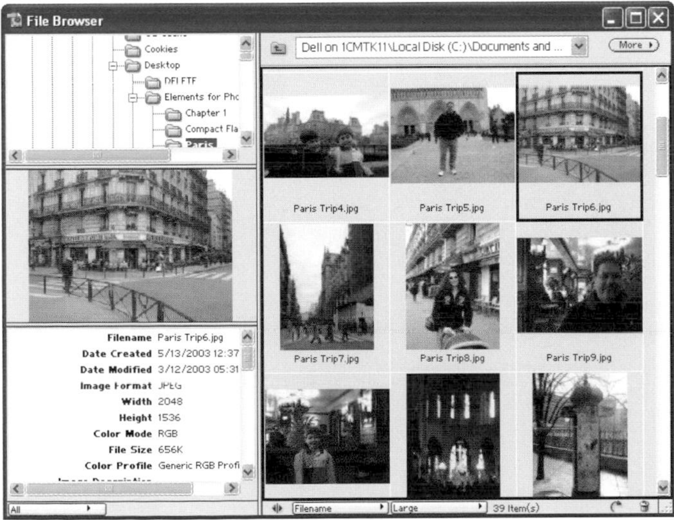

Editing in the Browser

You can make a number of edits to your images right within the File Browser that can save you time later when you actually open the images in Photoshop Elements. Here are some of the edits you can perform:

Rotation:
Near the bottom right-hand corner of the Browser next to the Trash icon is a button with a little circular arrow on it. Clicking it rotates the currently selected photo in the Browser 90° clockwise. This is incredibly handy if you turned the camera vertically for a tall (portrait) shot rather than a wide (landscape) shot. When these tall photos originally appear within the browser, you'll see them lying on their side, and they'll need to be rotated until they're right side up (which, incidentally may take three clicks of the rotation button, depending on which way the photo is facing).

When you rotate an image in the Browser, Elements gives you a warning dialog box (shown bottom) telling you that it's just rotating the preview thumbnail, and not actually rotating the file itself. So the rotation of this photo won't really take place until you actually double-click on the file to open it in Elements, then it rotates the way you want it.

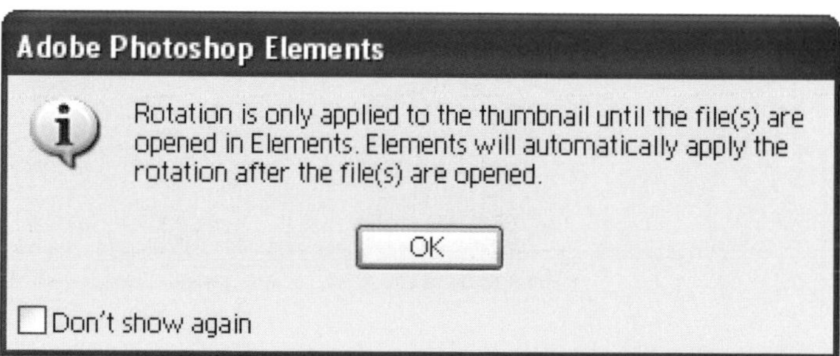

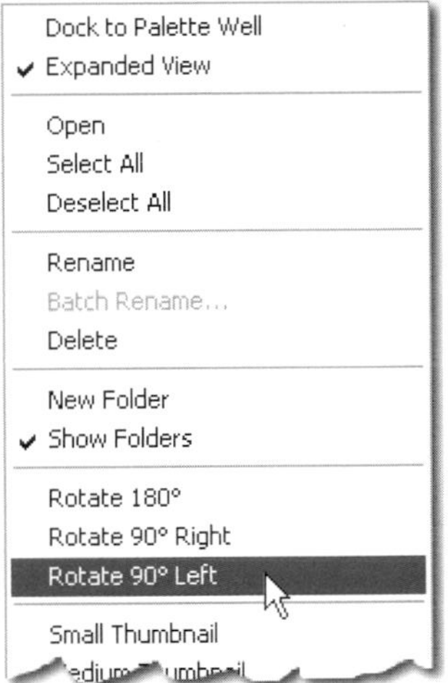

TIP: You can save yourself some clicks when rotating your image with this little shortcut: Hold the Alt key (Mac: Option key) then click on the rotation button. This will rotate the image counterclockwise (rather than the default rotation of clockwise), letting you correct that "sideways" picture in just one click. If you forget the shortcut, you can always choose Rotate 90° Left from the File Browser's More pop-down menu (shown here).

Deleting Photos:

If you burned a CD when you first inserted your memory card (and I know you did, because now you know how important it is to keep your negatives safely stored), then you can safely delete any image you don't want in your new folder by clicking on the thumbnail within the Browser and dragging it to the Trash icon at the bottom right-hand corner of the window.

You can also use this keyboard shortcut: Click on the file to be deleted and press the Delete key (Mac: Option-Delete) and that file will be moved to your Recycling Bin (Mac: the Trash) until you choose to "Empty Recycling Bin"

Photographer | Carol Freeman

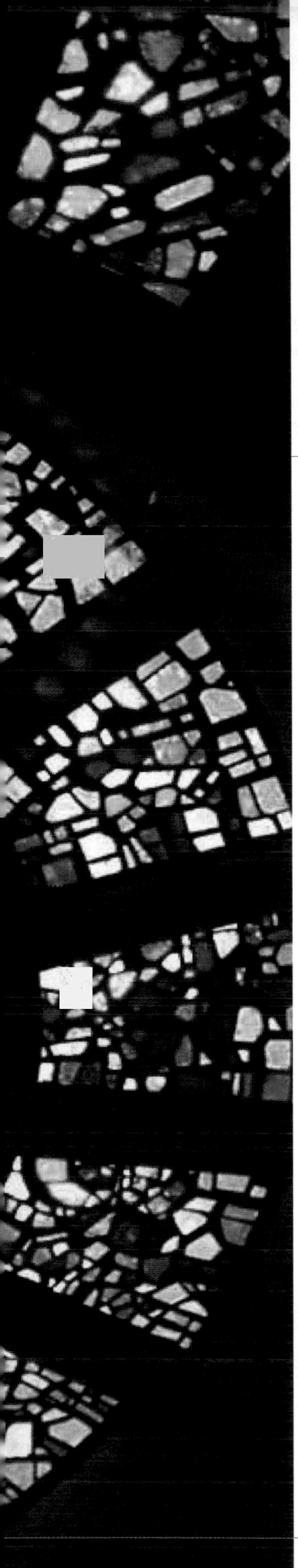

If a chapter on cropping and resizing doesn't sound exciting, really, what does? It's sad, but a good portion of our lives is spent doing just that—cropping and resizing. Why is that? It's because nothing, and

Cream of the Crop

cropping and resizing

I mean nothing, is ever the right size. Think about it. If everything were already the right size, there'd be no opportunity to "Super Size it." You'd go to McDonald's, order a Value Meal, and instead of hearing, "Would you care to Super Size your order?" there would just be a long uncomfortable pause. And frankly, I'm uncomfortable enough at the McDonald's drive-thru, what with all the cropping and resizing I'm constantly doing. Anyway, although having a chapter on cropping and resizing isn't the kind of thing that sells books (though I hear books on crop circles do fairly well), both are important and necessary, especially if you ever plan on cropping or resizing things in Elements. Actually, you'll be happy to learn that there's more than just cropping and resizing in this chapter. That's right—I super sized the chapter with other cool techniques that honestly are probably a bit too cool to wind up in a chapter called "Cropping and Resizing," but it's the only place they'd fit. But don't let the extra techniques throw you; if this chapter seems too long to you, flip to the end of the chapter and rip out a few pages, and you have effectively cropped the chapter down to size. (And by ripping the pages out yourself, you have transformed what was originally a mere book into an "interactive experience," which thereby enhances the value of the book, making you feel like a pretty darn smart shopper.) See, it almost makes you want to read it now, doesn't it?

Custom Sizes for Photographers

Photoshop Elements' dialog for creating new documents has a pop-up menu with a list of Preset Sizes. You're probably thinking, "Hey, there's a 4x6, 5x7, and 8x10—I'm set." The problem is there's no way to switch the orientation of these presets (so a 4x6 will always be a 4″ wide by 6″ tall portrait-orientated document). That's why creating your own custom new document sizes is so important. Here's how:

Step One:
Go under the File menu and choose New. When the New dialog box appears, click on the Preset Sizes pop-up menu to reveal the list of preset sizes.

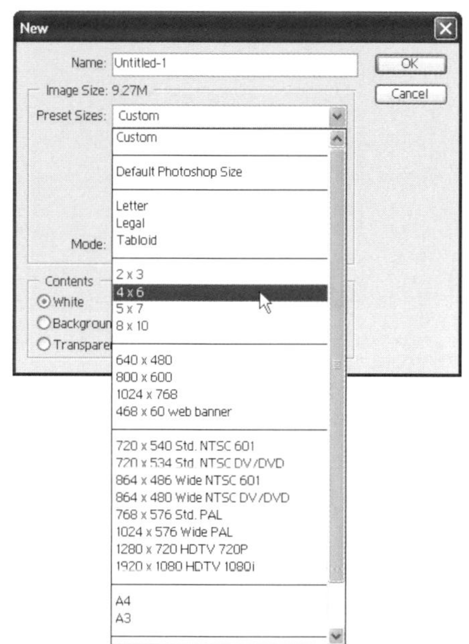

Step Two:
Go ahead and hit Cancel in the New dialog (now that you've seen the preset list where you'll be adding your own custom settings) instead of actually creating a document. Now, find the Photoshop Elements folder on your hard drive. Inside that folder, you'll find a folder called Presets and in that folder you'll find a text document named New Doc Sizes.txt.

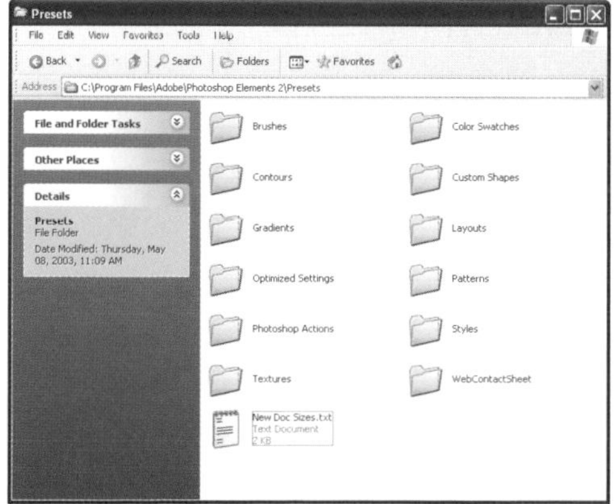

```
New Doc Sizes.txt - Notepad
File  Edit  Format  View  Help
;       "Preset Name" requires quotes around it

;       Width is the decimal width of the preset, in units

;       Height is the decimal height of the preset, in units

;       Units is the units for the preset and is one of the following:
;               pixels
;               inches
;               cm
;               mm
;               points
;               picas

;       If a Resolution value is not present, the resolution in the
;       dialog will not be changed.

;       Otherwise resolution is one of the following:
;               print
;               screen
;               an actual numeric value in dpi or dpcm, e.g. 72 dpi, or 300
dpcm

; Example: for a size named "My Paper Size" that is 8.5 in. wide x
; 4 in. tall at 72 dpi:

; "My Paper Size"       8.5         4               inches  72 dpi

; Example: for a size named "My Web Size" that is 800 pixels wide x
; 600 pixels tall at the resolution specified in preferences for
; "screen" documents:

; "My Web Size"         800         600             pixels  screen
```

Step Three:

Double-click on that text document to open it in your word processor or other text editor. Scroll to the bottom of the document and you'll see some examples of how to create your own presets. Rather than trying to decipher the instructions in this document, just highlight the line of text that starts out "My Paper Size." Don't get the semicolon (;) at the beginning of the line; start with the opening quote and highlight down to the last letter of "dpi." Now press Control-C (Mac: Command-C) to copy that selected text. Note: If you accidentally select the semicolon—it won't work. Also, if you miss the opening quote, it won't work either, so make sure you've selected that text exactly as shown here at left.

```
New Doc Sizes.txt - Notepad
File  Edit  Format  View  Help

;       Width is the decimal width of the preset, in units

;       Height is the decimal height of the preset, in units

;       Units is the units for the preset and is one of the following:
;               pixels
;               inches
;               cm
;               mm
;               points
;               picas

;       If a Resolution value is not present, the resolution in the
;       dialog will not be changed.

;       Otherwise resolution is one of the following:
;               print
;               screen
;               an actual numeric value in dpi or dpcm, e.g. 72 dpi, or 300
dpcm

; Example: for a size named "My Paper Size" that is 8.5 in. wide x
; 4 in. tall at 72 dpi:

; "My Paper Size"       8.5         4               inches  72 dpi

; Example: for a size named "My Web Size" that is 800 pixels wide x
; 600 pixels tall at the resolution specified in preferences for
; "screen" documents:

; "My Web Size"         800         600             pixels  screen

"My Paper Size" 8.5          4              inches  72 dpi
```

Step Four:

Now go to the very last line in the document, the one that begins "My Web Size", and click your cursor once right after the letter "n" in the word "screen" at the end of the line. Press Enter (Mac: Return) twice to move down two lines, then press Control-V (Mac: Command-V) to paste the line you copied earlier into this space (as shown here).

Continued

Step Five:

The hard part's over—now all you have to do is highlight the name "My Paper Size" (just the words, not the quotes around them), and then type in the name that you want for your custom preset (for example, we'll call this one "Scott's 6x4") as shown at right. (Needless to say, don't start your preset name with "Scott's" unless your name happens to be Scott. If that's the case, then I applaud you for having such an unusually cool name.)

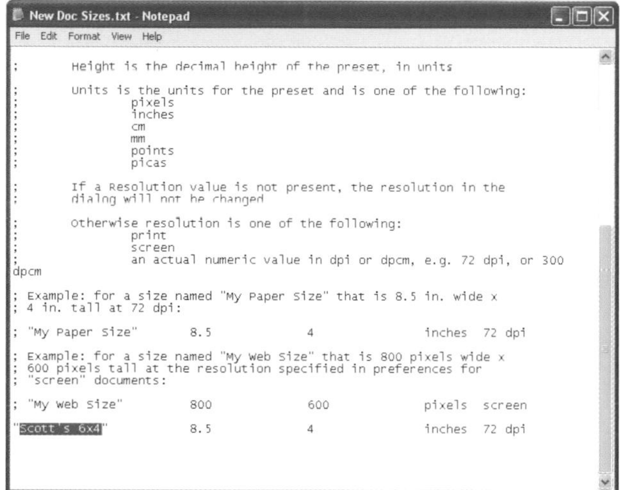

New Doc Sizes.txt - Notepad

File Edit Format View Help

```
;       Height is the decimal height of the preset, in units

;       Units is the units for the preset and is one of the following:
;               pixels
;               inches
;               cm
;               mm
;               points
;               picas

;       If a Resolution value is not present, the resolution in the
;       dialog will not be changed

;       Otherwise resolution is one of the following:
;               print
;               screen
;               an actual numeric value in dpi or dpcm, e.g. 72 dpi, or 300
dpcm

; Example: for a size named "My Paper Size" that is 8.5 in. wide x
; 4 in. tall at 72 dpi:

; "My Paper Size"       8.5             4               inches  72 dpi

; Example: for a size named "My Web Size" that is 800 pixels wide x
; 600 pixels tall at the resolution specified in preferences for
; "screen" documents:

; "My Web Size"         800             600             pixels  screen

"Scott's 6x4"           8.5             4               inches  72 dpi
```

Step Six:

Next, highlight the 8.5, and type in your desired width (in this case 6), then highlight the 4 and type in...well, it's already a 4, but you won't always get that lucky (unless, of course, you're really into 4-inch height for everything). Note: Don't add a quote for inches after you enter your width or height settings, because that will mess with the script, and it won't work, so just enter the number with no inch marks.

New Doc Sizes.txt - Notepad

File Edit Format View Help

```
;       Height is the decimal height of the preset, in units

;       Units is the units for the preset and is one of the following:
;               pixels
;               inches
;               cm
;               mm
;               points
;               picas

;       If a Resolution value is not present, the resolution in the
;       dialog will not be changed.

;       Otherwise resolution is one of the following:
;               print
;               screen
;               an actual numeric value in dpi or dpcm, e.g. 72 dpi, or 300
dpcm

; Example: for a size named "My Paper Size" that is 8.5 in. wide x
; 4 in. tall at 72 dpi:

; "My Paper Size"       8.5             4               inches  72 dpi

; Example: for a size named "My Web Size" that is 800 pixels wide x
; 600 pixels tall at the resolution specified in preferences for
; "screen" documents:

; "My Web Size"         800             600             pixels  screen

"Scott's 6x4"           6               4               inches  72 dpi
```

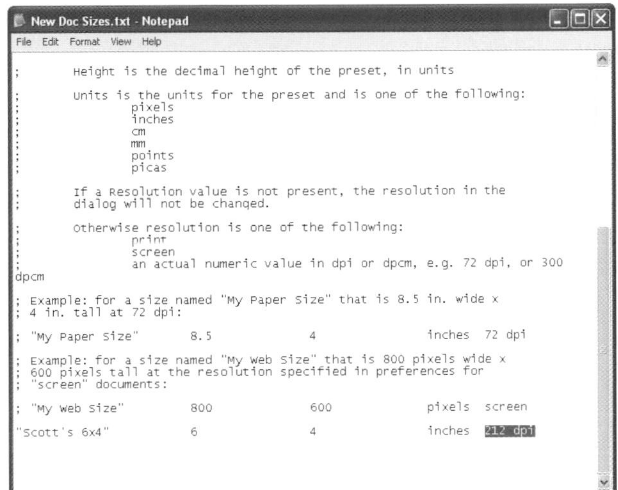

Step Seven:

In this case, since we're creating a new document that's measured in inches, we don't have to change the next word—it's already inches, but if you did want to change it to pixels, just highlight the word "inches" and replace it with the word "pixels." Of course, you can type in any unit of measure, if you're so inclined, such as picas, millimeters, centimeters, kilometers, miles, acres, etc. (Okay, you can't really enter kilometers, miles, or acres. I just wanted to see if you're paying attention.)

Next, you need to choose a resolution, so highlight the number that appears before "dpi." Here, we've changed it to "212" for print. For low-res or the Web you can leave it at "72."

Now, save this file and close it. In Mac OS X, be sure to save as plain Text. That's it, nothing fancy—just save and close.

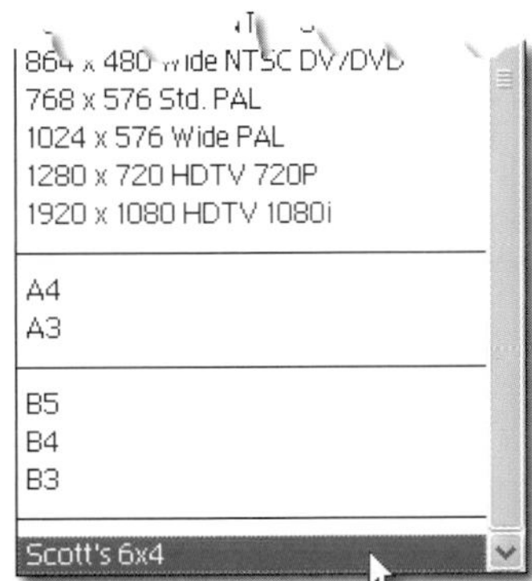

Step Eight:

This last step is critically important—you must quit Elements and restart for your custom presets to appear. This one catches a lot of people, so don't forget to do it or you won't see your preset. Once you restart Elements, go under the File menu and choose New, and when you click the Preset Sizes pop-up menu, scroll all the way to the bottom and there your new custom preset will appear. (I know what you're thinking—shouldn't my custom settings appear at the top of the list, rather than all the way at the bottom? Yup. That'd be nice. Sadly, that's just not the way it works.)

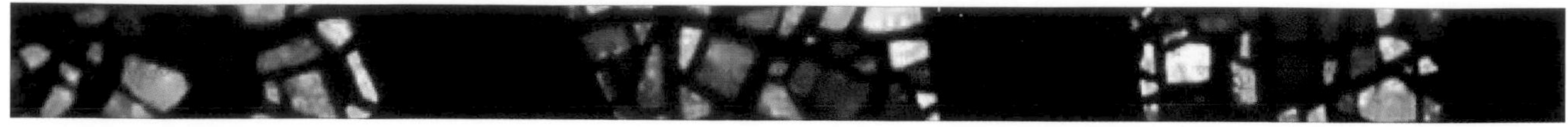

Cropping Photos

After you've sorted your images in the Browser, one of the first editing tasks you'll probably undertake is cropping a photo. There are a number of different ways to crop a photo in Elements. We'll start with the basic garden variety, and then we'll look at some ways to make the task faster and easier.

Step One:

Press the letter "C" to get the Crop tool (you could always select it directly from the Toolbox but I only recommend doing so if you're charging by the hour).

Step Two:

Click within your photo and drag out a cropping border (as shown here). The area to be cropped away will appear dimmed (shaded). You don't have to worry about getting your crop border right when you first drag it out, because you can edit the border by dragging the control points that appear in each corner and at the centers of all four sides.

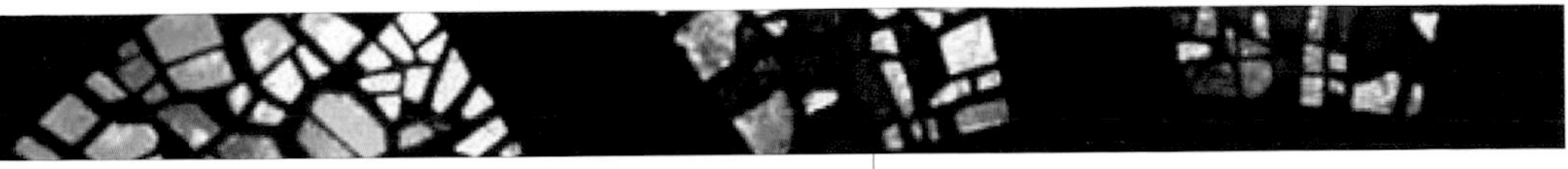

TIP: If you don't like seeing your photo with the cropped-away areas appearing shaded (as in the previous step), you can toggle this shading feature off/on by pressing the Forward Slash key on your keyboard. When you press the Forward Slash key, the border remains in place but the shading is turned off (as shown here).

Step Three:

While you have the crop border in place, you can rotate the entire border by moving your cursor outside the border (note the cursor's position in the lower right-hand corner of the image shown here), and when you do, the cursor changes into a double-headed arrow. Just click-and-drag and the cropping border will rotate in the direction that you drag (this is a great way to save time if you have a crooked image, because it lets you crop and rotate at the same time).

Continued

Step Four:
Once you have the cropping border where you want it, you can choose any one of the following to actually crop the image to size:

(1) Press the Enter key (Mac: Return key).

(2) Click any other tool in the Toolbox.

(3) Click the Checkmark up in the top right side of the Options Bar.

Doing any of those three will crop your image (the final crop is shown below).

TIP: Changing Your Mind
If you've dragged out a cropping border and then decide you don't want to crop the image, there are two ways to cancel your crop:

(1) Press the Escape (esc) key on your keyboard and the crop will be canceled and the photo will remain untouched.

(2) Look up in the Options Bar, and you'll see the International symbol for "No way." Click the circle with the diagonal line through it to cancel your crop.

Before

After

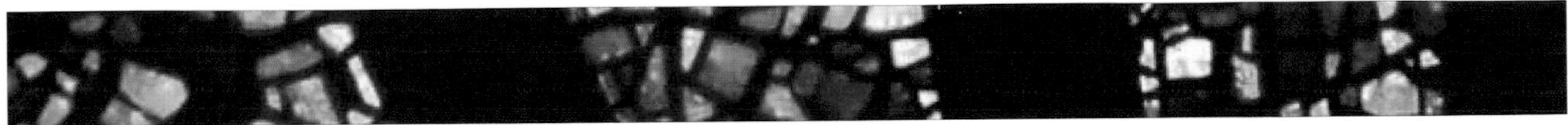

Cropping to a Specific Size

If you're outputting photos for clients, chances are they're going to want them in standard sizes so they can easily find frames to fit. If that's the case, you'll find this technique handy, because it lets you crop any image to a predetermined size (like a 5x7, 8x10, etc.).

Step One:
The portrait shown here measures 5.917"x7.194" and we want to crop it to be a perfect 5"x7". First, get the Crop tool, and up in the Options Bar on the left you'll see fields for Width and Height. Enter the size you want for Width, followed by the unit of measure you want to use (e.g., use "in" for inches, "px" for pixels, "cm" for centimeters, "mm" for millimeters, etc.). Next, press the Tab key to jump over to the Height field and enter your desired height, again followed by the unit of measure (as shown in the inset).

Step Two:
Once you've entered these figures in the Options Bar, click within your photo with the Crop tool and drag out a cropping border. You'll notice that as you drag, the border is constrained to a vertical shape, and no side points are visible–only corner points. Whatever size you make your border, the area within that border will become a 5"x7" photo. In the example shown here, I dragged the border so it almost touched the top and bottom, to get as much of the subject as possible.

Continued

Step Three:
Once your cropping border is onscreen, you can reposition it by moving your cursor inside the border, and your cursor will change to a Move arrow. You can now drag the border into place, or use the Arrow keys on your keyboard for more precise control. When it looks right to you, press Enter (Mac: Return) to finalize your crop, and the area inside your cropping border becomes 5"x7". (I made the rulers visible so you could see that the image measures exactly 5"x7".)

TIP: Once you've entered a Width and Height in the Options Bar, those dimensions will remain there. To clear the fields, just choose the Crop tool, and up in the Options Bar, click on the Clear button (shown here). This will clear the Width and Height fields, and now you can use the Crop tool for freeform cropping (you can drag it in any direction—it's no longer constrained to a vertical 5x7).

COOLER TIP: If you already have one photo that is the exact size and resolution you'd like, you can use it to enter the crop dimensions for you. First, open the photo you'd like to resize, then open your "ideal-size-and-resolution" photo. Get the Crop tool, then go up in the Options Bar and click on the Front Image button. Photoshop will automatically input that photo's Width, Height, and Resolution in the Crop tool's fields—all you have to do is crop, and the other image will now share the exact same specs.

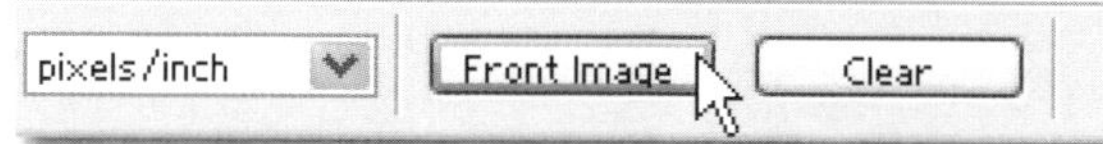

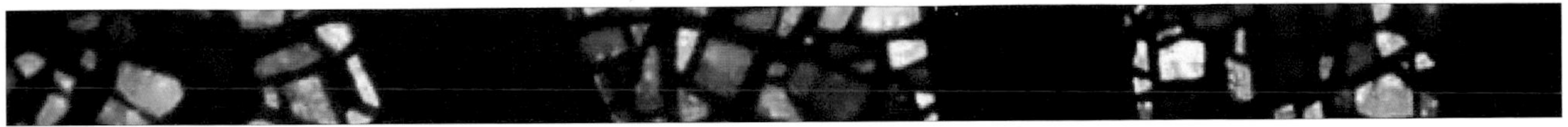

Sometimes it's quicker to crop your photo using some of Elements' other tools and features than it is to reach for the Crop tool every time you need a simple crop.

Cropping Without the Crop Tool

© BRAND X PICTURES

Step One:
This is the method I probably use the most for cropping images of all kinds (primarily when I'm not trying to make a perfect 5x7, 8x10, etc.—I'm basically just "eyeing" it). Start by pressing "m" to get the Rectangular Marquee tool. (I use this tool so much that I usually don't have to switch to it—maybe that's why I use this method all the time.) Drag out a selection around the area you want to keep (leaving all the other areas to be cropped away outside the selection) as shown.

Step Two:
Go under the Image menu and choose Crop (as shown here).

Continued

Step Three:
When you choose Crop, the image is immediately cropped (as shown). There are no crop handles, no dialogs—bang—it just gets cropped—down and dirty, and that's why I like it.

TIP: One instance of where you'll often use the Crop command from the Image menu is when you're creating collages. When you drag photos from other documents onto your main document and position them within your collage, the parts of the image that extend beyond the document borders are actually still there. So to keep our file size manageable, we choose All from the Select menu (as shown) or press Control-A (Mac: Command-A), then we choose Crop from the Image menu. This deletes all the excess layer data that extends beyond the image border, and brings our file size back in line.

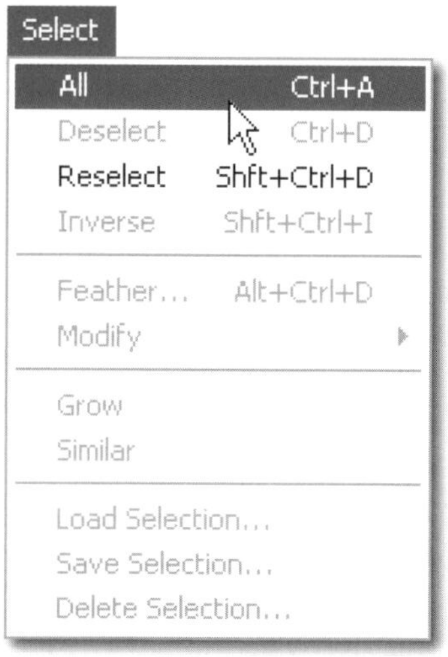

Select
All Ctrl+A
Deselect Ctrl+D
Reselect Shft+Ctrl+D
Inverse Shft+Ctrl+I
Feather... Alt+Ctrl+D
Modify
Grow
Similar
Load Selection...
Save Selection...
Delete Selection...

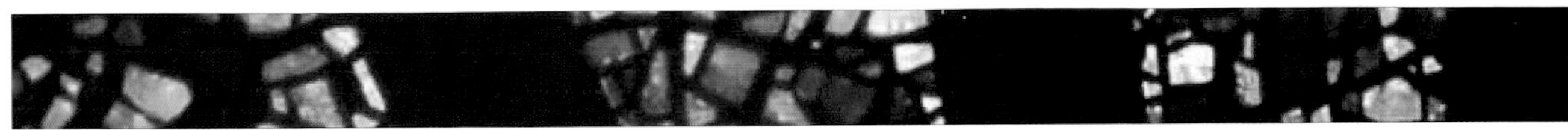

Using the Crop Tool to Add More Canvas Area

I know the heading at right doesn't make much sense—Using the Crop Tool to Add More Canvas Area. How can the Crop tool (which is designed to crop photos to a smaller size) actually make the Canvas area (white space) around your photo larger? That's what I'm going to show you.

© JIM PATTERSON

Step One:

Open the image that you want to give additional blank Canvas area. Press the letter "d" to set your Background color to its default color of white.

Step Two:

Press Control-minus (Mac: Command-minus) to zoom out a bit (so your image doesn't take up your whole screen), then press the Maximize button in the top right-hand corner of the document window to see the gray desktop area around your image. (Mac: Grab the bottom right-hand corner of your document window and drag it out until you see the gray desktop area that surrounds your image.)

Continued

Step Three:

Press the letter "C" to switch to the Crop tool, and drag a cropping marquee border out to any random size, as shown here (it doesn't matter how big or little the marquee is at this point).

Step Four:

Now, grab any one of the side or corner points and drag outside the image area, out into the gray desktop area that surrounds your image (as shown here). The area that your cropping border extends outside the image is the area that will be added as white Canvas space, so position it where you want to add the blank Canvas space.

Step Five:

Now, just press the Enter key (Mac: Return key) to finalize your crop, and when you do, the area outside your image will become white Canvas area.

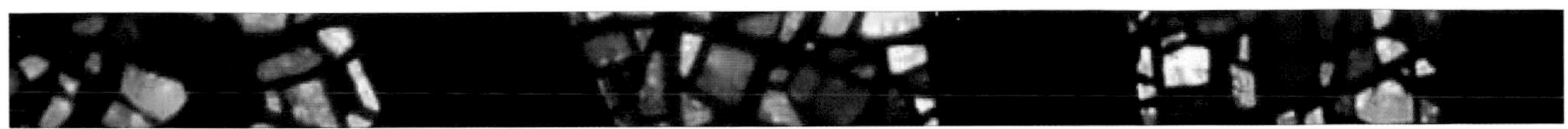

Straightening Crooked Photos

If you handhold your digital camera for most of your shots rather than using a tripod, you can be sure that some of your photos are going to come out a bit crooked. Well, I have good news and bad news. First, the good news: Elements has a built-in function for straightening crooked images. Now, the bad news: It doesn't always work. That's why I included a pretty slick workaround for when the auto-straighten function doesn't work.

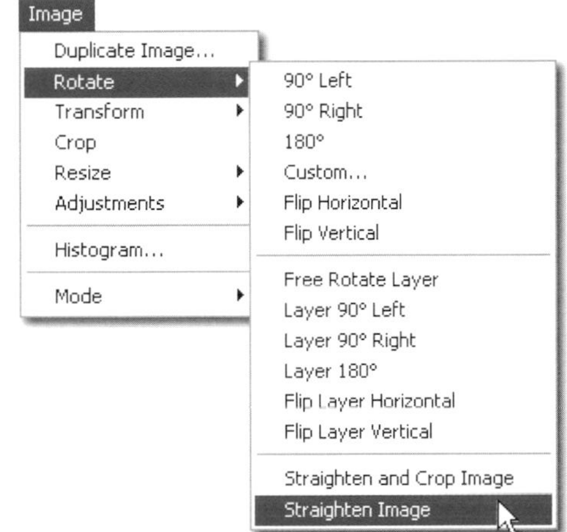

Step One (The Only One):
Automated Straightening:
Open the photo that needs straightening. To use Elements' automated straightening (which works fairly well in many cases), simply go under the Image menu, under Rotate, and choose Straighten Image, and if it can find a straight edge, it'll straighten your image (well, most of the time). Note: Oftentimes when the image is rotated, you'll see white Canvas area around the image, so if you want to straighten and crop at the same time, choose (do I even have to say it?) "Straighten and Crop Image" instead. That does it (there is no Step Two).

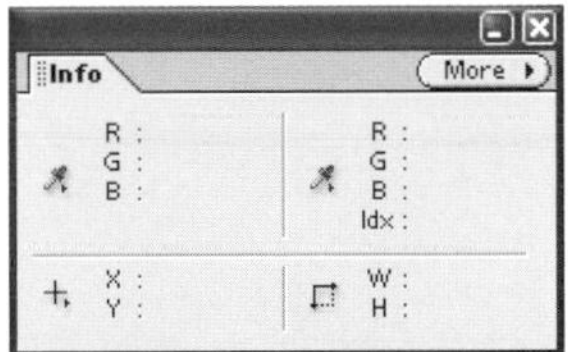

Step One:
Manual Straightening:
Open the photo that needs straightening. Go under the Window menu and choose Info to bring up the Info palette (shown here).

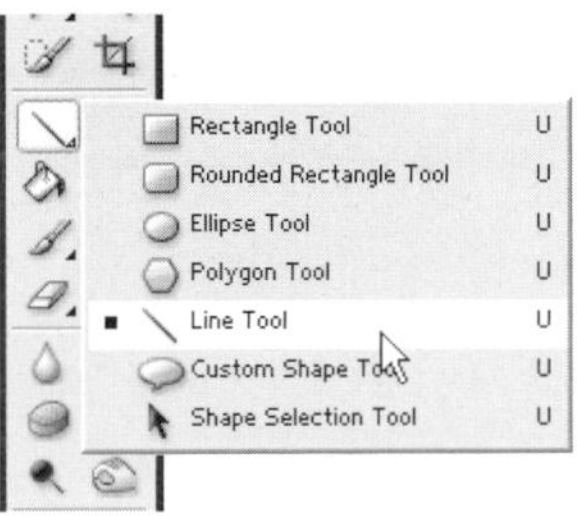

Step Two:
Next choose the Line tool from Element's Toolbox (it's in the Custom Shape tool flyout menu just to the left of the Type tool, as shown here).

Continued

Step Three:
Find something in your photo that is supposed to be straight (such as the photo's border, or even something within the photo itself, such as the horizon, a table, a window, etc., that you think should be straight). Click-and-drag the Line tool horizontally along this straight edge in your photo (as shown), starting from the left and extending right, but don't let go of the mouse button (that's important).

© DAVE MOSER

Step Four:
While you're still holding the mouse button down, look over on the right side of the Info palette, and third from the top is the letter "A" representing "Angle." Look at the amount (here it's 1.8°) and remember that number. Now you can release the mouse button.

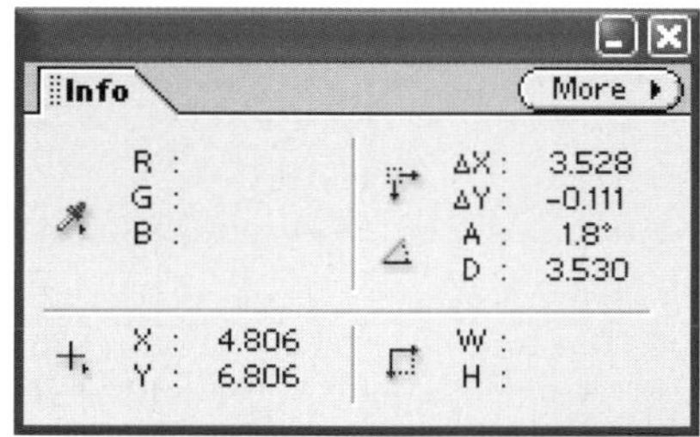

Step Five:
Using the Line tool in this fashion creates a Shape Layer, so press Control-Z (Mac: Command-Z) to Undo this layer (it's no longer needed). Next, go under the Image menu, under Rotate, and choose Custom to bring up the Rotate Canvas dialog box. Now, remember that angle you were supposed to remember? (It was 1.8° in case you forgot.) That goes in the Angle field in this dialog. You also have to click on the radio button for whether it should rotate 1.8° to the Left or Right, then click OK and whammo! (whammo! being a technical term), your image is straightened.

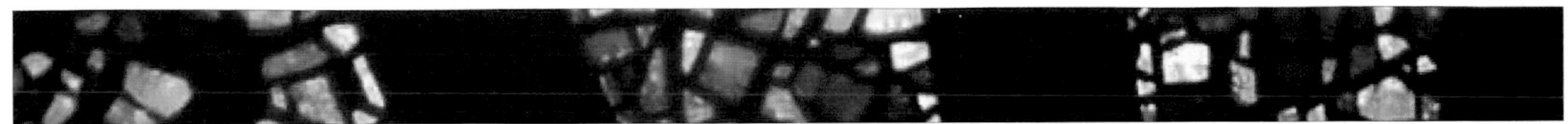

Using a Visible Grid for Straightening Photos

Here's another popular technique for straightening photos that works particularly well when you're having trouble finding a straight edge within your image.

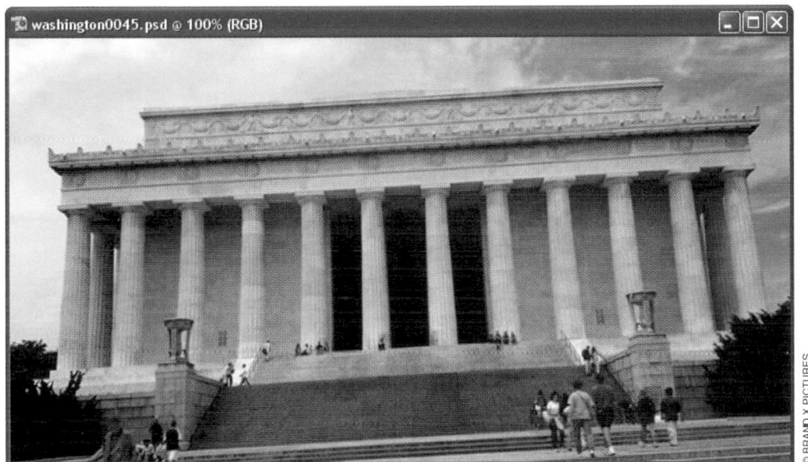

© BRAND X PICTURES

Step One:
Open a photo that needs straightening. (The example here is a photo taken with a handheld digital camera, and as you can see, the image is tilted a bit to the left.)

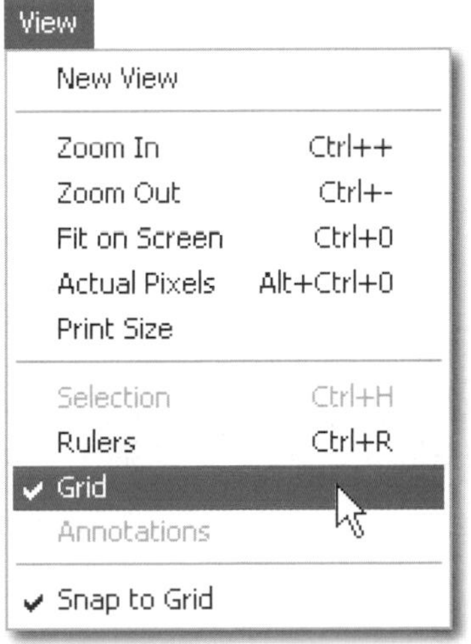

Step Two:
Go under the View menu and choose Grid. Elements will put a non-printing grid of squares over your entire photo (as shown on the following page).

Continued

Step Three:
Grab the bottom right-hand corner of your image window and drag outward to reveal the gray desktop area around your photo (as shown here). Press Control-A (Mac: Command-A) to select the entire photo, and then press Control-T (Mac: Command-T) to bring up the Free Transform bounding box around your photo.

Step Four:
Move your cursor outside the bounding box and click-and-drag upward or downward to rotate your image (using the grid as a straight edge to align your image). If one of the horizontal grid lines isn't close enough to a part of your image that's supposed to be straight, just move your cursor inside the bounding box, then use the Up/Down Arrow keys on your keyboard to temporarily nudge your photo up/down until it reaches a grid line.

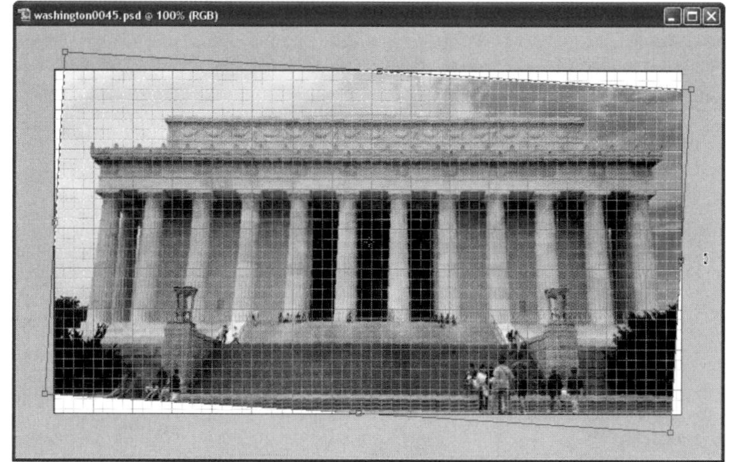

TIP: If you want more control of your rotation (and this is particularly helpful when you're trying to align to a grid, rather than just "eyeing it"), try this: While you have Free Transform in place, go up to the Options Bar and click once inside the rotation field (as shown here). Then use the up/down arrow on your keyboard which will rotate your photo in 1/10˚ increments, giving you maximum control.

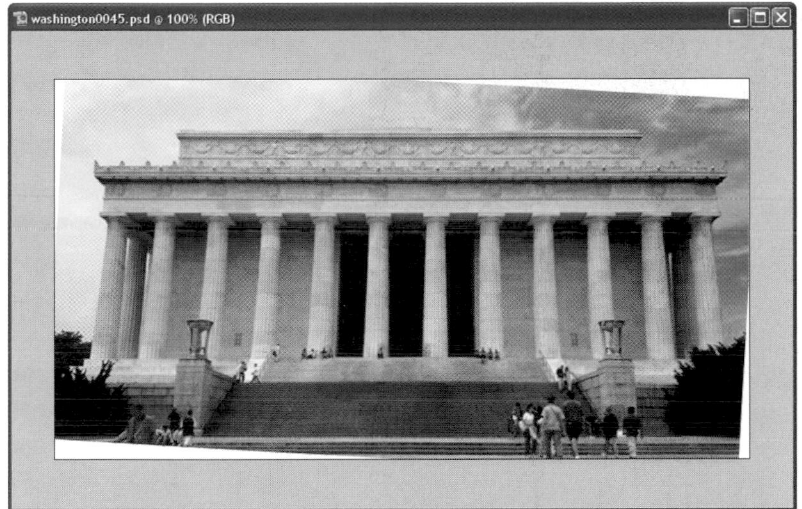

Step Five:

Go back under the View menu, and choose Grid to remove the grid. Once you remove the grid, you'll notice that there are white Canvas areas visible in the corners of your image, so you'll have to crop the image to hide these from view.

Step Six:

Press the letter "C" to switch to the Crop tool, then drag out a cropping border that will crop your image so none of the white corners are showing. When your border is in place, press Enter (Mac: Return). The final cropped image is shown here.

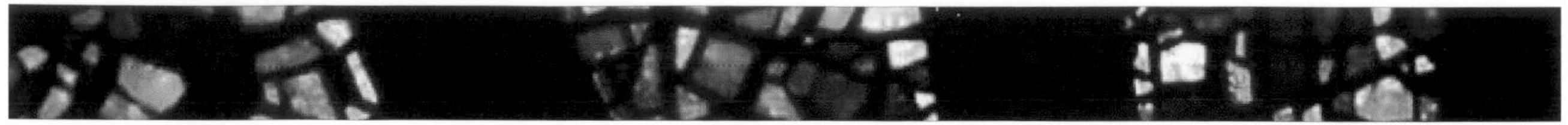

Resizing Digital Camera Photos

If you're used to resizing scans, you'll find that resizing images from digital cameras is a bit different, primarily because scanners create high-resolution scans (usually 300 ppi or more), but the default setting for digital cameras usually produces an image that is large in physical dimensions, but lower in ppi (usually 72 ppi). The trick is to decrease the size of your digital camera image (and increase its resolution) without losing any quality in your photo. Here's the trick:

Step One:

Open the digital camera image that you want to resize. Press Control-R (Mac: Command-R) to make Elements' Rulers visible. As you can see from the Rulers, the photo is just a little more than 13″ wide by nearly 9″ high.

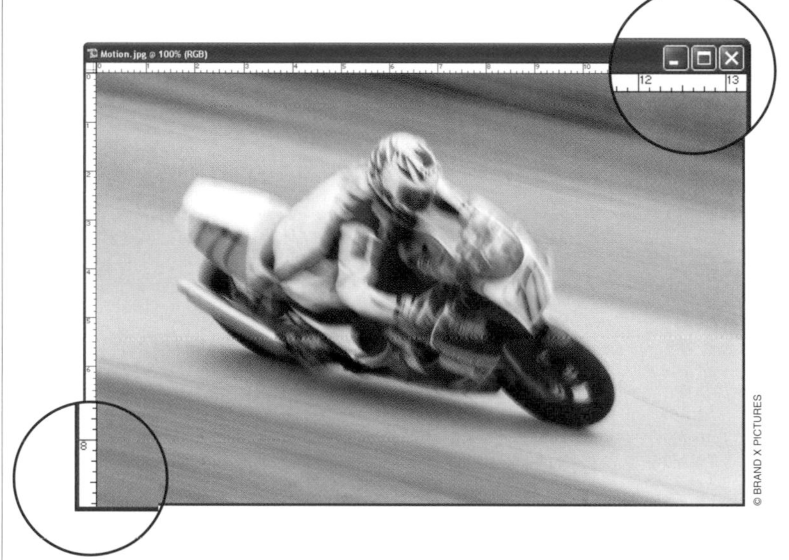

© BRAND X PICTURES

Step Two:

Go under the Image menu, under Resize, and choose Image Size to bring up the Image Size dialog box shown here. Under the Document Size section, the Resolution setting is 72 pixels/inch (ppi). A resolution of 72 ppi is considered "low resolution" and is ideal for photos that will only be viewed onscreen (such as Web graphics, slideshows, etc.), but is too low to get high-quality results from a color inkjet printer, color laser printer, or for use on a printing press.

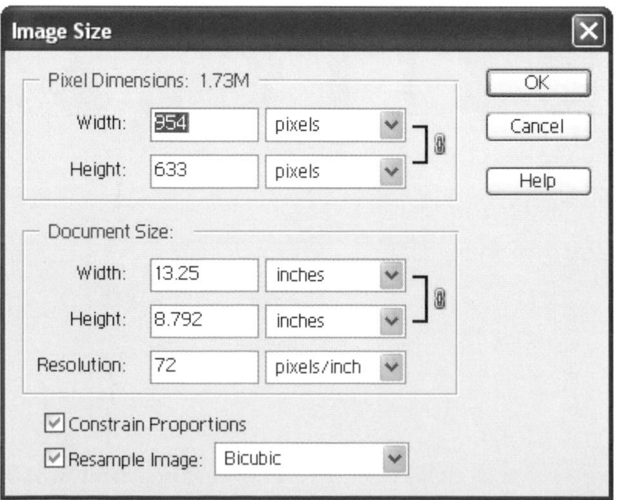

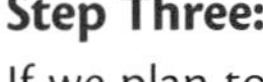

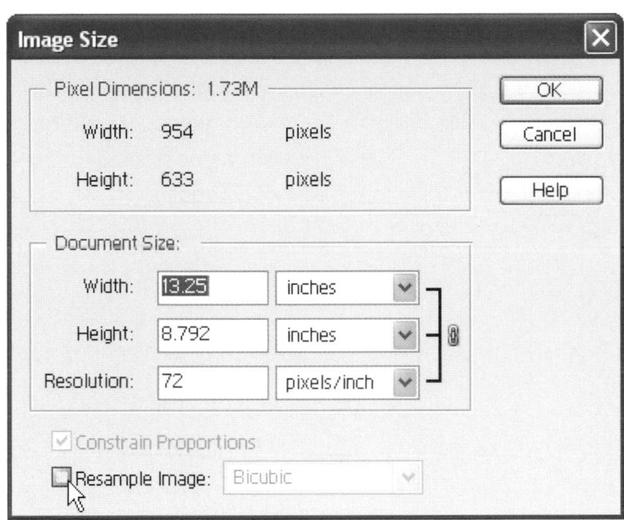

Step Three:

If we plan to output this photo to any printing device, it's pretty clear that we'll need to increase the resolution to get good results. I wish we could just type in the resolution we'd like it to be in the Resolution field (such as 200 or 300 ppi), but unfortunately, this "resampling" makes our low-resolution photo appear soft (blurry) and pixelated. That's why we need to turn the Resample Image checkbox off (it's on by default). That way, when we type in a resolution setting that we need, Elements automatically adjusts the Width and Height of the image down in the exact same proportion. As your Width and Height come down (with Resample Image turned off) your resolution goes up. Best of all, there's absolutely no loss of quality. Pretty cool!

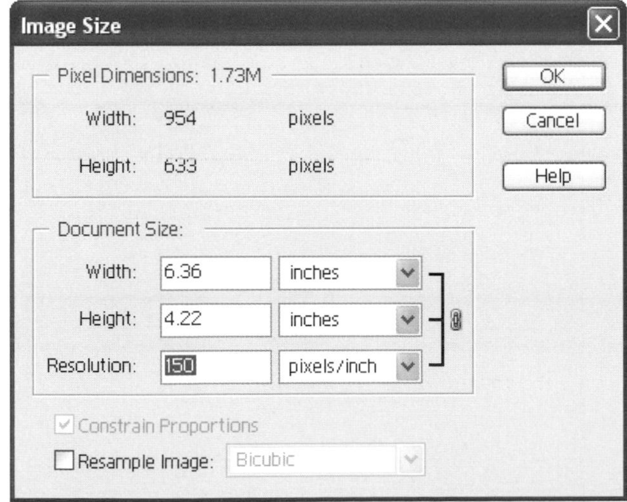

Step Four:

Here I've turned off Resample Image, then I typed 150 in the Resolution field (for output to a color inkjet printer. I know, you probably think you need a lot more resolution, but you usually don't). At a resolution of only 150 ppi, I can actually print a photo that is 6" wide by almost 4" high.

Continued

Step Five:

Here's the Image Size dialog for our source photo, and this time I've increased the Resolution setting to 212 ppi (for output to a printing press. Again, you don't need nearly as much resolution as you'd think). As you can see, the Width of my image is no longer 13.25"—it's now just 4.5". The Height is no longer 8.792"—now it's 2.986".

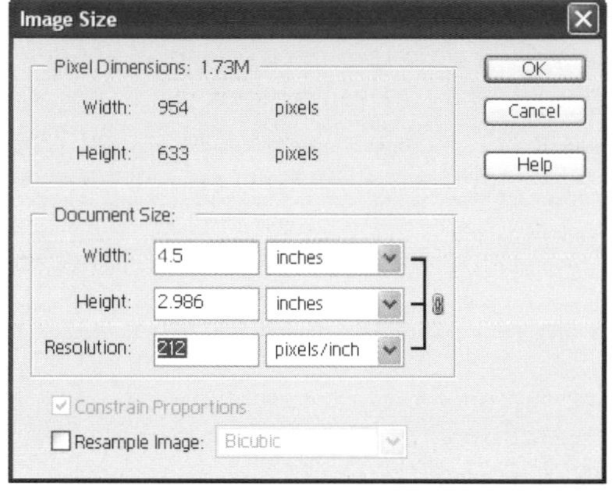

Step Six:

When you click OK, you won't see the image window change at all—it will appear at the exact same size on screen. But now look at the rulers—you can see that it's now just 4.5" wide by almost 3" high.

Resizing using this technique does three big things: (1) It gets your physical dimensions down to size (the photo now fits on an 8x10 sheet); (2) it increases the resolution enough so you can even output this image on a printing press; and (3) you haven't softened, blurred, or pixelated the image in any way—the quality remains the same—all because you turned off Resample Image.

Note: Do not turn off Resample Image for images that you scan on a scanner—they start as high-resolution images in the first place. *Turning off Resample Image is only for photos taken with a digital camera.*

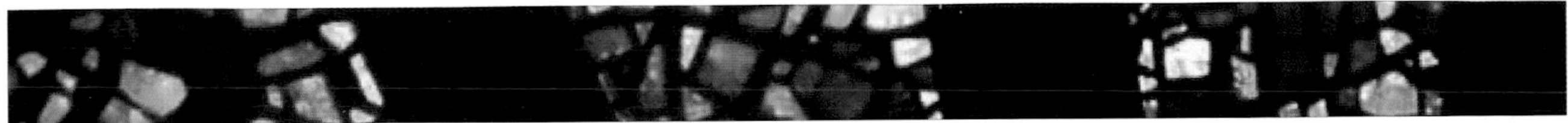

Resizing and How to Reach Those Hidden Free Transform Handles

What happens if you drag a large photo onto a smaller photo in Elements? (This happens all the time, especially if you're collaging or combining two or more photos.) You have to resize the photo using Free Transform, right? Right. But here's the catch—when you bring up Free Transform, at least two, or more likely all four of the handles you need to resize the image are out of reach. You see the center point (as shown in the photo below), but not the handles you need to reach to resize. Here's how to get around that hurdle quickly and easily.

© BRAND X PICTURES

Step One:

In the example shown here, we opened two photos and used the Move tool to drag one on top of the other (the photo that you drag appears on its own layer automatically). To resize a photo on a layer, press Control-T (Mac: Command-T) to bring up the Free Transform function. Next, hold the Shift key (to constrain your proportions), grab one of the Free Transform corner points and (a) drag inward to shrink the photo, or (b) drag outward to increase its size (not more than 20%, to keep from making the photo look soft and pixelated). But the problem is—you can't even see the Free Transform handles in this image.

Step Two:

To instantly have full access to all of Free Transform's handles, just press Control-0 (Mac: Command-0 [that's zero, not "O"]) and Elements will instantly zoom out your document window and surround your photo with gray desktop, making every handle well within reach. Try it once, and you'll use this trick again and again. Note: You must choose Free Transform first for this trick to work.

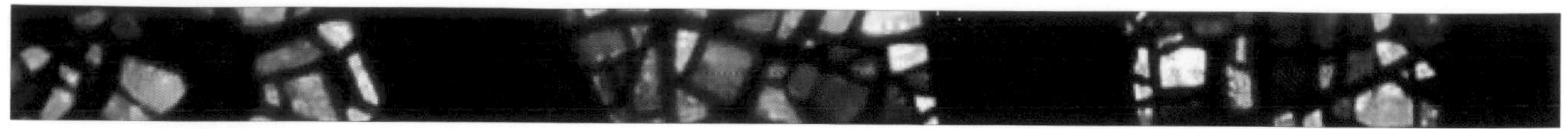

The Cool Trick for Turning Small Photos into Poster-Sized Prints

Generally speaking, shrinking the physical dimensions of a photo does not create a quality problem—you can make an 8x10 into a 4x5 with little visible loss of quality. It's increasing the size of an image where you run into problems (the photo often gets visibly blurry, softer, and even pixelated). However, digital photography guru (and *Photoshop User* columnist) Jim DiVitale showed me a trick he swears by that lets you increase your digital camera images up to full poster size, with hardly any visible loss of quality to the naked eye, and I tell ya, it'll make a believer out of you.

Step One:

Open the digital camera image you want to increase to poster size. The image shown here was taken with a 3-megapixel Nikon digital camera. It's physically more than 6″ wide by 10″ high, at 72 ppi.

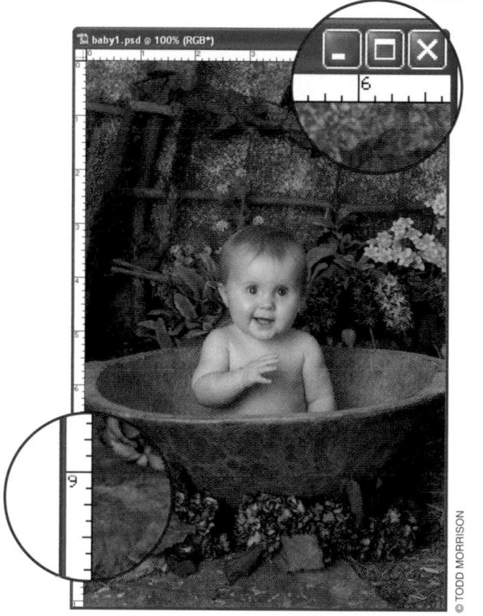

© TODD MORRISON

Step Two

Go under the Image menu, under Resize, and choose Image Size. When the Image Size dialog box appears, make sure Resample Image is turned on. Switch the unit of measure pop-up menus in the dialog from Inches to Percent (as shown) and type in 110, which will increase your image by 10%. Believe it or not, when you increase in 10% increments, for some reason it doesn't seem to soften or blur the image. It's freaky, I know, but to believe it you just have to try it yourself.

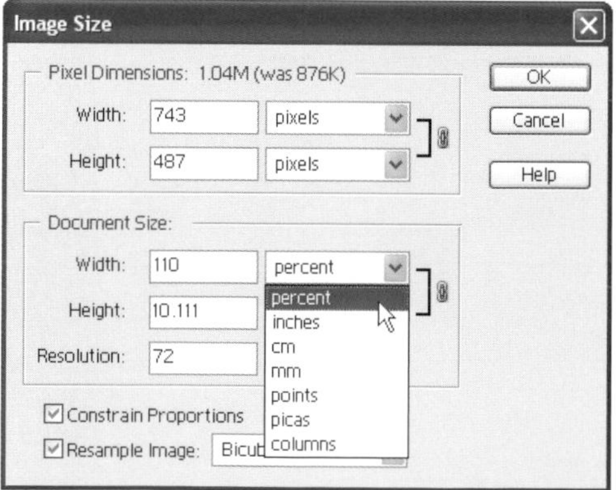

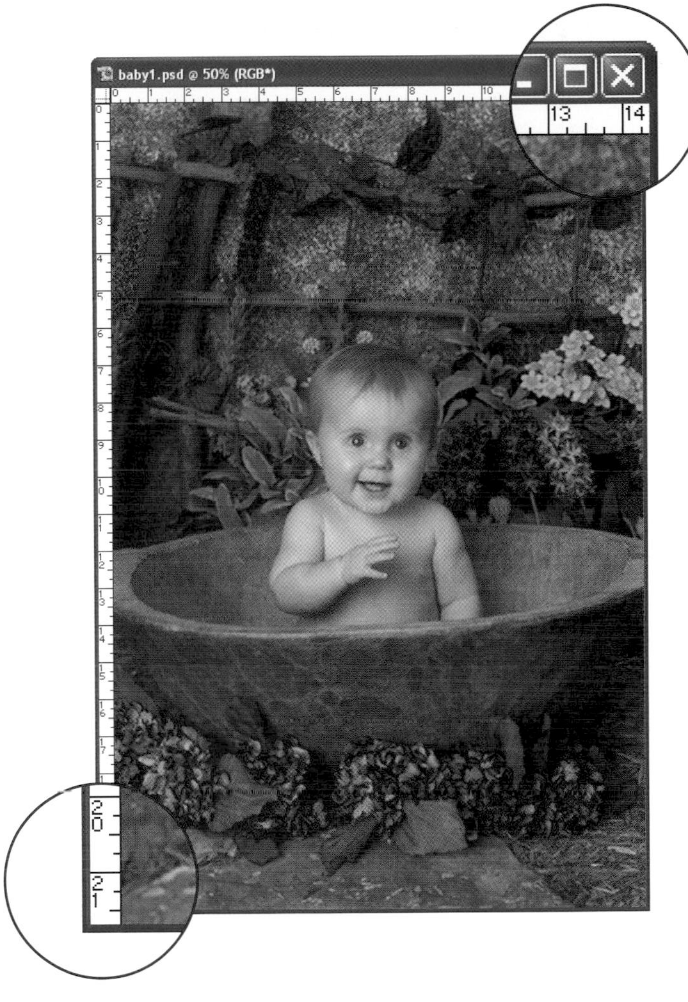

Step Three:

To get this image up to poster size, it's going to take quite a few passes with this "increase-by-10%" technique, so make sure you've got a comfy chair before you start. But if you need to make your prints big, and keep as much clarity and definition as possible, it's worth the extra effort.

Here's the final image, increased from approximately 6.5″x10″ to approximately 14″x21″, and even onscreen, the loss of quality is almost negligible; yet the image is almost the size of a standard, full-sized poster. I had to increase the size by 10% about 12 times to get up to that size. Thanks to Jimmy D for sharing this amazing, yet deceptively simple technique with us. Jim rocks!

Photographer | Todd Morrison

The Big Fixx

digital camera image problems

Okay, did you catch that reference to the band The Fixx in the title? You did? Great. That means that you're at least in your mid-thirties to early forties. (I myself am only in my mid- to early twenties, but I listen to oldies stations just to keep in touch with baby boomers and other people who at one time or another tried to break-dance.) Well, the Fixx had a big hit in the early '80s (around the time I was born) called "One Thing Leads to Another" and that's a totally appropriate title for this chapter because one thing (using a digital camera) leads to another (having to deal with things like digital noise, color aliasing, and other nasties that pop up when you've finally kicked the film habit and gone totally digital). Admittedly, some of the problems we bring upon ourselves (like leaving the lens cap on; or forgetting to bring our camera to the shoot, where the shoot is, who hired us, or what day it is; or we immersed our flash into a tub of Jell-O, you know—the standard stuff). And other things are problems caused by the hardware itself (the slave won't fire when it's submerged in Jell-O, you got some Camembert on the lens, etc.). Whatever the problem, and regardless of whose fault it is, problems are going to happen, and you're going to need to fix them in Elements. Some of the fixes are easy, like running the "Remove Camembert" filter, and then changing the Blend Mode to Fromage. Others will have you jumping through some major Elements hoops, but fear not, the problems you'll most likely run into are all covered here in a step-by-step format that will have you wiping cold congealed water off your flash unit faster than you can say, "How can Scott possibly be in his mid-twenties?"

Compensating for "Too Much Flash" or Overexposure

Don't ya hate it when you open a photo and realize that either (a) the flash fired when it shouldn't have; (b) you were too close to the subject to use the flash and they're totally "blown out"; or (c) you're simply not qualified to use a flash at all, and your flash unit should be forcibly taken from you, even if that means ripping it from the camera body? Here's a quick fix to get your photo back from the "flash graveyard" while keeping your reputation, and camera parts, intact.

Step One:
Open the photo that is suffering from "flashaphobia." In the example shown here the flash, mounted on the camera body, washed out the entire subject.

© BRAND X PICTURES

Step Two:
Make a copy of the photo by dragging your Background layer to the Create New Layer icon at the bottom of the Layers palette. This will create a layer titled "Background copy."

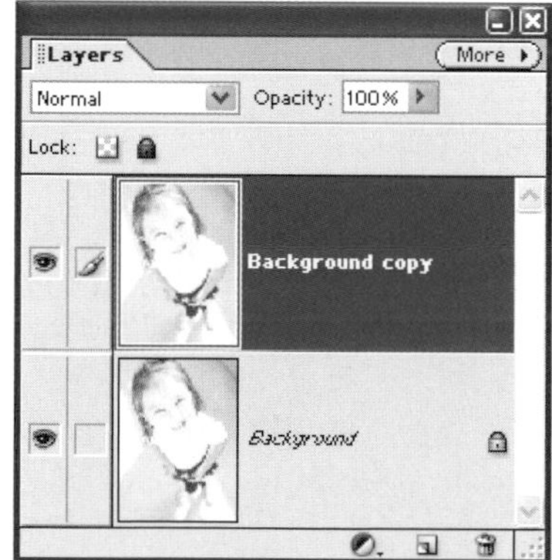

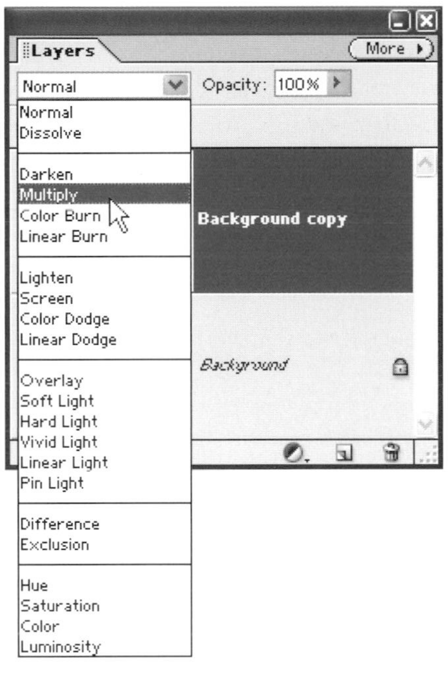

Step Three:

Next, change the Blend Mode of Background copy from Normal to Multiply from the pop-up menu at the top of the Layers palette. This Blend Mode has a "multiplier" effect, and brings back a lot of the original detail the flash "blew out."

Step Four:

If the photo still looks washed out, you may need to make a duplicate of the Background copy layer. Just drag this background copy layer to the Create New Layer icon at the bottom of the Layers palette. This additional copy of the Background Layer copy will already be in Multiply mode. Incidentally, because of the immutable laws of life, chances are that creating one layer with its Blend Mode set to Multiply won't be enough, but adding another layer (in Multiply mode) will be "too much." If that's the case, just go to the Layers palette and lower the Opacity setting of the top layer to 50% or less—this way you can "dial in" just the right amount, and get the amount of flash looking right.

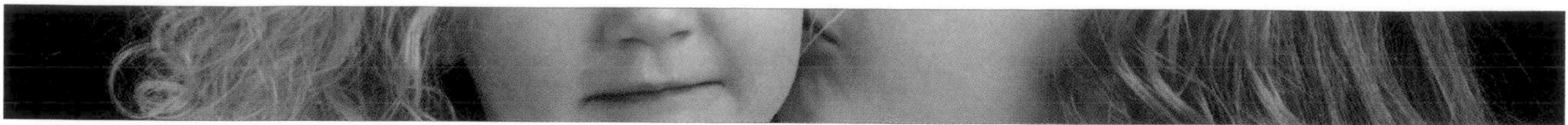

Removing Digital Noise (AKA Color Aliasing)

Here's a quick trick Jim DiVitale and Kevin Ames use for reducing digital noise (those nasty red, green, and blue little dots). This noise (also called color aliasing) will often appear in digital photos shot in low lighting situations. This is one of those "the cheaper the digital camera, the more noise it creates" situations, so if you're shooting with an "el cheapo" digital camera, this is one technique you'll be using a lot. This technique won't remove all the noise, but it will remove the red, green, and blue color from the noise, so it will appear much less prevalent in the photo.

Step One:

Open the photo that has visible digital noise. Make a copy of the Background layer by dragging it to the Create New Layer icon at the bottom of the Layers palette. This will create a layer titled "Background copy."

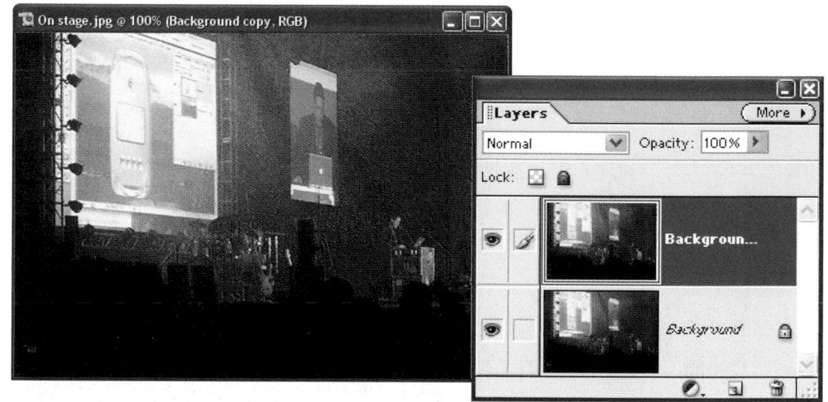

Step Two:

Go under the Filter menu, under Blur, and choose Gaussian Blur. Drag the Radius slider all the way to the left, then start dragging to the right until the digital noise is blurred enough that you can't see it (of course, the rest of the photo will look mighty blurry too, but don't sweat that, just blur it until the digital noise goes away, even if the photo gets very blurry). Click OK to apply the blur.

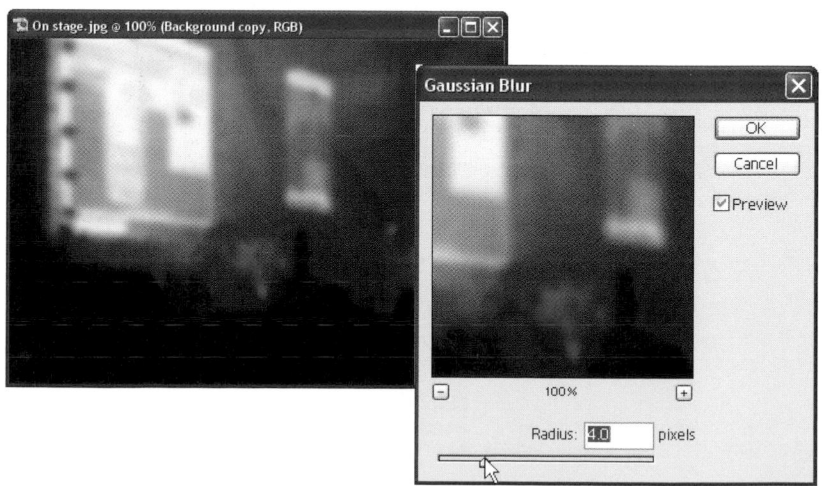

Step Three:
Go to the Layers palette and change the Blend Mode of this layer from Normal to Color.

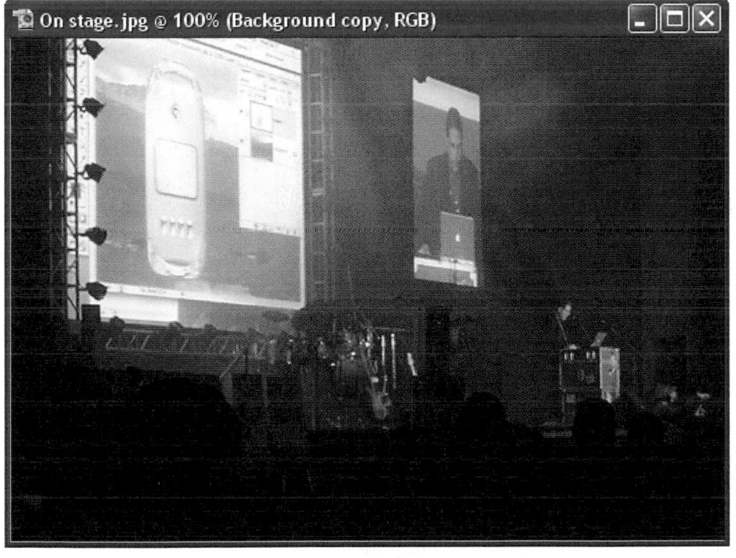

© LESA SNIDER

Step Four:
Changing the Blend Mode to Color removes the visible blurring, but at the same time, it removes the red, green, and blue colors from the noise, leaving you with a much cleaner-looking photo. Remember, this technique does not remove all the noise that your camera introduced. Instead, it removes the color from the noise, which makes the overall amount of noise less visible to the eye.

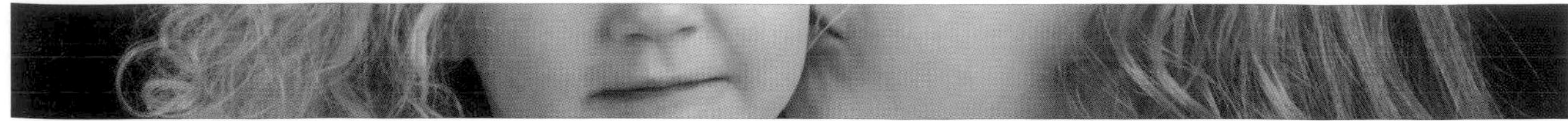

Fixing Photos Where You Wish You Hadn't Used Flash

There's a natural tendency for some photographers to react to their immediate surroundings, rather than what they see through the lens. For example, if you're shooting an indoor concert, there are often hundreds of lights illuminating the stage. However, some photographers think it's one light short—their flash—because where they're sitting, it's dark. When you look at your photos later, you see that your flash lit everyone in front of you (which wasn't the way it really looked—the crowd is usually in the dark), which ruins an otherwise great shot. Here's a quick fix to make it look as if your flash never fired at all.

Step One:

Open a photo where shooting with the flash has ruined part of the image (like the image shown here taken during a seminar presentation, where the back ten rows are lit by the flash, when they should be dark. Just the stage lit by the stage lighting should appear out of the darkness).

Step Two:

Press the letter "L" to get the Lasso tool, and draw a loose selection over the area where the flash affected the shot. In the image shown here, all the people in the audience have been selected.

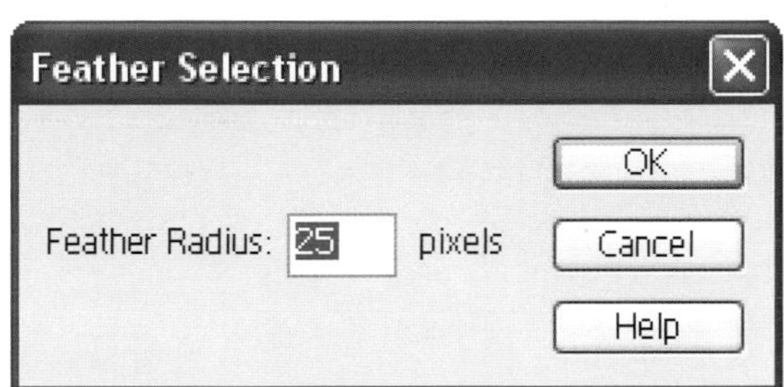

Step Three:

In the next step, we're going to adjust the tonal range of this selected area, but we don't want that adjustment to appear obvious. We'll need to soften the edges of our selection quite a bit so our adjustment blends in smoothly with the rest of the photo. To do this, go under the Select menu and choose Feather. When the Feather Selection dialog box appears, enter 25 pixels to soften the selection edge. (By the way, 25 pixels is just my guess for how much this particular selection might need. The rule of thumb is: the higher the resolution of the image, the more Feathering you'll need, so don't be afraid to use more than 25 if your edge is visible when you finish.)

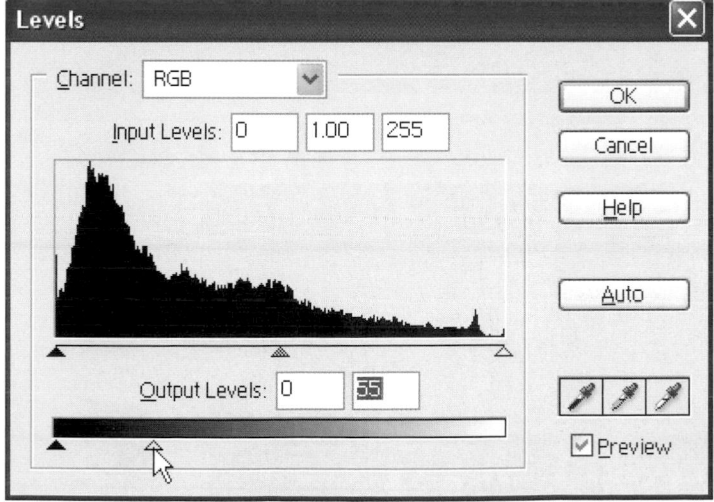

Step Four:

It will help you make a better adjustment if you hide the selection border (we call it "the marching ants") from view. Note: We don't want to deselect—we want our selection to remain intact but we don't want to see the annoying border, so press Control-H (Mac: Command-H) to hide the selection border. Now, press Control-L (Mac: Command-L) to bring up the Levels dialog. At the bottom of the dialog, drag the right Output Levels slider to the left to darken your selected area. Because you've hidden the selection border, it should be very easy to match the surroundings of your photo by just dragging this slider to your left.

Continued

Step Five:
When the photo looks about right, click OK to apply your Levels adjustment. Then, press Control-H (Mac: Command-H) to make your selection visible again (this trips up a lot of people who, since they don't see the selection anymore, forget it's there and then nothing reacts as it should from that point on).

Step Six:
Last, press Control-D (Mac: Command-D) to deselect and view your repaired "flash-free" photo.

Before

After

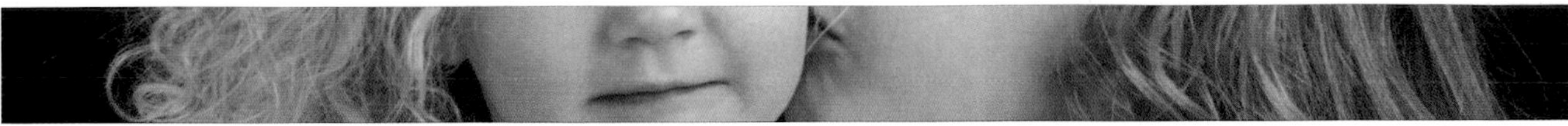

Fixing Underexposed Photos

This is a tonal correction for people who don't like making tonal corrections (over 60 million Americans suffer from the paralyzing fear of MTC [Making Tonal Corrections]). Since this technique requires no knowledge of tonal corrections (like using Levels), it's very popular, and even though it's incredibly simple to perform, it does a pretty incredible job of fixing underexposed photos.

© BRAND X PICTURES

Step One:
Open an underexposed photo. The photo shown here, shot indoors without a flash, could've used either a fill flash or a better exposure setting.

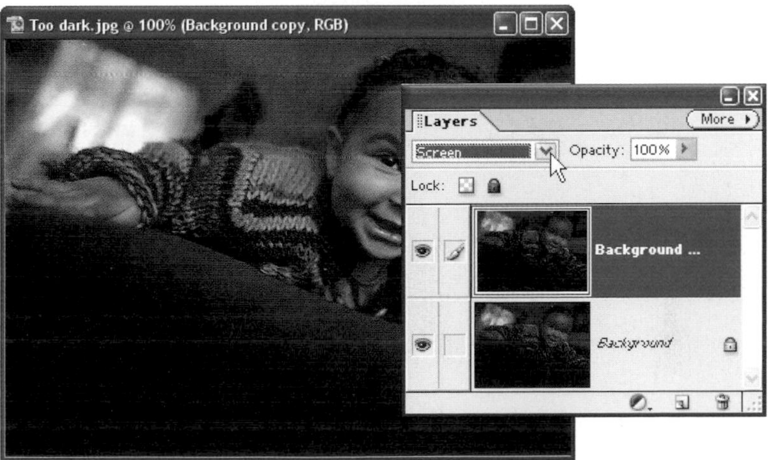

Step Two:
Make a copy of the Background layer by dragging it to the Create New Layer icon at the bottom of the Layers palette. This will create a layer titled "Background copy." In the Layers palette change the Blend Mode of this new layer from Normal to Screen to lighten the entire photo.

Continued

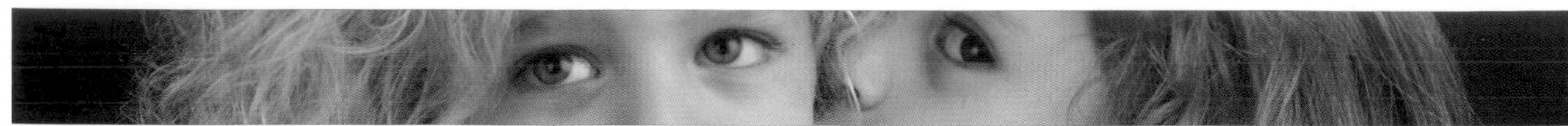

Step Three:

If the photo still isn't properly exposed, keep dragging this Screen layer to the Create New Layer icon at the bottom of the Layers palette to duplicate it until the exposure looks about right (this may take a few layers, but don't be shy about it—keep duplicating layers until it looks right).

Step Four:

There's a good chance that at some point your photo will still look a bit underexposed, so you'll duplicate the layer again, but now it looks overexposed. What you need is "half a layer." Half as much lightening. Here's what to do: Lower the Opacity of your top layer to "dial in" the perfect amount of light, giving you something between the full intensity of the layer (at 100%) and no layer at all (at 0%). For half the intensity, try 50%. (Did I really even have to say that last line? Didn't think so.) Once the photo looks properly exposed, click the "More" button at the top right of the Layers palette to access the palette's pop-down menu, and choose Flatten Image.

Before

After

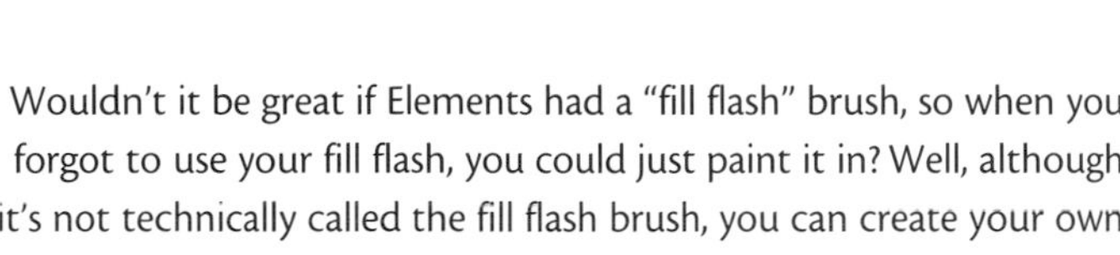

When you Forget to Use Fill Flash

Wouldn't it be great if Elements had a "fill flash" brush, so when you forgot to use your fill flash, you could just paint it in? Well, although it's not technically called the fill flash brush, you can create your own brush and get the same effect. There's also a "built-in" Fill Flash fixer, so I'll show you that first, but I predict you'll like the fill flash brush that you'll create even better. Hey, it's just a prediction.

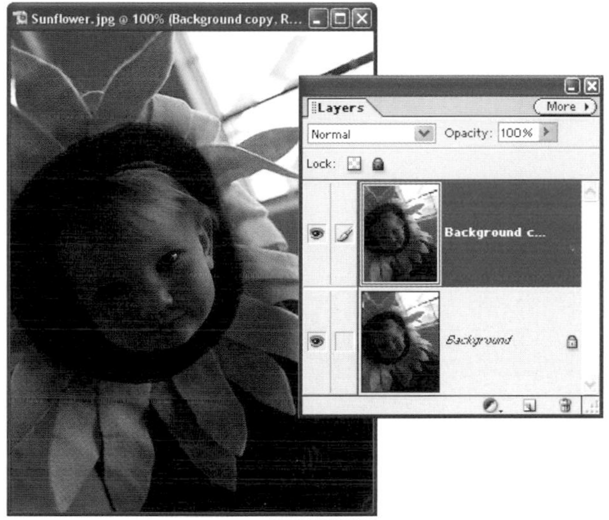

© BRAND X PICTURES

Step One:

Open a photo where the subject of the image appears in shadows. Make a copy of the photo by dragging your Background layer to the Create New Layer icon at the bottom of the Layers palette. This will create a layer titled "Background copy."

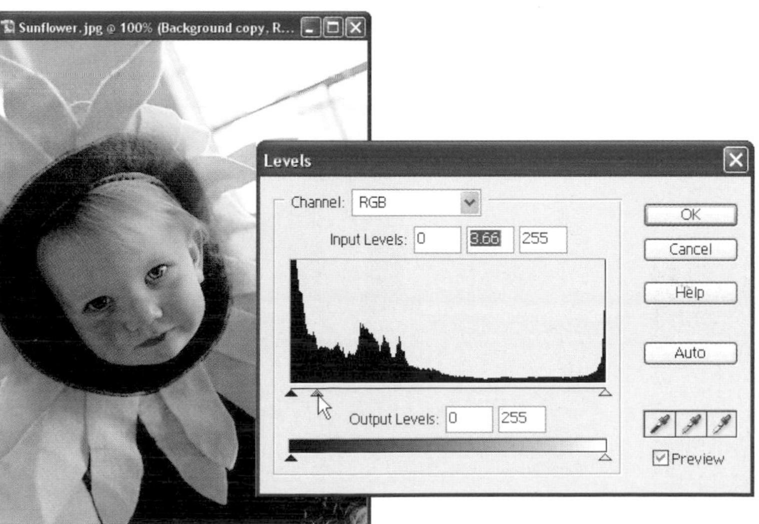

Step Two:

Go under the Enhance menu, under Adjust Brightness/Contrast, and choose Levels. Drag the middle Input Levels slider (the gray one) to the left until your subject looks properly exposed. (Note: Don't worry about how the background looks—it will probably become completely "blown out" but you'll fix that later; for now, just focus on making your subject look right.) If the midtone slider doesn't bring out the subject enough, you may have to increase the highlights as well, so drag the far right Input Levels slider to the left to increase the highlights. When your subject looks properly exposed, click OK.

Continued

Step Three:
Hold the Control key (Mac: Command key) and click on the Create New Layer icon at the bottom of the Layers palette. This creates a new blank layer beneath your duplicate layer (shown here, left). In the Layers palette, click on the top layer (your duplicate of the Background layer), then press Control-G (Mac: Command-G) to group this photo layer with the blank layer beneath it. This removes the brightening of the photo you did in Step Two (shown here, right).

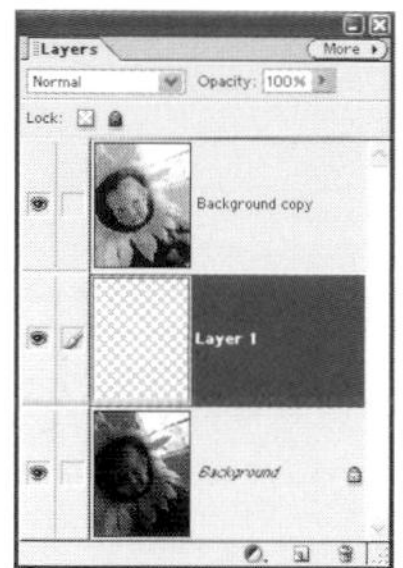

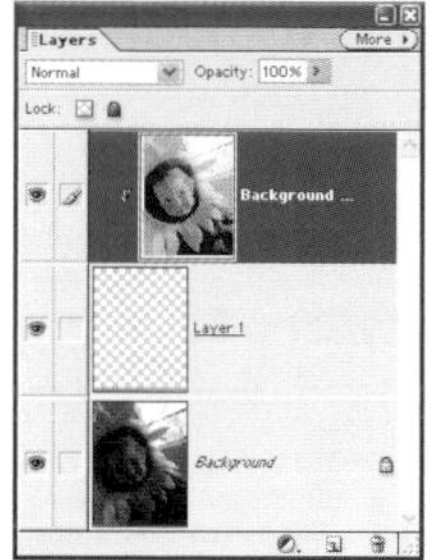

Step Four:
In the Layers palette, click on the blank layer beneath your grouped, top layer. Get the Brush tool from the Toolbox and choose a soft-edged brush from the Brush Picker in the Options Bar. Set black as your Foreground color, and begin to paint (on this blank layer) over the areas of the image that need a fill flash with your newly created "fill flash" brush. As you paint, the areas you paint over will appear lighter, because you're "painting in" the lighter version of your image on this layer. Continue painting until it looks as if you had used a fill flash. When you're painting, if it appears too intense, just lower the Opacity of the layer you're painting on.

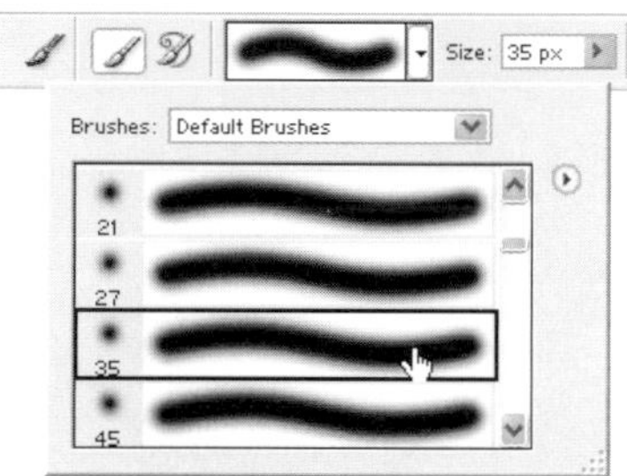

Before

After

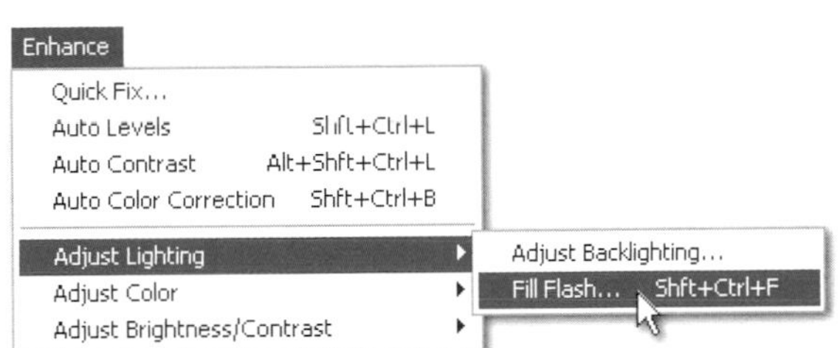

The "Built-in" Fill Flash

Step One:

If you're not as concerned about keeping the background from being lightened as well, you can use Elements' built-in Fill Flash correction. Go under the Enhance menu, under Adjust Lighting, and choose Fill Flash.

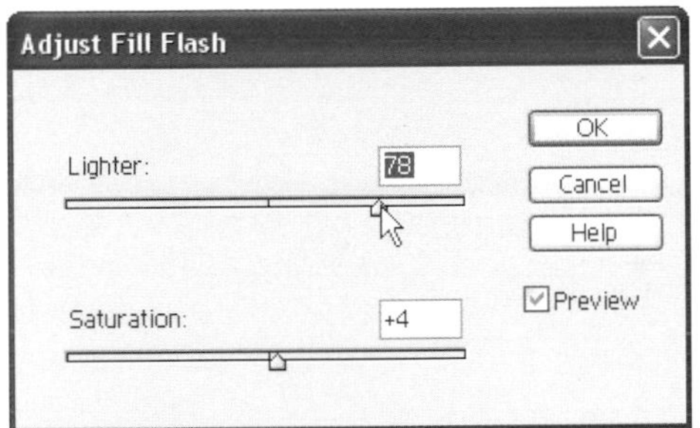

Step Two:

When the Fill Flash dialog appears, drag the Lighter slider to the right to simulate the effect of a fill flash. If making the photo lighter makes it look less saturated, you can increase the saturation by dragging the Saturation slider at the bottom of the dialog to the right (as shown here).

Step Three:

Click OK and the Fill Flash effect is applied. If you don't want the Fill Flash to affect your entire photo, you could make a selection of the area that you want to apply the effect to (like putting a selection around a person in shadows), but if you're going to go through all that trouble, you might as well just use the "fill flash" brush technique shown on the previous pages.

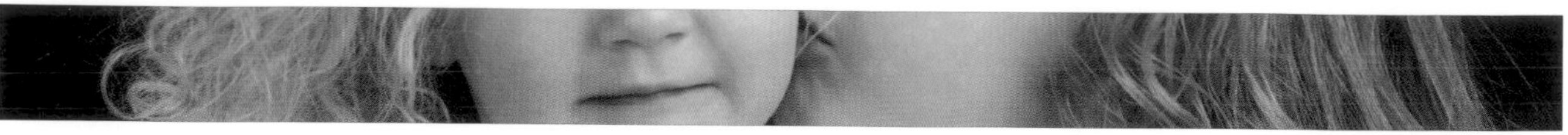

Instant Red-Eye Removal

When I see a digital camera with the flash mounted directly above the lens, I think, "Hey, there's an automated red-eye machine." In studio situations, you don't have to deal with this as much, because your flash probably wouldn't be mounted directly above your lens—you're using bounce flash, holding the flash separately, you've got studio strobes, or one of a dozen other techniques. Here's the quick "I-just-want-it-gone" technique for getting rid of red eye fast.

Step One:

Open a photo where the subject has red eye. Get the Zoom tool from the Toolbox (it looks like a magnifying glass) and drag out a selection with it right around the eyes (this zooms you in on the eyes).

© LEO & EILEEN GILLIS

Step Two:

Now, press the letter "Y" to switch to the Red Eye Brush tool (it looks like a brush with an "eye" icon). Set your Foreground color to black (or just click the Default Colors button up in the Options Bar).

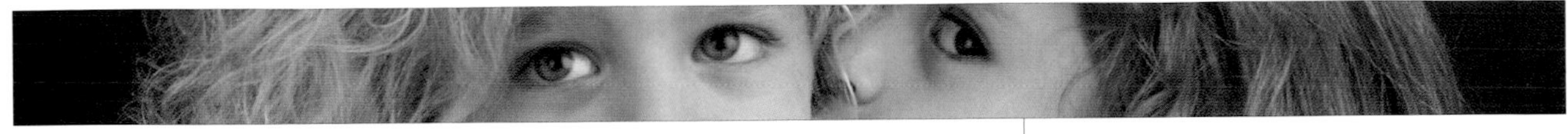

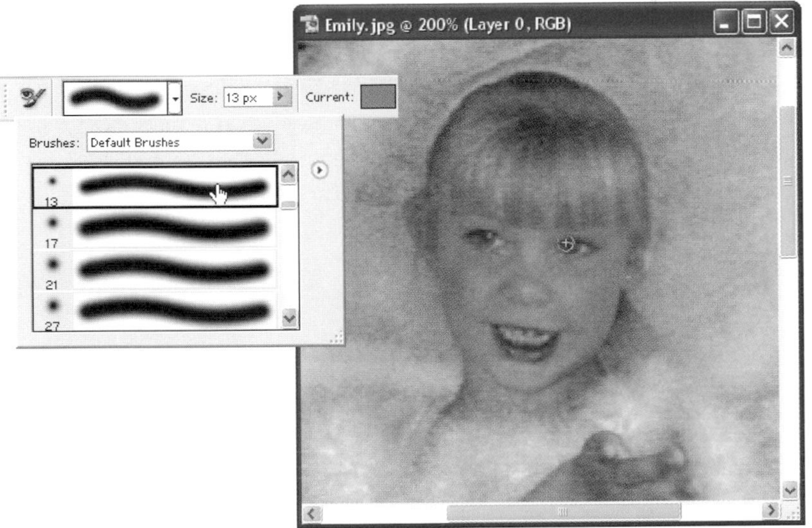

Step Three:
Choose a soft-edged brush from the Brush Picker up in the Options Bar, then use the Red Eye Brush tool to paint directly over the red eye (you can even dab if you like). As you paint, the red disappears. Note: Your Background layer changes to Layer 0 in the Layers palette when you use the Red Eye Brush.

Step Four:
While your cursor moves over the eye, you'll see a swatch called "Current" changing color up in the Options Bar. That's the "sample" color, which can be very helpful in pointing on any areas that are still red. Just move your cursor around the eye (without painting) and anytime you see a red color appear in the sample, paint it away. Continue painting over any other eyes in the photo (hey, the photo could have more than one person in it, meaning more than just one other eye to fix) and you're done. No more red eye. Instead, now you have gray eye, which doesn't look spectacular, but it's a heck of a lot better than red eye.

Removing Red Eye and Recoloring the Eye

This technique is a little more complicated (not hard, it just has a few more steps) but the result is more professional because you're not just going to remove the red eye (like in the previous "Instant Red-Eye Removal" trick) and replace it with the more pleasing "gray eye"; instead, we're going to restore the eye to its original color.

Step One:

Open a photo where the subject has red eye.

Step Two:

Zoom in close on one of the eyes using the Zoom tool (the magnifying glass). Note: You might not want to do this late at night if you're home alone, because seeing a huge scary eye on your screen can really give you the willies. Use the technique shown on the previous two pages, which removes the red eye, and replaces it with gray eye.

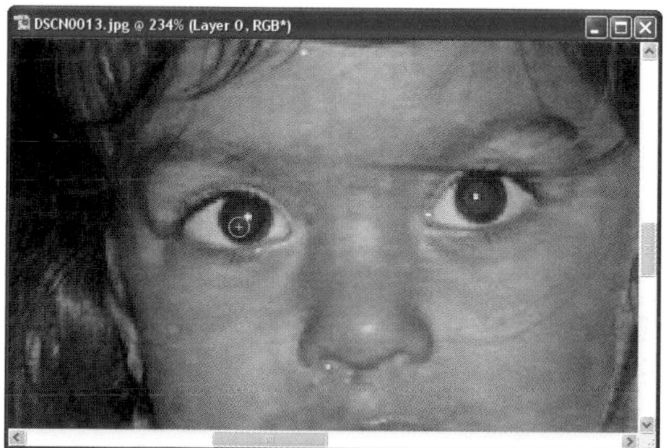

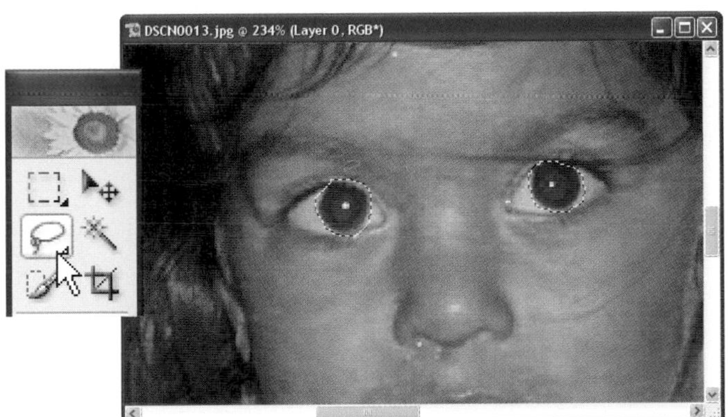

Step Three:

Press the "L" key to switch to the Lasso tool, and draw a very loose selection around the entire left eye (as shown). The key word here is loose—stay well outside the iris itself, and don't try to make a precise selection. Selecting the eyelids, eyelashes, etc. will not create a problem. Once the left eye is selected, hold the Shift key, and then use the Lasso tool to select the right eye in the same fashion (giving you both eyes as selections).

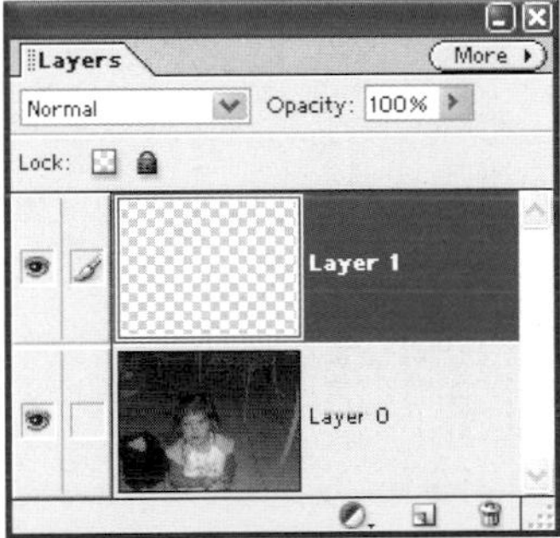

Step Four:

Once you have a loose selection around both eyes, press Control-C (Mac: Command-C) to copy the selection of the eyes in Elements' clipboard memory. Then, without deselecting, go to the Layers palette and create a new blank layer by clicking on the Create New Layer icon at the bottom of the Layers palette.

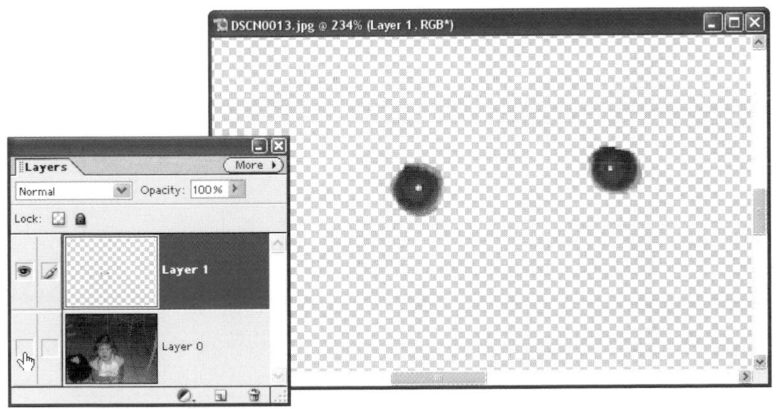

Step Five:

Next, press Control-V (Mac: Command-V) to paste the eyes into the selection on this new layer. This does two things: (1) It pastes the copied eyes on this layer in the exact same position as they are on the Background layer, and (2) it automatically deselects for you. Now you have just a pair of eyes on this layer (you may have to hide your Background layer for just a moment, to see the eyes by themselves. Just click the Eye icon in the first column beside the Background layer to hide it).

Continued

Step Six:
While you're on this "eyes" layer, go under the Enhance menu, under Adjust Color, and choose Hue/Saturation. In the dialog box, click on the Colorize checkbox (in the bottom right-hand corner). Now you can choose the color you'd like for the eyes by moving the Hue slider. In this case, we're going to colorize the iris blue. Don't worry about the color being too intense at this point, you can totally adjust that later, so if you want blue eyes, choose a deep blue and we'll dial in the exact blue later. Click OK to apply the blue to the irises and the area around them as well. (Don't let this freak you out that other areas right around the iris appear blue. We'll fix that in the next step.)

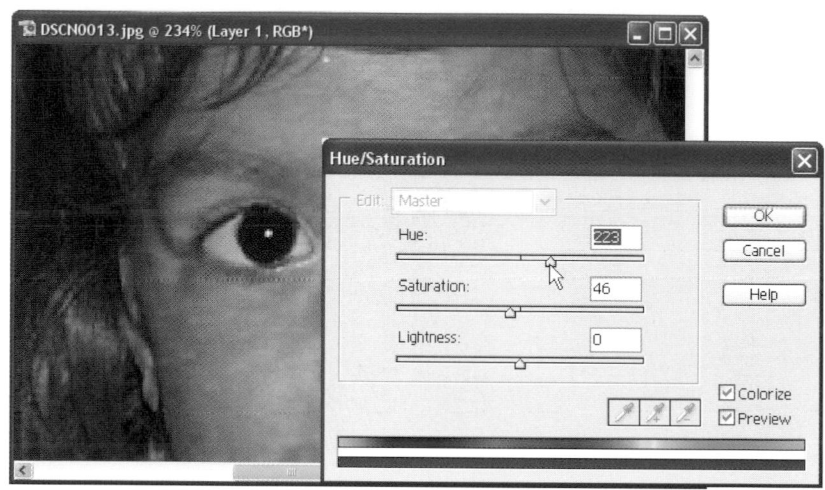

Step Seven:
Press the "E" key to switch to the Eraser tool. Press "D" to make sure your background color is white. Choose a hard-edged brush (from the Brush Picker up in the Options Bar), and then simply erase the extra areas around the iris. This sounds much harder than it is—it's actually very easy—just erase everything but the blue iris. Don't forget to erase over the whites of the person's eyes. Remember, the eyes are on their own layer, so you can't accidentally damage any other parts of the photo.

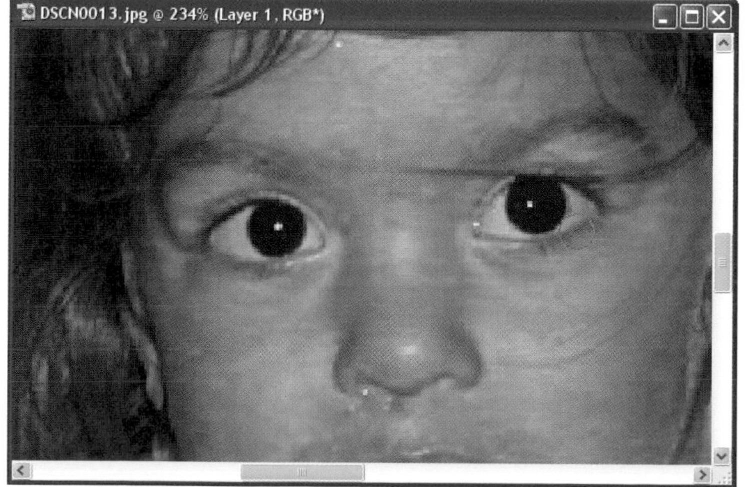

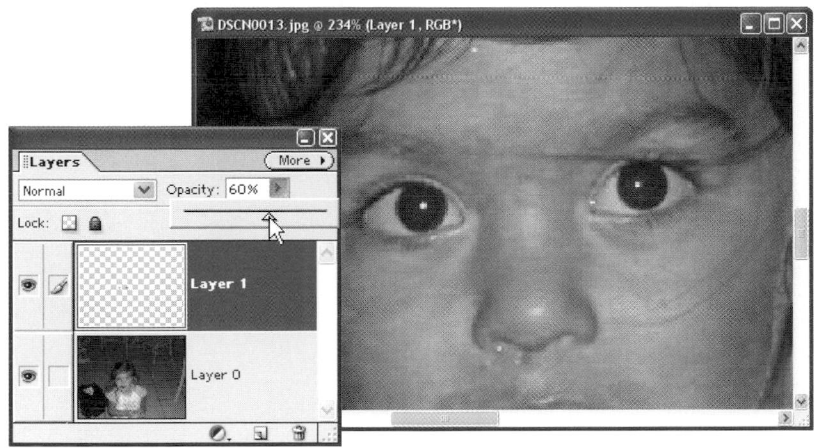

Step Eight:

If the eye color seems too intense (and chances are, it will), you can lower the intensity of the color in the Layers palette by simply lowering the Opacity of this layer (using the Opacity slider in the upper right-hand corner of the Layers palette) until the eyes look natural.

Step Nine:

To finish the red-eye correction and recolor, press Control-E (Mac: Command-E) to merge the colored eye layer with the Background layer, completing the repair.

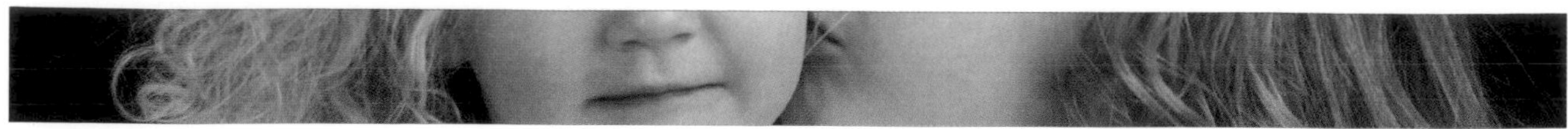

Repairing Keystoning

Keystoning is often found in photos with buildings or tall objects, where the buildings look as if they're falling away from the viewer (giving the impression that the tops of these buildings are narrower than their bases). Here's how to use Elements' Free Transform function, and one simple filter, to fix the problem fast.

Step One:
Open an image that has a keystoning problem (such as the photo shown here, where the building seems to be leaning away from the viewer).

Step Two:
Grab the bottom right corner of your image window and drag outward to reveal the gray desktop background. Click on the Foreground color swatch (at the bottom of the Toolbox) to bring up the Color Picker. In the R (red) field enter 74, for G (green) enter 132, and in the B (blue) field enter 255, then click OK to set your Foreground color to a light blue.

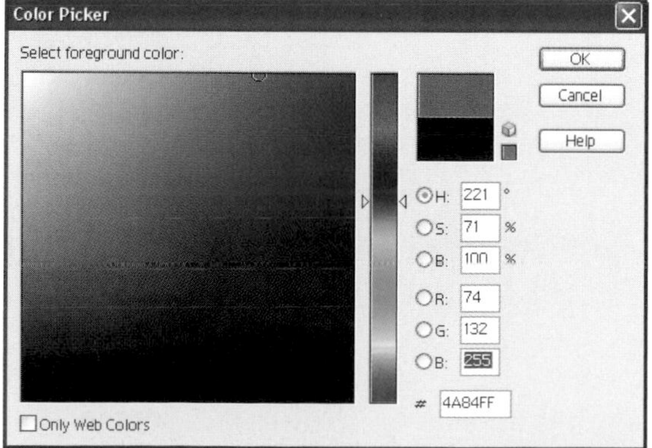

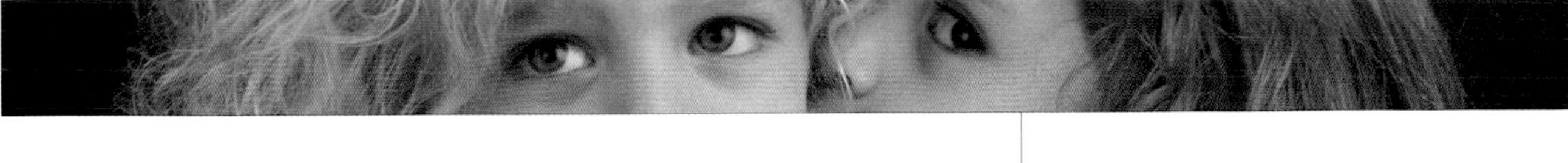

Step Three:
Switch to the Line tool (it's to the left of the Type tool in the Toolbox). Go up in the Options Bar and set the Width to 2 pixels, then hold the Shift key, and draw a straight, blue, 2-pixel line from the top of your image down to the bottom near a part of the building that should be straight (as shown here). This will add a Shape layer in your Layers palette.

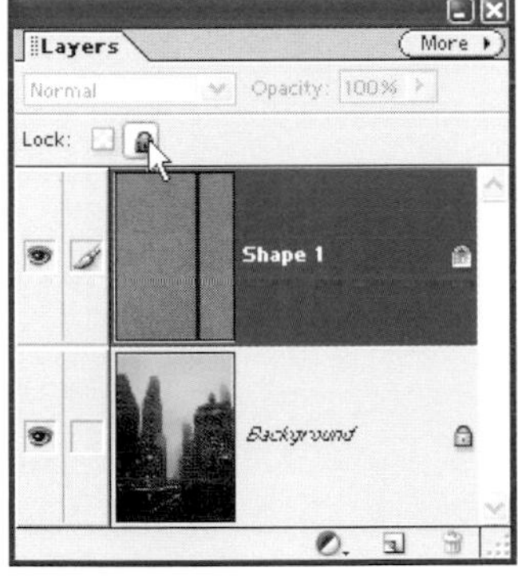

Step Four:
This blue line will act as your visual guide. (Note: If it's not positioned where you want it, then you can drag it with the Move tool. If this layer is locked, click on the Lock icon near the top left of the Layers palette to unlock it). Next, in the Layers palette, click back on the Background layer. Press Control-A (Mac: Command-A) to put a selection around your entire photo, then press Control-T (Mac: Command-T) to bring up the Free Transform bounding box.

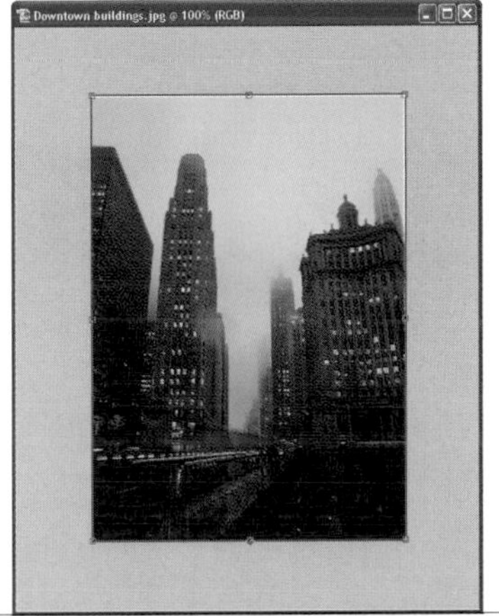

Step Five:
Go up to the Options Bar and you'll see a grid which represents the bounding box around the photo. Click the bottom center box (as shown) so any transformation you apply will have the bottom center locked in place.

Continued

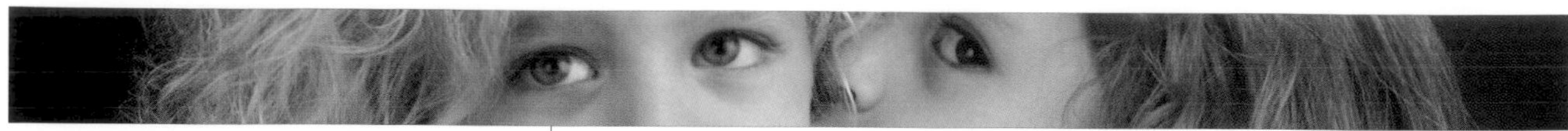

Step Six:

Hold Shift-Alt-Control (Mac: Shift-Option-Command) and drag either the top left and/or right corner points of the bounding box outward until the corner of the building aligns with your guide. Making this correction can sometimes make your building look a bit "smushed" and "squatty" (my official technical terms), so you can release the Shift-Alt-Control/Shift-Option-Command keys, grab the top center point, and drag upward to stretch the photo back out and fix the "squattyness" (another technical term).

Step Seven:

When the building looks right, press Enter (Mac: Return) to lock in your transformation. Now you can go to the Layers palette, click on your blue-line guide Shape layer, and drag it into the Trash icon at the bottom of the Layers palette to delete it. There's still one more thing you'll probably have to do to complete this repair job.

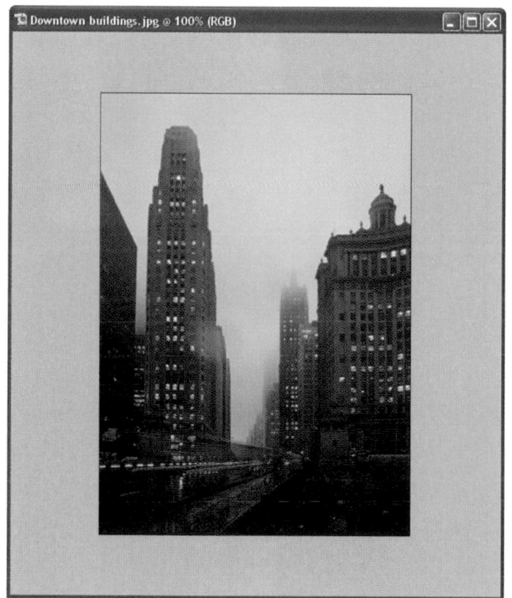

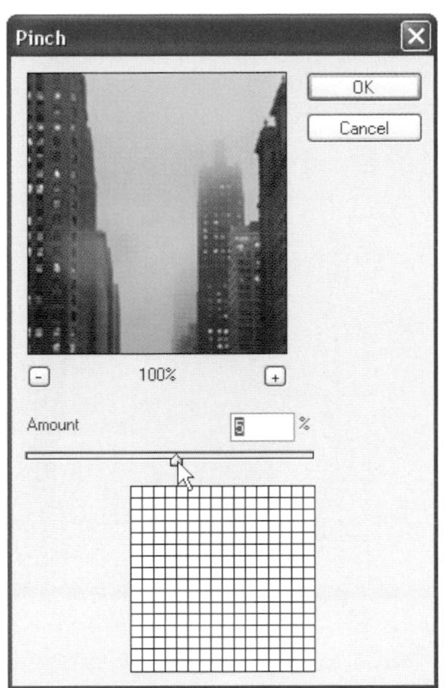

Step Eight:

If after making this adjustment the building looks "round" and "bloated," you can repair that problem by going under the Filter menu, under Distort, and choosing Pinch. Drag the Amount slider to 0%, and then slowly drag it to the right (increasing the amount of Pinch), while looking at the preview in the filter dialog, until you see the roundness and bloating go away. (In the example shown here, I used 5% for my Amount setting.) When it looks right, click OK to complete your keystoning repair. A before and after are shown here.

In the original photo, the building appears to be "falling away."

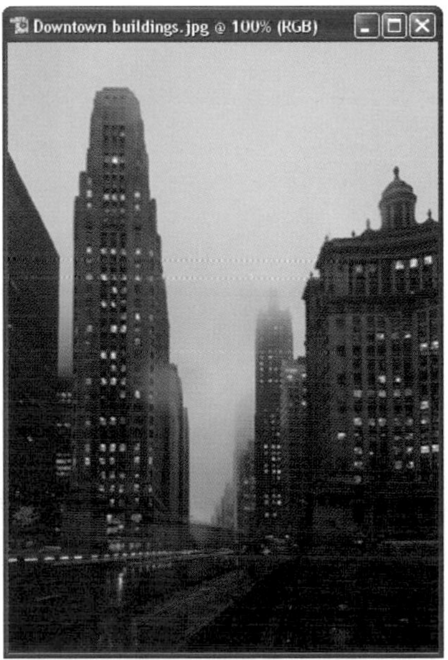

The same photo after repairing the keystoning and bloating

Photographer | Dave Moser

Color Me Badd

color correction for photographers

The subtitle for this chapter is "Color Correction for Photographers," which invites the question "How is color correction for photographers different from color correction for anybody else?" Actually, it's quite a bit different, because photographers generally work in RGB or black-and-white. And in reality, digital photographers mostly work in RGB because, although we can manage to build reusable spacecrafts and have GPS satellites orbiting in space so golfers here on earth know how far it is from their golf cart to the green, for some reason creating a color inkjet printer that prints a decent black-and-white print is still apparently beyond our grasp. Don't get me started. Anyway, this chapter isn't about black and white, and now that I think about it, I'm sorry I brought it up in the first place. So forget I ever mentioned it, and let's talk about color correction. Why do we even need color correction? Honestly, it's a technology thing. Even with traditional film cameras, every photo needs some sort of color tweaking (either during processing or afterward in Elements) because if it didn't need some correction, we'd have about 20-something pages in this book that would be blank, and that would make my publisher pretty hopping mad (and if you haven't seen her hop, let me tell you, it's not pretty). So, for the sake of sheer page count, let's all be glad that we don't live in a perfect world where every photo comes out perfect and 6-megapixel cameras are only 200 bucks and come with free 1-GB memory cards.

Before you Color Correct Anything, Do This First!

Before we color correct even a single photo, we need to consider a couple of settings that can affect the results you will get. It's important to note that the changes you make will remain as your defaults until you change them again, and that, particularly with Color Settings, you may change your setting from time to time based on individual projects.

Step One:

From the Edit menu, choose Color Settings (or press Shift-Control-K [Mac: Shift-Command-K]). Note: In Mac OS X, Color Settings can be found under the Photoshop Elements menu.

Step Two:

Choose from the three options: No color management, Limited color management, or Full color management. To a large degree, your choice will depend on your final output; but for photographers we recommend using Full color management because it reproduces such a wide gamut of colors, and it's ideal if your photos will wind up in print.

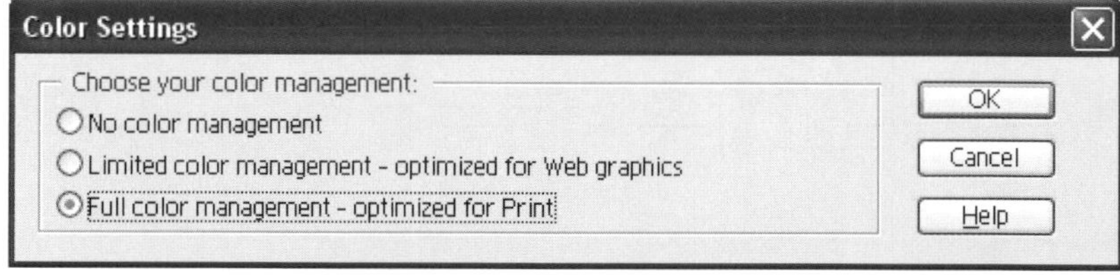

Note: Unfortunately, color management is beyond the scope of this book. In fact, entire books have been dedicated to the subject. So for now, just switch your Color Settings to Full color management and let's move on.

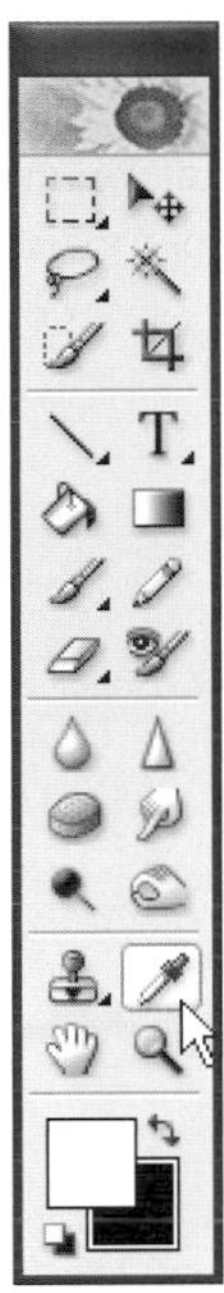

Step Three:

Now we're moving to a completely different area. In the Toolbox, click on the Eyedropper tool. In the Options Bar, the Sample Size setting for this tool (Point Sample) is fine for using the Eyedropper to steal a color from within a photo and making it your Foreground color. However, Point Sample doesn't work well when you're trying to read values in a particular area (like flesh tones), because it gives you the reading from just one individual pixel, rather than a reading of the area under your cursor.

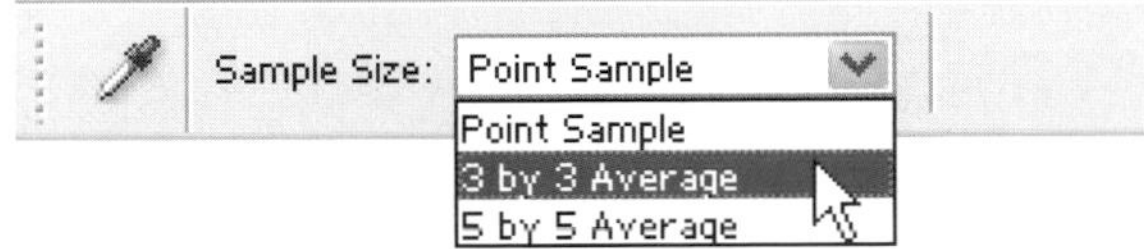

Step Four:

For example, flesh tone is actually composed of dozens of different colored pixels (just zoom way in and you'll see what I mean); and if you're color correcting, you want a reading that is representative of the area under your Eyedropper, not just one of the pixels within that area, which could hurt your correction decision making. That's why you'll go up in the Options Bar, under Sample Size, and choose 3 by 3 Average from the pop-up menu. This changes the Eyedropper to give you a 3-by-3 pixel average of the area you're reading. Once you've completed the changes on these two pages, it's safe to go ahead with the rest of the chapter and start correcting your photos.

Continued

Color Correcting Digital Camera Images

As far as digital technology has come, there's still one thing that digital cameras won't do—give you perfect color every time. In fact, if they gave us perfect color 50% of the time, that would be incredible but unfortunately, every digital camera (and every scanner that captures traditional photos) sneaks some kind of color cast into your image. Generally, it's a red cast but, depending on the camera, it could be blue. Either way, you can be pretty sure—there's a cast. (Figure it this way, if there wasn't, the term "color correction" wouldn't be used.) Here's how to get your color in line.

Step One:
Open the digital camera photo you want to color correct. (The photo shown here doesn't look too bad, but as we go through the correction process, you'll see that, like most photos, it really needed a correction.)

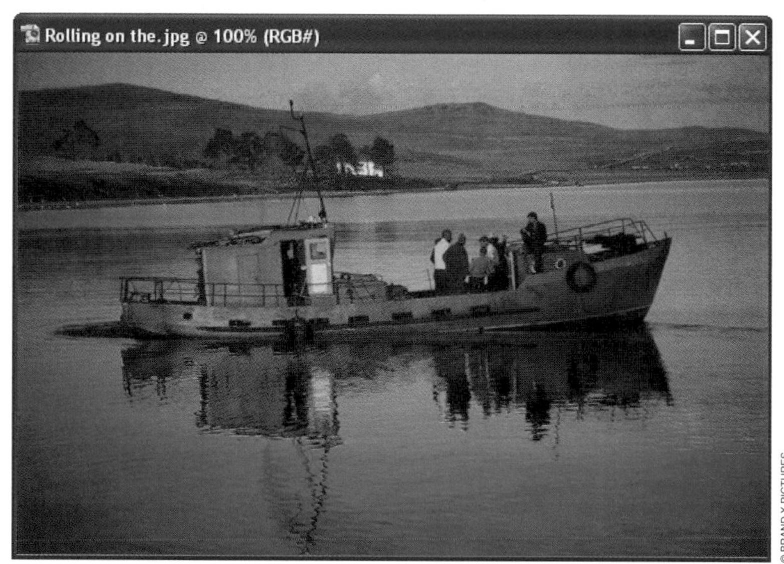

Step Two:
Go under the Enhance menu, under Adjust Brightness/Contrast, and choose Levels. The dialog box may look intimidating at first, but the technique you're going to learn here requires no previous knowledge of Levels, and it's so easy, you'll be correcting photos using Levels immediately.

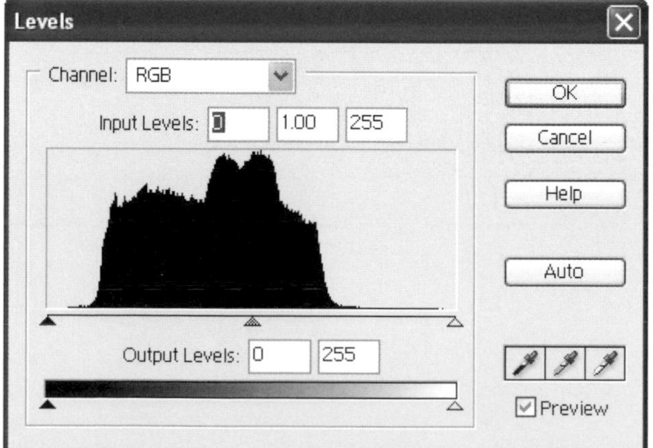

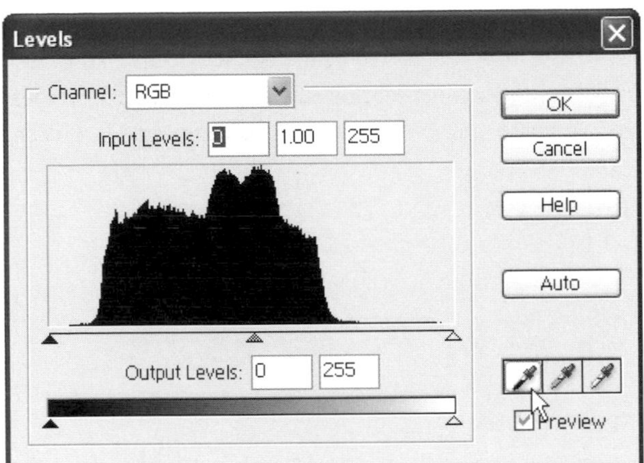

Step Three:

First, we need to set some preferences in the Levels dialog box so we'll get the results we're after when we start correcting. We'll start by setting a target color for our shadow areas. To set this preference, in the Levels dialog, double-click on the black Eyedropper tool (it's on the lower right-hand side of the dialog box, the first Eyedropper from the left). A Color Picker will appear asking you to "Select target shadow color." This is where we'll enter values that, when applied, will help remove any color casts your camera introduced in the shadow areas of your photo.

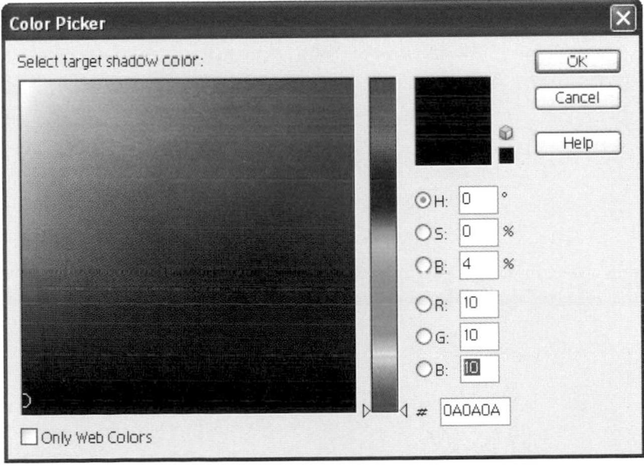

Step Four:

We're going to enter values in the R, G, and B (red, green, and blue) fields of this dialog box (the blue field is highlighted here).

For "R," enter 10
For "G," enter 10
For "B," enter 10

TIP: To move from field to field, just press the Tab key.

Then click OK. Because these figures are evenly balanced (neutral), they help ensure that your shadow area won't have too much of one color (which is exactly what causes a color cast—too much of one color).

Continued

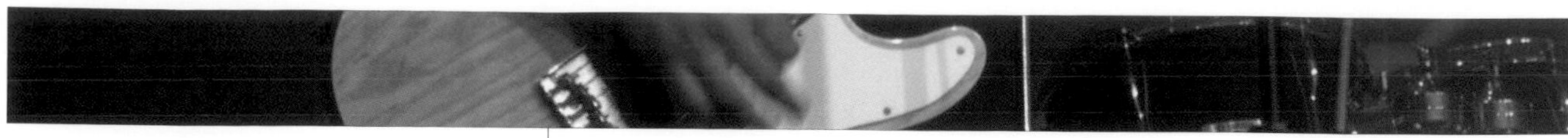

Step Five:

Now we'll set a preference to make our highlight areas neutral. Double-click on the highlight Eyedropper (the third of the three Eyedroppers in the Levels dialog). The Color Picker will appear asking you to "Select target highlight color." Click in the "R" field, and then enter these values:

For "R," enter 240
For "G," enter 240
For "B," enter 240

Then click OK to set those values as your highlight target.

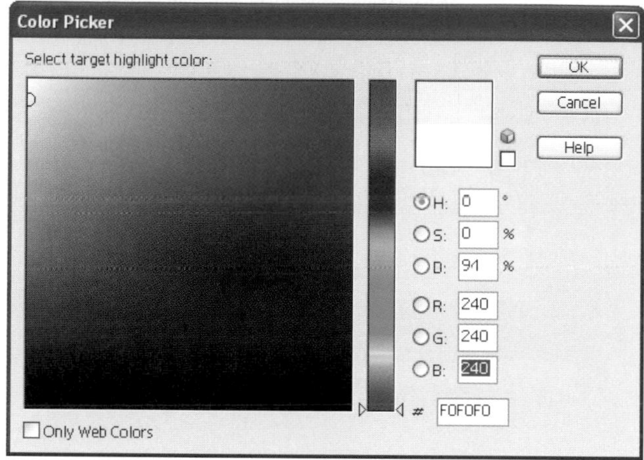

Step Six:

Last, set your midtone preference. You know the drill—double-click on the midtone Eyedropper (the middle of the three Eyedroppers) so you can "Select target midtone color." Enter these values in the RGB fields (if they're not already there by default):

For "R," enter 128
For "G," enter 128
For "B," enter 128

Then click OK to set those values as your midtone target.

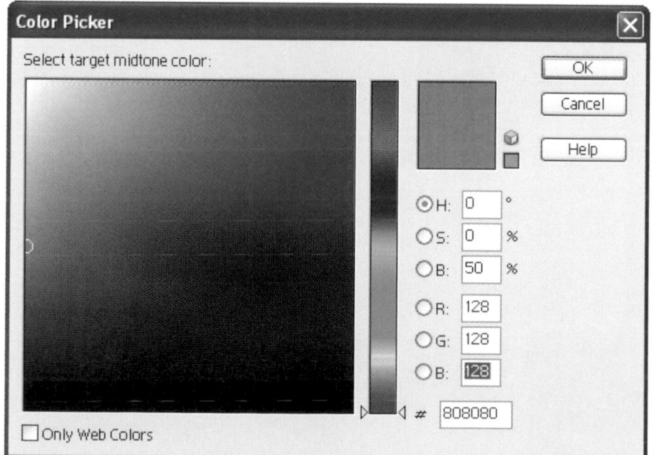

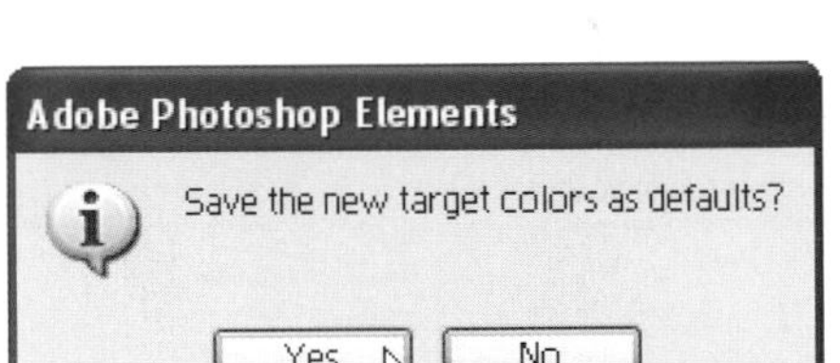

Step Seven:

Okay, you've entered your preferences (target colors) in the Levels dialog. Once you make your adjustments and finally click OK in the Levels dialog box, you'll get an alert dialog asking you if you want to Save the new target colors as defaults. Click Yes, and from that point on, you won't have to enter these values each time you correct a photo, because they'll already be entered for you—they're now the default settings.

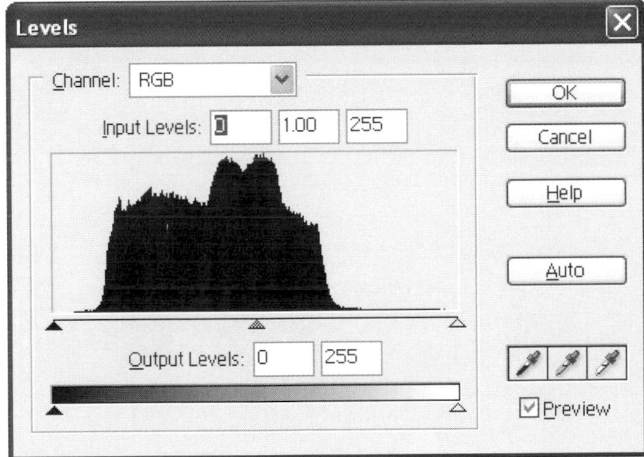

Step Eight:

Now that you've entered all these values, you're going to use these Eyedropper tools that reside in the Levels dialog box to do most of your correction work. Your job is to determine where the shadow, midtone, and highlight areas are, and click the right Eyedropper in the right place (you'll learn how to do that in just a moment). So remember, your job—find the shadow, midtone, and highlight areas and click the right Eyedropper in the right spot. Sounds easy, right? It is.

You start by setting the shadows first, so you'll need to find an area in your photo that's supposed to be black. If you can't find something that's supposed to be the color black, then it gets a bit trickier—in the absence of something black, you have to determine which area in the image is the darkest. If you're not sure where the darkest part of the photo is, you can use the following trick to have Elements tell you exactly where it is.

Continued

Step Nine:
If you still have the Levels dialog open, click OK to exit it for now. Go to the Layers palette and click on the half white/half black circle icon to bring up the Adjustment Layer pop-up menu (it's the first icon from the left at the bottom of the palette). When the menu appears, choose Threshold (this brings up a dialog with a histogram and a slider under it).

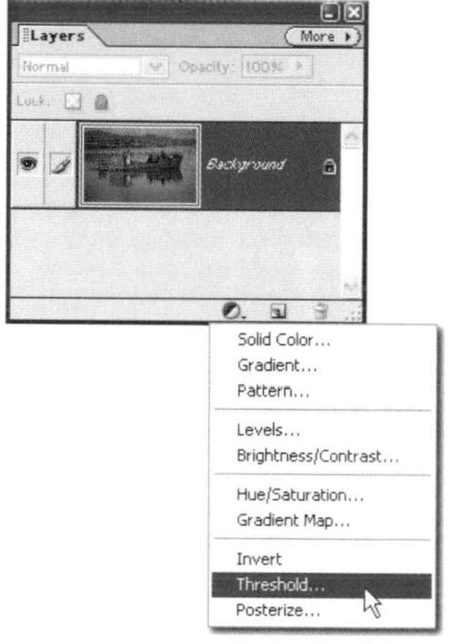

Step Ten:
When the Threshold dialog box appears, drag the Threshold Level slider under the histogram all the way to the left. Your photo will turn completely white. Slowly drag the Threshold slider back to the right, and as you do, you'll start to see some of your photo reappear. The first area that appears is the darkest part of your image. That's it—that's Elements telling you exactly where the darkest part of the image is.

Now that you know where your shadow area is, make a mental note of its location. Now to find a white area in your image.

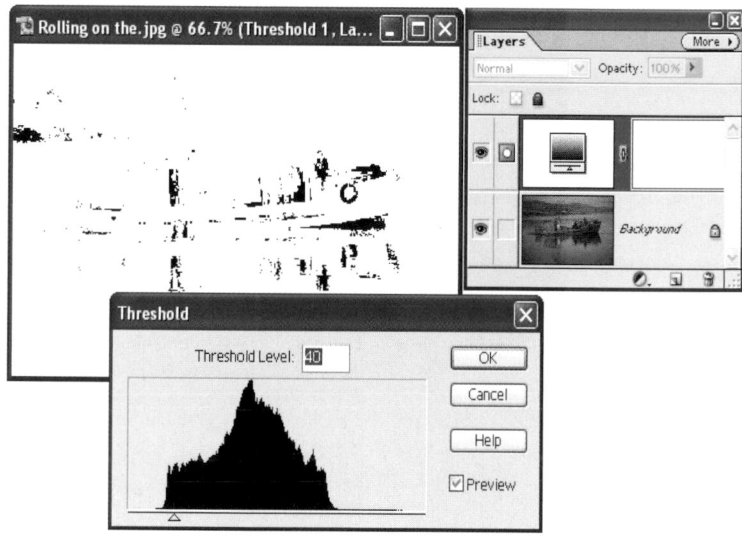

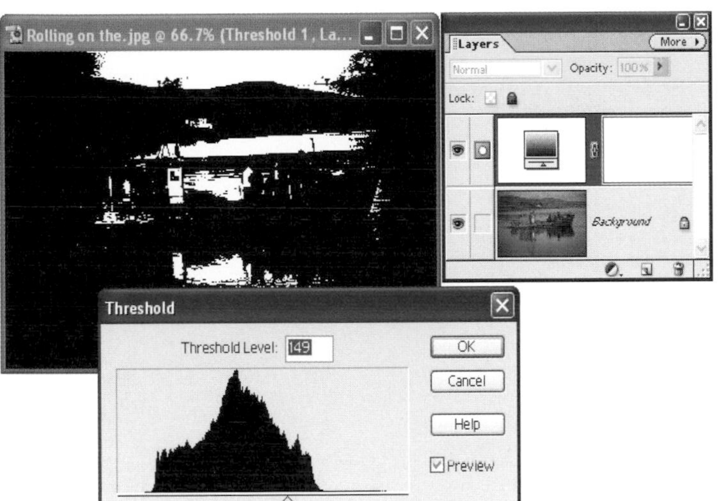

Step Eleven:

If you can't find an area in your image that you know is supposed to be white, you can use the same technique to find the highlight areas that you just used to find the shadow areas. With the Threshold dialog box still open, drag the slider all the way to the right. Your photo will turn black. Slowly drag the Threshold slider back toward the left, and as you do, you'll start to see some of your photo reappear (as shown top left). The first area that appears is the lightest part of your image. Make a mental note of this area as well (yes, you have to remember two things, but you have to admit, it's easier than remembering two PIN numbers).

Step Twelve:

You're now done with your Threshold so just click Cancel because we don't actually need the Adjustment Layer anymore.

Step Thirteen:

Press Control-L (Mac: Command-L) to bring up the Levels dialog. First, select the shadow Eyedropper (the one half filled with black) from the bottom right of the Levels dialog. Move your cursor outside the Levels dialog box into your photo and click once in the area that Elements showed you was the darkest part of the photo. When you click there, you'll see the shadow areas correct. (Basically, you just reassigned the shadow areas to your new neutral shadow color—the one you entered earlier as a preference in Step Four). If you click in that spot and your photo now looks

Continued

horrible, you either clicked in the wrong spot, or what you thought was the shadow point actually wasn't. Undo the setting of your shadow point by pressing Alt-Control-Z (Mac: Option-Command-Z) and try again. If that doesn't work, don't sweat it; just keep clicking in areas that look like the darkest part of your photo until it looks right.

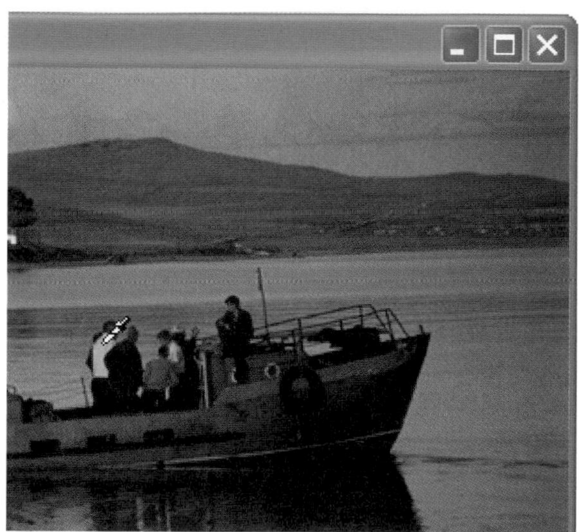

Step Fourteen:
While still in the Levels dialog box, switch to the highlight Eyedropper (the one filled with white). Move your cursor over your photo and click once on the lightest part (the one you committed to memory earlier) to assign that as your highlight. You'll see the highlight colors correct.

Step Fifteen:
Now that the shadows and highlights are set, you'll need to set the midtones in the photo. It may not look as if you need to set them, because the photo may look properly corrected, but chances are there's a cast in the midtone areas. You may not recognize the cast until you've corrected it and it's gone, so it's worth giving it a shot to see the effect (which will often be surprisingly dramatic).

Unfortunately, there's no Threshold Adjustment Layer trick that works well for finding the midtone areas, so you have to use some good old-fashioned guesswork. Ideally, something in the photo would be the color gray, but not every photo has a "gray" area, so look for a neutral area (one that's obviously not a shadow, but not a highlight either). Click the middle (gray) eyedropper in that area. If it's not right, you'll see that instantly, and you can undo it.

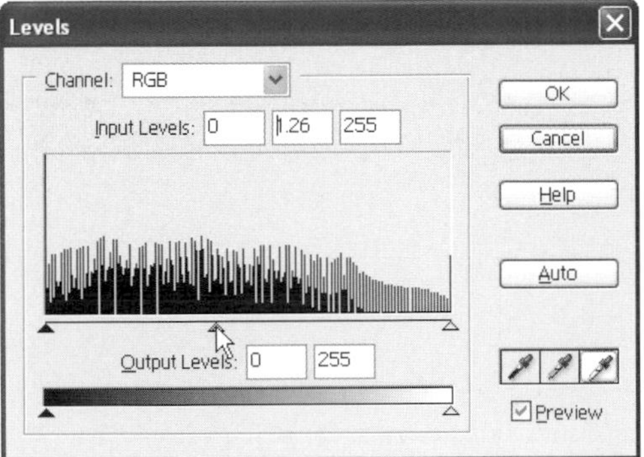

Step Sixteen:

There's one more important adjustment to make before you click OK in the Levels dialog and apply your correction. Under the Histogram (that's the black mountain-range-looking thing), click on the center slider (that's the Midtone slider—that's why it's gray) and drag it to the left a bit to brighten the midtones of the image (as shown). This is a visual adjustment, so it's up to you to determine how much to adjust, but it should be subtle—just enough to brighten the midtones a bit and bring out the midtone detail. When it looks right to you, click OK to apply your correction to the highlights, midtones, and shadows, removing any color casts and brightening the overall contrast.

Before

After

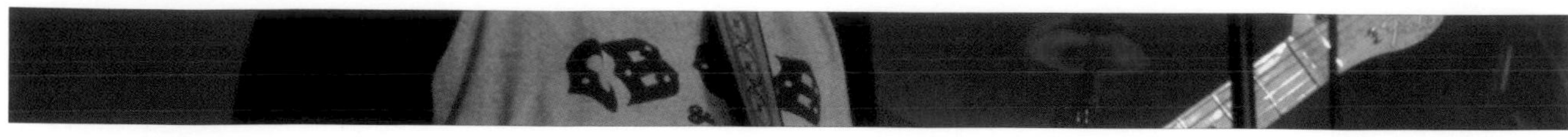

Drag-and-Drop Instant Color Correction

This is a wonderful timesaving trick for quickly correcting an entire group of photos that have similar lighting. It's ideal for shots where the lighting conditions are controlled, but works equally well for outdoor shots, or really any situation where the lighting for your group of shots is fairly consistent. Once you try this, you'll use it again and again and again.

Step One:

First, here's a tip-within-a-tip: If you're opening a group of photos, you don't have to open them one by one. Just go under the File menu and choose Open. In the Open dialog, click on the first photo you want to open, then hold the Control key (Mac: Command key) and click on any other photos you want to open. Then, when you click the Open button, Elements will open all the selected photos. (If all your photos are consecutive, hold the Shift key and click on the first and last photo in the list to select them all.) So now that you know that tip, go ahead and open at least four or five images, just to get you started.

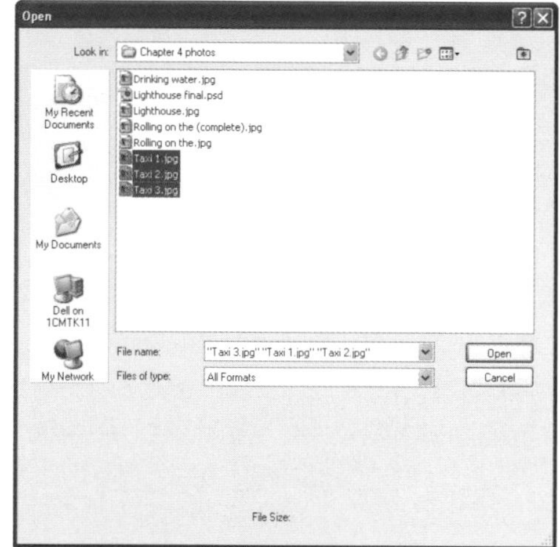

Step Two:

At the bottom of the Layers palette, there's a pop-up menu for adding Adjustment Layers. Click on it and choose Levels. Note: An Adjustment Layer is a special layer that contains the tonal adjustment of your choice (such as Levels, Brightness/Contrast, etc.). There are a number of advantages of having this correction applied as a layer, as you'll soon see, but the main advantage is that you can edit or delete this tonal adjustment

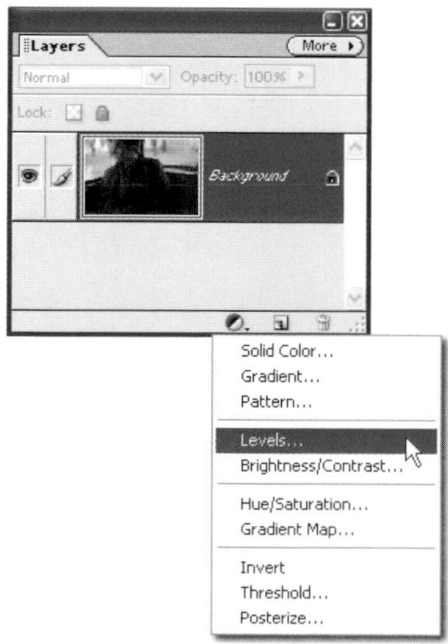

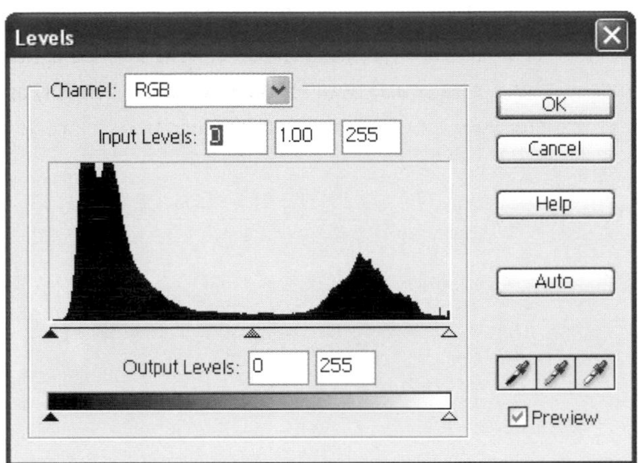

at any time while you're working, plus you can save this adjustment with your file as a layer.

Step Three:
When you choose this Adjustment Layer, you'll notice that the regular Levels dialog box appears, just like always. Go ahead and make your corrections, just as you did in the previous tutorial (setting highlights, midtones, shadows, etc. with the Eyedropper tools), and when your correction looks good, click OK.

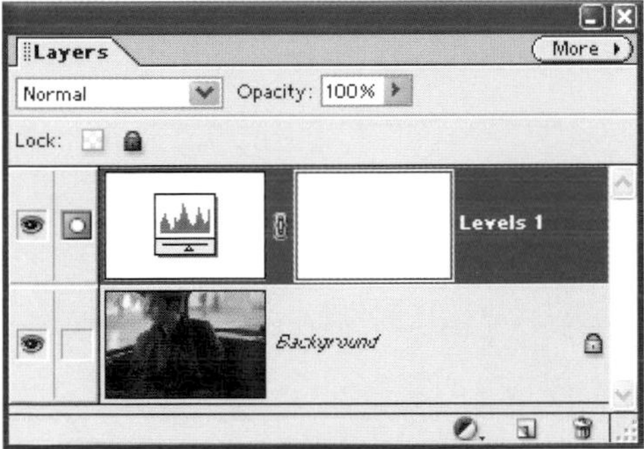

Step Four:
In the Layers palette, you'll see a new Adjustment Layer is created, and if you expand the width of your Layers palette (click-and-drag on the very bottom right-hand corner of the palette), you can actually read the word "Levels," as shown here.

Continued

Step Five:
Because you applied this correction as an Adjustment Layer, you can treat this adjustment just like a regular layer, right? Right! Now, Elements lets you drag layers between open documents, right? So, go to the Layers palette, and simply drag this layer right onto one of your other open photos, and that photo will instantly have the same correction applied to it. This technique works because you're correcting photos that share similar lighting conditions. Need to correct 12 photos? Just drag-and-drop it 12 times (making it the fastest correction in town!). In the example shown here, the original corrected image is on the far left, and I've dragged-and-dropped that Levels Adjustment Layer onto one of the other open photos.

© BRAND X PICTURES

Step Six:
Okay, what if one of the "dragged corrections" doesn't look right? That's the beauty of these Adjustment Layers. Just double-click directly on the Adjustment Layer icon for that photo, and the Levels dialog will reappear with the last settings you applied still in place. You can then adjust this individual photo separately from the rest. Try this "dragging-and-dropping-Adjustment-Layers" trick once, and you'll use it again and again to save time when correcting a digital roll with similar lighting conditions.

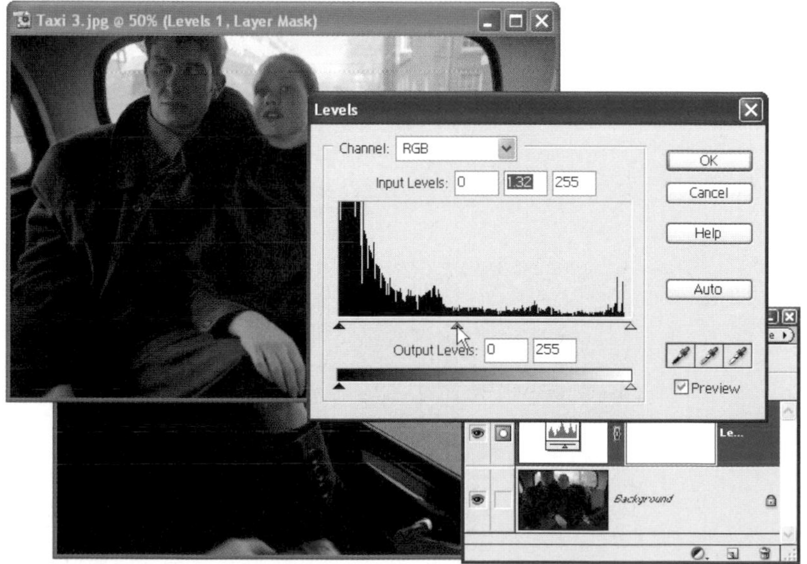

Automated Color Correction (Correction for Chickens)

Elements 1.0 had two automated color correction tools: Auto Levels and Auto Contrast, both of which were fairly lame. But in Photoshop Elements 2, Adobe introduced Auto Color Correction, which is much better than either Auto Levels or Auto Contrast, because it goes beyond just automating the setting of shadows and highlights, it adds the all-important midtone correction at the same time.

Step One:

Open a photo that needs correcting, but you don't feel warrants the time for a full manual color correction using Levels.

Step Two:

Go under the Enhance menu and choose Auto Color Correction to apply an auto correction to your photo. When you apply Auto Color Correction, it just does its thing. It doesn't ask you to input numbers or make decisions (see, I told you this was correction for chickens)—basically, it's a one-trick pony which tries to neutralize the highlight, midtone, and shadow areas of your photo. In some cases, it does a pretty darn decent job, in others, well...let's just say it falls a bit short (and that's why Levels exists). By the way, since this Auto Color Correction is so simple, there is no step three. It only takes two steps. Okay, it's really just one.

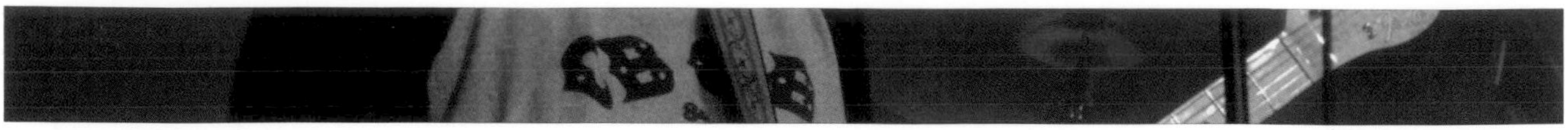

Adjusting Flesh Tones

So what do you do if you've used Levels to properly set the highlights, midtones, and shadows, but the flesh tones in your photo still look too red? Try this quick trick for getting your flesh tones in line by removing the excess red with one small adjustment that makes a world of difference.

Step One:

Open the photo you corrected with Levels earlier. If the whole image appears too red, skip this step and go on to Step Three. However, if it's just the flesh tone areas that appear too red, get the Lasso tool and make a selection around all the flesh tone areas in your photo. (Hold the Shift key to add other flesh tone areas to the selection, such as arms, hands, legs, etc.)

Step Two:

Next, go under the Select menu and choose Feather. Enter a Feather Radius of 3 pixels, then click OK. By adding this feather, you're softening the edges of your selection, and this will keep you from having a hard visible edge show up where you made your adjustment.

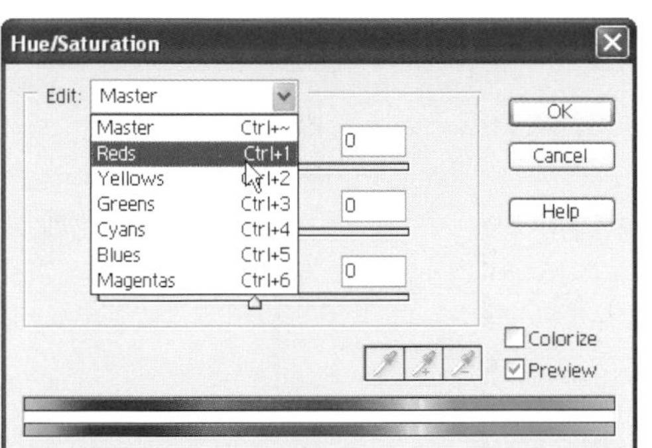

Step Three:

Go under the Enhance menu, under Adjust Color, and choose Hue/Saturation. When the dialog box appears, click-and-hold on the Edit pop-up menu and choose Reds (as shown here) so you're just adjusting the reds in your photo (or in your selected areas if you put a selection around just the flesh tones).

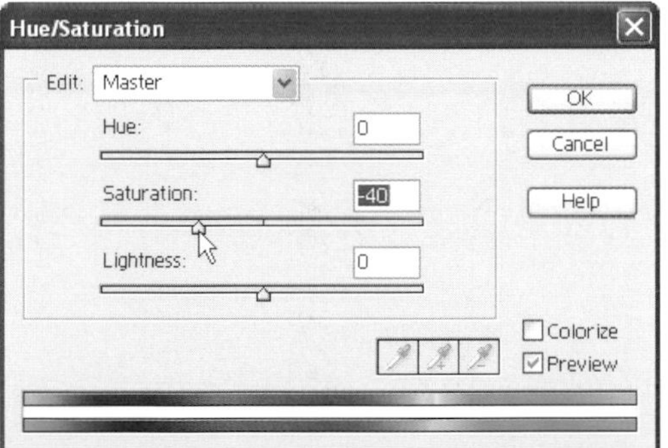

Step Four:

The rest is easy—you're simply going to reduce the amount of saturation so the flesh tones appear more natural. Drag the Saturation slider to the left (as shown) to reduce the amount of red. You'll be able to see the effect of removing the red as you lower the Saturation slider.

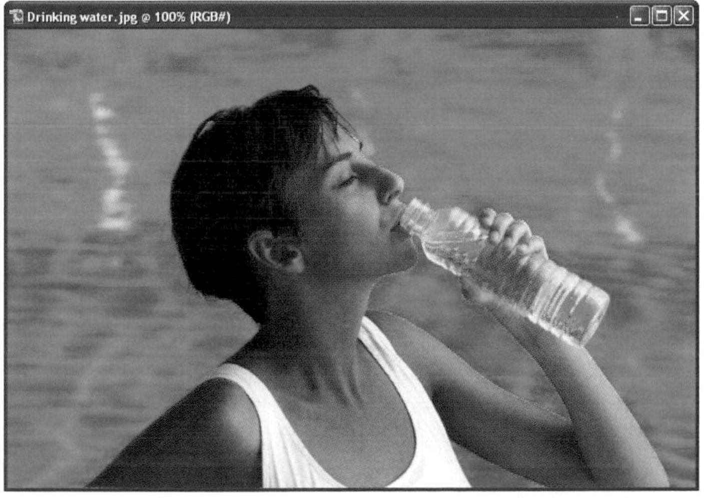

TIP: If you made a selection of the flesh tone areas, you might find it easier if you hide the selection border from view (that makes it easier to see what you're correcting) by pressing Control-H (Mac: Command-H). You can even hide the selection border while the Hue/Saturation dialog box is open. When the flesh tones look right, just click the OK button and you're set.

Continued

Color Correcting One Problem Area Fast!

This technique really comes in handy when shooting outdoor scenes because it lets you enhance the color in one particular area of the photo, while leaving the rest of it untouched. Real estate photographers often use this trick because they want to present the house on a bright sunny day, but the weather doesn't always cooperate. With this technique, a gray cloudy sky can become a beautiful blue sky in just seconds, and brownish grass in the front can quickly become a lush green yard (like it really looks in summer).

Step One:

Open the image that has an area of color you would like to enhance. In this example, we want to make the sky and water blue (rather than gray).

© BRAND X PICTURES

Step Two:

Go to the Layers palette and choose Hue/Saturation from the Adjustment Layer pop-up menu at the bottom of the Layers palette (it's the half black, half white circle icon, first from the left). A new layer named Hue/Saturation will be added to your Layers palette (as shown here), but the name will probably be cut off by default. If you want to see the layer's name, you'll have to widen your Layers palette.

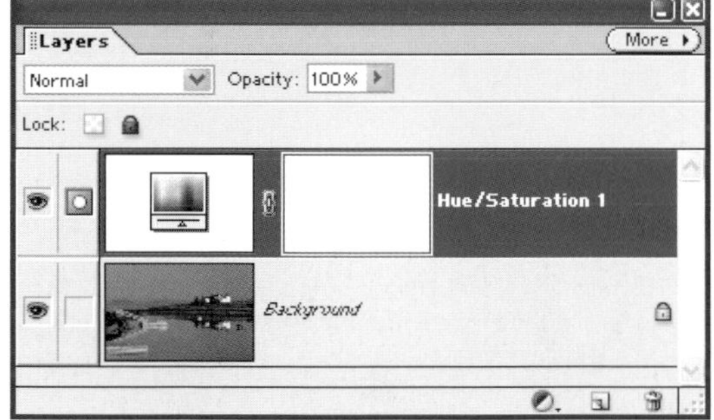

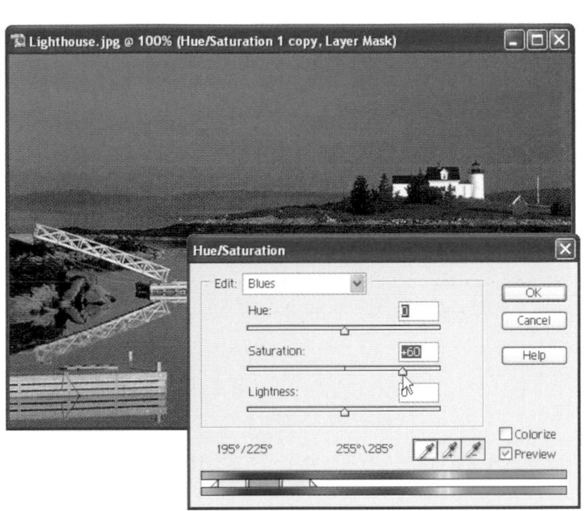

Step Three:

When you choose Hue/Saturation, the Hue/Saturation dialog box will appear (shown here). From the Edit menu at the top of the dialog, choose Blues, then drag the Saturation slider to the right to add more blue into the sky and water. You might also choose Cyans from the Edit pop-up menu and do the same thing there—drag the Saturation slider to the right, adding some cyan to "blue-up" your sky even more. When the sky looks as blue as you'd like it, click OK.

Step Four:

Now your sky and water is probably much bluer, but so is everything else. That's okay, you can fix that easily enough. Switch your Foreground color to black, then press Alt-Backspace (Mac: Option-Delete) to fill the Hue/Saturation's Layer Mask with black. Doing this removes all the blue that you just added, but that's okay, because now you can selectively add (actually paint) the blue and water back in only where you want it (which is the sky and water, not the rest of the photo).

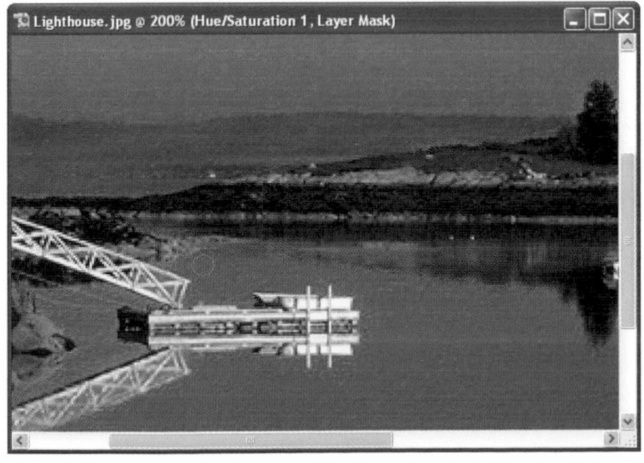

Step Five:

Now, switch your Foreground color to white, and begin painting over either the sky or the water. As you paint, the version of your photo where you added the blue will appear. While you're painting over the areas you want to make bluer, you may have to go up to the Options Bar to switch to a smaller, hard-edged brush to paint along well-defined areas such as where the sky meets the land in this photo.

Continued

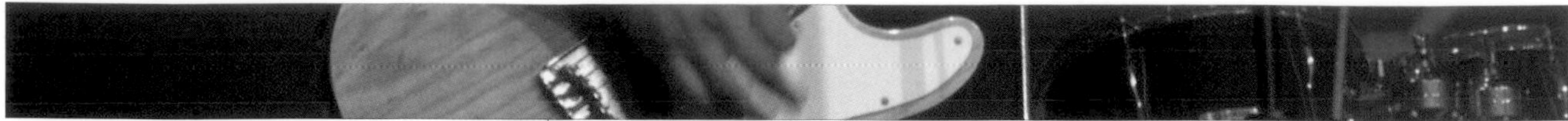

Step Six:

If you make a mistake and paint over an area you shouldn't have—no problem—just switch your Foreground color to black and paint over the mistake—it will disappear. Then, switch back to white and continue painting. When you're done, the photo will look like the one shown below right, with much bluer, brighter-looking sky and water.

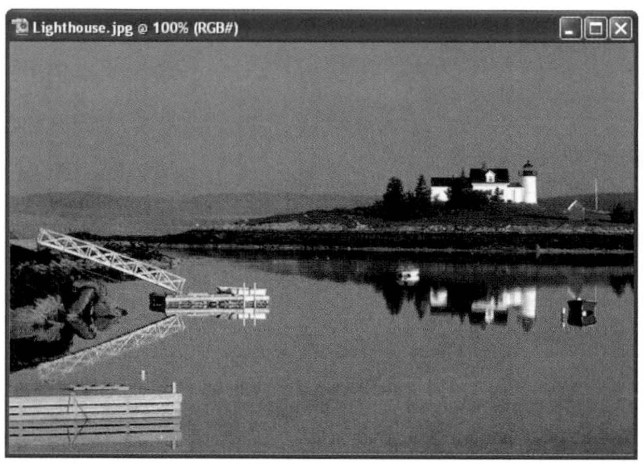

Before

After

Getting a Better Conversion from Color to Black & White

If you've ever converted a color photo to black-and-white, chances are you were fairly disappointed with the results. That's because Elements simply throws away the color, leaving a fairly bland black-and-white photo in its wake. In the full version of Adobe Photoshop, they have a feature called "Channel Mixer" that lets you custom create a better black-and-white. Unfortunately, that feature isn't in Elements, but I figured out a way to get similar control using a little workaround here in Elements. Here's how:

© TODD MORRISON

Step One:

Open the color photo you want to convert to black-and-white.

Step Two:

To really appreciate this technique, it wouldn't hurt if you went ahead and did a regular conversion to black-and-white, just so you can see how lame it is. Go under the Image menu, under Mode and choose Grayscale. When the "Discard Color Information?" dialog appears, click OK, and behold the somewhat lame conversion. Now that we agree it looks pretty bland, press Control-Z (Mac: Command-Z) to undo the conversion, so now you can try something better.

Continued

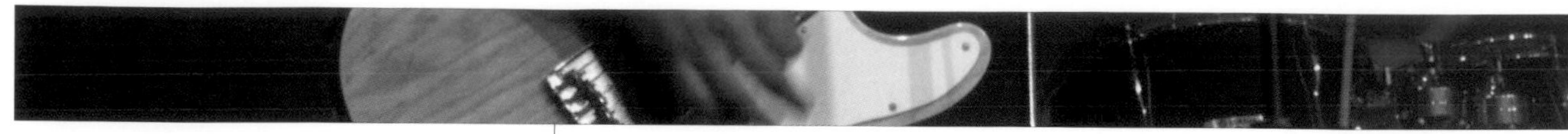

Step Three:
Go to the Layers palette, and choose Levels from the Adjustment Layer pop-up menu (shown here) at the bottom of the palette (it's the first icon from the left, the half-black, half-white circle). When the Levels dialog appears, don't make any changes, just click OK. This will add a layer to your Layers palette named Levels.

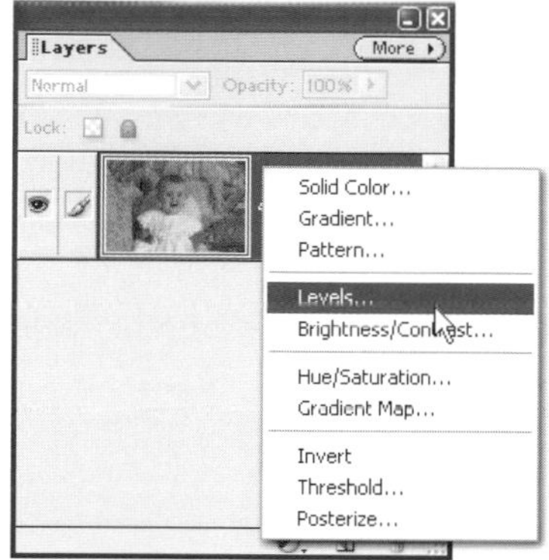

Step Four:
In the Layers palette, choose Hue/Saturation from the Adjustment Layer pop-up menu at the bottom of the palette (as shown here) to bring up the Hue/Saturation dialog.

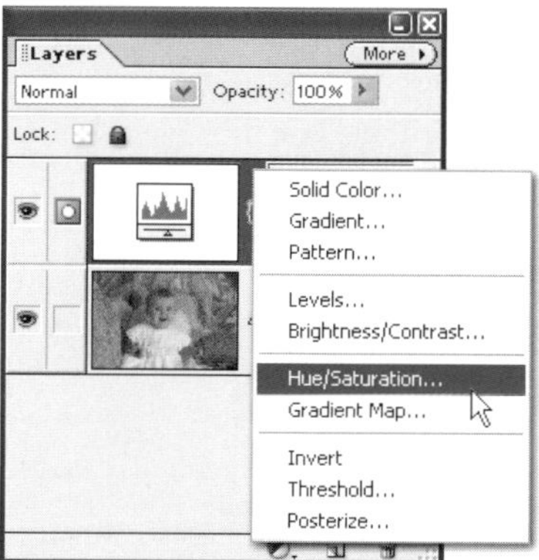

Step Five:
When the Hue/Saturation dialog appears, drag the Saturation slider all the way to the left to remove all the color from the photo, then click OK. This will add another layer to the Layers palette (above your Levels layer) named Hue/Saturation.

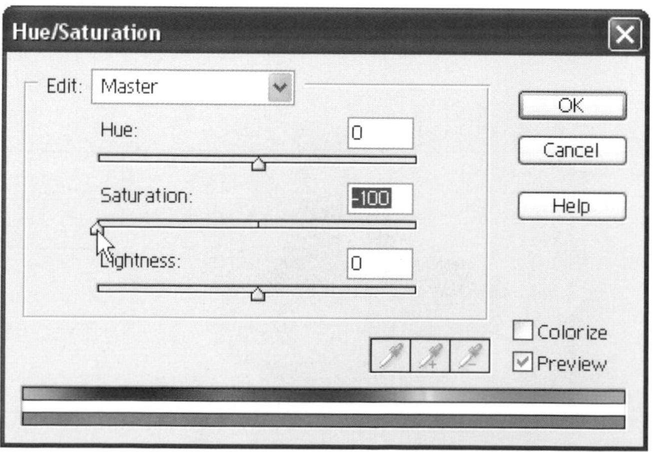

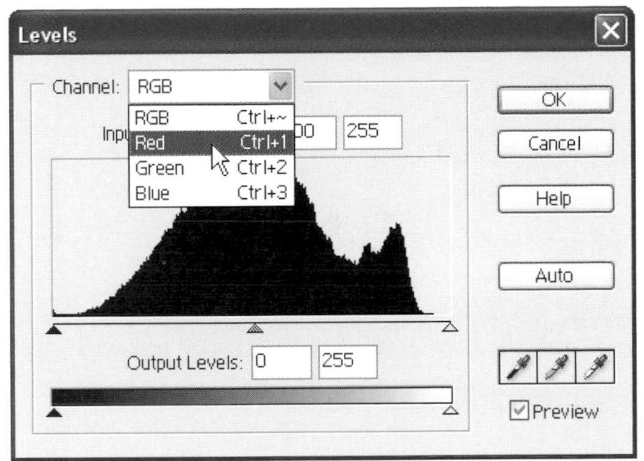

Step Six:

In the Layers palette, double-click directly on the Levels thumbnail in the Levels layer to bring up the Levels dialog box again. At the top of the dialog, you can choose individual color channels to edit (kind of like you would with Photoshop 7.0's Channel Mixer). Choose the Red color channel (as shown here).

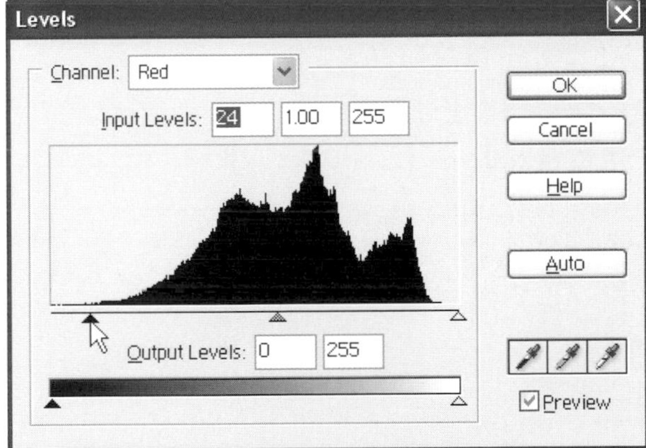

Step Seven:

Now, you can adjust the Red channel, and you'll see the adjustments live onscreen as you tweak your black-and-white photo (it appears as a black-and-white photo because of the Hue/Saturation Adjustment Layer on the layer above the Levels layer. Pretty sneaky, eh?) In the example shown here, I dragged the shadow Input Levels slider to the right a bit to increase the shadows in the Red channel.

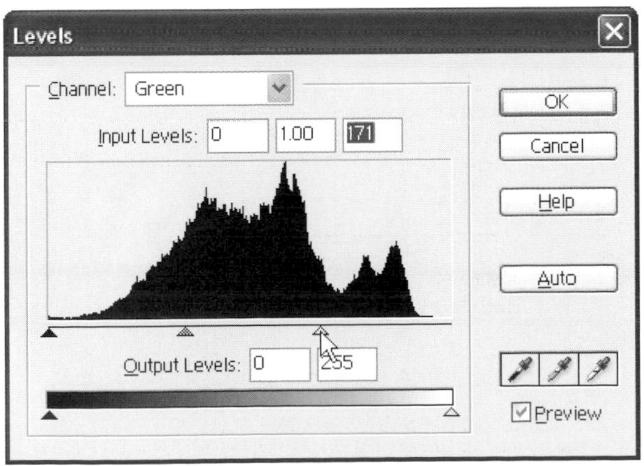

Step Eight:

Now switch to the Green channel. You can make adjustments here as well. In this case, I increased the highlights in the Green channel by dragging the highlight Input Levels slider to the left (as shown). Don't click OK yet.

Continued

Step Nine:

Lastly, choose the Blue channel from the pop-up menu. In the example shown here, I increased the highlights quite a bit, and the shadows just a little bit. These adjustments are not standards, nor suggested settings for every photo; I just experimented by dragging the sliders, and when the photo looked better—I stopped dragging. When the black-and-white photo looks good to you (good contrast and good shadow and highlight details), click OK.

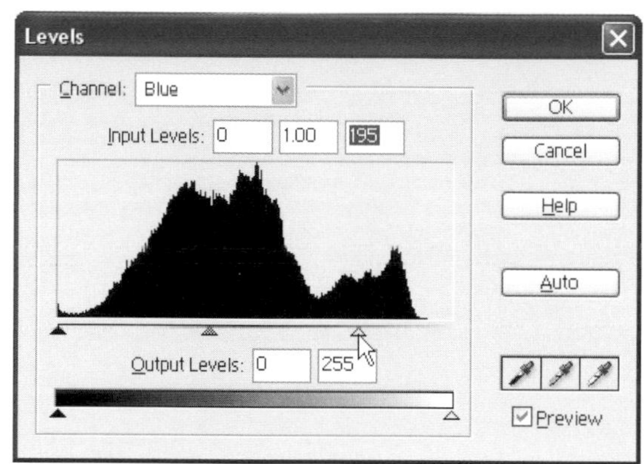

Step Ten:

To complete your conversion, go to the Layers palette, click on the More button to bring up the palette's pop-down menu, then choose Flatten Image to flatten the Adjustment Layers down to the Background. Although your photo looks like a black-and-white, technically, it's still in RGB Color, so if you want a grayscale file, go under the Image menu, under Mode, and choose Grayscale.

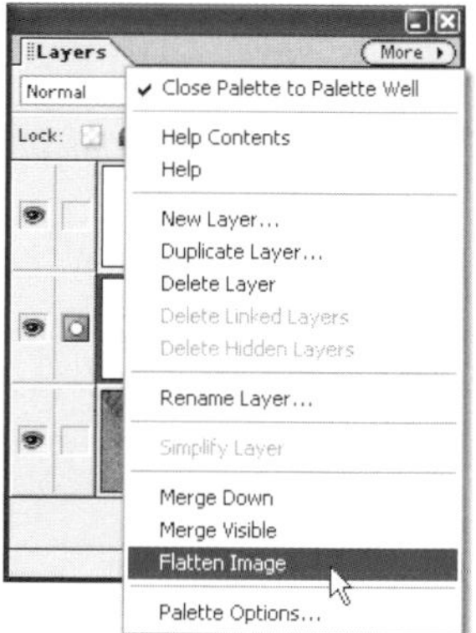

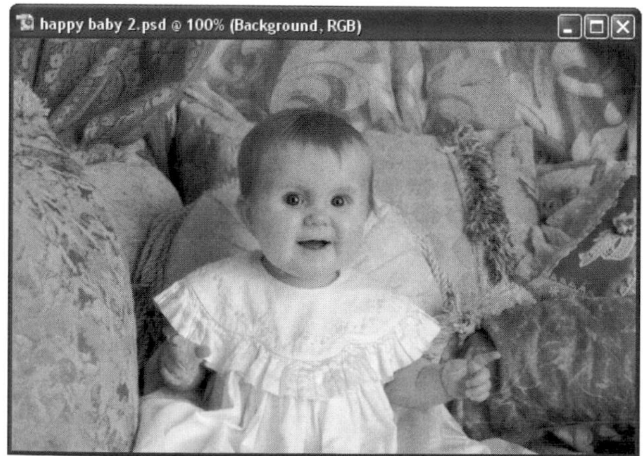

A standard color to black-and-white conversion

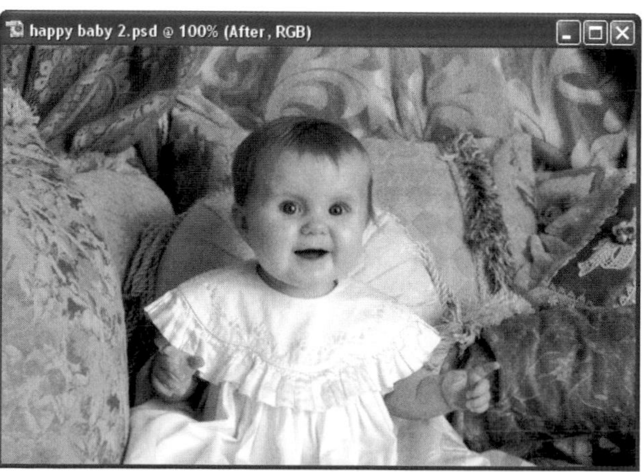

The conversion using the method shown here

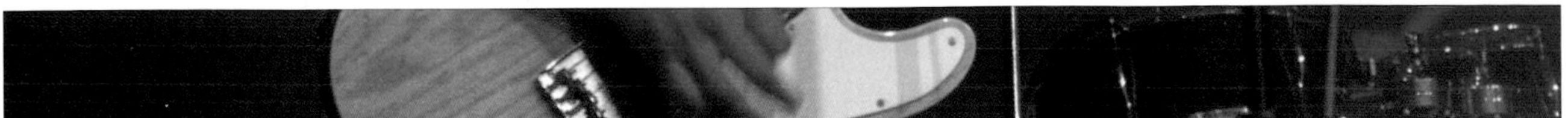

Photographer | Carol Freeman

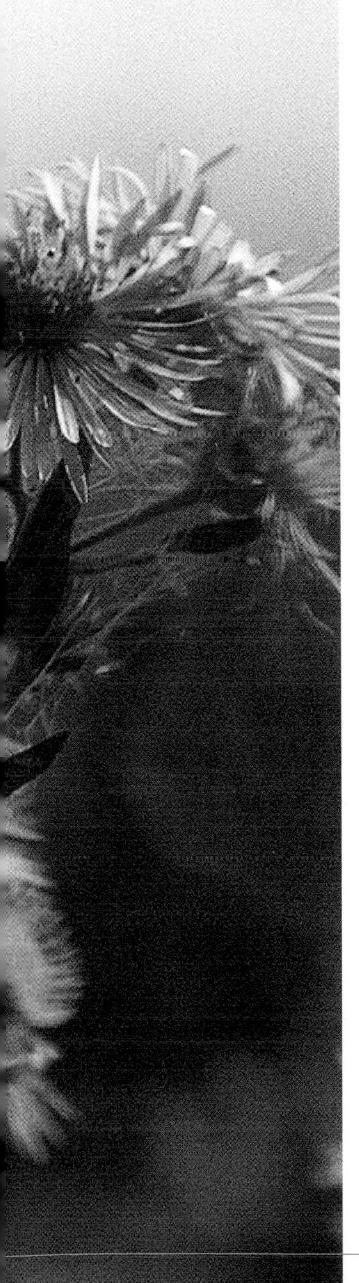

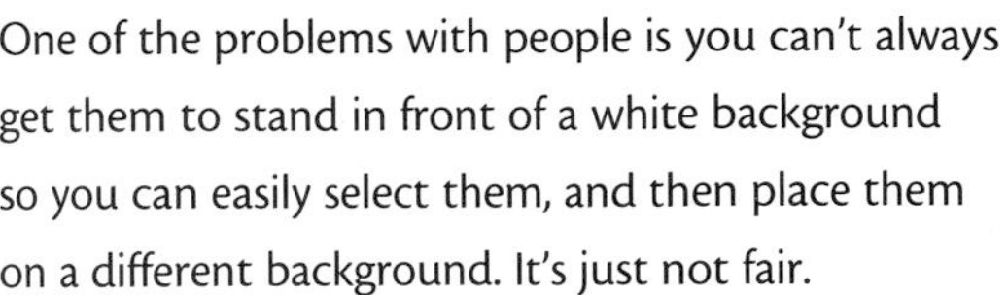

One of the problems with people is you can't always get them to stand in front of a white background so you can easily select them, and then place them on a different background. It's just not fair.

The Mask
selection techniques

If I were elected president, one of my first priorities would be to sign an executive order requiring all registered voters to carry with them a white seamless roll at all times. Can you imagine how much easier life would be? For example, let's say you're a sports photographer and you're shooting an *NFL Monday Night Football* game with one of those Canon telephoto lenses that are longer than the underground tube for a particle accelerator; and just as the quarterback steps into the pocket to complete a pass, a fullback comes up from behind, quickly unfurls a white, seamless backdrop, and lets you make the shot. Do you know how fast you'd get a job at *Sports Illustrated?* Do you know how long I've waited to use "unfurl" in a sentence and actually use it in the proper context? Well, let's just say at least since I was 12 (three long years ago). In this chapter, you'll learn how to treat everyone, every object, everything, as though it was shot on a white seamless background.

Selecting Square, Rectangular or Round Areas

Selections are an incredibly important part of working in Elements. That's because without them, everything you do, every filter you run, etc. would affect the entire photo. By being able to "select" an area, you can apply these effects only in the areas you want, giving you a much greater control. Believe it or not, the most basic selections (selecting square areas, rectangular areas, and round areas) are the ones you'll use the most, so we'll start with them.

Step One:
To make a rectangular selection, choose (big surprise) the Rectangular Marquee tool (shown here). Adobe's word for selection is "marquee." (Why? Because calling it a marquee makes it more complicated than calling it what it really is—a selection tool, and giving tools complicated names is what Adobe does for fun.)

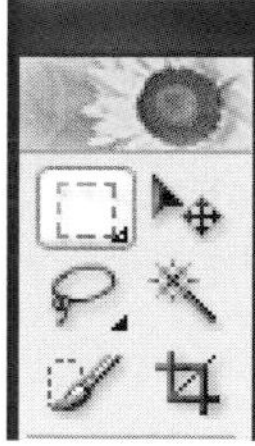

Step Two:
We're going to select one of the panes of glass in this photo, so click your cursor in the upper left-hand corner of the second pane and drag down and to the right until your selection covers the entire pane (as shown), then release the mouse button. That's it! You've got a selection, and anything you do now will affect only that selected pane.

© BRAND X PICTURES

Step Three:
Now, let's add another pane. To add another selection to your current selection, just hold the Shift key, then draw another selection. Try the top right pane (as shown).

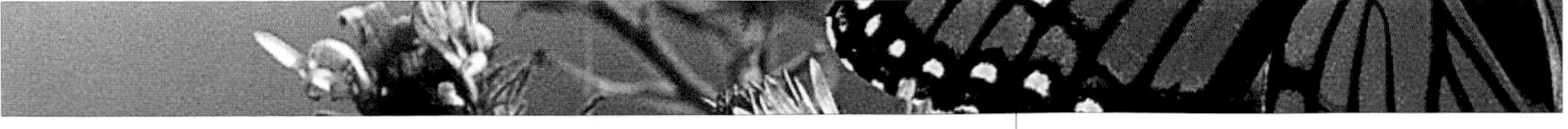

Step Four:
Now, go under the Filter menu, under Render, and choose Difference Clouds, and you'll notice that the Clouds effect is applied only to your selected areas. That's why making selections is so important. To deselect (make your selection go away), just press Control-D (Mac: Command-D).

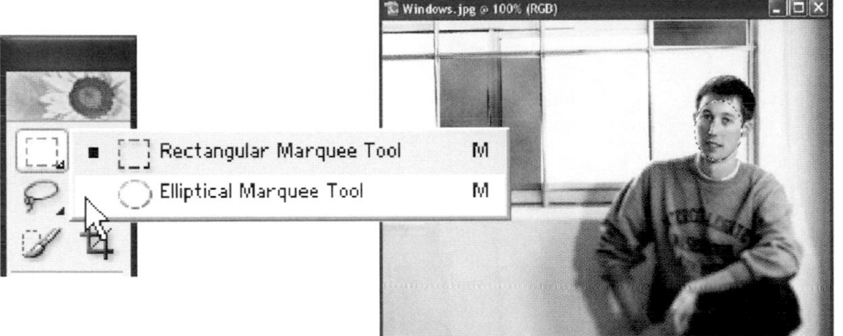

Step Five:
Now, let's make a circular selection. Click-and-hold on the Rectangular Marquee tool and a pop-out menu will appear. Choose the Elliptical Marquee tool. We're going to put an oval-shaped selection around the man's face, so start at the top left of his face and drag out a selection around his face (it won't fit perfectly, of course, so just get close, as shown here).

Step Six:
Press Control-F (Mac: Command-F) to apply the Difference Clouds filter we used earlier to his face. Okay, it looks pretty lame, but you get the idea. So far we've drawn freeform rectangles and ovals (which again, you'll wind up doing a lot). So, how do you make a perfect square or a perfect circular selection?

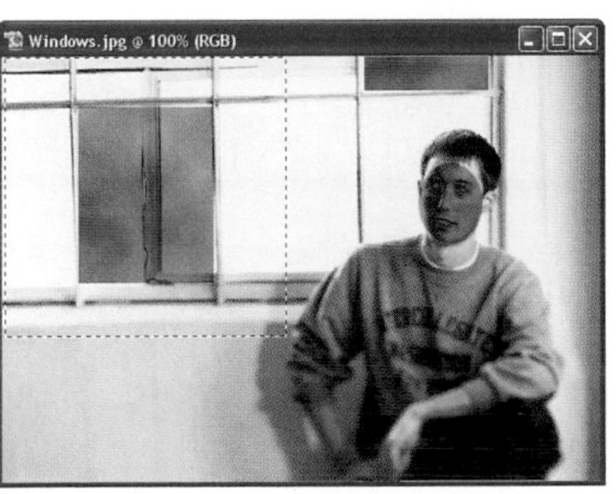

Step Seven:
To make a perfect square or rectangle, just hold the Shift key as you drag out your selection, and Elements will constrain your shape into perfectly square (or circular) proportions (a large square selection is shown here).

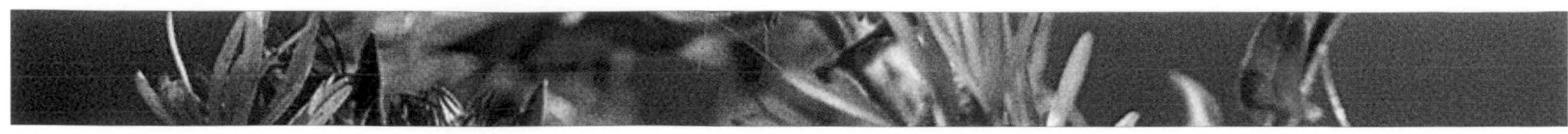

Softening Those Harsh Edges

When you make an adjustment to a selected area in a photo, your adjustment stays fully inside your selected area. That's great in many cases, but if you're making an adjustment to one selected area, such as adding Fill Flash or something like that, when you finally deselect, you'll see a hard edge around the area you adjusted, making the change look fairly obvious. However, softening those hard edges, thereby "hiding your tracks," is easy—here's how:

Step One:
First, we'll look at the problem. In this photo, we want to add some Fill Flash around this little guy's head, so drag out a rectangular selection slightly larger than his head. Press Shift-Control-F (Mac: Shift-Command-F) to bring up Fill Flash (or Enhance>Adjust Lighting>Fill Flash), then drag the Lighter slider to 25, and click OK. When you deselect, you can clearly see the border around the area you adjusted.

Step Two:
So let's start over (choose Revert from the File menu). Select around the little guy's head again, but before you make any adjustments, go under the Select menu and choose Feather. This brings up the Feather Selection dialog box, where you'll enter the desired amount of Feathering. The higher the amount you enter, the softer the edges. Enter 20 pixels (just a starting point) and click OK. Now apply the Fill Flash (as in Step One).

Step Three:
Now deselect and look at the difference. You don't see the hard edges, because the Feathering you applied softened them. Cool.

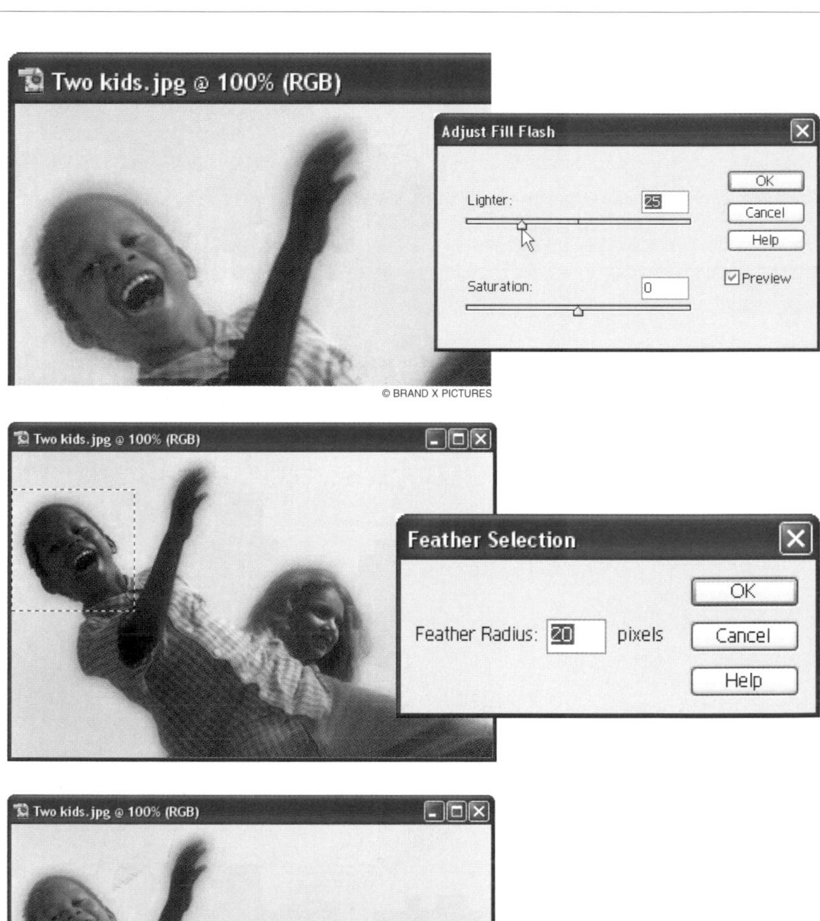

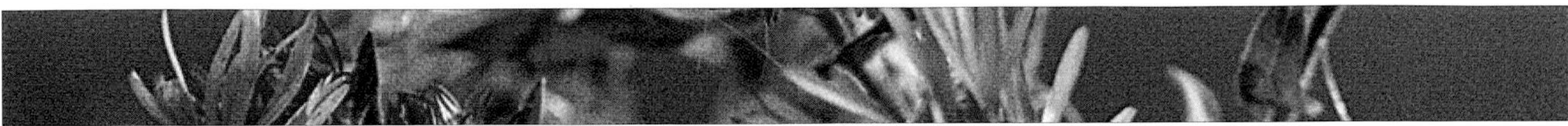

How to Select Things that Aren't Round, Square, or Rectangular

By now you know that selecting squares, rectangles, circles, ovals, etc. is a total no-brainer. But things get a little stickier when the area you want to select isn't square, or rectangular, or, well...you get the idea. Luckily, although it's not quite the no-brainer of the Marquee tools, if you don't mind being just a little patient, they're not hard, and making these "non-conformist" selections can actually be fun. Here's a quick project to get your feet wet.

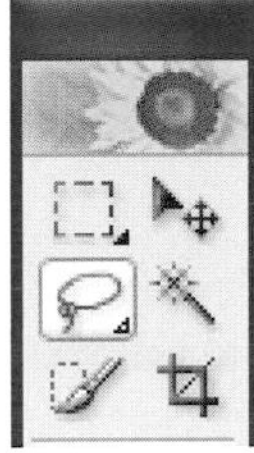

Step One:

In the photo shown here, you're going to select the bristles of the brush (which, as you can see, is not rectangular, square, etc). This is what the Lasso tool was born for, so choose it from the Toolbox (as shown).

© BRAND X PICTURES

Step Two:

Start at the bottom-left side of the brush tip, click, and slowly (the key word here is SLOWLY) drag the lasso tool around the brush tip, tracing the edges (as shown). If after you're done, you missed a spot, just hold the Shift key and select that missing spot—it will be added right to your selection. If you selected too much, hold the Alt key (Mac: Option) and draw over the area you shouldn't have selected.

Continued

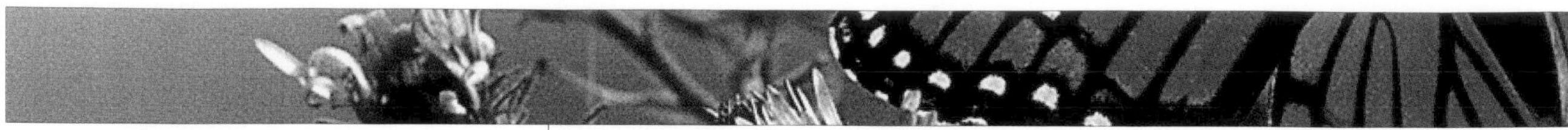

Step Three:
When the bristles are fully selected, go under the Select menu and choose Feather (we're doing this to soften the edges of the selected area). Enter 3 pixels (just a slight bit of softening), then click OK. Now that our edges are softened, we can make adjustments to the brush tip without "getting caught."

Step Four:
Now press Control-U (Mac: Command-U) to bring up Hue/Saturation, then drag the Hue slider either left or right to change the color of your brush tip. If the color looks too intense, just lower the amount of Saturation by dragging the Saturation slider to the left. Remember, these adjustments affect only the brush tip, not the whole photo, because you selected the brush tip with the Lasso tool before you made any adjustments.

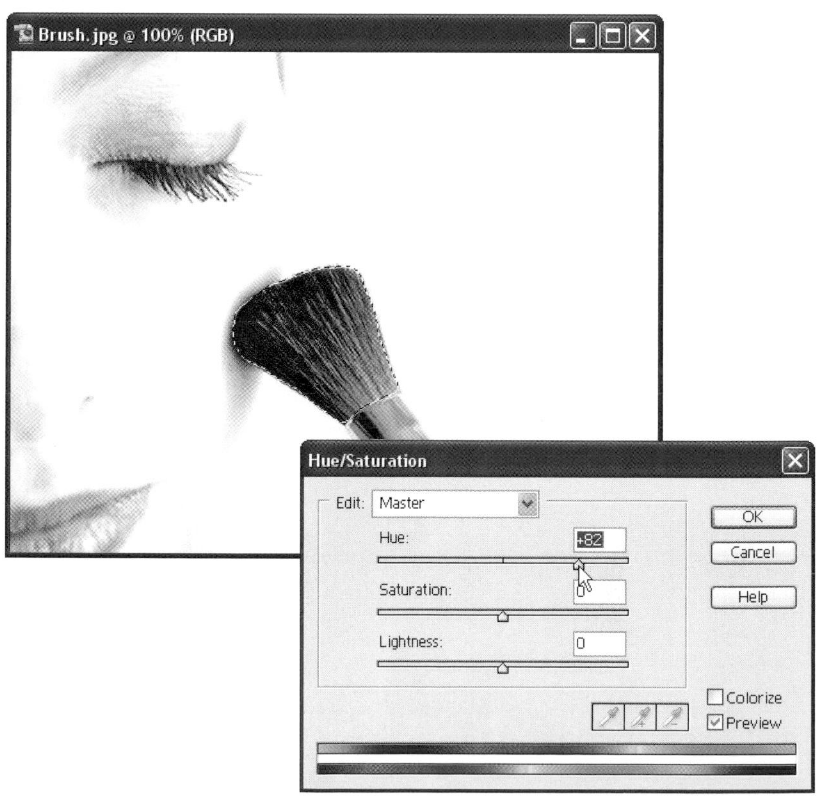

Selecting Areas by Their Color

How would you select an entire sky using the Rectangular Marquee tool? You probably wouldn't. Oh, you might use a combination of the Lasso and Rectangular Marquee, but even then it could be somewhat of a nightmare (depending on the photo). That's where the Magic Wand tool comes in. It selects by ranges of color, so instead of selecting by clicking-and-dragging, you click once in the blue sky, and the Magic Wand selects things in your photo that are colored fairly close to the color blue in your sky. It's pretty amazing by itself, but you can make it work even better.

© BRAND X PICTURES

Step One:

In this project, you'll select the sky (visible between the columns) using the Magic Wand tool. Start by choosing the Magic Wand tool from the Toolbox. Then, click it once in the middle opening between the columns, and it selects the blue sky in that area (as shown).

Step Two:

Now let's select the rest of the sky between the columns. With your first area still selected, just hold the Shift key and click on the area between another set of columns to add it to the selection. Keep holding the Shift key and clicking on other areas of the sky and they'll be added right along, until the entire sky is selected. Now you can use Hue/Saturation to change the color of the sky, just like you did in Step Four of the previous project.

TIP: If you click in an area of the sky with the Magic Wand and not all of that sky area gets selected, then you need to deselect, go up to the Options Bar, and increase the Tolerance setting. The higher the setting, the more colors it will select, so as a rule of thumb: If the Magic Wand doesn't select enough colors, increase the amount of Tolerance. If it selects too much, decrease it.

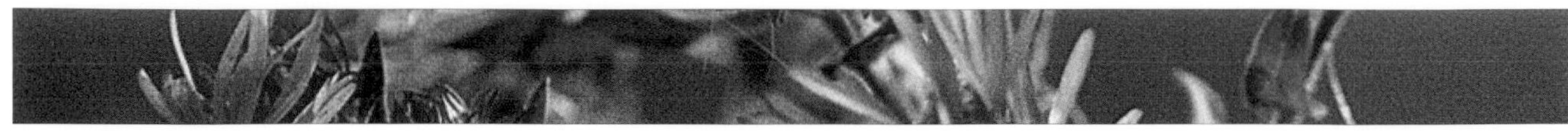

Making Selections Using a Brush

A lot of people are more comfortable using brushes than using Marquee tools, and if you're one of them (you know who you are) then you're in luck—you can make your selections by painting over the areas you want selected. Even if this sounds weird, it's worth a try—you might really like it (it's the same way with sushi). A major advantage of painting your selections is that you can choose a soft-edged brush (if you like), so you get feathered edges automatically. Here's how it works:

Step One:
Choose the Selection Brush tool from the Toolbox (as shown). Before you start you'll want to choose your brush size from up in the Options Bar. If you want a soft-edged selection (roughly equivalent to a feathered selection), change the Hardness setting: 0% gives a very soft edge, while 100% creates a very hard edge to your selection.

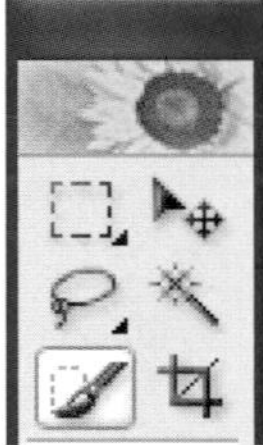

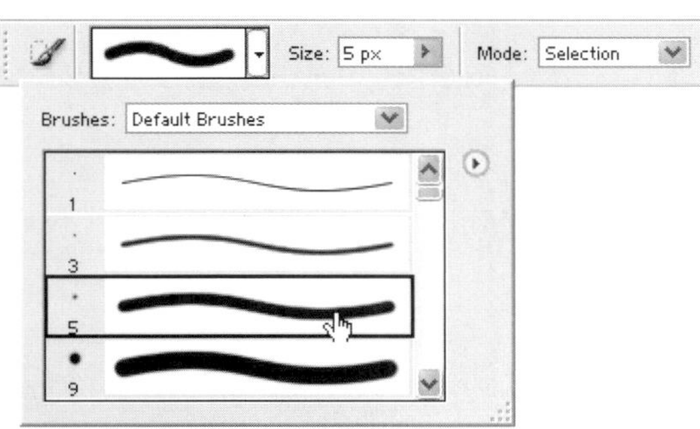

Step Two:
Now you can click-and-drag to "paint" the area you want selected. In this case, we're going to a select the lotus bud by painting over it. When you release the mouse, the selection becomes active. Note: You don't have to hold down the Shift key to add to your selection when using this brush—just start painting somewhere else and it's added.

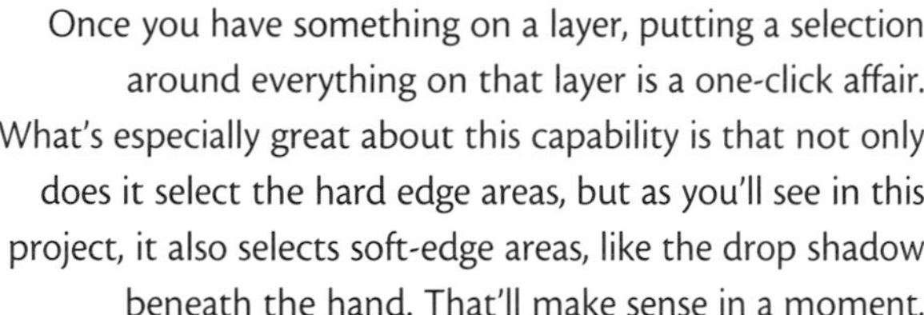

Selecting Everything On a Layer at Once!

Once you have something on a layer, putting a selection around everything on that layer is a one-click affair. What's especially great about this capability is that not only does it select the hard edge areas, but as you'll see in this project, it also selects soft-edge areas, like the drop shadow beneath the hand. That'll make sense in a moment.

Step One:

In the example shown here, we have a hand holding some poker cards (4-card stud?). The hand, the cards, and the drop shadow are all on the same layer (as shown here in the Layers palette).

Step Two:

To instantly put a selection around everything on that layer, just Control-click (Mac: Command-click) on the layer in the Layers palette. For just one (of many) examples of why you might want to do this, go to the Layers palette while your selection is still in place and add a new blank layer. Now, choose a medium blue for your Foreground color, then press Alt-Backspace (Mac: Option-Delete) to fill your selected area with blue. Now deselect. Next, change the Blend Mode of this blue layer in the Layers palette to Color, so now you have blue cards. Lower the Opacity of this layer to 20% and this removes the yellowish fluorescent lighting cast from the cards.

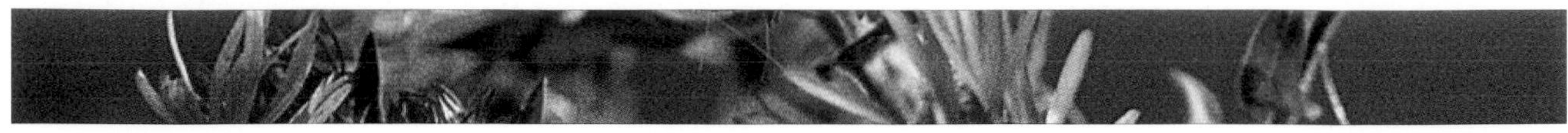

Saving Your Selections

If you've spent 15 or 20 minutes (or even more) putting together an intricate selection, once you deselect it, it's gone. (Well, you might be able to get it back by choosing Reselect from the Select menu, as long as you haven't made any other selections in the meantime, so don't count on it. Ever.) Here's how to save your finely honed selections and bring them back into place any time you need them.

Step One:

Put a selection around an object in your photo using whichever tool you want.

© BRAND X PICTURES

Step Two:

Once your selection is in place, to save it (to use again later), go under the Select menu and choose Save Selection. This brings up the Save Selection dialog box (as shown). Enter a name and click OK to save your selection.

Step Three:

You can get that selection back (known as "reloading" by Elements wizards) by going to the Select menu and choosing Load Selection. If you've saved more than one selection, they'll be listed in the pull-down menu—just choose which one you want to "load" then click OK—and the saved selection will appear in your image.

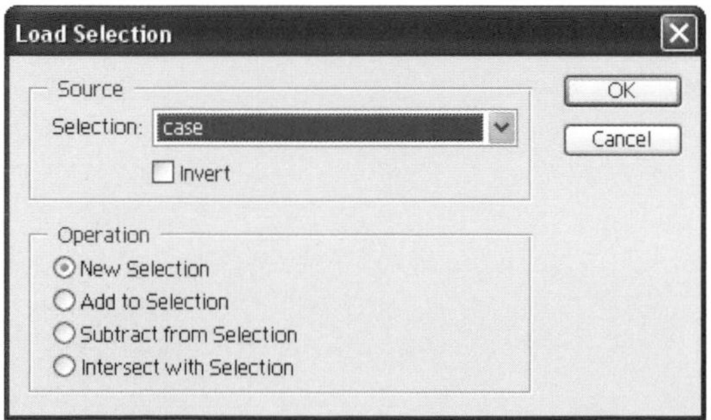

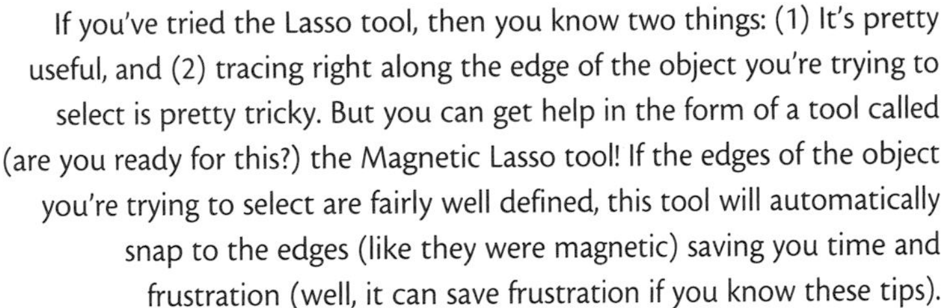

Getting Elements to Help You Make Tricky Selections

If you've tried the Lasso tool, then you know two things: (1) It's pretty useful, and (2) tracing right along the edge of the object you're trying to select is pretty tricky. But you can get help in the form of a tool called (are you ready for this?) the Magnetic Lasso tool! If the edges of the object you're trying to select are fairly well defined, this tool will automatically snap to the edges (like they were magnetic) saving you time and frustration (well, it can save frustration if you know these tips).

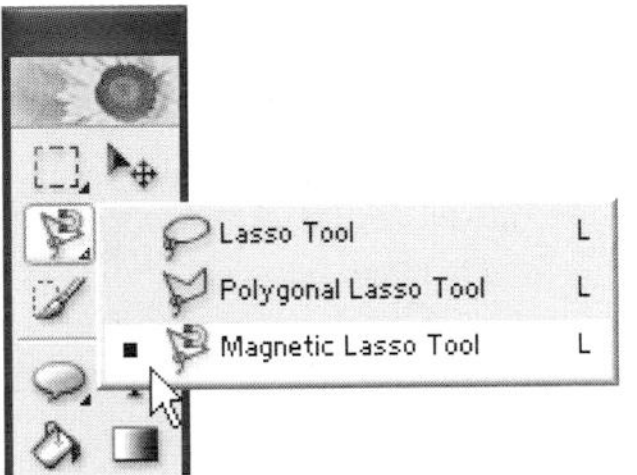

Step One:
Click-and-hold for a moment on the Lasso tool, and a menu pops out where you can choose the Magnetic Lasso tool (as shown).

© BRAND X PICTURES

Step Two:
Go to any edge of the object you want to select. Click once, then let go of the mouse button, and just move the mouse near the edge you want to select, and the Magnetic Lasso will snap right to it. Don't get too far away, stay kind of the near the edge for the best results.

Step Three:
As you drag, it lays down little points as it finds the edge. If you're dragging the mouse and it misses an edge, just press Backspace (Mac: Delete) to remove the last point and try again. If it still misses, hold the Alt key (Mac: Option key), which temporarily switches you to the regular Lasso tool. Then hold down the mouse button and drag a Lasso selection around the trouble area. Then, release the Alt key (Mac: Option key), then the mouse button, and you're back to the Magnetic Lasso to finish up the job.

Photographer | Todd Morrison

This should be called "The Kevin Ames Chapter." Actually, it really should be called the "I Hate Kevin Ames Chapter" because I already had this entire chapter written, until I stopped by Kevin's studio in

Head Games
retouching portraits

Atlanta one night to show him the rough draft of the book. What should have been a 15-minute visit went on until after midnight with him showing me some amazing portrait retouching tricks for the book. So I had to go back home and basically rewrite, update, and tweak the entire chapter. Which I can tell you, is no fun once you think a chapter is done and you're about a week from deadline, but the stuff he showed me was so cool, I literally couldn't sleep that night because I knew his techniques would take this chapter to the next level. And even though Kevin was incredibly gracious to let me share his techniques with my readers (that's the kind of guy Kevin is), there was no real way I was going to name this chapter "The Kevin Ames Chapter." That's when it became clear to me—I would have to kill him. But then I remembered Kevin had mentioned that Jim DiVitale had developed some of the techniques that he had showed me, so now it was going to be a double murder. I thought, "Hey, they both live in Atlanta, how hard could this be?" but the more I thought about it, what with having to fly back up there and having to fly on Delta (stuffed in like human cattle), I figured I'd just give them the credit they deserve and go on with my life. Thus far, it's worked out okay.

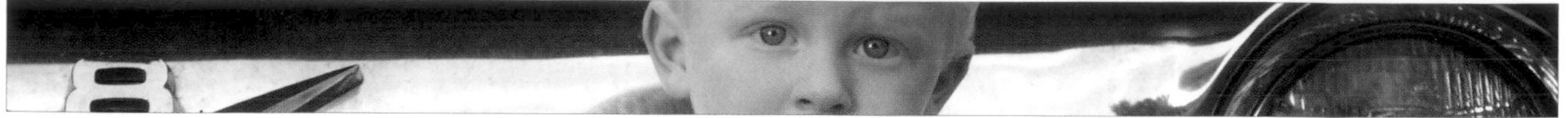

Removing Blemishes

When it comes to removing blemishes, acne, or any other imperfections of the skin, our goal is to maintain as much of the original skin texture as possible. That way, our retouch doesn't look pasty and obvious. Here are two techniques we use that work pretty nicely.

Technique #1
Step One:
Open a photo containing some skin imperfections you want to remove.

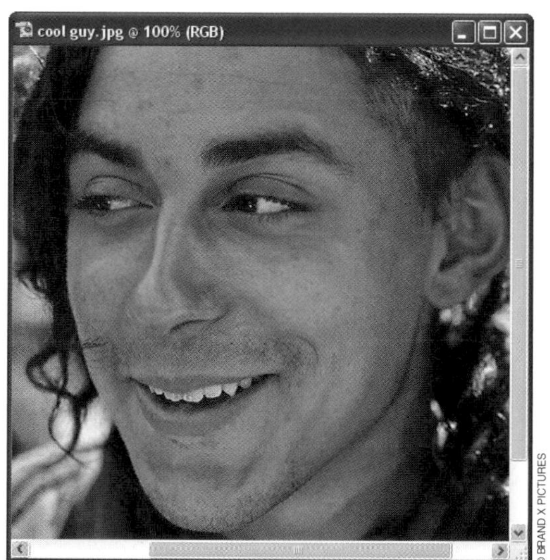

© BRAND X PICTURES

Step Two:
Choose the Clone Stamp tool in the Toolbox. From the Brush Picker up in the Options Bar (click on the Brush thumbnail on the left-hand side), choose a soft-edged brush that's slightly larger than the blemish you want to remove. Once you're working, if you need to quickly adjust the brush size up or down, use the Bracket keys on your keyboard: the Left Bracket key makes your brush smaller; the Right larger.

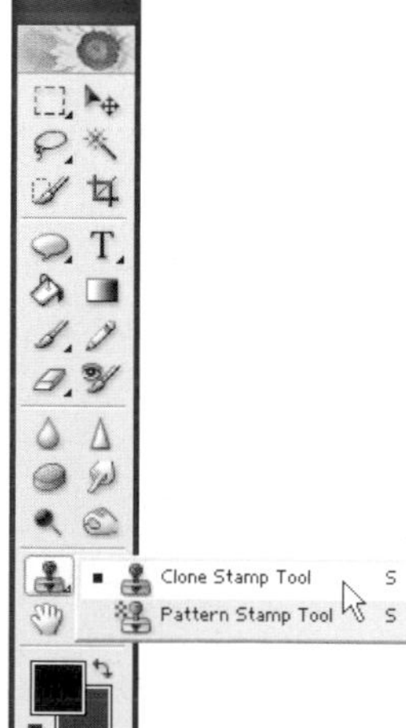

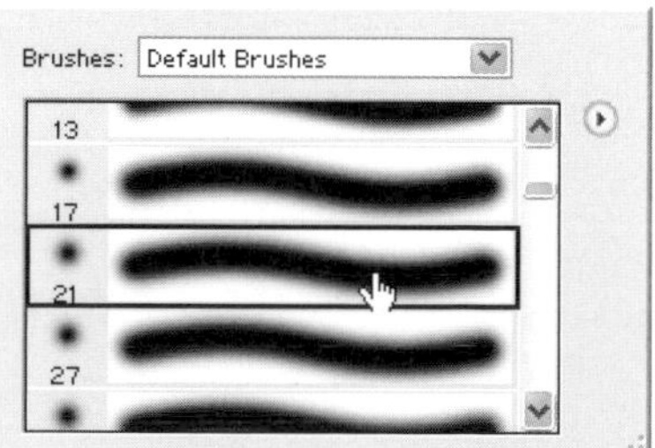

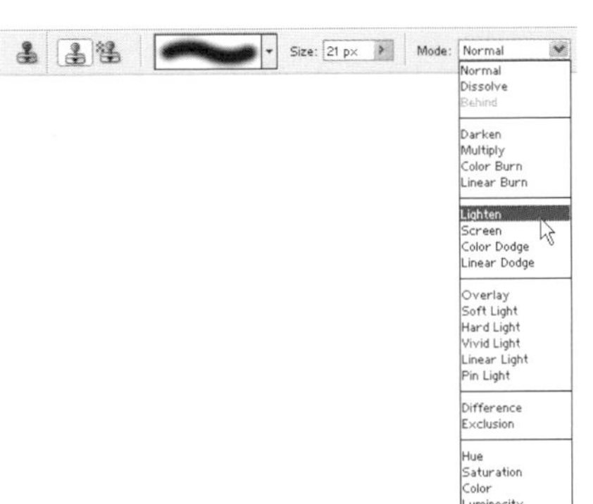

Step Three:
Up in the Options Bar, change the Blend Mode of the Clone Stamp tool to Lighten. With its Mode set to Lighten, the Clone Stamp will affect only pixels that are darker than the area you're going to sample. The lighter pixels (the regular flesh tone) will pretty much stay intact, and only the darker pixels (the blemish) will be affected.

Step Four:
Find an area right near the blemish that's pretty clean (no visible spots, blemishes, etc.), hold the Alt key (Mac: Option key), and click once. This samples the skin from that area. Try to make sure this sample area is very near the blemish so the skin tones will match. If you move too far away, you risk having your repair appear in a slightly different color, which is a dead giveaway of a repair.

Step Five:
Now, move your cursor directly over the blemish and click just once. Don't paint! Just click. The click will do it—it will remove the blemish instantly (as shown here), while leaving the skin texture intact. But what if the blemish is lighter than the skin, rather than darker? Simply go up in the Options Bar change the Blend Mode of the Clone Stamp tool to Darken instead of lighten—it's that easy. On to Technique #2.

Continued

Technique #2

Step One:

Switch to the Lasso tool in the Toolbox. Find a clean area (no blemishes, spots, etc.) near the blemish that you want to remove. In this clean area, use the Lasso tool to make a selection that is slightly larger than the blemish (as shown here).

Step Two:

Once your selection is in place, go under the Select menu and choose Feather. When the Feather Selection dialog box appears, enter 2 pixels as your Feather Radius and click OK. Feathering blurs the edges of our selected area, which will help hide the traces of our retouch. Feathering (softening) the edges of a selection is a very important part of facial retouching, and you'll do this quite a bit, to "hide your tracks," so to speak.

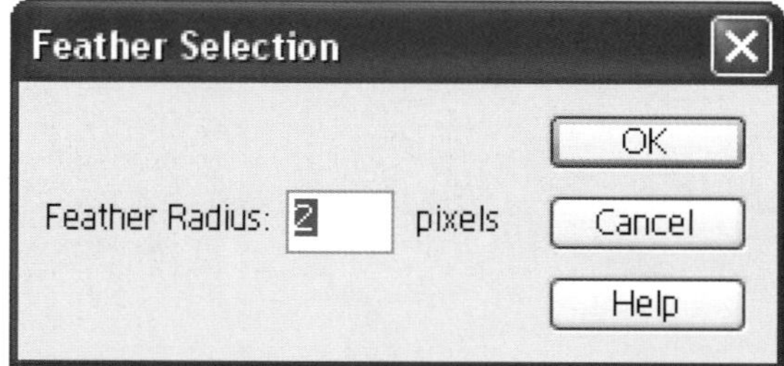

Step Three:

Now that you've softened the edges of the selection, hold Alt-Control (Mac: Option-Command), and you'll see your cursor change into two arrowheads—a white one with a black one overlapping it. This is telling you that you're about to copy the selected area. Click within your selection and drag this clean skin area right over the blemish to completely cover it.

Step Four:

When the clean area covers the blemish, release the keys (and the mouse button, of course) to drop this selected area down onto your photo. Now, press Control-D (Mac: Command-D) to deselect. The photo at left shows the final results, and as you can see, the blemish is gone. Best of all, because you dragged skin over from a nearby area, the full skin texture is perfectly intact, making your repair nearly impossible to detect.

Before

After

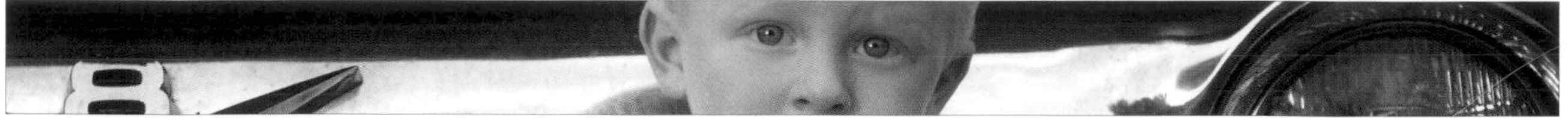

Removing Dark Circles Under Eyes

Here's a quick technique for removing the dark circles that sometimes appear under a person's eyes—especially after a hard night of drinking. At least, that's what I've been told.

Step One:
Open the photo that has the dark circles you want to lessen. Select the Clone Stamp tool in the Toolbox. Then (from the Brush Picker in the Options Bar) choose a soft-edged brush that's half as wide as the area you want to repair.

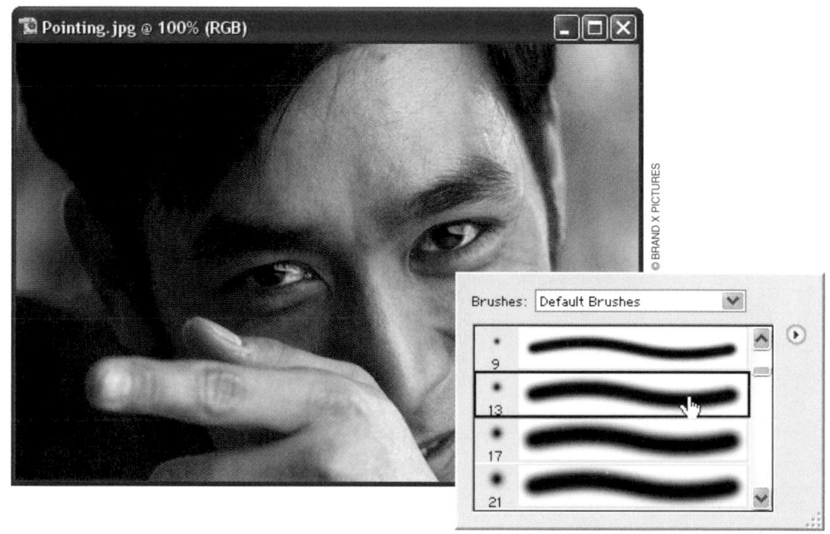

Step Three:
Go up to the Options Bar and lower the Opacity of the Clone Stamp tool to 50%. Then, change the Blend Mode to Lighten (so you'll only affect areas that are darker than where you'll sample from).

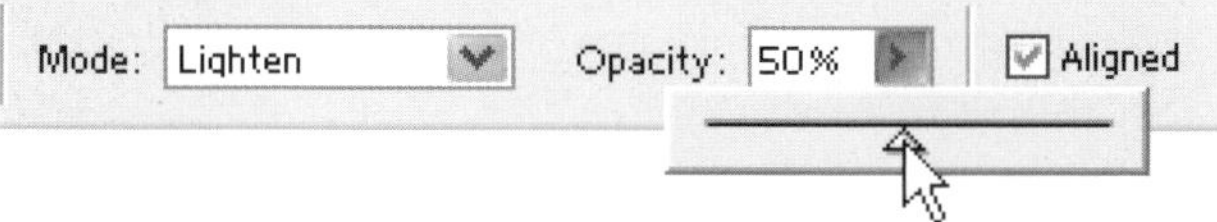

Step Four:

Hold the Alt key (Mac: Option key) and click once in an area near the eye that isn't affected by the dark circles. If the cheeks aren't too rosy, you can click there, but more likely you'll click (sample) on an area just below the dark circles under the eyes.

Step Five:

Now, take the Clone Stamp tool and paint over the dark circles to lessen or remove them (the result is shown here). It may take two or more strokes for the dark circles to pretty much disappear, so don't be afraid to go back over the same spot if the first stroke didn't work.

Before

After

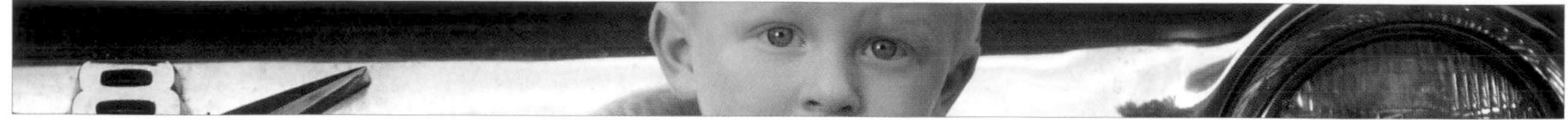

Lessening Freckles or Facial Acne

This technique is popular with senior class portrait photographers who need to lessen or remove large areas of acne, pockmarks, or freckles. This is especially useful when you have a lot of photos to retouch (like a senior portrait retoucher) and don't have the time to use the methods shown previously, where you deal with each blemish individually.

Step One:
Open the photo that you need to retouch. Make a duplicate of the Background layer by dragging it to the Create New Layer icon at the bottom of the Layers palette. We'll perform our retouch on this duplicate of the background layer.

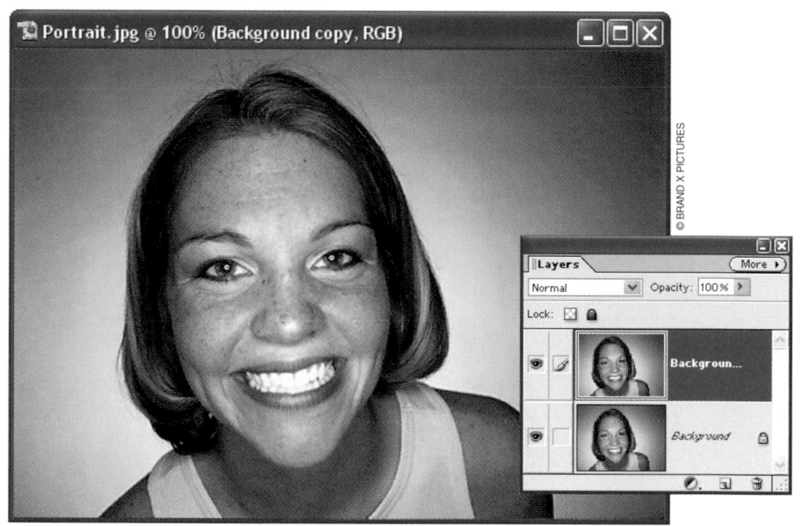

Step Two:
Go under the Filter menu, under Blur, and choose Gaussian Blur. When the Gaussian Blur dialog appears, drag the slider all the way to the left, then drag it slowly to the right until you see the freckles blurred away. The photo should look very blurry, but we'll fix that in just a minute, so don't let that throw you off—make sure it's blurry enough that the freckles are no longer visible.

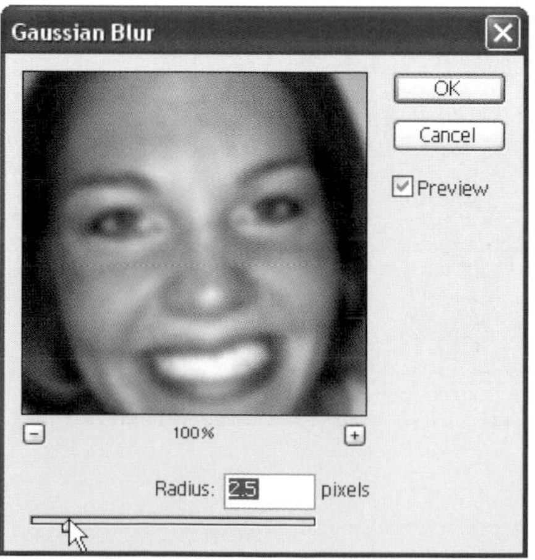

Step Three:
Hold the Control key (Mac: Command key) and click once on the Create New Layer icon at the bottom of the Layers palette. This creates a new blank layer directly beneath your current layer (the blurry layer).

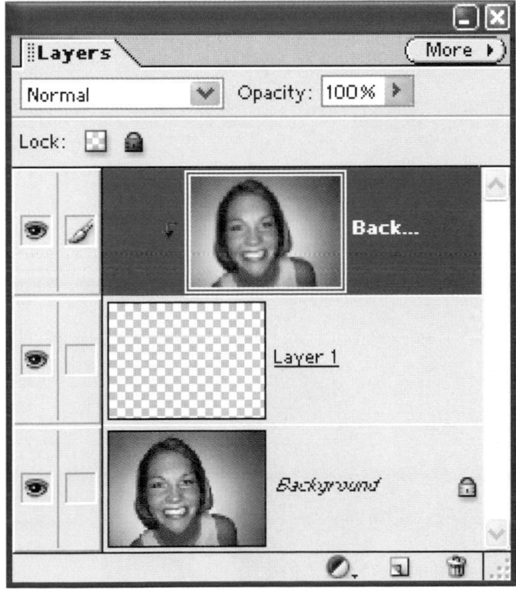

Step Four:
Now, in the Layers palette, click back on the top layer (the blurry layer), then press Control-G (Mac: Command-G) to Group the blurry layer with the blank layer beneath it. You'll notice that doing this removes all the blurriness from view (and that's exactly what we want to do at this point).

Continued

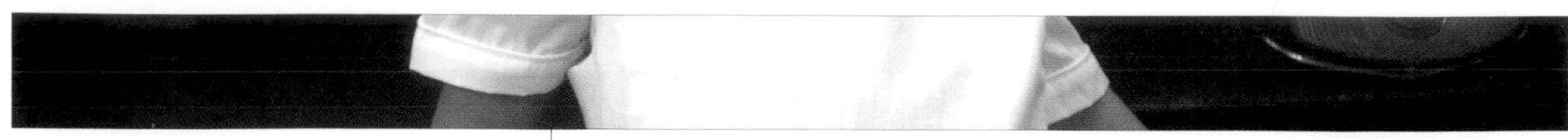

Step Five:
In the Layers palette, click on the middle layer (the blank layer) as you're going to paint on this layer. Press the letter "D" to set your Foreground color to black. Switch to the Brush tool in the Toolbox, then choose a soft-edged brush from the Brush Picker in the Options Bar.

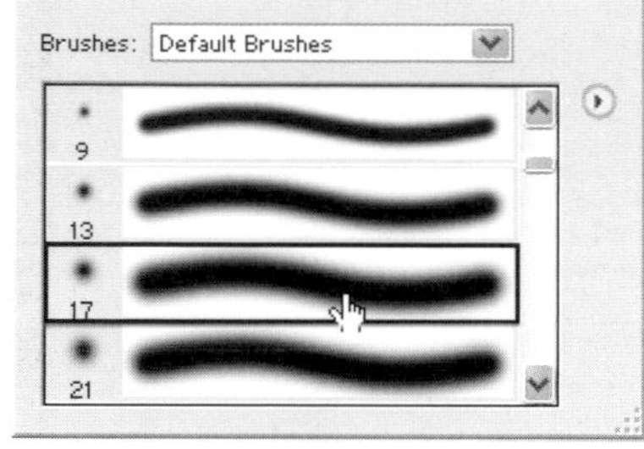

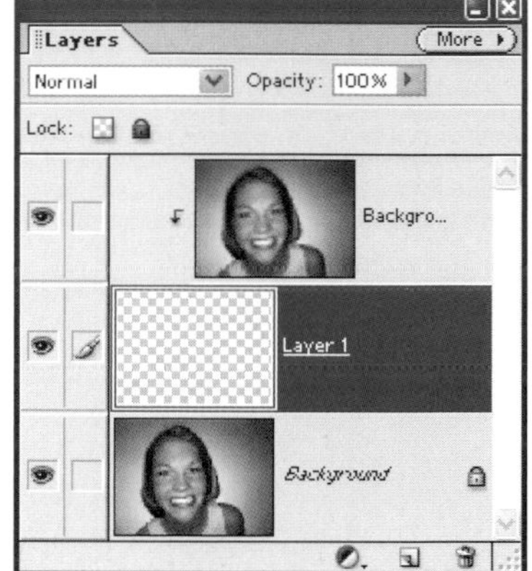

Step Six:
Lower the Opacity setting of your brush (in the Options Bar) to 50%, and change the Blend Mode from Normal to Lighten. Now when you paint, it will affect only the pixels that are darker than the blurred state. Ahhh, do you see where this is going?

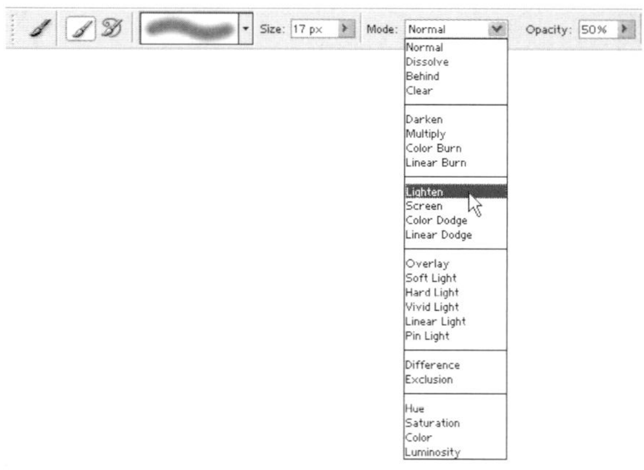

Step Seven:
Now you can paint over the freckle areas, and as you paint you'll see them diminish quite a bit (as shown here). If they diminish too much, and the person looks "too clean," undo, then try lowering the Opacity of the brush to 25% and try again.

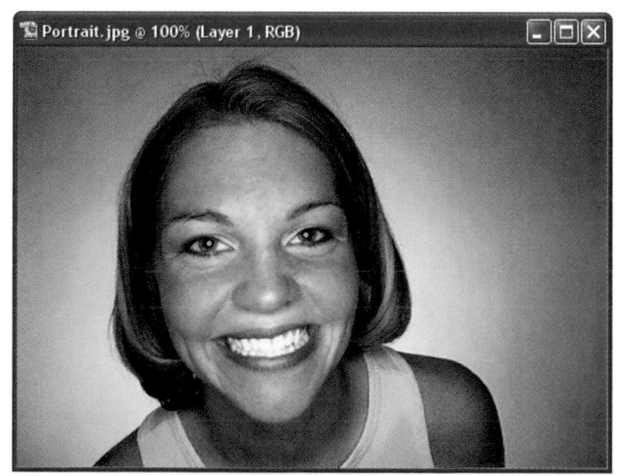

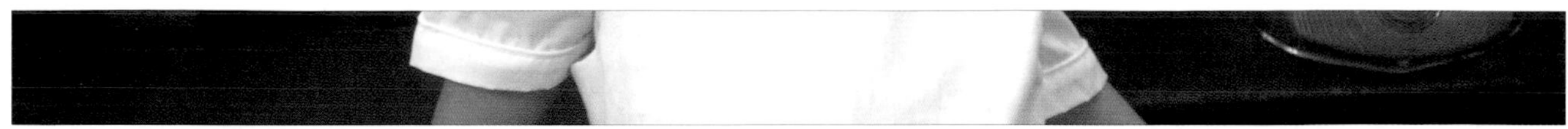

Before

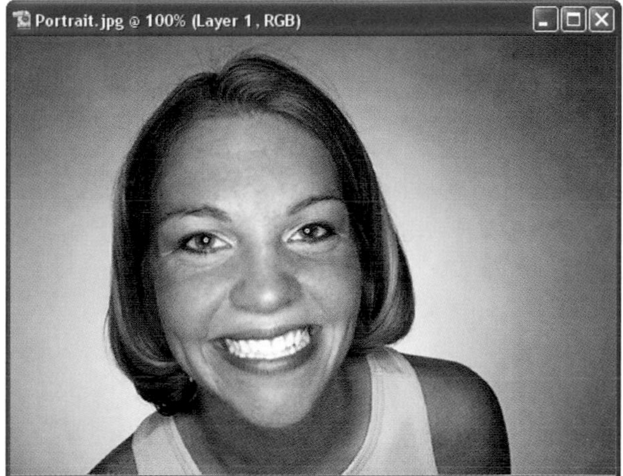

After

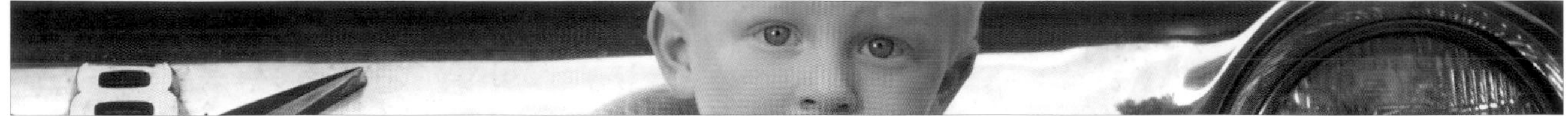

Removing or Lessening Wrinkles

This is a great trick for removing wrinkles, with a little twist at the end (courtesy of my buddy Kevin Ames) that helps make the technique look more realistic. His little tweak makes a big difference because (depending on the age of the subject) removing every wrinkle would probably make the photo look obviously retouched (in other words, if you're retouching someone in their 70s and you make them look as if they're 20 years old, it's just going to look weird). Here's how to get a more realistic wrinkle removal.

Step One:

Open the photo that needs some wrinkles or crows feet lessened.

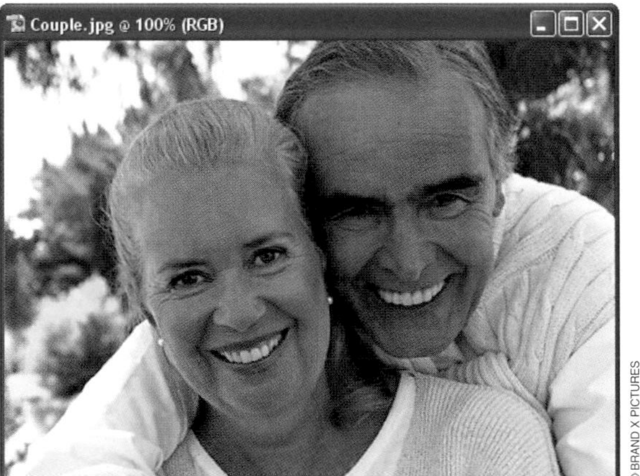

Step Two:

Duplicate the Background layer by dragging it to the Create New Layer icon at the bottom of the Layers palette. You'll perform your "wrinkle removal" on this duplicate layer.

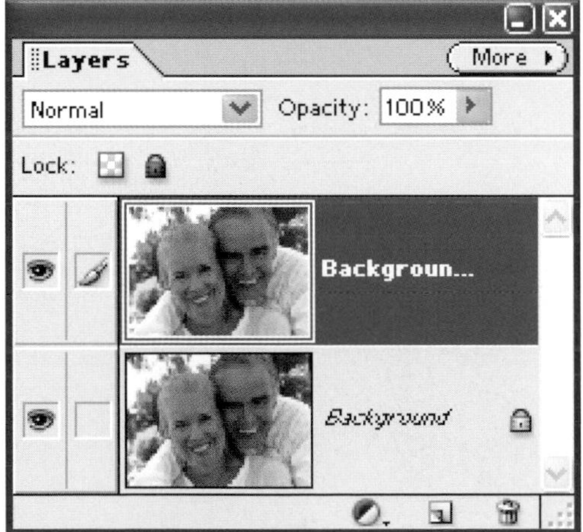

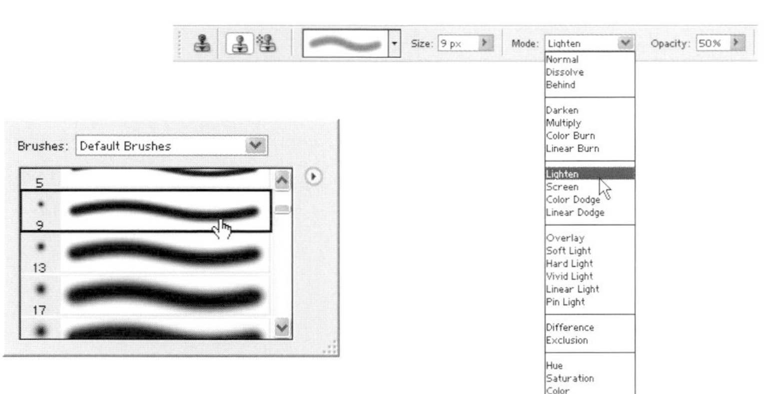

Step Three:

Select the Clone Stamp tool in the Toolbox. Then (from the Brush Picker in the Options Bar) choose a soft-edged brush that's close to the size of the wrinkles you want to remove. Go up to the Options Bar and lower the Opacity of the Clone Stamp tool to 50%. Then, change the Blend Mode to Lighten, so we only affect the darker pixels.

Step Four:

Find a clean area that's somewhere near the wrinkles (perhaps the upper cheek if you're removing crows feet, or if you're removing forehead wrinkles, perhaps just above or below the wrinkle), hold the Alt key (Mac: Option key), and click once to sample the smooth skin from that area. Now, take the Clone Stamp tool and paint over the wrinkles. As you paint, you're cloning smooth skin over the wrinkles. It may take more than one pass over the wrinkles to remove them adequately.

Step Five:

Now that the wrinkles are gone, it's time to bring just enough of them back to make it look realistic. Simply go to the Layers palette and reduce the Opacity of this layer to bring back some of the original wrinkles. This lets a small amount of the original photo (the Background layer, with all its wrinkles still intact) show through. Keep lowering the Opacity until you see the wrinkles so they're visible but not nearly as prominent (as shown here).

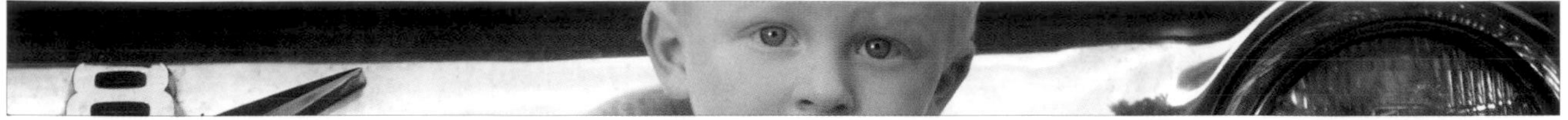

Dodging and Burning Done Right

If you've ever used Elements' Dodge and Burn tools, you already know how lame they are. That's why the pros choose this method instead—it gives them a level of control that the Dodge and Burn tools just don't offer, and best of all, it doesn't "bruise the pixels." (That's digital retoucher-speak for "it doesn't mess up your original image data while you're editing.")

Step One:
In this tutorial, we're going to dodge areas of this person to add some highlights, then we're going to burn in the background a bit to darken some of those areas. Start by opening the photo you want to dodge and burn.

© BRAND X PICTURES

Step Two:
Go to the Layers palette, and from the More pop-down menu choose New Layer. The reason you need to do this (rather than just clicking on the Create New Layer icon) is that you need to access the New Layer dialog box for this technique to work, and you don't get the dialog when you use the Create New Layer icon.

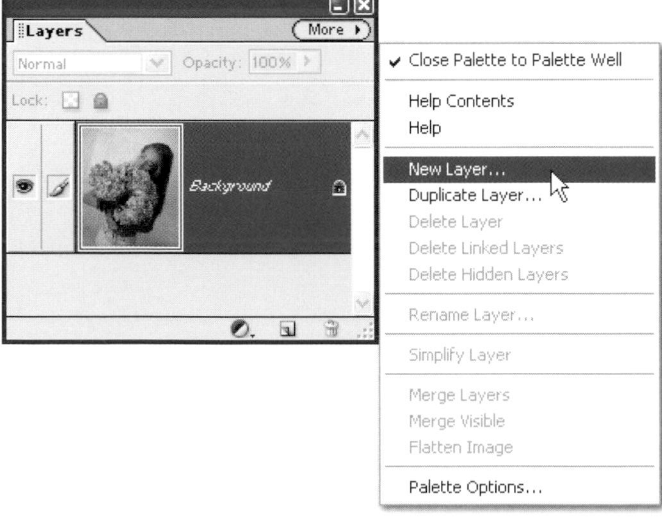

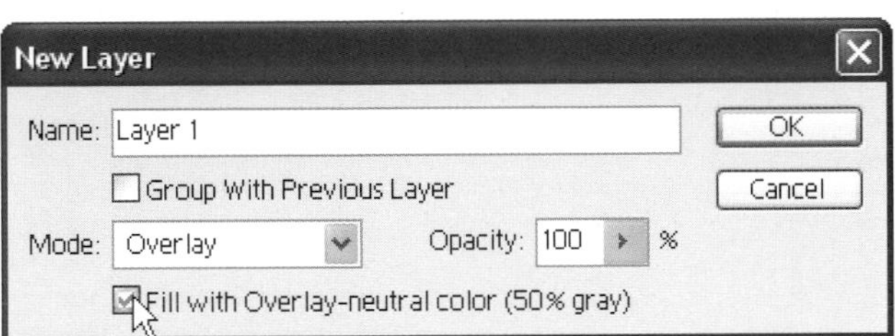

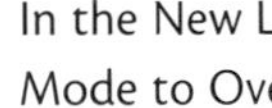

Step Three:

In the New Layer dialog box, change the Mode to Overlay, then right below it, choose "Fill with Overlay-neutral color (50% gray)." This is normally grayed out, but when you switch to Overlay mode, this choice becomes available. Click the checkbox to make it active, then click OK.

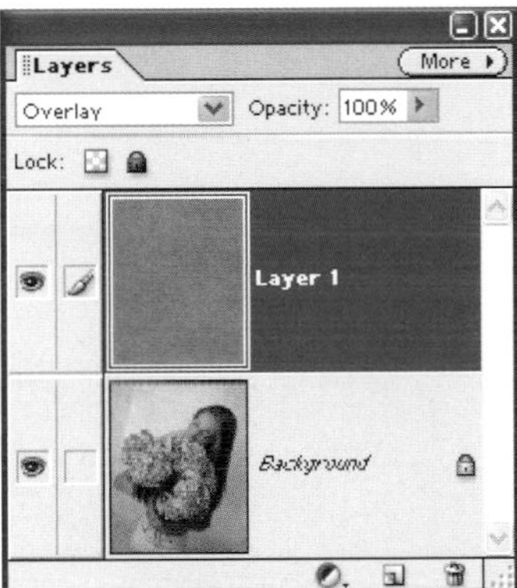

Step Four:

This creates a new layer, filled with 50% gray, above your Background layer. (When you fill a layer with 50% gray and change the Mode to Overlay, Elements ignores the color. You'll see a gray thumbnail in the Layers palette, but the layer will appear transparent in your image window.)

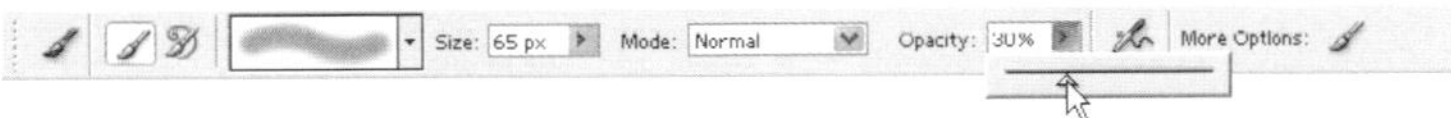

Step Five:

Switch to the Brush tool, choose a large soft-edged brush, then go up to the Options Bar and lower the Opacity to approximately 30%.

Continued

Step Six:

Press "D" then "X" to set your Foreground color to white. Begin painting over the areas that you want to highlight (dodge). As you paint, you'll see white strokes appear in the thumbnail of your gray transparent layer, and in the image window you'll see soft highlights.

Step Seven:

If your first stab at dodging isn't as intense as you'd like, just release the mouse button, click again, and paint over the same area. Since you're dodging at a low Opacity, the highlights will "build up" as you paint over previous strokes. If the highlights appear too intense, just go to the Layers palette and lower the Opacity setting until they blend in.

Step Eight:

If there are areas you want to darken (burn), just press "D" to switch your Foreground color to black and begin painting in the areas that need darkening. In this example, the background looked a little light, so I burned it in a bit to darken it and make it less prominent. Okay, ready for another dodging and burning method? Good, 'cause I've got a great one.

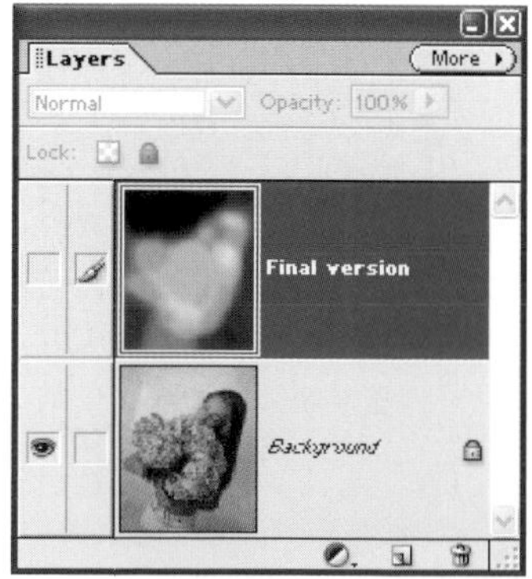

Alternate Technique:
Just click the Create New Layer icon, then change the Blend Mode in the Layers palette to Soft Light. Now, just set white as your Foreground color and you can dodge right on this layer using the Brush tool set to 30% Opacity. To burn, just as before—switch to black. The dodging and burning using this Soft Light layer does appear a bit softer and milder than the previous technique, and you should definitely try both to see which one you prefer.

Before

After

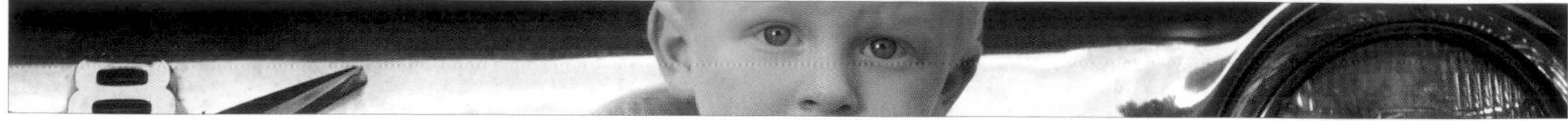

Colorizing Hair

This technique (that I learned from Kevin Ames) gives you maximum control and flexibility while changing or adjusting hair color, and because of the use of an Adjustment Layer, you're not "bruising the pixels." Instead, you're following the enlightened path of "non-destructive retouching."

Step One:

Open the photo you want to retouch.

© BRAND X PICTURES

Step Two:

Choose Hue/Saturation from the Adjustment Layer pop-up menu at the bottom of the Layers palette. When the dialog appears, click on the checkbox for Colorize (in the bottom right-hand corner of the dialog) and then drag the Hue slider to the approximate color you'd like for the hair. Doing this will colorize the entire image, but don't let that throw you—just focus on the hair color. You may also have to drag the Saturation slider to the right a bit to make the color more vibrant.

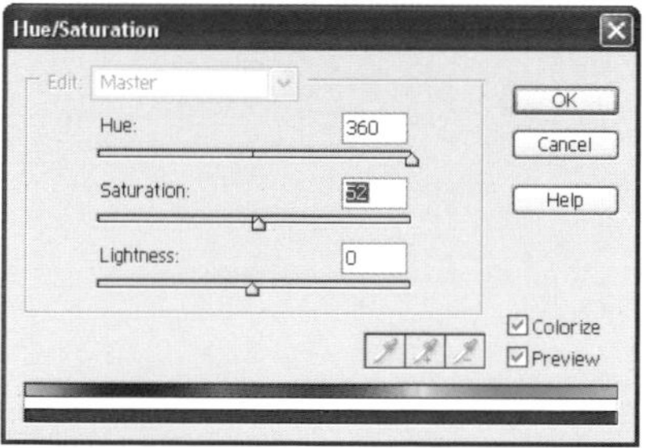

Step Three:

In this case, we want to make the hair more red, so move the top slider (Hue) to the far right, then drag the Saturation slider (the middle slider) to the right to increase the intensity of the red. Now, click OK and the entire photo will have a heavy red cast over it (as shown).

Step Four:

Press "X" until your Foreground color is black, and press Alt-Backspace (Mac: Option-Delete) to fill the Hue/Saturation mask with black. Doing so removes the red tint from the photo.

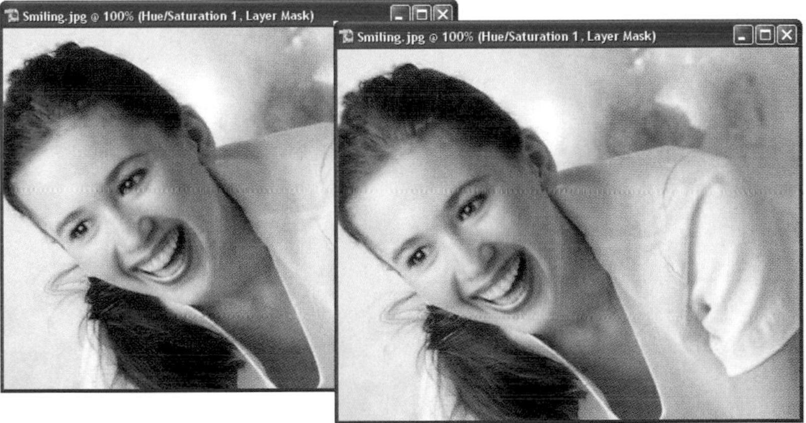

Step Five:

Get the Brush tool in the Toolbox, choose a soft-edged brush, press "X" to set your Foreground color to white and begin painting over her hair. As you paint, the red tint you added with Hue/Saturation is painted back in (as shown). Once the hair is fully painted, change the Blend Mode of your Hue/Saturation Adjustment Layer to Color, then lower the Opacity until the hair color looks natural (as shown at near left).

Before

After

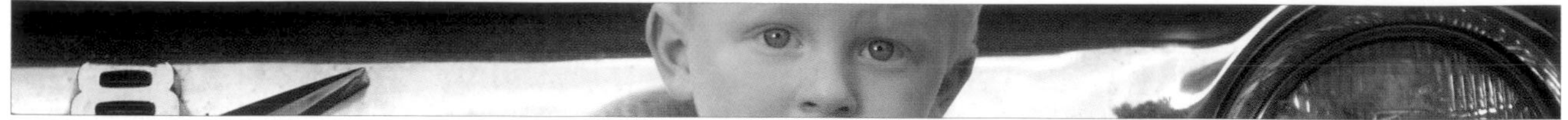

Whitening the Eyes

This is a great little technique for quickly whitening the whites of the eyes, and it has the added benefit of removing any redness in the eye along the way. Note: by redness, I mean the "bloodshot-I-stayed-up-too-late" type of redness, not the "red-eye-from-a-flash-mounted-above-the-lens" type of redness, which is addressed in Chapter 3, "The Big Fixx."

Step One:

Open the photo where the subject's eyes need whitening.

© BRAND X PICTURES

Step Two:

Choose the Lasso tool from the Toolbox and draw a selection around the whites of one of the eyes. Hold the Shift key and draw selections around the whites of the other eye, until all the whites are selected in both eyes (as shown here).

Step Three:

Go under the Select menu and choose Feather. You'll need to use Feather to soften the edges of your selection so your retouch isn't obvious. In the Feather Selection dialog box, enter 2 pixels and click OK.

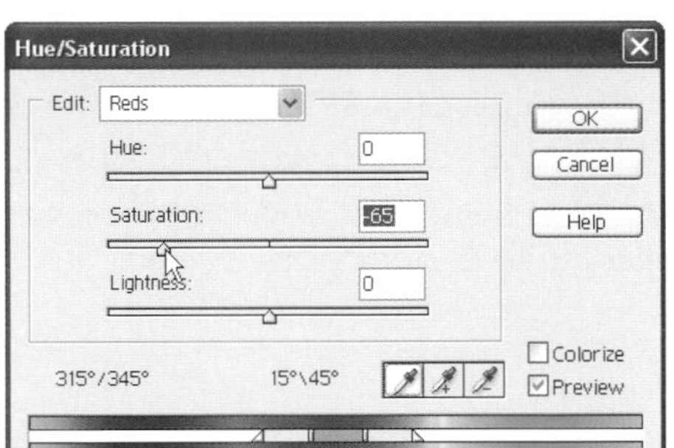

Step Four:

Go under the Enhance menu, under Adjust Color, and choose Hue/Saturation. When the Hue/Saturation dialog box appears, choose Reds from the Edit pop-up menu at the top (to edit just the reds in the photo). Now, drag the Saturation slider to the left to lower the amount of saturation in the reds (which removes any bloodshot appearance in the whites of the eyes).

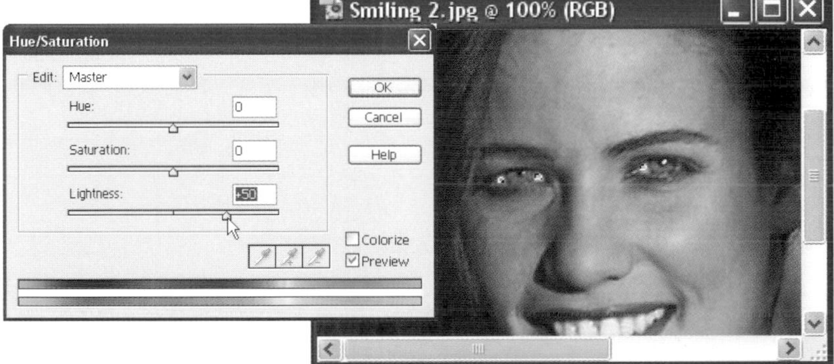

Step Five:

While you're still in the Hue/Saturation dialog, from the Edit menu switch back to Master. Drag the Lightness slider to the right to increase the lightness of the whites of the eyes (as shown here).

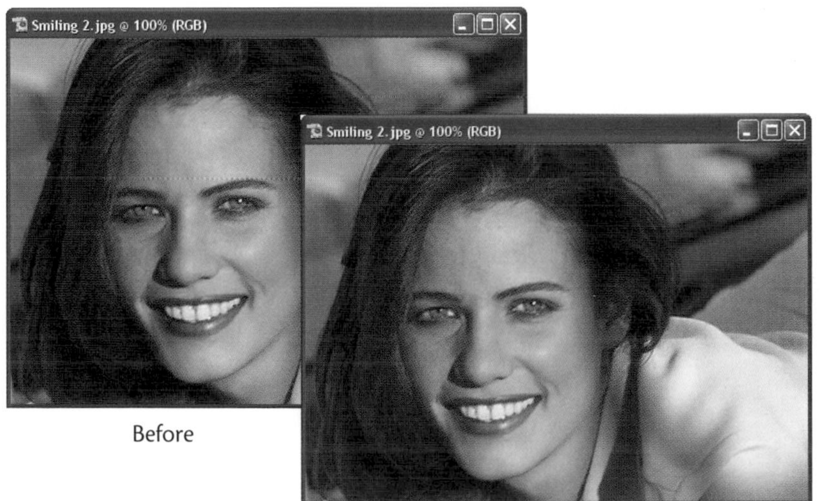

Before

After

Step Six:

Click OK in the Hue/Saturation dialog to apply your adjustments, then press Control-D (Mac: Command-D) to deselect and complete the enhancement.

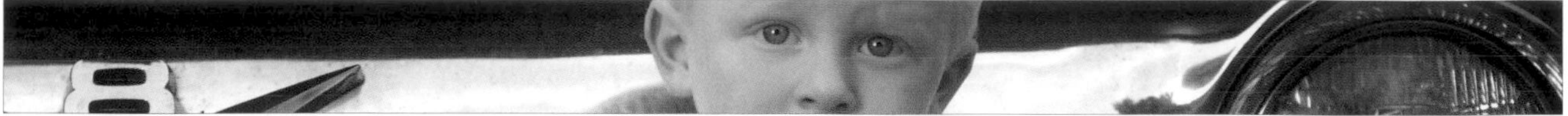

Making Eyes that Sparkle

This is another one of those "30-second miracles" for making eyes seem to sparkle by enhancing the catch lights, and generally drawing attention to the eyes by making them look sharp and crisp (crisp in the "sharp and clean" sense, not crisp in the "I-burned-my-retina-while-looking-at-the-sun" sense).

Step One:
Open the photo that you want to retouch. Make a duplicate of the Background layer by dragging it to the Create New Layer icon at the bottom of the Layers palette.

© BRAND X PICTURES

Step Two:
Go under the Filter menu, under Sharpen, and choose Unsharp Mask. (It sounds like this filter would make things blurry, but it's actually for sharpening photos.) When the Unsharp Mask dialog appears, enter your settings. (If you need some settings, go to the first technique in Chapter 10, "Sharp Dressed Man" or you can use my favorite all-around sharpening settings of Amount: 85%, Radius: 1, Threshold: 4 for now), then click OK to sharpen the entire photo.

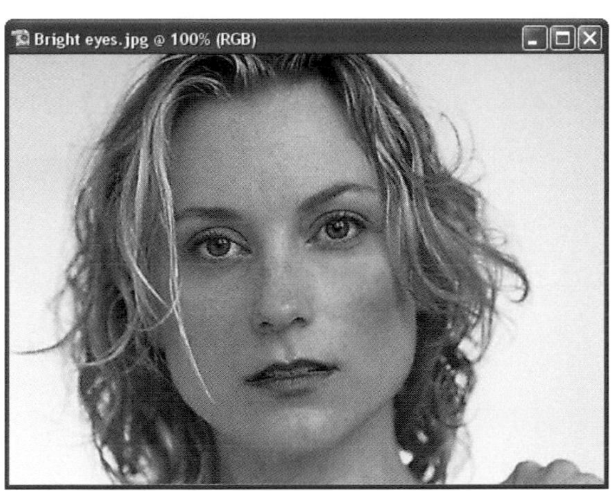

Step Three:

After you've applied the Unsharp Mask filter, apply it again using the same settings by pressing Control-F (Mac: Command-F), and then apply it one more time using the same keyboard shortcut (you'll apply it three times in all). The eyes will probably look nice and crisp at this point, but the rest of the person will be severely oversharpened, and you'll probably see lots of noise and other unpleasant artifacts.

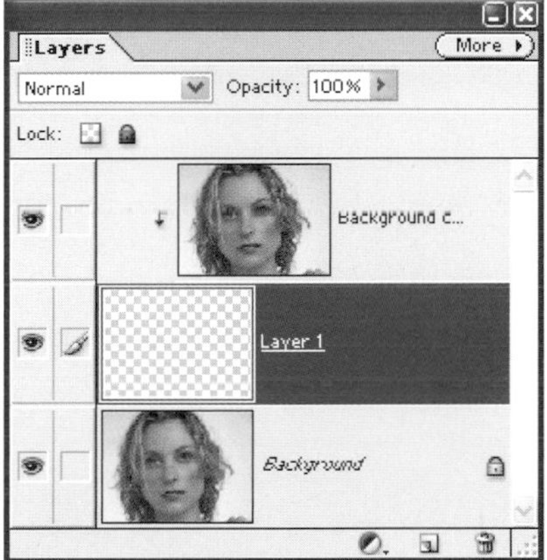

Step Four:

Hold the Control key (Mac: Command key) and click once on the Create New Layer icon at the bottom of the Layers palette. This creates a new blank layer directly beneath your sharpened layer. Now, in the Layers palette, click back on the top layer (the sharpened layer), then press Control-G (Mac: Command-G) to Group the sharpened layer with the blank layer beneath it. This removes all the visible sharpness (at least for now).

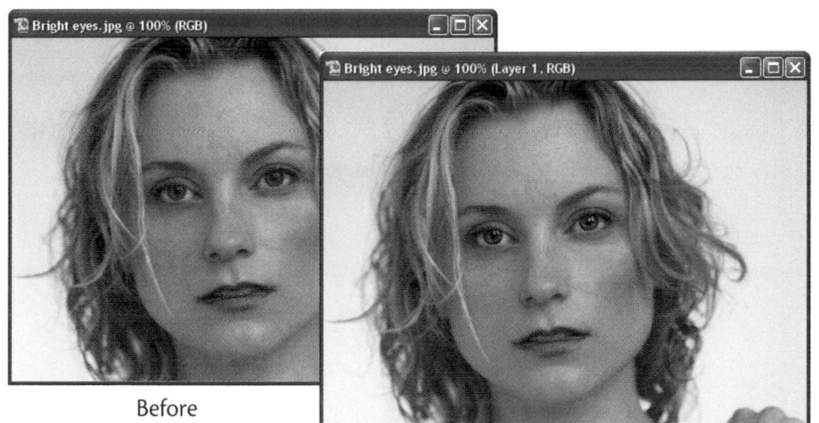

Before

After

Step Five:

In the Layers palette, click on the middle layer (the blank layer) as you're going to paint on this layer. Press the letter "D" to set your Foreground color to black. Then, switch to the Brush tool and choose a soft-edged brush that's a little smaller than your subject's eyes from the Brush Picker in the Options Bar. Now paint over just the irises and pupils of the eyes to reveal the sharpening, making the eyes really sparkle and completing the effect.

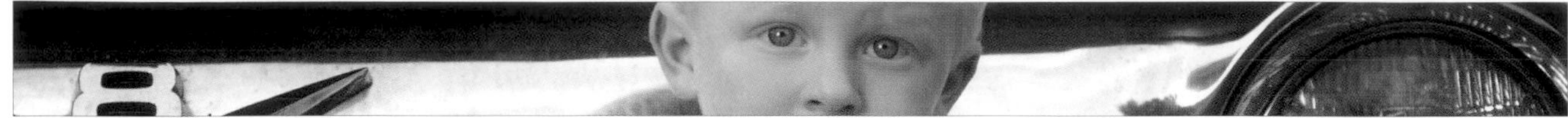

Enhancing Eyebrows and Eyelashes

After Kevin Ames showed me this technique for enhancing eyebrows and eyelashes, I completely abandoned the method I'd used for years. I switched over to this method because it's faster, easier, and equally, if not more effective than any technique I've seen yet.

Step One:
Open the photo that you want to enhance.

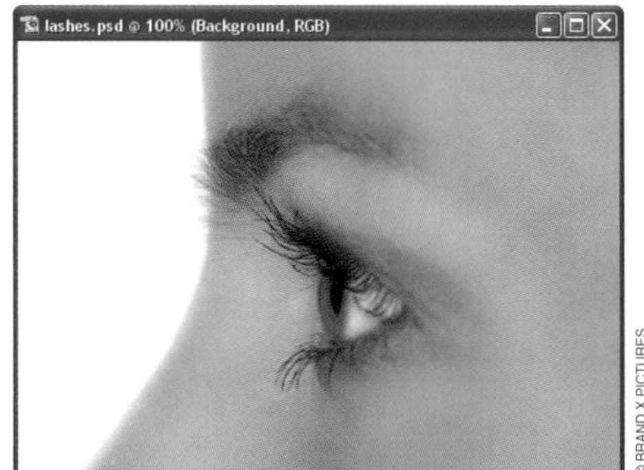

© BRAND X PICTURES

Step Two:
Get the Lasso tool from the Toolbox and draw a loose selection around the eyebrow. It isn't necessary to make a precise selection; make it loose like the one shown here. In this example, there's only one eyebrow, but if there are two (meaning they don't have a uni-brow), after you select one eyebrow, hold the Shift key down and select the other eyebrow.

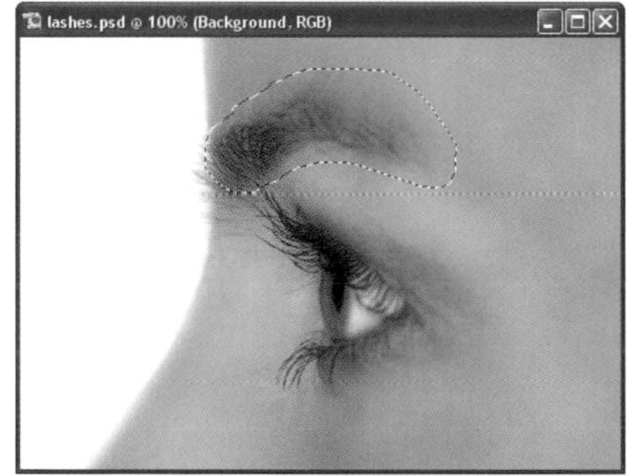

Step Three:
Once your eyebrow(s) is selected, go under the Layer menu, under New, and choose Layer via Copy. This will copy just the selected area to a new layer (Layer 1).

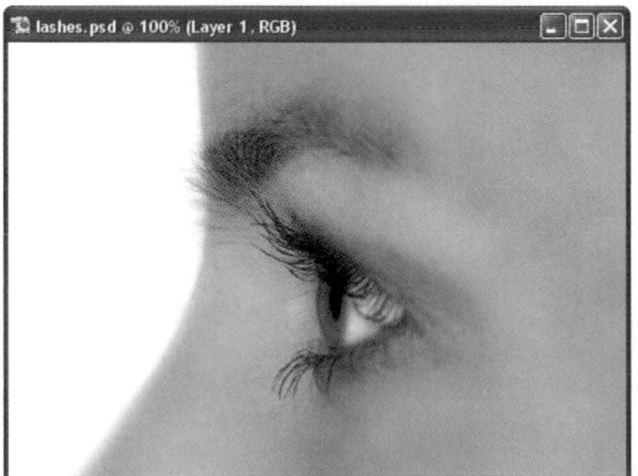

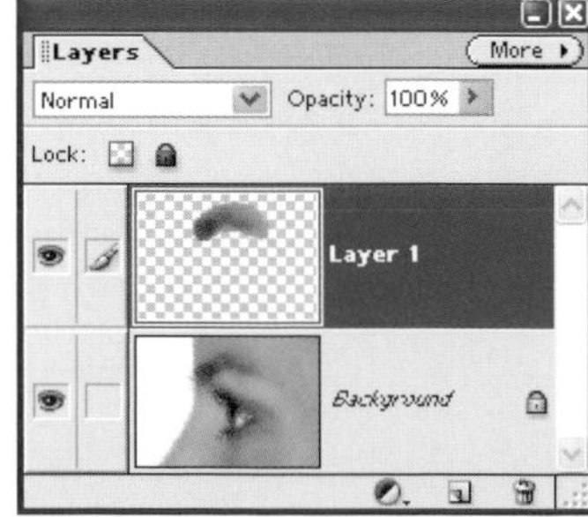

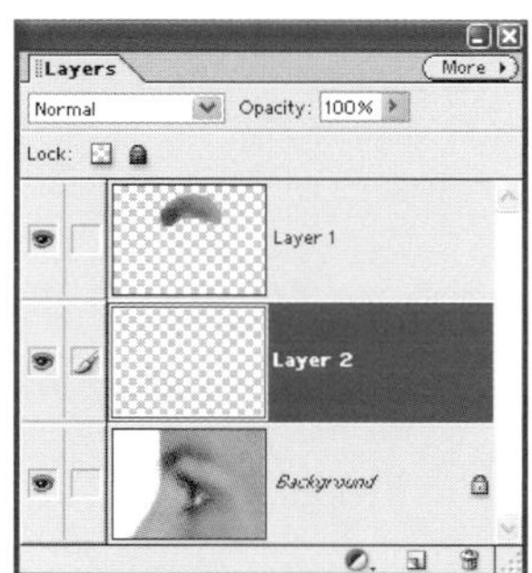

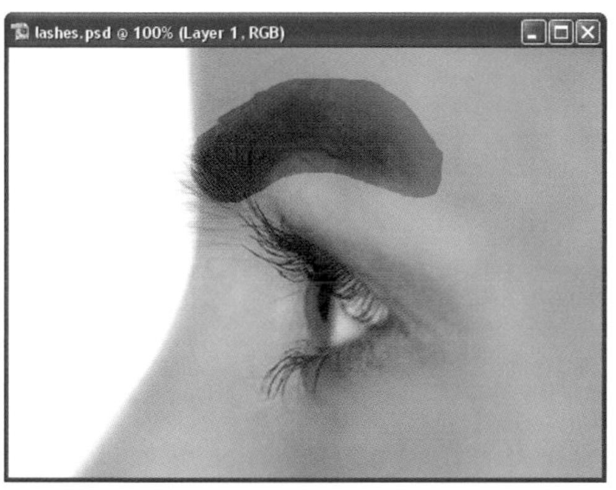

Step Four:

In the Layers palette, switch the Blend Mode of this eyebrow layer from Normal to Multiply, which will darken the entire layer (as shown here). Hold the Control key (Mac: Command key) and click once on the Create New Layer icon at the bottom of the Layers palette. This creates a new blank layer directly beneath your Multiplied eyebrow layer.

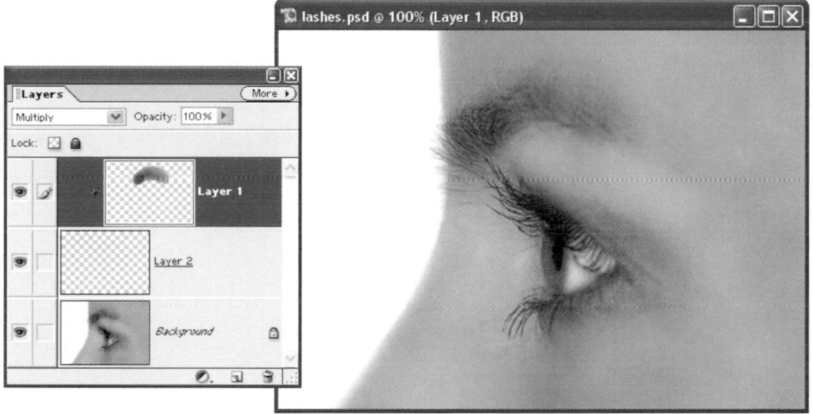

Step Five:

Now, in the Layers palette, click back on the top layer (the Multiplied eyebrow layer), then press Control-G (Mac: Command-G) to Group the Multiplied layer with the blank layer beneath it. This removes the darker Multiplied version of the layer from view, so your photo looks untouched, like it did when you first opened it. In the Layers palette, click on the middle layer (the blank layer) to make it the active layer.

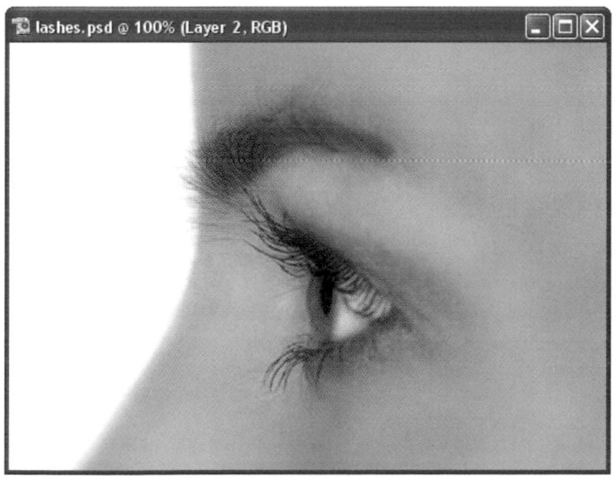

Step Six:

Press the letter "D" to set your Foreground color to black. Switch to the Brush tool and choose a soft-edged brush that's about the size of the largest part of the eyebrow. Go up in the Options Bar and lower the Opacity of your brush to 50%. Now, paint over the eyebrows, starting at the widest part. As you paint, hold the Left Bracket key to make your brush smaller as you trace the eyebrow. As you do, it darkens the eyebrow by revealing the Multiply layer.

Continued

Step Seven:
Now on to the eyelashes. Get the Lasso tool again and draw a loose selection around the eye(s), and make sure your loose selection fully encompasses the eyelashes (as shown here).

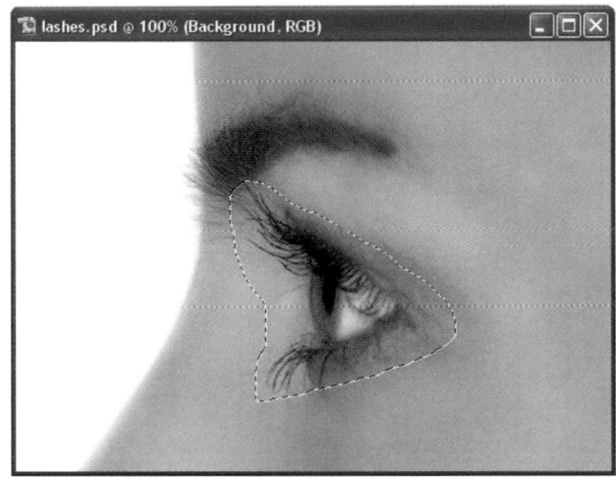

Step Eight:
Once the eye and eyelash area is fully selected, click on the Background layer in the Layers palette. Then, go under the Layer menu, under New, and choose Layer via Copy. This will copy just the selected area to a new layer (Layer 3).

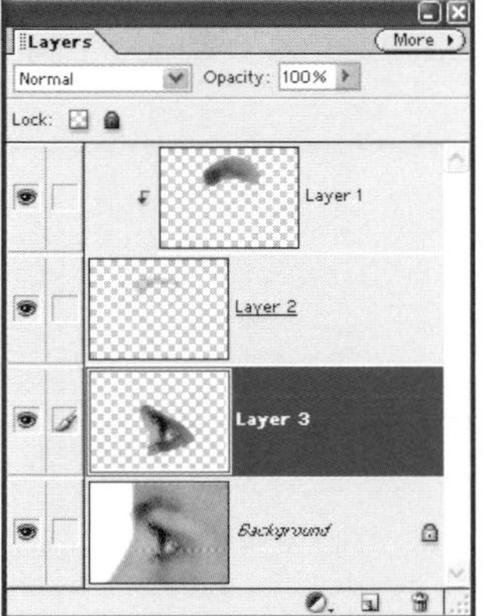

Step Nine:
Change the Blend Mode of this layer to Multiply, which darkens the entire layer (as shown). Hold the Control key (Mac: Command key) and click once on the Create New Layer icon at the bottom of the Layers palette. This creates a new blank layer directly beneath your Multiply eye layer. In the Layers palette, click back on Layer 3 (the Multiplied eye layer), then press Control-G (Mac: Command-G) to Group the Multiplied layer with the blank layer beneath it to remove the Multiply effect.

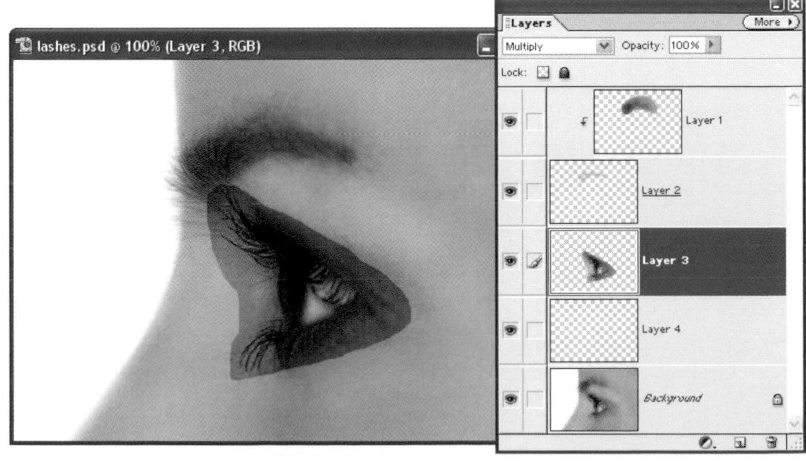

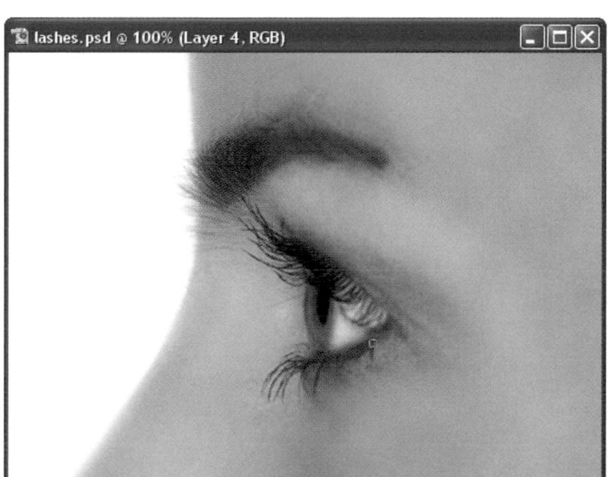

Step Ten:

Make sure your Foreground color is still set to black, then choose a very small soft-edged brush and paint along the base of the eyelashes to darken that area (as shown). Also paint along the top eyelid and at the base of the eyelashes to make the lashes appear thicker, fuller, longer, and more luxurious. (Maybe she's born with it, maybe it's Maybelline, or just maybe it's an Elements Multiply layer. Only her digital retoucher knows for sure).

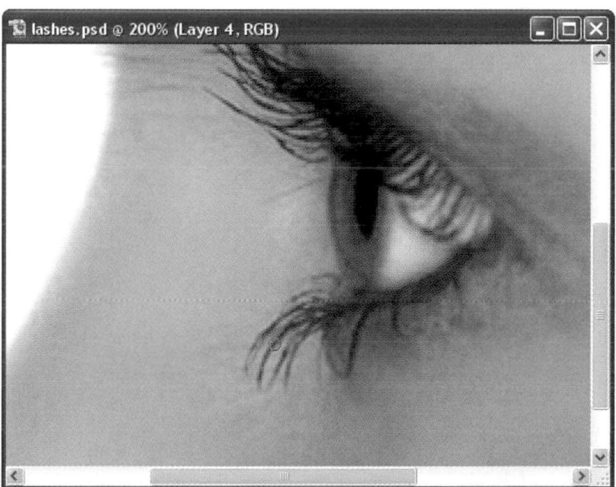

Step Eleven:

When it comes to enhancing individual lashes, zoom in close on the eye and choose a very, very small brush (as shown). Then start at the base of the eyelash (where it meets the lid) and trace the eyelash, following its contours to darken them. You may have to use a 1- or 2-pixel-sized brush to trace the lashes, but it will be worth it.

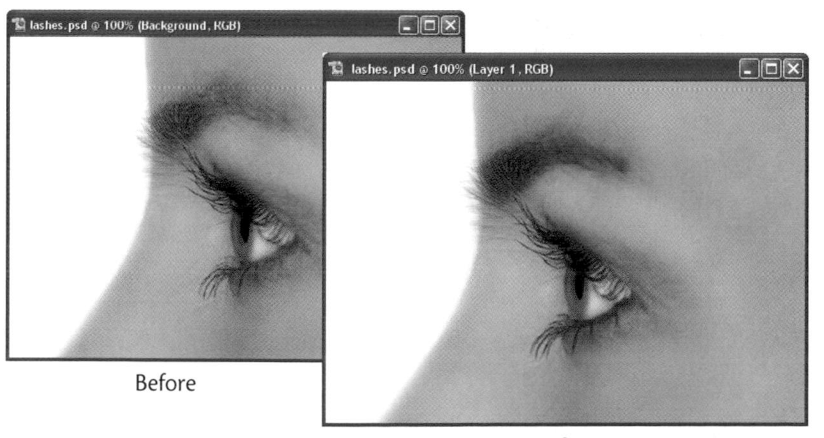

Before

After

Step Twelve:

When you're done painting over the eyelashes, zoom back out to reveal your final retouch (as shown here). Compare the eyelashes shown here with the ones in Step Seven to see the difference. If the effect seems a bit too intense to you, just lower the Opacity of either layer. (Incidentally, the reason we put the eyelashes and eyebrows on separate layers, rather than doing them at the same time, is so you can control the Opacity of each part individually.)

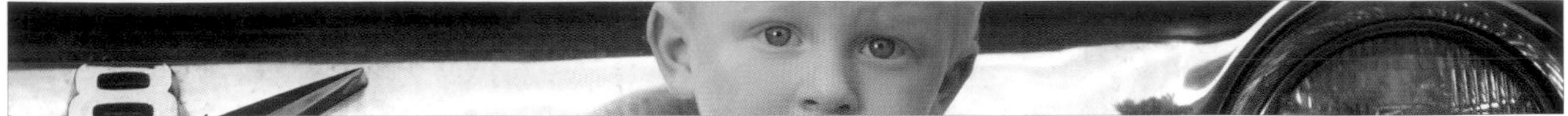

Whitening and Brightening Teeth

This really should be called "Removing Yellowing, Then Whitening Teeth" because almost everyone has some yellowing, so we remove that first before we move on to the whitening process. This is a simple technique, but the results have a big impact on the overall look of the portrait, and that's why I do this to every single portrait where the subject is smiling.

Step One:
Open the photo you need to retouch.

© BRAND X PICTURES

Step Two:
Switch to the Lasso tool, and carefully draw a selection around the teeth, being careful not to select any of the gums (as shown here).

Step Three:
Go under the Select menu and choose Feather. When the Feather Selection dialog appears, enter 1 pixel and click OK to smooth the edges of your selection. That way, you won't see a hard edge along the area you selected once you've whitened the teeth.

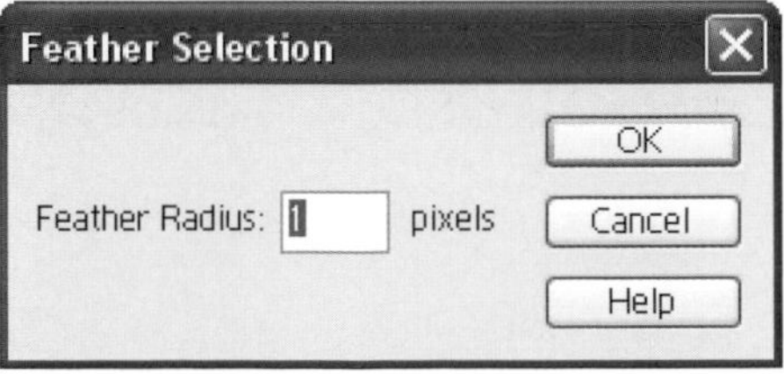

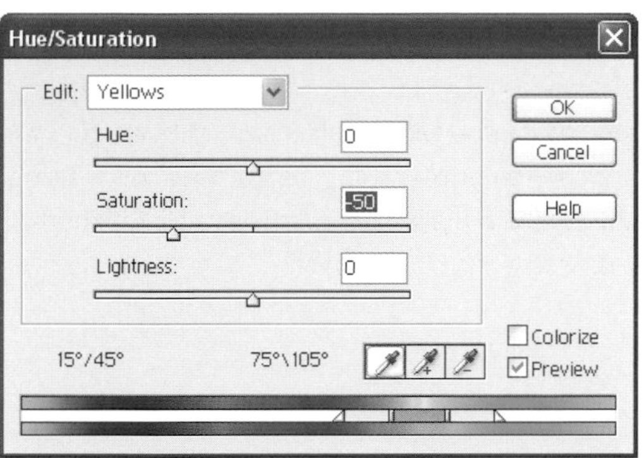

Step Four:
Go under the Enhance menu, under Adjust Color, and choose Hue/Saturation. When the dialog appears, choose Yellows from the Edit pop-up menu at the top. Then, drag the Saturation slider to the left to remove the yellowing from the teeth.

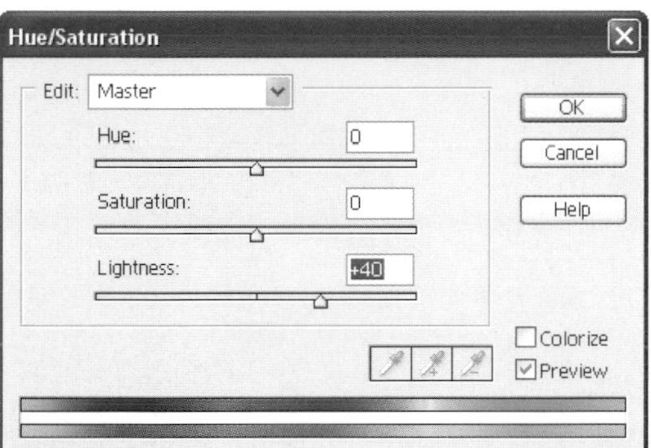

Step Five:
Now that the yellowing is removed, switch the Edit pop-up menu back to Master, and drag the Lightness slider to the right to whiten and brighten the teeth. Be careful not to drag it too far, or the retouch will be obvious. Click OK in the Hue/Saturation dialog and your enhancements will be applied. Last, press Control-D (Mac: Command-D) to deselect and see your finished retouch.

Before

After

Removing Hot Spots

If you've ever had to deal with hot spots (shiny areas on your subject's face caused by uneven lighting, or the flash reflecting off shiny surfaces, making your subject look as if they're sweating), you know they can be pretty tough to correct. That is, unless you know this trick.

Step One:

Open the photo that has hot spots that need to be toned down. Select the Clone Stamp tool in the Toolbox. Up in the Options Bar, change the Blend Mode from Normal to Darken, and lower the Opacity to 50%. By changing the Blend Mode to Darken, we'll only affect pixels that are lighter than the area we're sampling, and those lighter pixels are the hot spots.

© BRAND X PICTURES

Step Two:

Make sure you have a large, soft-edged brush, then hold the Alt key (Mac: Option key) and click once in a clean area of skin (an area with no hot spot) as shown here, on her left cheek. This will be your sample area, or reference point, so Elements knows to affect only pixels that are lighter than this.

Step Three:
Start gently painting over the hot spot areas with the Clone Stamp tool, and as you do, the hot spots will fade away. As you work on different hot spots, you'll have to resample (Alt-/Option-click) on nearby areas of skin so the skin tone matches. For example, when you work on the hot spots on her nose, sample an area of skin from the bridge of her nose where no hot spots exist.

Step Four:
Here's the result after about 60 seconds of hot-spot retouching using this technique. Notice how the hot spots on her forehead and tip of her nose are now gone. Much of this was done with brush strokes, but just clicking once or twice with the Clone Stamp tool often works too.

Before

After

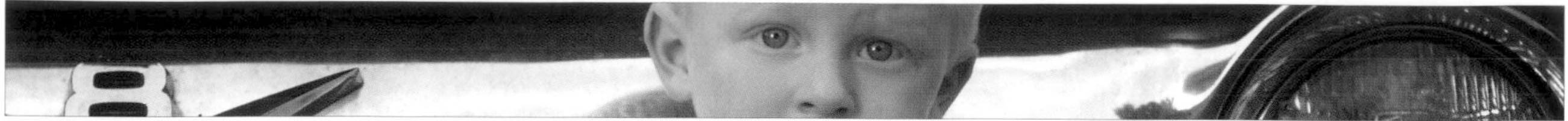

Glamour Skin Softening

This is another technique I learned from Chicago-based retoucher David Cuerdon. David uses this technique in fashion and glamour photography to give skin a smooth, silky feel, and it's also popular in shots of female seniors (not high school seniors—the other seniors).

Step One:

Open the photo that you want to give the glamour skin-softening effect and duplicate the Background layer by dragging it to the Create New Layer icon at the bottom of the Layers palette.

© BRAND X PICTURES

Step Two:

Go under the Filter menu, under Blur, and choose Gaussian Blur. When the dialog box appears, enter between 3 and 6 pixels of blur (depending on how soft you want the skin), to put a blur over the entire photo.

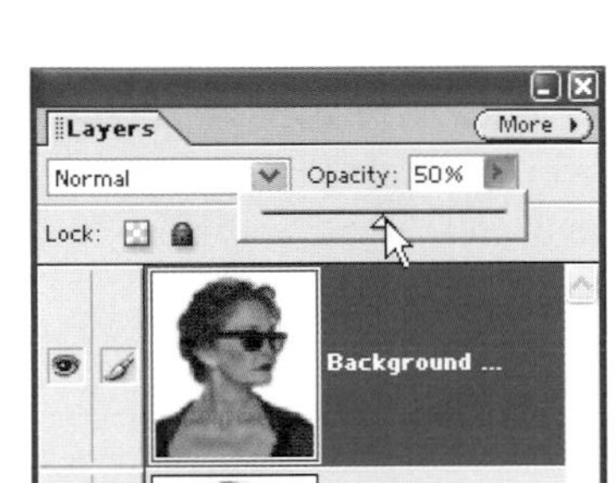

Step Three:
Next, lower the Opacity of this layer by 50% (as shown at left). At this point, the blurring effect is reduced and now the photo has a soft glow to it. In some cases, you may want to leave it at this, with an overall soft, glamorous effect (you sometimes see portraits of people over 60 with this overall softening), so your retouch is complete. If this is too much softening for your subject, go on to the next step.

Step Four:
What really pulls this technique together is selectively bringing back details in some of the facial areas. Switch to the Eraser tool, choose a soft-edged brush, and erase over the facial areas that are supposed to have sharp detail (her sunglasses, eyebrows, lips, and teeth). What you're doing is erasing the blurry sunglasses, eyebrows, lips, and teeth, and thereby revealing the original features on the layer beneath your blurry layer.

Before

After

Step Five:
David completes his retouch at Step Four, leaving the subject's clothes, hair, background, etc. with the soft glow. I prefer to switch to a larger soft-edged Eraser tool and erase over everything else except her skin—so I erase over her hair, and the background so everything has sharp detail except her skin. This is totally a personal preference, so I recommend trying both and seeing which fits your particular needs.

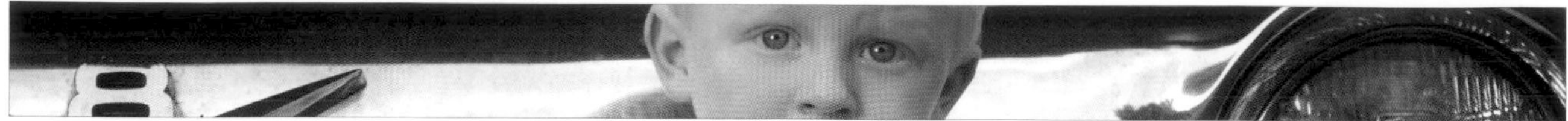

Transforming a Frown into a Smile

This is a pretty slick technique for taking a photo where the subject was frowning and tweaking it just a bit to add a pleasant smile in its place—which can often save a photo that otherwise would've been ignored.

Step One:
Open the photo that you want to retouch.

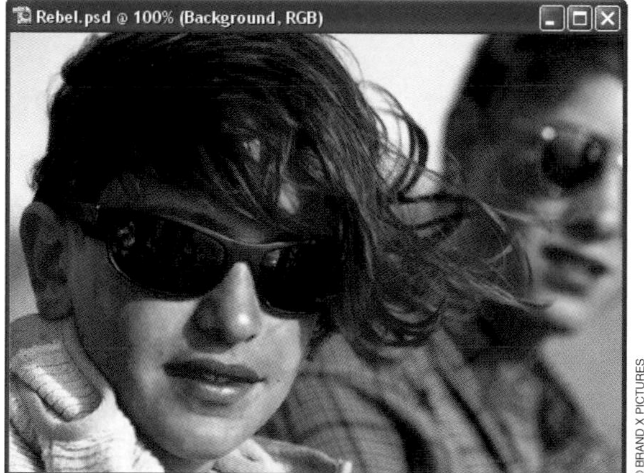

© BRAND X PICTURES

Step Two:
Go under the Filter menu, under Distort, and choose Liquify. When the Liquify dialog appears, choose the Zoom tool (it looks like a magnifying glass) from the Liquify Toolbar (found along the left edge of the dialog box). Click it once or twice within the preview window to zoom in closer on your subject's face. Then, choose the Warp tool (it's the top tool in Liquify's Toolbar, as shown here).

Step Three:

Press the Left/Right Bracket keys on your keyboard to adjust the brush size until it's about the size of the person's cheek. Place the brush at the base of their cheek (as shown), click-and-"tug" slightly up. This tugging of the cheek makes the corner of the mouth turn up, creating a smile.

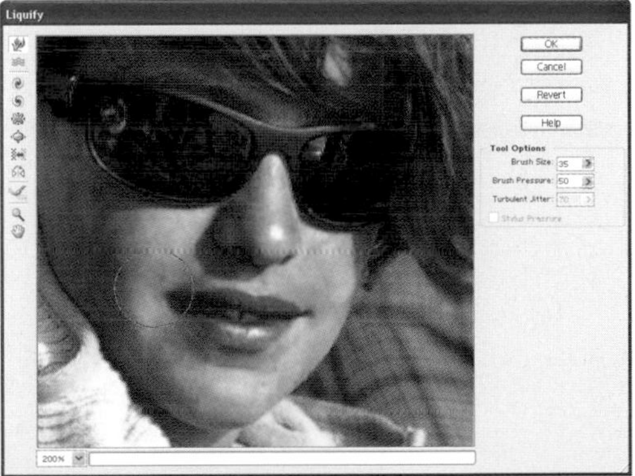

Step Four:

Repeat the "tug" on the opposite side of the mouth, using the already tugged side as a visual guide as to how far to tug. Be careful not to tug too far, or you'll turn your subject into the Joker from *Batman Returns.* Click OK in Liquify to apply the change, and the retouch is applied to your photo.

Before

After

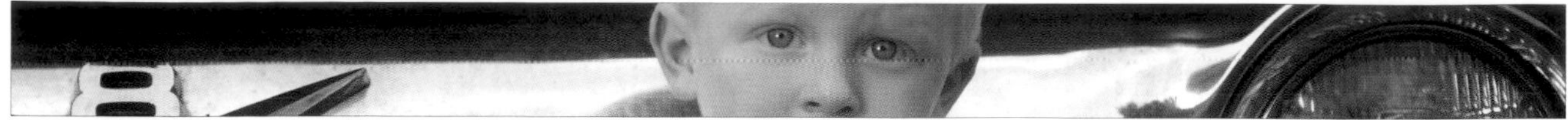

Digital Nose Job

This is a very simple technique for decreasing the size of your subject's nose by 15 to 20%. The actual shrinking of the nose part is a breeze and only takes a minute or two—you may spend a little bit of time cloning away the sides of the original nose, but since the new nose winds up on its own layer, it makes this cloning a lot easier. Here's how it's done:

Step One:
Open the photo that you want to retouch. Get the Lasso tool, and draw a loose selection around your subject's nose. Make sure you don't make this selection too close or too precise—you need to capture some flesh tone area around the nose as well (as shown here).

© BRAND X PICTURES

Step Two
To soften the edges of your selection, go under the Select menu and choose Feather. When the Feather Selection dialog box appears, for Feather Radius enter 10 pixels (for high-res, 300-ppi images, enter 22 pixels), then click OK.

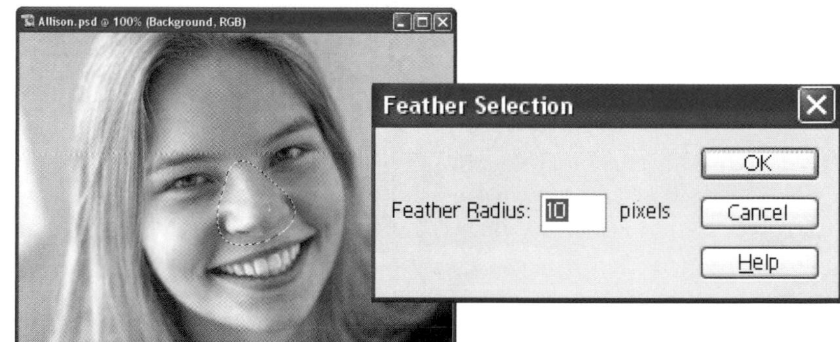

Step Three:
Now, go under the Layer menu, under New, and choose Layer via Copy. This will copy just the selected area to a new layer (Layer 1).

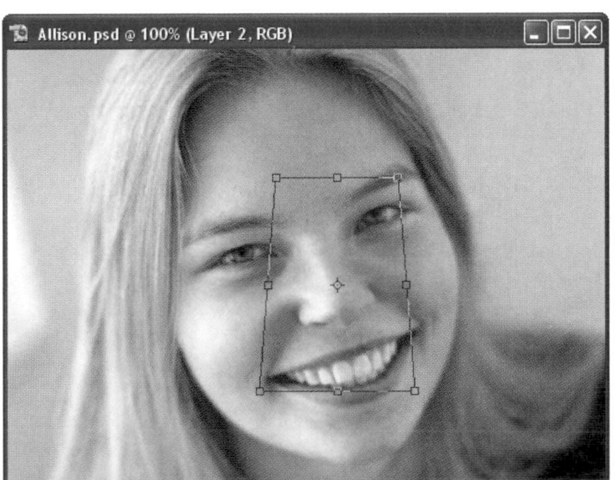

Step Four:

Press Control-T (Mac: Command-T) to bring up the Free Transform bounding box. Hold Shift-Alt-Control (Mac: Shift-Option-Command) then grab the upper right-hand corner point of the bounding box and drag inward to add a perspective effect to the nose. Doing this gives the person a pug nose, so release all the keys, then grab the top center point (as shown) and drag straight downward to undo the "pug effect" and make the nose look natural again, but now it's smaller.

Step Five:

When the new size looks about right, press Enter (Mac: Return) to lock in your changes. If any of the old nose peeks out from behind the new nose, in the Layers palette click on the Background layer and then use the Clone Stamp tool to clone away those areas: Sample an area next to the nose, and then clone right over it. Compare the before and after shots (below) and you can see what a dramatic change our 1-minute retouch made in the photo.

Before

After

Photographer | Jim Patterson

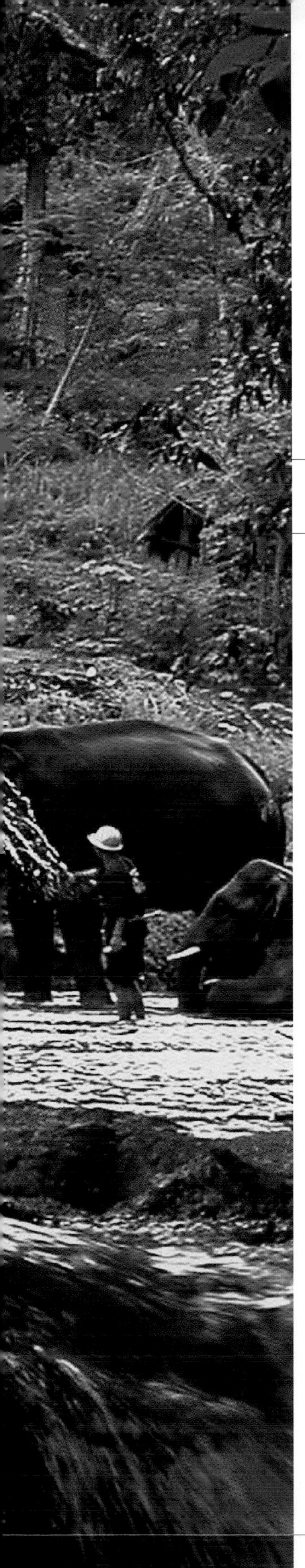

Okay, if you remember that movie (*Invasion of the Body Snatchers*) you're way older than I am (remember, I'm only 19), and therefore, for the rest of this chapter intro, I'll refer to you as either "gramps" or

Invasion of the Body Snatchers
body sculpting

"meemaa" (depending on your gender and what kind of mood I'm in). This chapter is a testament to the fact that people's bodies are simply not perfect, with the possible exception of my own, which I might say is pretty darn fine because of all the healthy food I eat at sundry drive-thru eating establishments that shall remain nameless (Wendy's). Anyway, your goal (my goal, our common goal, etc.) is to make people look as good in photos as they look in real life. This is a constant challenge because many people eat at McDonald's. Luckily, there are a ton of tricks employed by professional retouchers (who use terms like digital plastic surgery, botox in a box, digital liposuction, liquid tummy tucks, noselectomies, stomalectomies, and big ol' nasty feetalectomies) that can take a person who hasn't seen a sit-up or a stomach crunch since they tested for the President's Council on Physical Fitness and Sports (which for me, was just one year ago, when I was a senior) and make them look like Wonder Woman or Superman on a good day. In this chapter, you'll learn the pros' secrets for transforming people who basically look like Shrek into people who look like the person who produced *Shrek* (I don't really know who that is, but those Hollywood types always look good, what with their personal trainers and all).

Slimming and Trimming

This is an incredibly popular technique because it consistently works so well, and because just about everyone would like to look about 10 to 15 pounds thinner. I've never applied this technique to a photo and (a) been caught, or (b) not had the client absolutely love the way they look. The most important part of this technique may be not telling the client you used it.

Step One:
Open the photo of the person that you want to put on a quick diet.

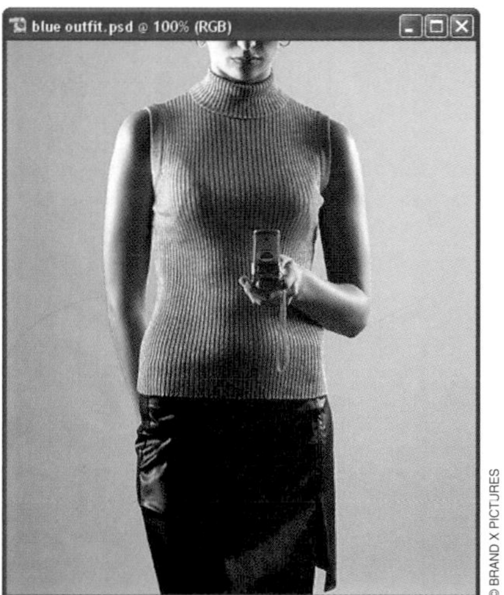

© BRAND X PICTURES

Step Two:
Press Control-A (Mac: Command-A) to put a selection around the entire photo. Then, press Control-T (Mac: Command-T) to bring up the Free Transform function. The Free Transform handles will appear at the corners and sides of your photo. These handles might be a little hard to reach, so I recommend expanding your image window a little bit by dragging its bottom-right corner outward. This makes some of the gray desktop area visible (as shown here) and makes grabbing the Free Transform handles much easier.

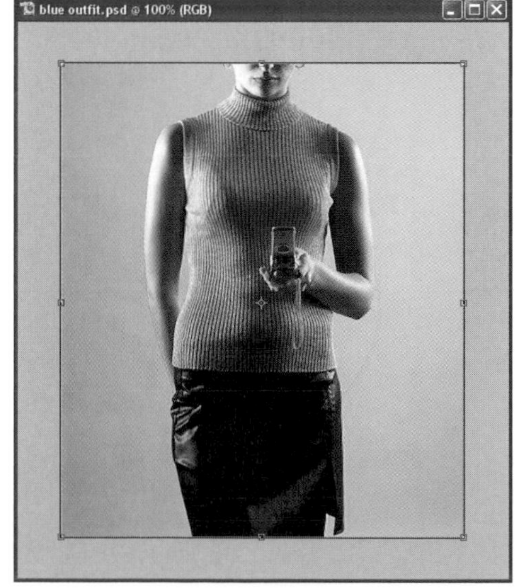

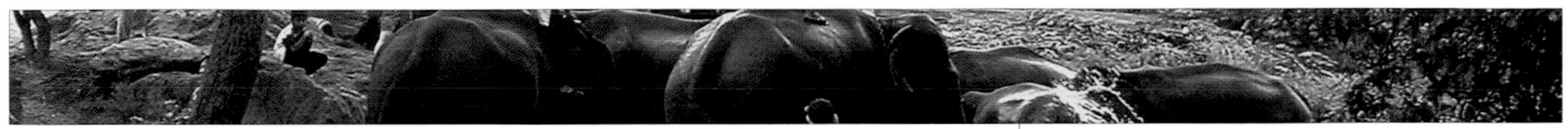

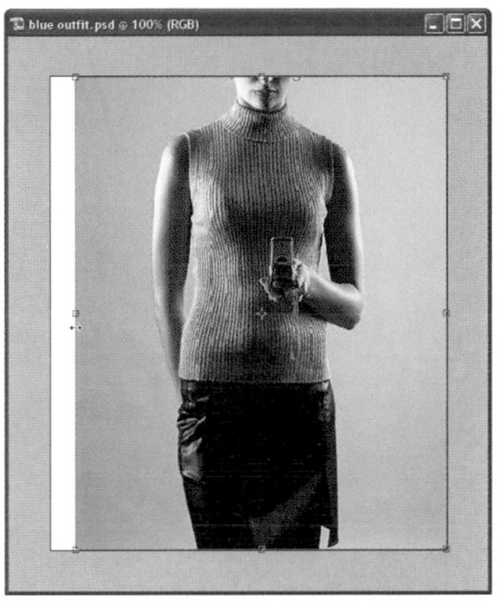

Step Three:

Grab the left-center handle and drag it horizontally toward the right to slim the subject. The farther you drag, the slimmer they become. How far is too far (in other words, how far can you drag before people start looking like they've been retouched)? Look up in the Options Bar at the W (width) field as a guide.

Step Four:

You're pretty safe to drag inward to around 95%, although I've been known to go to 94% or even 93% once in a while (it depends on the photo).

Before

After

Step Five:

Press Enter (Mac: Return) to lock in your transformation. Now that you've moved the image area over a bit, you'll have to use the Crop tool to crop away the white background area that is now visible on the left side of your photo.

Step Six:

After you drag out your Crop border, press the Enter key (Mac: Return key) to complete your Crop. Compare the Before and After shown here, and you can see how effective this simple little trick is at slimming and trimming your subject. Also, notice that because we didn't drag too far, the subject still looks very natural.

Removing Love Handles

This is a very handy body-sculpting technique, and you'll probably be surprised at how many times you'll wind up using it. It uses Liquify, which many people first dismissed as a "toy for giving people bug-eyes and huge lips," but it didn't take long for professional retouchers to see how powerful this tool could really be.

Step One:

Open the photo that has a love handle repair just waiting to happen. (In the photo here, we're going to remove the love handles and baggy shirt on the man's sides.)

© BRAND X PICTURES

Step Two:

Go under the Filter menu, under Distort, and choose Liquify. When the Liquify dialog box appears, click on the Zoom tool in the Toolbar on the left-hand side of the dialog, and then drag out a selection around the area you want to work on to give you a close-up view for greater accuracy.

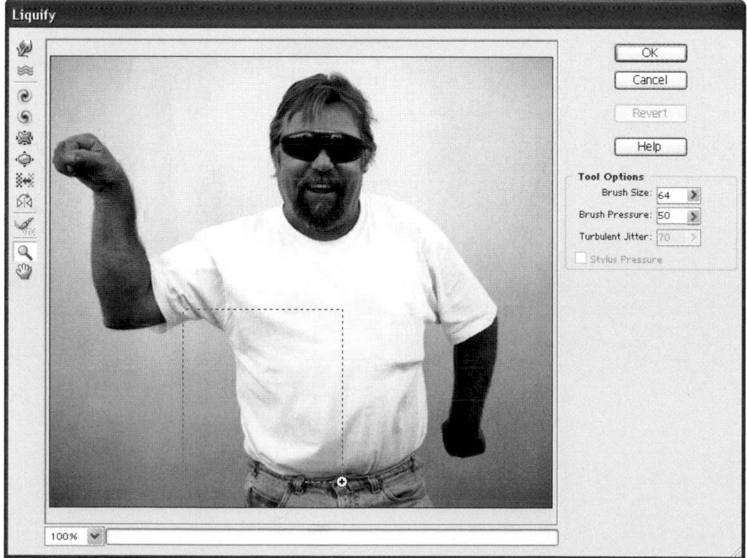

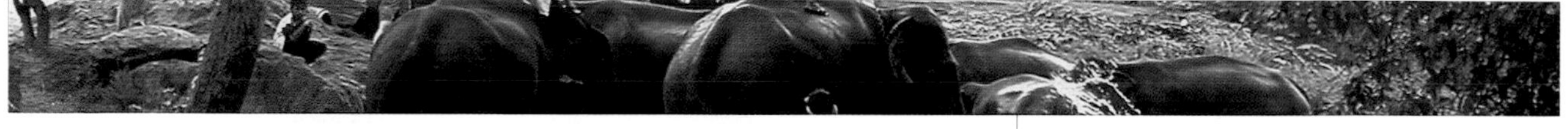

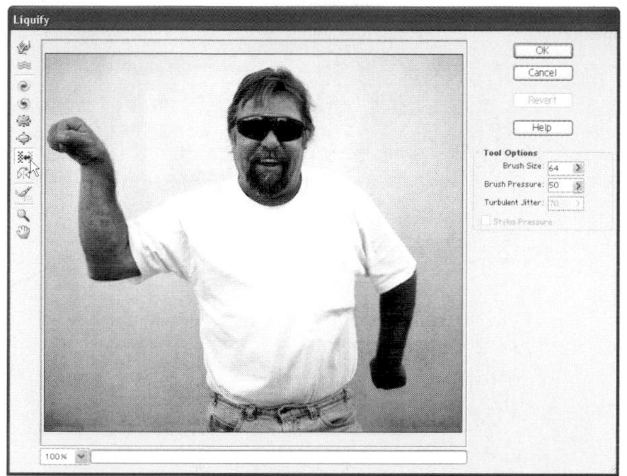

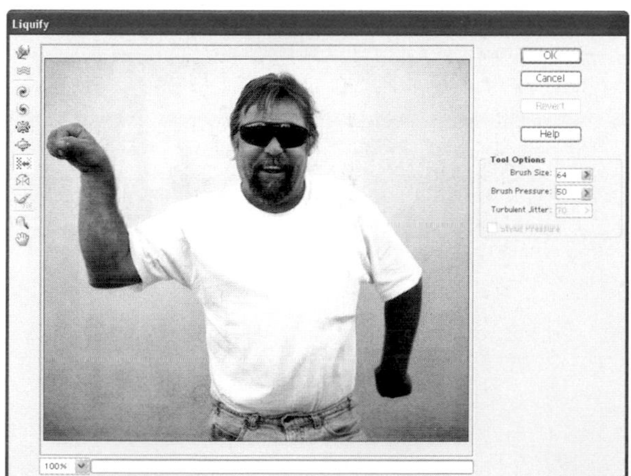

Step Three:

Get the Shift Pixels tool from Liquify's Toolbar (it's the seventh tool down). Choose a relatively small brush size using the Brush Size field near the top-right of the Liquify dialog. With it, paint a downward stroke starting just above and outside of the left love handle and continuing downward. The pixels will shift back in toward his body, removing the love handle as you paint. (Note: When removing love handles on his right side, paint upward rather than downward. Why? That's just the way it works.)

Step Four:

When you click OK, the love handle repair is complete.

Check out the Before and After shown below and you'll see the difference a quick 30-second retouch can make.

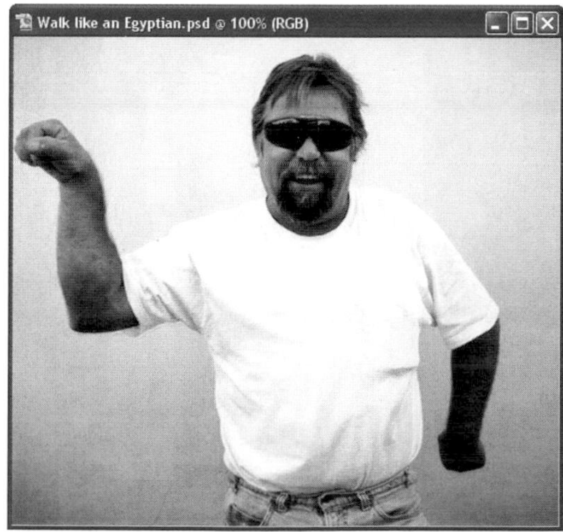

Before

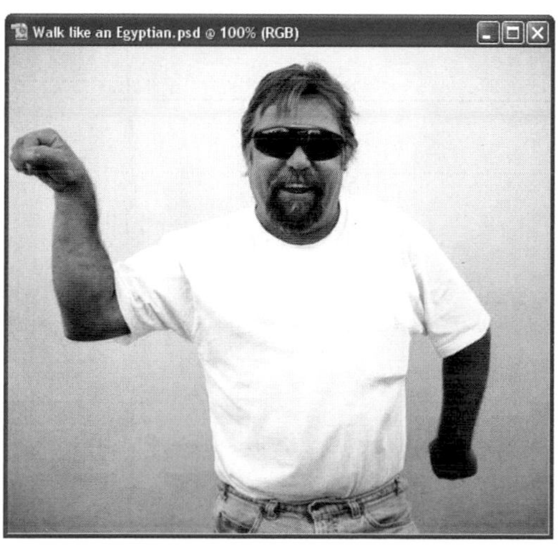

After

Slimming Buttocks, Thighs and Arms

This is a technique I picked up from Helene DeLillo that works great for trimming up thighs and buttocks by repositioning parts of the existing areas. It's deceptively simple and amazingly effective. At the end of this tutorial, I also show how to use the same technique to slim arms (helpful in getting rid of "grannies," which is an industry term for loose skin under a person's arm). Hey, I didn't make up the term, I just fix the problems.

Step One:

Open the photo that you need to retouch. In this case, we're going to reduce the size of this person's buttocks, which seem disproportionately large due to the low camera angle of the shot.

© BRAND X PICTURES

Step Two:

Get the Lasso tool from the Toolbox and make a selection loosely around the area you want to retouch. It's important to select some background area (as shown here) because that background will be used to cover over the existing area. Once you have your selection in place, soften the edges just a bit by going under the Select menu and choosing Feather. Enter 1 pixel and click OK to soften the edges of your selection.

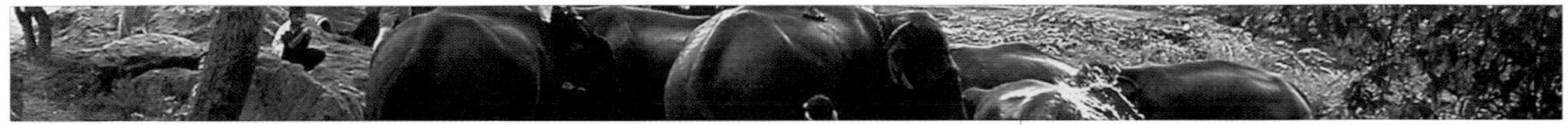

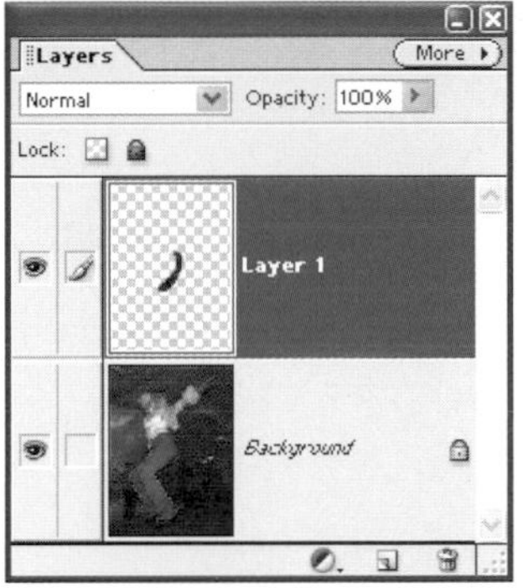

Step Three:
Go under the Layer menu, under New, and choose Layer via Copy. This will create a new layer with just your selected area on it.

Step Four:
Press "V" to switch to the Move tool, click on the area you had selected (it's on its own separate layer now) and drag inward toward the rest of her body. You're literally moving the edge of her body, thereby reducing the width of her thighs and buttocks at the same time (as shown).

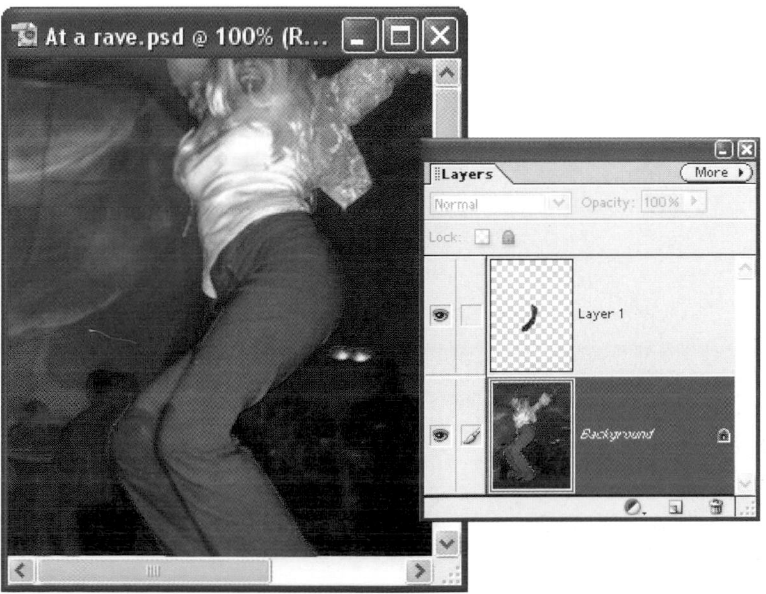

Step Five:
When you do this, you'll usually have a small chunk of the old body left over that you'll have to remove from the original Background layer. Use the Zoom tool to zoom in, then click on the Background layer. Get the Clone Stamp tool from the Toolbox, choose a small hard-edged brush, and Alt-click (Mac: Option-click) in an area very near where you need to retouch (as shown here, where I sampled from the area just below where her buttocks used to be). Then clone the background over the leftover body to produce smooth curves.

Continued

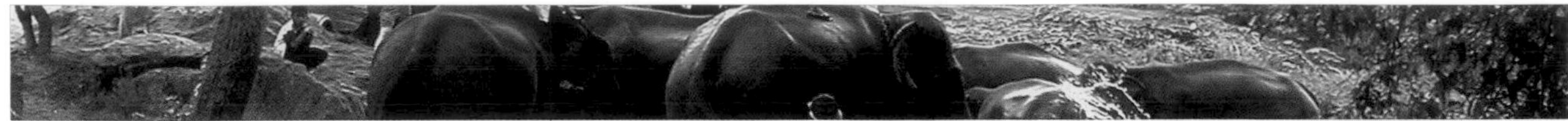

Step Six:

Once you've removed those little chunks (I know, "chunks" probably isn't the best word to use, but yet on some level, it fits), the retouch is done, as shown here in the Before and After.

Before

After

Just the Thighs

Step One:

This time, we're going to select the bottom of this person's thigh with the Lasso tool (as shown), and once it's selected, go under the Layer menu, under New, and choose Layer via Copy. This will create a new layer with just your selected area on it.

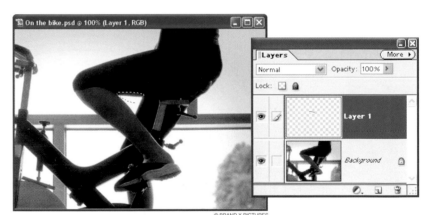

Step Two:

Switch to the Move tool, and drag upward to slim the thigh (as shown here). Depending on the photo, you may not have to feather the edges, but it probably wouldn't hurt.

Step Three:

Again, you'll probably have little chunks (Okay, how about "shards" or "pieces" instead? Nah. It's chunks.) that you'll have to remove, so switch to the Background layer, get the Clone Stamp tool again, Alt-click (Mac: Option-click) near the area you need to retouch and clone background area over the chunks.

Once you've cloned over all the chunks (this process is called "dechunk-inization"—not really, but it should be) the retouch is complete. Compare the Before photo (left) and the After photo (right) to see the difference. On the next page, we're going to apply the same effect to trim the subject's arm.

Before

After

Continued

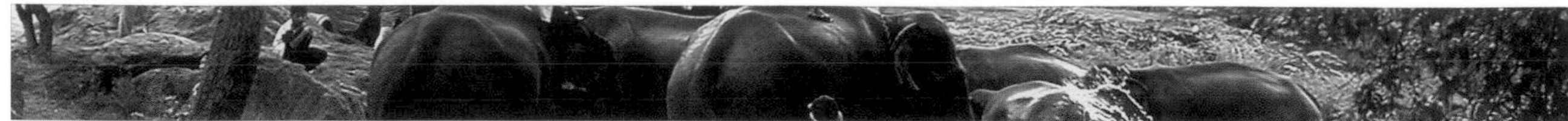

Slimming Arms

Step One:

Here's the technique applied to slimming the arms (clearly, the woman shown here doesn't really need her arms slimmed, but the photo works well to make the technique clear). Start by selecting the area you want to slim up with the Lasso tool (sound familiar?). Once it's selected, go under the Layer menu, under New, and choose Layer via Copy. This will create a new layer with just your selected area on it.

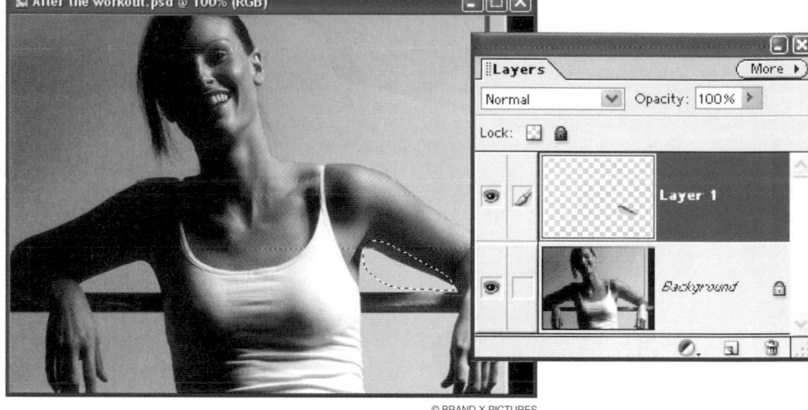

© BRAND X PICTURES

Step Two:

Switch to the Move tool and drag your selected arm area upward to slim the arm (as shown).

Step Three:

As usual, dragging this area upward will leave little chunks on the background, so go to the Layers palette and click on the Background layer, switch to the Clone Stamp tool, and clone away those excess areas (as shown here). The captures on the following page show the Before and After of the arm retouching. It's subtle in this photo, but on the right person, it's worth a million bucks (meaning, you can charge a million bucks).

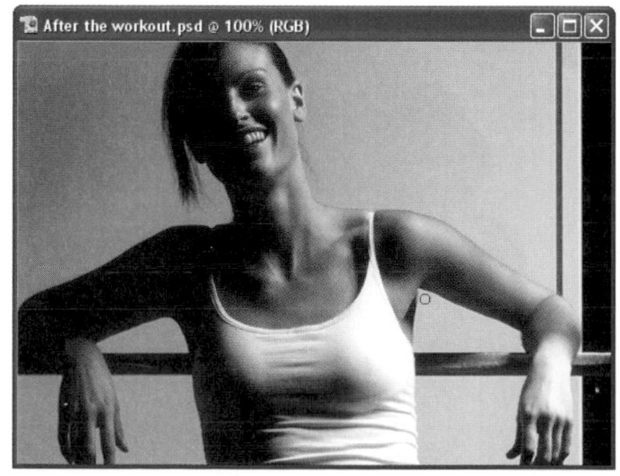

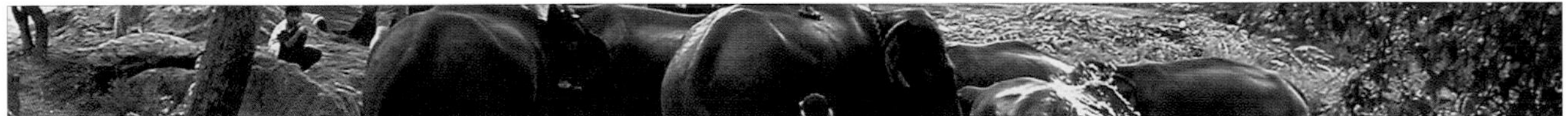

Before

After

Photographer | Todd Morrison

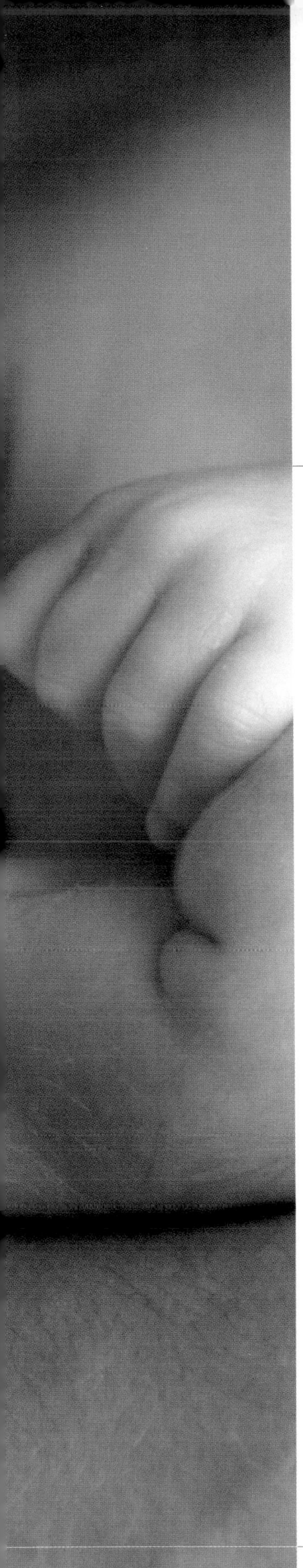

This is where the fun begins. Okay, I don't want to discount all the immeasurable fun you've had up to this point, but now it gets really fun. Mondo-crazy fun. This is where we get to play around in Elements

38 Special
photographic special effects

and change reality, and then send the client an invoice for our "playtime." Did the model not have the right color blouse on? No sweat, change it in Elements. Was it an overcast day when you shot the exterior of your client's house? Just drop in a new sky. Do you want to warm up a cold photo like you did in the old days by screwing on an 81A filter? Now you can do it digitally. Do you want to take your income to the next level? Just shoot a crisp shot of a $20 bill, retouch it a bit, print out a few hundred sheets on your color laser printer and head for Vegas. (Okay, forget that last one, but you get the idea.) This is where the rubber meets the road, where the nose gets put to the grindstone, where the meat meets the potatoes.... (Where the meat meets the potatoes? Hey, it's late.)

Blurred Lighting Vignette

This technique is very popular with portrait and wedding photographers. It creates a dramatic effect by giving the appearance that a soft light is focused on the subject, while dimming the surrounding area (which helps draw the eye to the subject).

Step One:

Open the photo that you want to add a soft light vignette to. Go under the Layer menu, under New, and choose Layer via Copy. This will duplicate the Background layer onto its own layer (Layer 1).

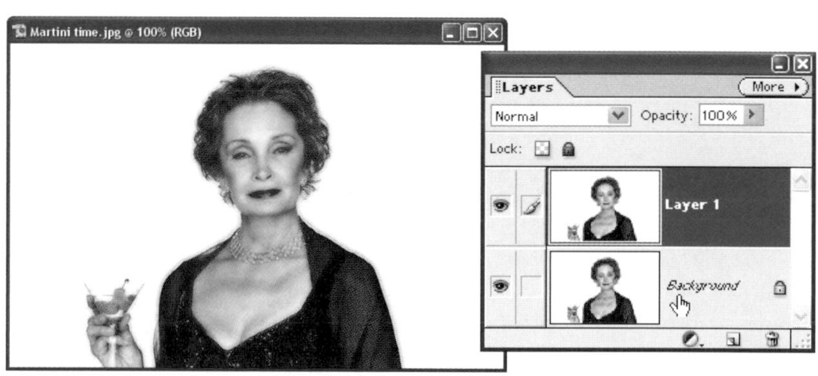

Step Two:

Get the Elliptical Marquee tool from the Toolbox and draw an oval-shaped selection where you'd like the soft light to fall on your subject. In the Layers palette, hold the Control-key (Mac: Command-key) and click on the Create New Layer icon. This creates a layer directly beneath your current layer.

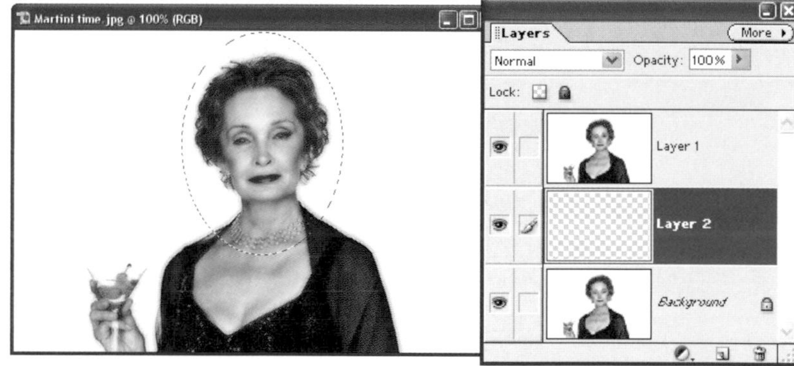

Step Three:

In the Layers palette, click back on the top layer. Now, press Control-G (Mac: Command-G) to Group your photo with the blank layer beneath it. Don't deselect yet.

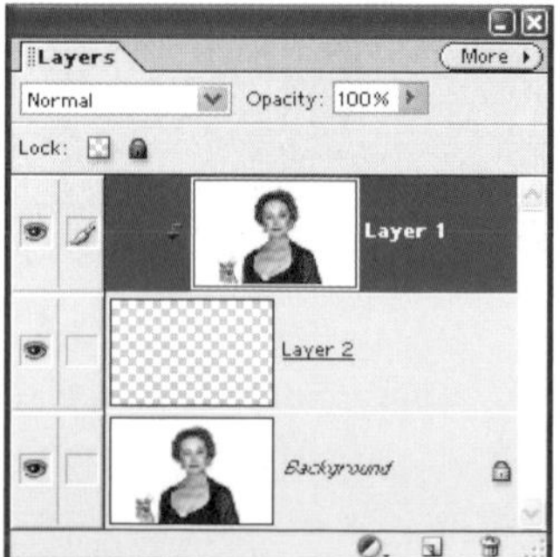

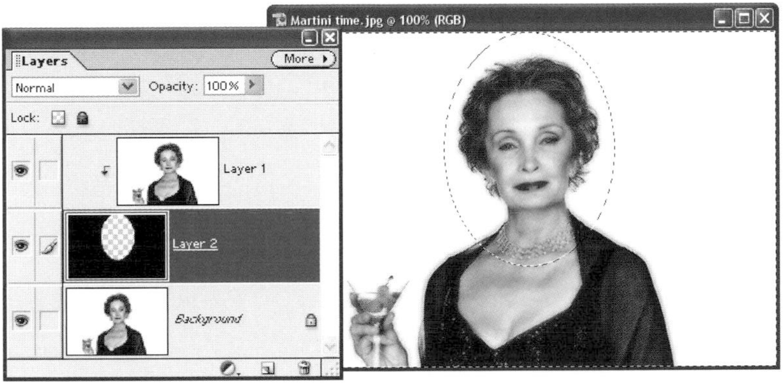

Step Four:
In the Layers palette, click on the middle layer (the blank one). Go under the Select menu and choose Inverse (which selects everything BUT the oval). Press the letter "D" to set your Foreground color to black, then press Alt-Backspace (Mac: Option-Delete) to fill the area around the oval with black. You won't see the black on screen, but you'll see it in the Layers palette thumbnail.

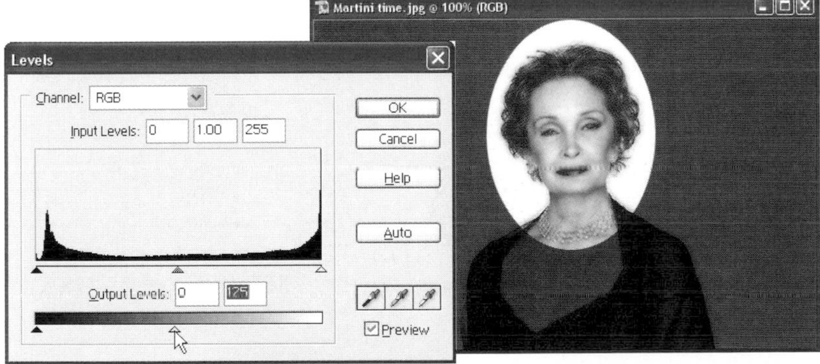

Step Five:
Press Control-D (Mac: Command-D) to deselect. In the Layers palette, click back on the top layer. Press Control-L (Mac: Command-L) to bring up the Levels dialog box. Grab the lower right-hand Output Levels slider and drag it to the left to darken the area outside the oval. When it looks fairly dark, click OK.

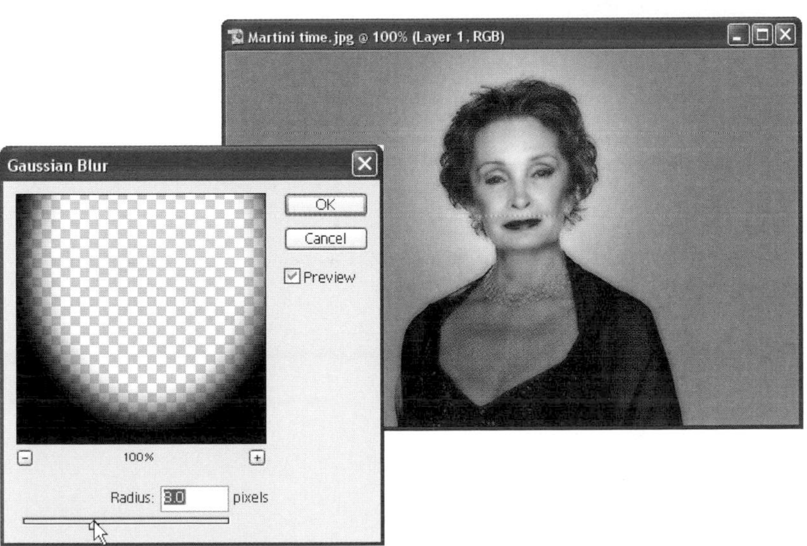

Step Six:
In the Layers palette, click on the middle layer again. Go under the Filter menu, under Blur, and choose Gaussian Blur. When the Gaussian Blur dialog appears, drag the slider all the way to the left, then start dragging it to the right to soften the edges of the oval until the oval area in your photo looks like a soft light. When you click OK to apply the Gaussian Blur, the effect is complete, and now you have a soft lighting vignette falling on your subject and fading as it moves farther away (as shown here).

Using Color for Emphasis

This is a popular technique for focusing attention by the use of color (or really, it's more like the use of less color—if everything's in black and white, anything that's in color will immediately draw the viewers eye). As popular as this technique is, it's absolutely a breeze to create. Here's how:

Step One:
Open a photo containing an object you want to emphasize through the use of color. Go under the Layer menu, under New, and choose Layer via Copy. This will duplicate the Background layer onto its own layer (Layer 1).

Step Two:
Get the Brush tool from the Toolbox and choose a large, hard-edged brush from the Brush Picker up in the Options Bar. Also in the Options Bar, change the Blend Mode of the Brush tool to Color.

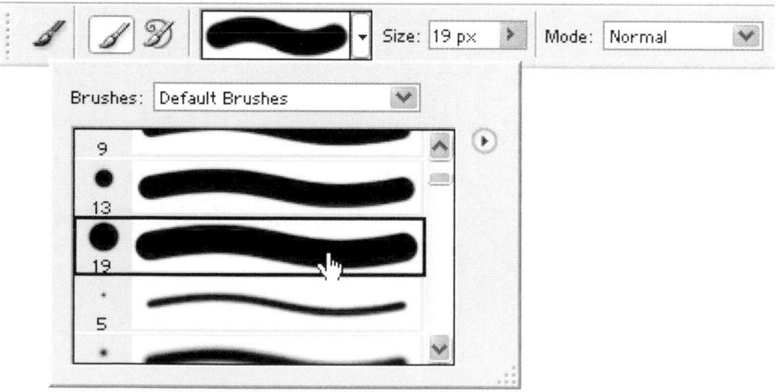

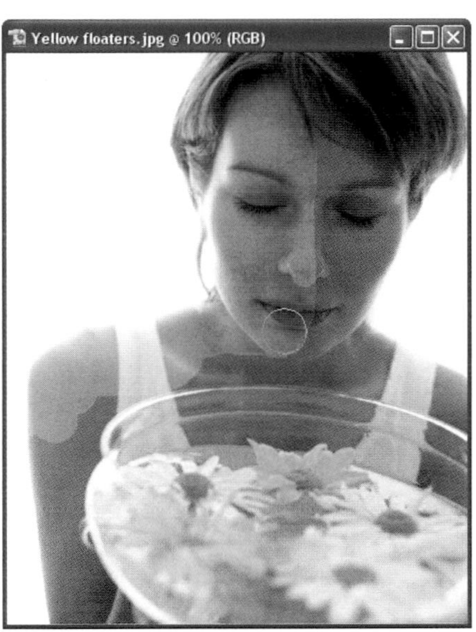

Step Three:
Set your Foreground color to black by pressing the letter "D" and begin painting on the photo. As you paint, the color in the photo will be removed. The goal is to paint away the color from all the areas except the areas you want emphasized with color.

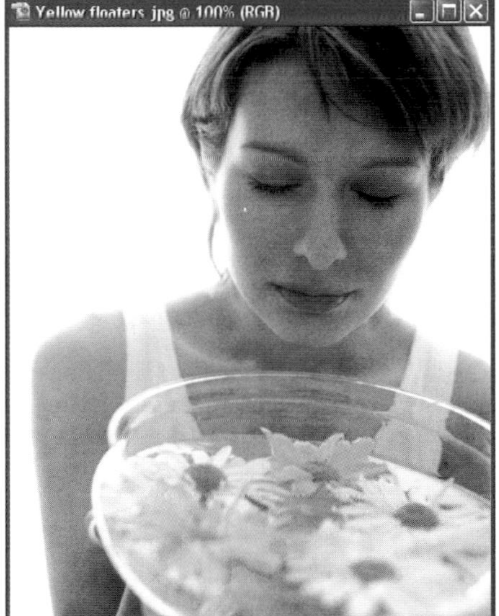

Step Four:
Here's the final image with the color clearly drawing your attention to the focal point.

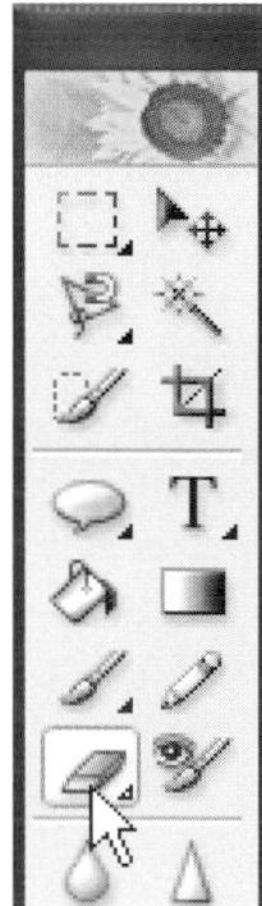

Step Five:
If you make a mistake while painting away the color, just switch to the Eraser tool, paint over the "mistake" area, and the original color will return as you paint (what you're really doing here is erasing part of the top layer, which is now mostly black and white, and as you erase, it reveals the original layer, which is still in full color).

Adding Motion Where You Want It

This is a painless way to add motion to a still photo, and because you're using a brush to apply the blur where you want it, you have a lot of flexibility in where the effect is applied.

Step One:
Open the photo you want to give a motion effect.

© BRAND X PICTURES

Step Two:
Duplicate the Background layer by going under the Layer menu, under New, and choosing Layer via Copy. This will duplicate the Background layer onto its own layer (Layer 1).

Step Three:
Go under the Filter menu, under Blur, and choose Motion Blur. The Motion Blur dialog appears, presenting two settings: Angle lets you choose which direction the blur comes from and Distance actually determines the amount of blur. In this case, set the Angle to 4° so the blur is almost horizontal, and increase the Distance slider (amount) until it looks realistic.

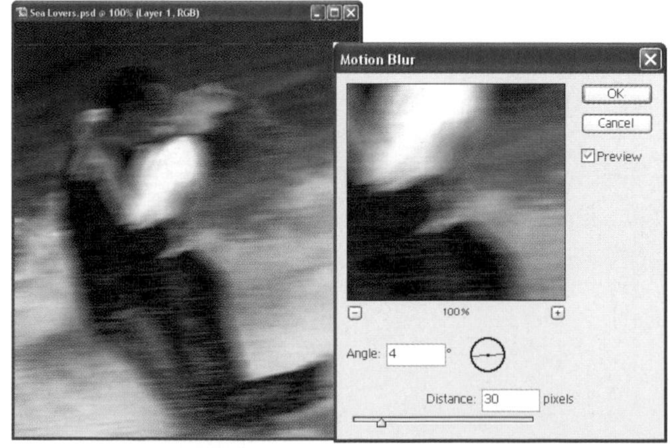

Step Four:

In the Layers palette, hold the Control key (Mac: Command key) and click on the Create New Layer icon. This creates a layer directly beneath your current layer. Now click back on the top layer, then press Control-G (Mac: Command-G) to Group your photo with the blank layer beneath it. Doing this hides the Motion Blur effect you applied to this layer.

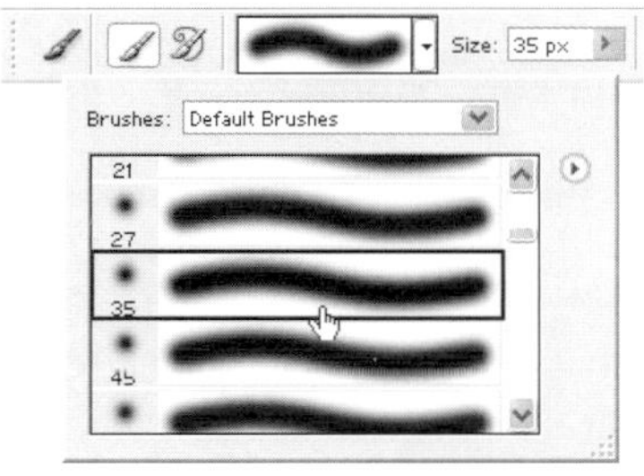

Step Five:

Click on the middle layer (the blank layer). Get the Brush tool from the Toolbox, and choose a medium-sized, soft-edged brush from the Brush Picker up in the Options Bar. Press the letter "D" to set your Foreground color to black, then begin painting over the areas you want to have motion (as shown). As you paint, you'll reveal the Motion Blur that's already applied to the top layer.

Before

After

Step Six:

Complete the effect by painting over all the areas that you want to have motion. If you make a mistake and reveal motion in an area where you don't want it, simply switch to the Eraser tool, then paint over the "mistake" area and the blur will be removed.

Changing an Object's Color

Have you ever wanted to change the color of one object in a photo (such as changing the color of a shirt, a car, etc.)? Here's perhaps the fastest, easiest way to change the color of, well…whatever.

Step One:
Open a photo containing an element that needs to be a different color. Put a selection around the area you want to recolor using any selection tool you'd like (Lasso tool, Magic Wand, Selection Brush, etc.—choose whichever you're most comfortable with).

Step Two:
Choose Hue/Saturation from the Adjustment Layer pop-up menu at the bottom of the Layers palette.

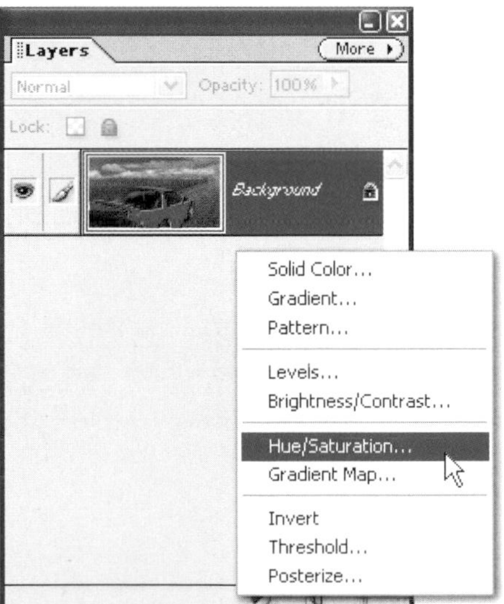

Step Three:

When the dialog appears, click on the Colorize checkbox at the bottom right of the dialog and then start dragging the Hue slider. As you drag, the color of the selected area will begin to change.

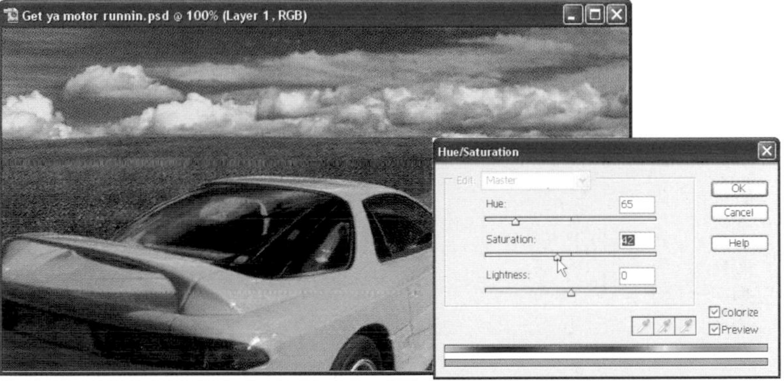

Step Four:

If the color appears too intense after dragging the Hue slider, just drag the Saturation slider (as shown) to the left to decrease the saturation of the color.

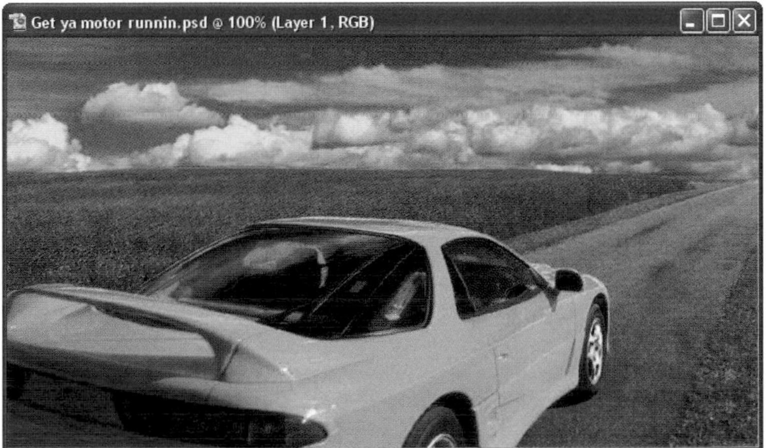

Step Five:

Click OK in the Hue/Saturation dialog to complete the color change. (Here we changed the color and lowered the Saturation.)

Replacing the Sky

When shooting, there's one thing you just can't count on—the sun. Yet, you surely don't want to take a photo of your house on a dreary day, or shoot a photo of your car on a gray overcast day. That's why having the ability to replace a gloomy gray sky with a bright sunny sky is so important. Is it cheating? Yes. Is it easy? You betcha. Do people do it every day? Of course.

Step One:
Open the photo that needs a new, brighter, bluer sky.

© BRAND X PICTURES

Step Two:
You have to select the sky, and in the example shown here I used the Magic Wand to select most of it. Then I chose Similar from the Select menu to select the rest of the sky, but as usual, it also selected part of the house. So I had to hold the Alt key (Mac: Option key) and use the Lasso tool to deselect some excess areas on the roof. You can use any combination of selection tools you'd like—the key is, select the entire sky area.

© BRAND X PICTURES

Step Three:

Shoot some nice sunny skies (like the one shown here) and keep them handy for projects like this. Open one of these "sunny sky" shots, and then go under the Select menu and choose All to select the entire photo. Then, press Control-C (Mac: Command-C) to copy this sky photo into memory.

Step Four:

Switch back to your original photo (the selection should still be in place). Create a new layer by clicking on the Create New Layer icon at the bottom of the Layers palette, then go under the Edit menu, and choose Paste Into. When you choose Paste Into, the sky will be pasted into your selected area in your new layer, appearing over the old sky.

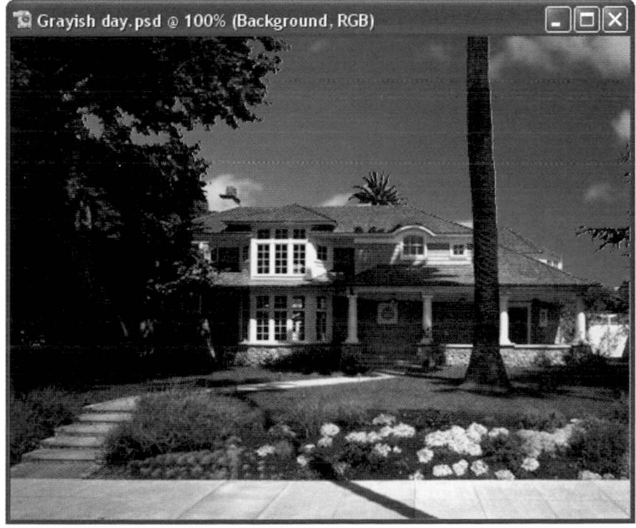

Step Five:

If the sky seems too bright for the photo, simply lower the Opacity of the layer in the Layers palette to help it blend in better with the rest of the photo. That's it—newer, bluer sky.

Replicating Photography Filters

This is a totally digital way to replicate some of the most popular photography filters, such as the 81A and 81B Color Correction filters used by many photographers. These are primarily used to warm photos, especially those taken outdoors where a bright sky radiates to give photos a bluish cast. They're also useful when shooting in shade on a sunny day, or for correcting bluish light from overcast days. Luckily, it's fairly easy to replicate both filters in Elements. (Note: The 81B filter normally provides more warming than the 81A.)

Step One:
Open the photo that needs the warming effect you'd get by applying an 81A Color Correction filter to your lens.

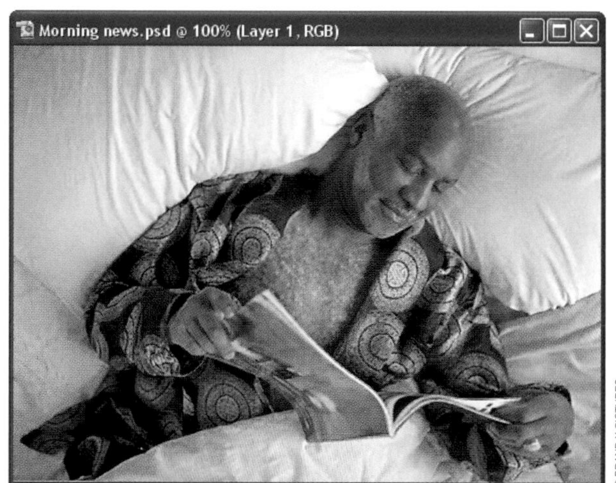

© BRAND X PICTURES

Step Two:
Click on the Foreground Color Swatch in the Toolbox to bring up the Color Picker and choose a cream color. (I used R=252, G=241, and B=211.)

Note: For an 81B filter, which provides more warmth than the 81A, try R=250, G=228, and B=181. To replicate the 80A and 80B filters (used by traditional photographers to correct the cast created by using daylight film in indoor artificial lighting), try a light blue shade instead. A starting point for the 80A might be R=101, G=102, and B=169; and for the 80B, which is more pronounced, try R=171, G=170 and B=214.

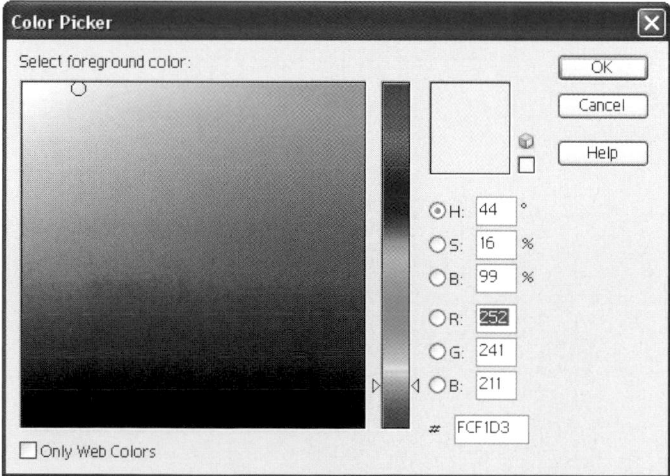

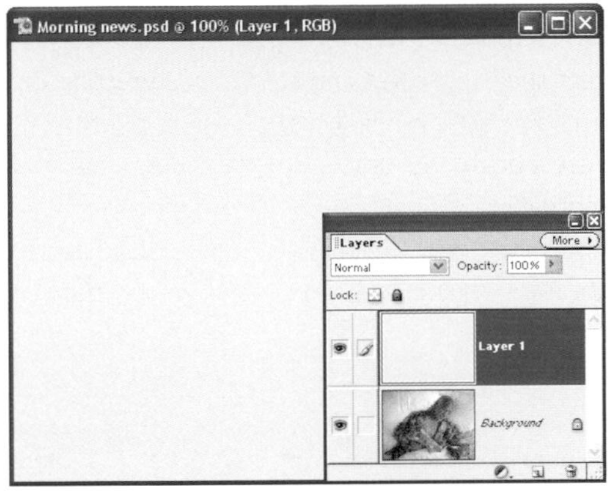

Step Three:

Go to the Layers palette and create a new blank layer by clicking on the Create New Layer icon at the bottom of the palette. Fill this new layer with your new Foreground color by pressing Alt-Backspace (Mac: Option-Delete).

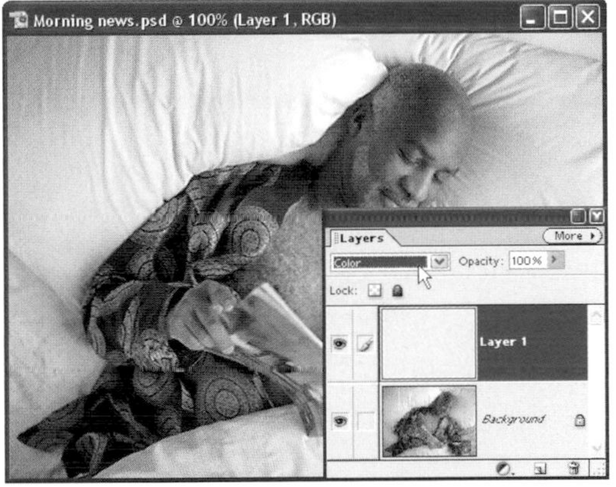

Step Four:

In the Layers palette, change the Blend Mode of this cream-colored layer from Normal to Color. This lets the color blend into the photo without covering the detail. The only problem is that it's way too warm. In fact, it looks as if it has an intentional tint, when what you're really after is a more natural appearance with no visible tint. But we'll fix that.

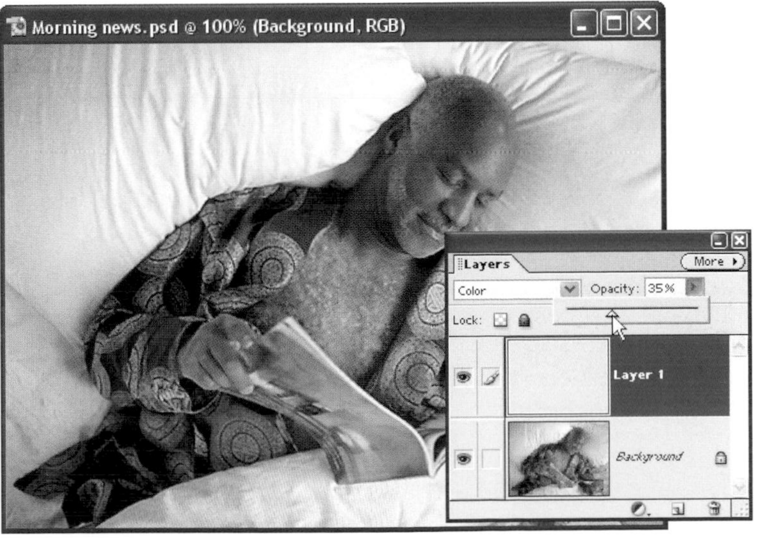

Step Five:

In the Layers palette, lower the Opacity of this Color layer until the color comes back and the photo looks balanced. In the example shown here, I lowered the Opacity of this layer to 35%, but you can go as low as 20% depending on how much effect you want the filter to have, and how blue the cast was when you started. If the 81A replication doesn't do the trick, try the 81B using the figures I listed in Step Two as a starting point.

Continued

Creating Photo Montages

Here's a great way to blend any two (or more) photos together to create a photo montage (also sometimes called collages).

Step One:

Open the photo that you want to use as your base photo (this will serve as the background of your collage). Open the first photo that you want to collage with your background photo.

© BRAND X PICTURES

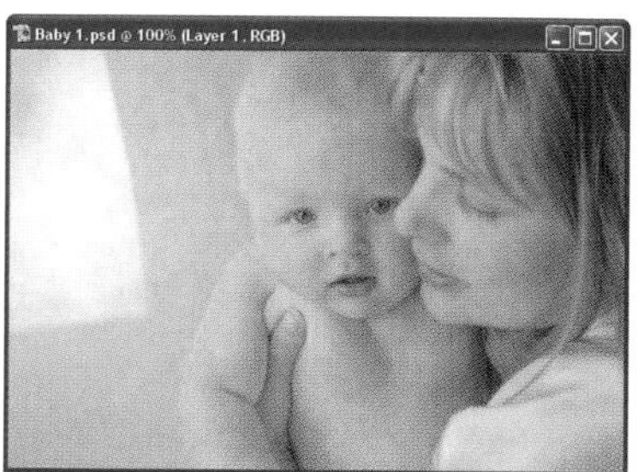

© BRAND X PICTURES

Step Two:

Switch to the Move tool in the Toolbox, and then click-and-drag the photo from this document right onto your background photo. It will appear on its own layer.

Step Three:

In the Layers palette, hold the Control key (Mac: Command key) and click on the Create New Layer icon. This creates a layer directly beneath your current layer. Now, click back on the top layer, then press Control-G (Mac: Command-G) to Group your photo with the blank layer beneath it. Press the letter "D" to set your Foreground color to black.

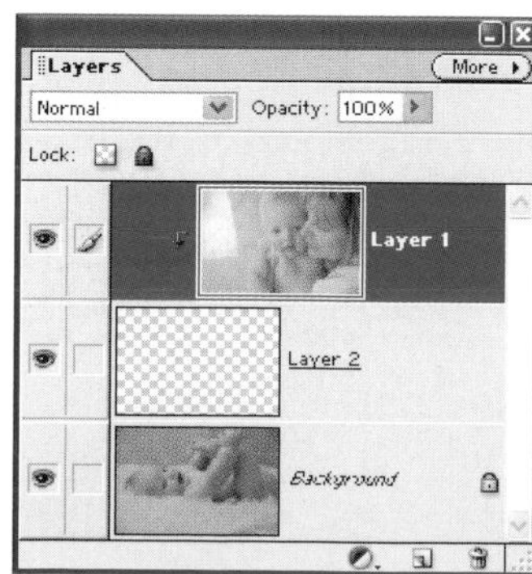

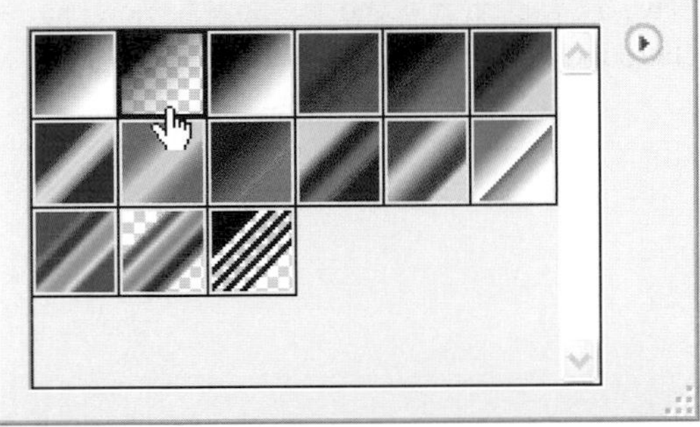

Step Four:
Get the Gradient tool from the Toolbox, and then press Enter (Mac: Return) to bring up the Gradient Picker (it appears at the location of your cursor within your image area). Choose the second gradient in the Picker, as shown (this is the Foreground to Transparent gradient).

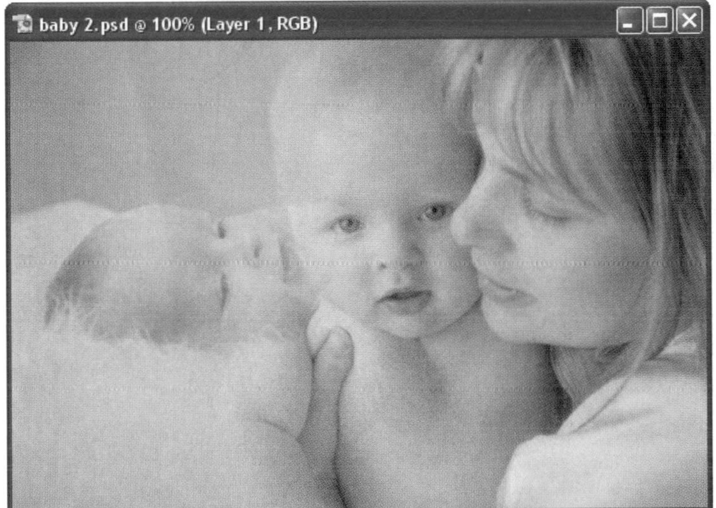

Step Five: Click on the middle, blank layer in the Layers palette to make it active. Click the Gradient tool in the center of your photo and drag upward. The point where you first click will make the top layer totally transparent, and the point where you stop dragging will have 100% opacity. Everything else will blend in between. If you want to start over—easy enough—just go under the Select menu, choose All, then press Backspace (Mac: Delete).

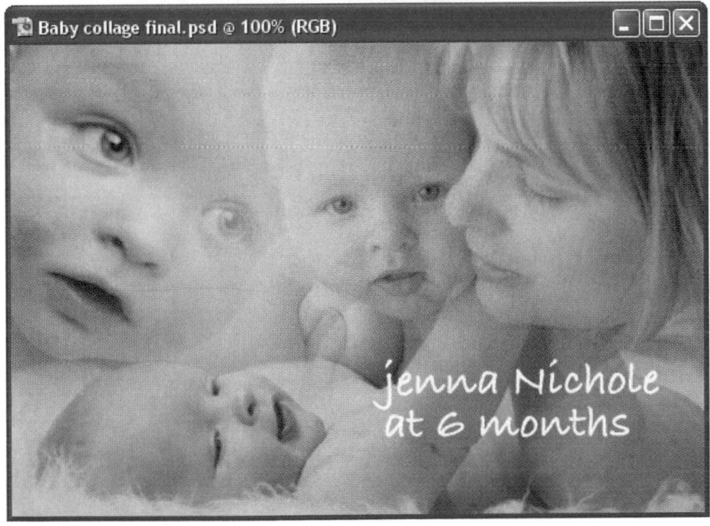

Step Six:
If you want to blend another photo into your montage, click on the top layer, then start again from Step Three. Here's an example of adding a third photo in the left corner, and adding some type in the right corner.

Adding Depth of Field

This is a digital way to create the classic in-camera depth-of-field effect, and thanks to Elements' Quick Mask, it's easy to pull off. Of course, for this technique to be effective, you have to start with the right photo, one that would benefit from a depth-of-field effect. (Close-up photos of people are ideal, as are product shots, as long as they're not shot straight on; or, if they are, they need to have a detailed background behind them.)

Step One:

Open the photo to which you want to apply a depth-of-field effect. Duplicate the Background layer by going under the Layer menu, under New, and choosing Layer via Copy. This will duplicate the Background layer onto its own layer (Layer 1).

Step Two:

Go under the Filter menu, under Blur, and choose Gaussian Blur. When the Gaussian Blur dialog box appears, drag the slider all the way to the left, then slowly drag it back to the right to blur your photo. Keep dragging until you reach the amount of blur you'd like for the area that's farthest away from the camera).

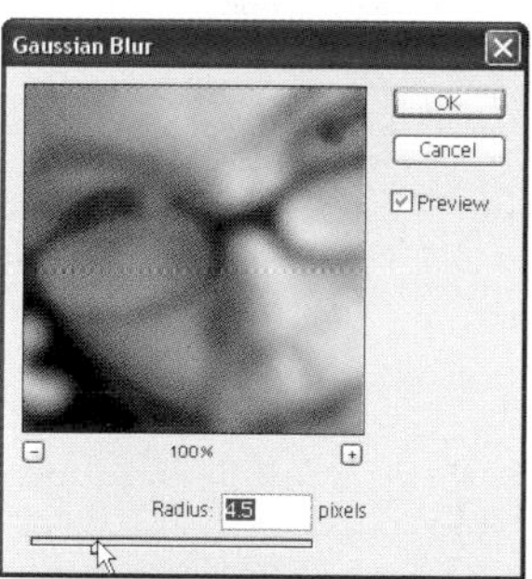

Step Three:

In the Layers palette, hold the Control key (Mac: Command key) and click on the Create New Layer icon to create a new blank layer beneath your current layer. Now, click back on the top layer, then press Control-G (Mac: Command-G) to Group your photo with the blank layer beneath it. Doing this hides the Gaussian Blur effect you applied to your top layer in Step Two.

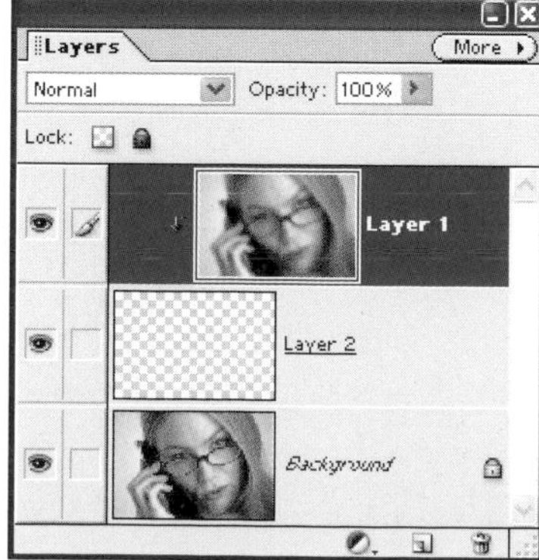

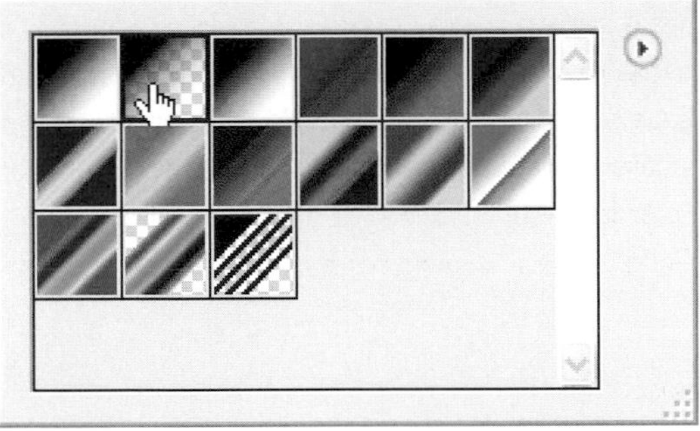

Step Four:
Press the letter "D" to set your Foreground color to black. Get the Gradient tool from the Toolbox, then press the Enter key (Mac: Return key) and the Gradient Picker will appear at the current location of your cursor within your image area. Choose the second gradient in the top row (Foreground to Transparent).

Step Five:
Click on the middle layer (the blank layer), then click the Gradient tool within your photo at the point that you want to be out of focus, and drag it to the point that you want to be in focus.

Step Six:
Once you release the mouse, you'll see a smooth blend from the non-blurred area to the blurred area. After you drag the gradient tool, you'll see what I mean because the left side of your photo should be blurred, and progressing to the right, the photo becomes less and less blurry.

Creating the Classic Vignette Effect

Here's how to create the classic soft-edged vignette that was originally made popular decades ago with portrait photographers, and still remains popular for wedding photos and portraits of children. A rectangular version is popular for photos used in print ads of high-priced items like fine homes, jewelry, perfume, etc.

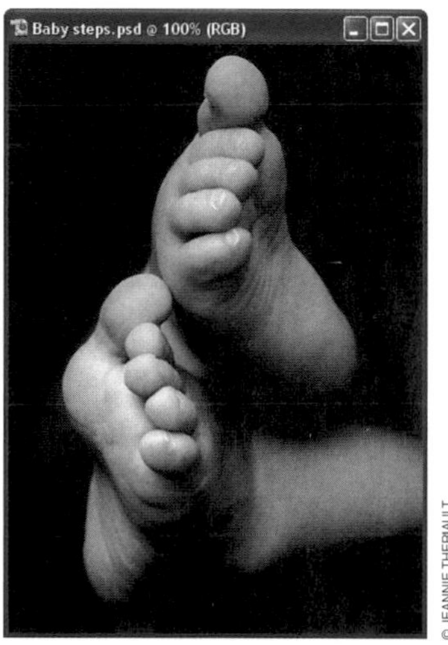

© JEANNIE THERIAULT

Step One:
Open the photo to which you want to apply the classic vignette effect.

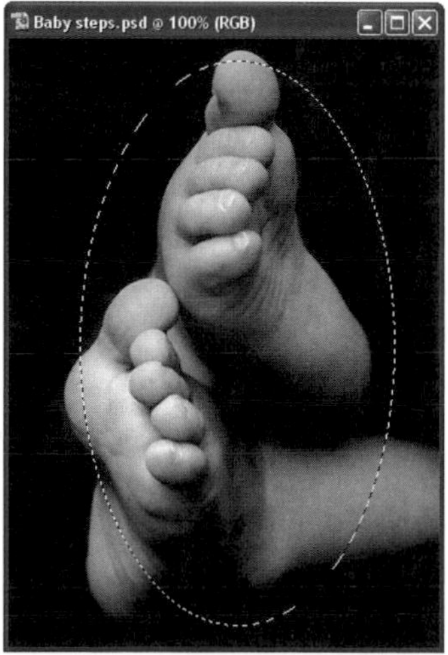

Step Two:
Get the Elliptical Marquee tool from the Toolbox and draw an oval-shaped selection around the part of the photo you want to remain visible.

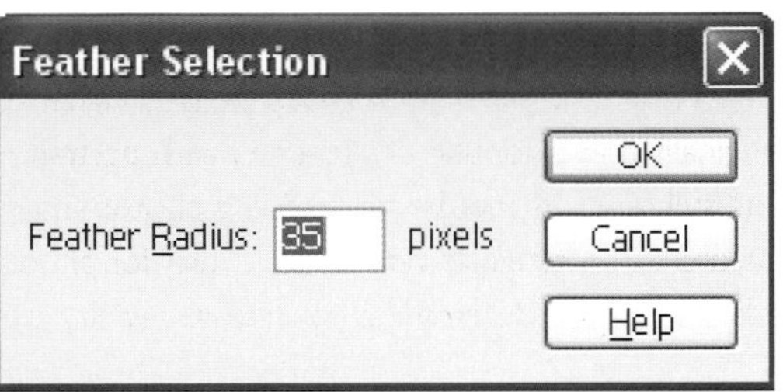

Step Three:

To soften the edge of your selection, go under the Select menu and choose Feather. When the Feather Selection dialog appears, enter 35 or more pixels (the higher the number, the softer the edge) and click OK.

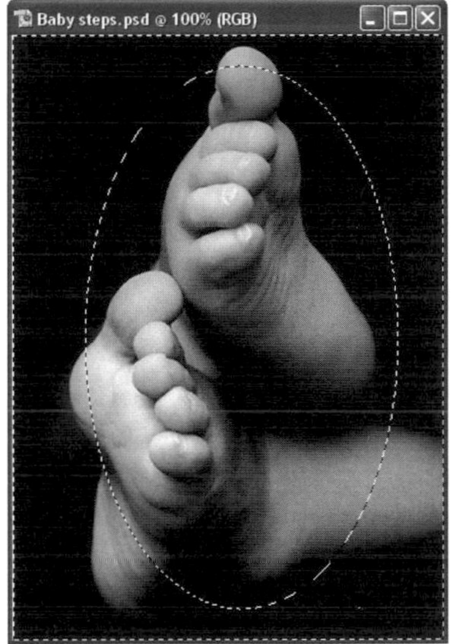

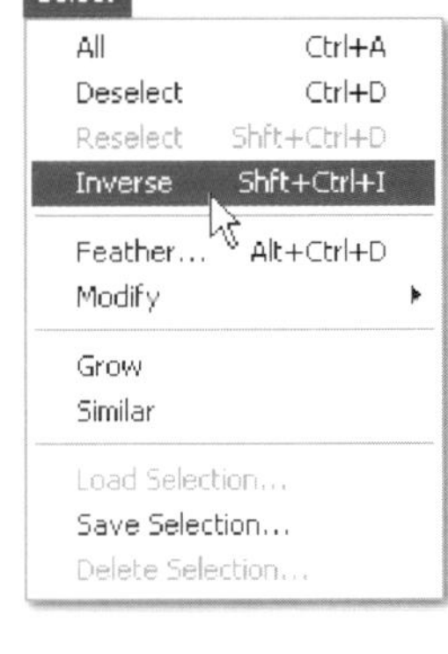

Step Four:

Here's the thing—you have your subject encircled in a selection, and that's the part you want to keep intact. However, you want everything else deleted, so go under the Select menu and choose Inverse. Doing this selects everything except the area you want to keep intact.

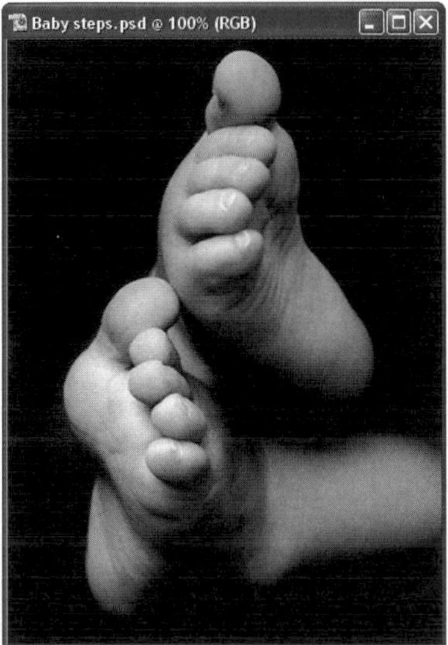

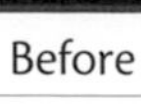
Before

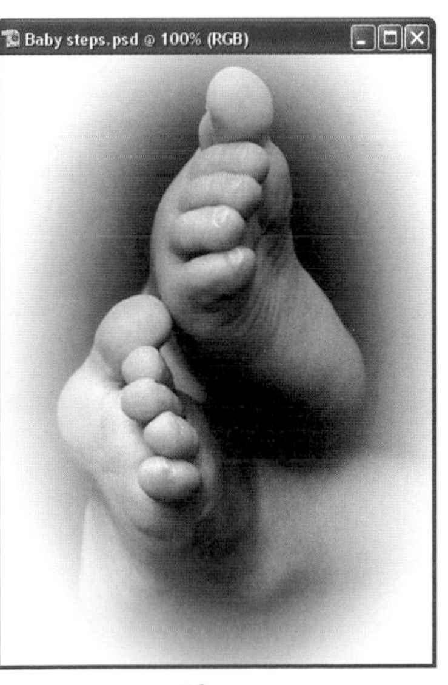

After

Step Five:

Now press Backspace (Mac: Delete) to remove the background areas. Because you feathered this oval in Step Three, the edges are soft, creating the vignette effect. That completes the effect; however, if you'd like to use this soft edge for collaging with other photos, you'll need the white areas outside the edge to be transparent and not solid white. To do that, just before Step Two, double-click on the Background layer in the Layers palette. A dialog box will appear; just click OK to change your Background layer to Layer 0, and then go on to Step Two.

Sepia Tone Effect

Here's another technique that was quite popular in the early days of photography. Today, it's normally used either as a special effect, or in photo-restoration projects where you sometimes have to remove the bad sepia tone from the original (during the tonal correction process), but then need to add it back in when your restoration is complete.

Step One:

Open the photo that you want to apply the sepia tone effect to.

© NANCY ADAMSON

Step Two:

Go under the Enhance menu, under Adjust Color, and choose Hue/Saturation. When the Hue/Saturation dialog appears, drag the Saturation slider all the way to the left (as shown here) to remove all the color from the image, making it look like a black-and-white photo.

Step Three:

Go under the Enhance menu, under Adjust Color, and choose Color Variations. This dialog shows you what your color photo would look like by adding or subtracting different colors, and you do so by clicking on the buttons at the bottom of the dialog. However, in this case, there is no color in the photo, so clicking on a swatch will actually add color in (even if it says it's decreasing it). So start by clicking once on the tiny thumbnail preview named "Decrease Blue." As you can see from the "After" preview up top, it added in a bit of a sepia tone effect to our photo.

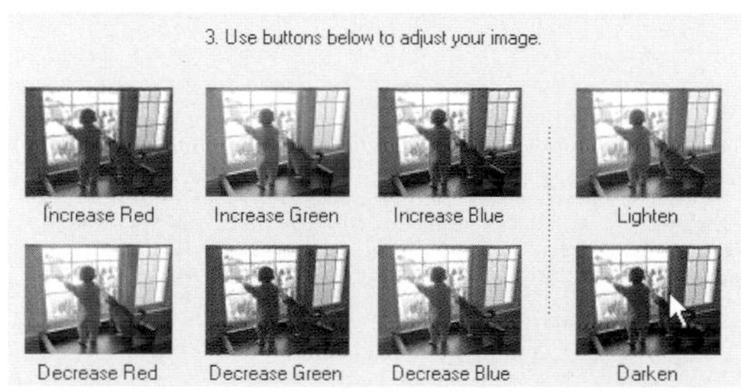

Step Four:

The rest is easy—just click on any of the thumbnail previews at the bottom of dialog that look more like a sepia tone than what you already have. Keep an eye on the preview up top to see how you're doing. In the example shown here, I clicked once on Increase Red, and once on Darken.

Before

After

Step Five:

Click OK and the sepia tone effect is applied to your photo (as shown here). Note: If you click a swatch and it doesn't look right, there's an Undo button on the right side of the dialog. Just click it and it undoes your swatch clicking (known as "swatch-clickination" in some circles).

Creating a Photo Backdrop

This is a quick technique for creating a traditional photographic background (a muslin, a backdrop, etc.) that you can composite portraits into. This technique is pretty handy if you need to take a headshot of a person from a snapshot, and make it look like a studio shot.

Step One:
Start by creating a custom gradient that will form the basis of the backdrop. Get the Gradient tool from the Toolbox, then up in the Options Bar click on the Edit button (as shown here).

Step Two:
When the Gradient Editor appears, you're going to create a simple custom gradient that goes from light gray to dark gray. Here's how: double-click on the left Color Stop (circled in red at right) to bring up the Color Picker. When the Color Picker appears, to create a light gray color, enter these figures: R=220, G=220, and B=220 (as shown) then click OK to assign that gray color for the left side of your gradient.

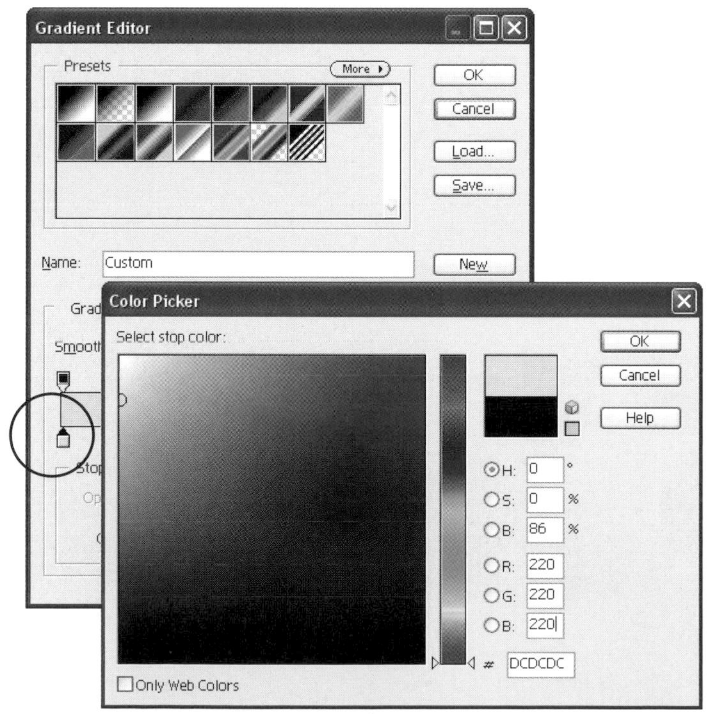

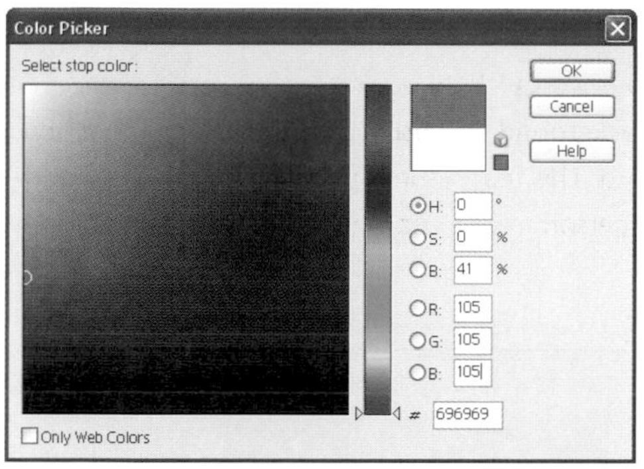

Step Three:

Now double-click on the Color Stop on the right side of the Gradient Picker, and this time you'll want to choose a dark gray, so enter R=105, G=105, and B=105, then click OK. Last, to save your gradient for future use, just click on the New button in the Gradient Editor, then click OK to save this gradient.

Step Four:

Open a new document in RGB mode (the one shown here is a 5″x7″). Take the Gradient tool, click near the bottom of your image area and drag upward (as shown here). Make sure the lighter gray appears at the bottom of the image. Next, press the letter "d" to set your Foreground color to black.

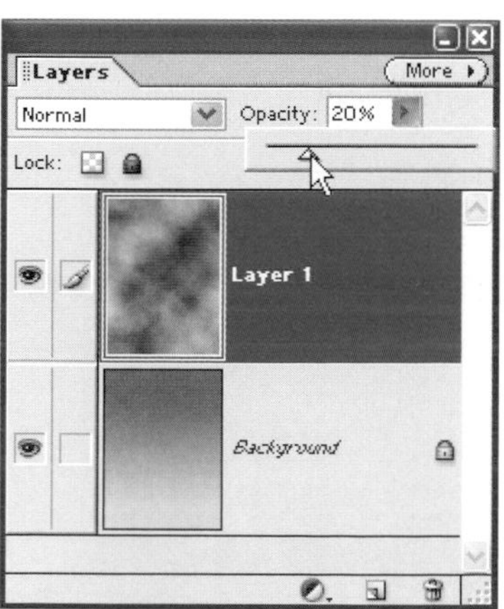

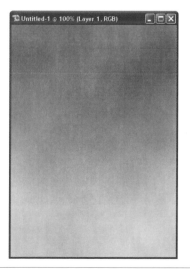

Step Five:

In the Layers palette click on the Create New Layer icon to create a new blank layer. Then, go under the Filter menu, under Render, and choose Clouds. The effect is way too intense, so to tone it down and have it blend in with the background, lower the opacity of this layer to 20% (as shown here).

Continued

Step Six:
To keep the background from looking too synthetic, we'll add a little "noise" to give it a bit of grain. Go under the Filter menu, under Noise, and choose Add Noise. Lower the Amount to 2%, set the Distribution to Gaussian, and then click on the Monochromatic checkbox (as shown here). Then click OK to add this slight bit of noise to the background.

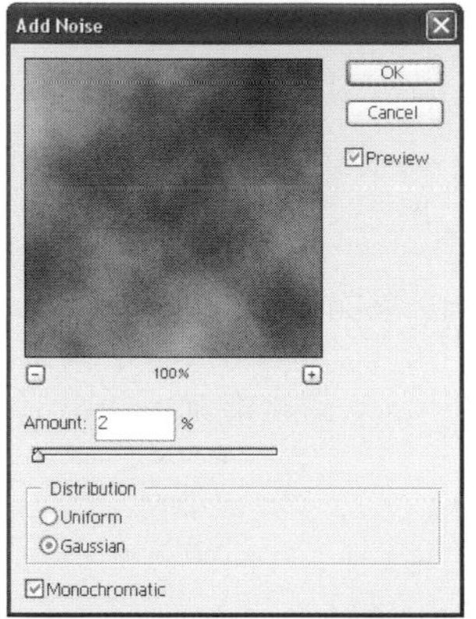

Step Seven:
In the Layers palette click on the Create New Layer icon to create a new blank layer. Get the Elliptical Marquee tool (it's behind the Rectangular Marquee tool in the Toolbox—just click-and-hold and it will appear). Hold the Shift key, and draw a circular selection in the top ¼ of the image area (as shown). Press the letter "X" to set your Foreground color to white, then fill your selection with white by pressing Alt-Backspace (Mac: Option-Delete).

Step Eight:
Press Control-D (Mac: Command-D) to deselect your circle. Go under the Filter menu, under Blur, and choose Gaussian Blur. You're going to use this filter to soften the edges of the white circle to make it look like a spotlight aiming at the gray background. In this example (a 72-ppi photo) I used a Radius (amount of blur) of slightly more than 30. On a high-resolution, 300-ppi image, try 60 or 70. Click OK when the edges look nice and soft (like the one shown here).

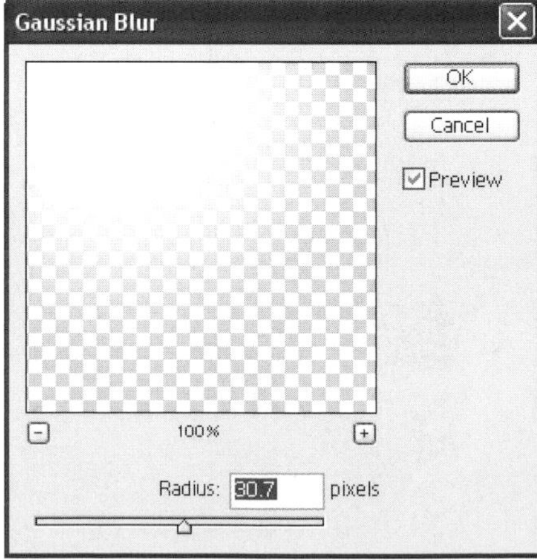

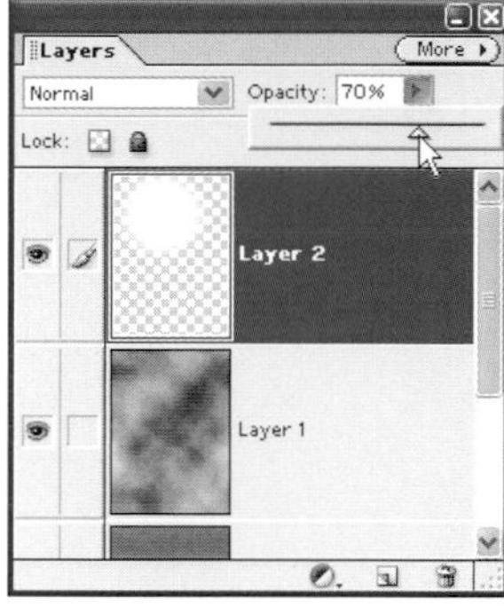

Step Nine:

To help the spotlight blend into the background more realistically, lower the Opacity of this layer to around 70% (as shown).

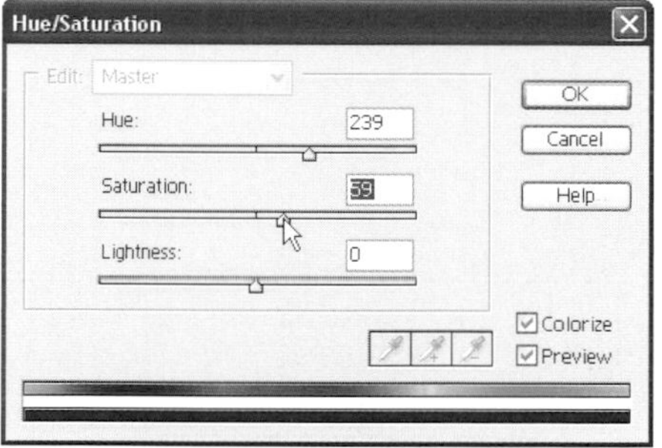

Step Ten:

You can use the background as is for a realistic looking backdrop, or you can add some color by switching back to the cloud layer in the Layers palette, going under the Enhance menu, under Adjust Color, and choosing Hue/Saturation. When the dialog appears, click the Colorize checkbox in the lower right-hand corner (as shown), then move the Hue slider to the color you'd like (in this case, a light blue). If the intensity of the color isn't right, drag the Saturation slider until it looks good to you. Click OK to apply the color to the background.

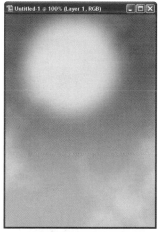

© BRAND X PICTURES

Step Eleven:

The final step is to put a person (an object, etc.) on the background. In the example shown here, I used the Lasso tool to draw a selection around the person, then I switched to the Move tool and dragged them from their photo onto my background to create the finished effect shown here.

Turning photos into drawings

This is a simple technique that yields big results. It lets you start with a photograph, and by applying a filter here, a layer trick there, in just a minute or two you've got a great-looking drawing that looks like it took hours to complete.

Step One:

Open the photograph that you want to convert into a drawing.

© BRAND X PICTURES

Step Two:

Make a duplicate of this background layer by going under the Layer menu, under New, and choosing Layer via Copy. Go to the Layers palette and hide this new duplicate Background layer by clicking on the Eye icon in the first column beside Layer 1. (Note: You're not deleting the layer, just hiding it from view for now.) Now, in the Layers palette click once on the Background layer because that's where you'll be applying the effect.

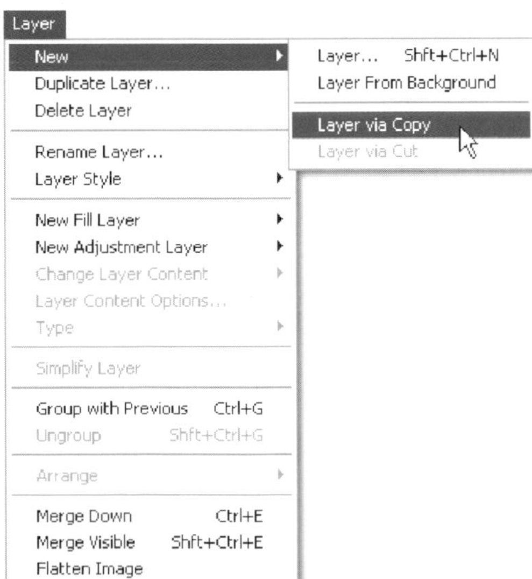

Step Three:

Go under the Filter menu, under Stylize, and choose Find Edges, and the filter will trace any edges it finds within the photo (as shown here). Note: The more clearly defined the edges are, the better job the Find Edges filter will do.

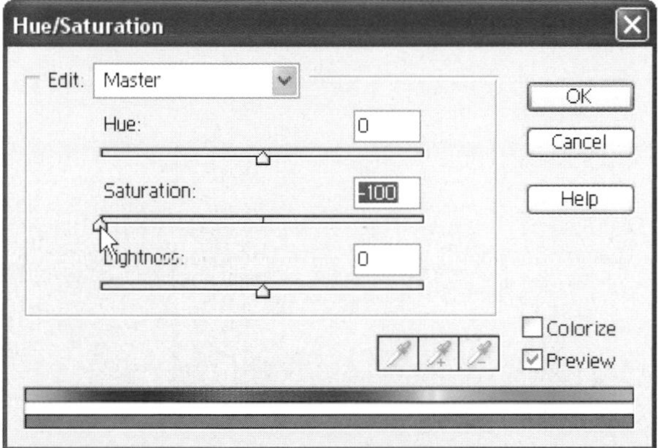

Step Four:

Running the Find Edges filter usually introduces some garish neon-like colors that you'll have to remove before your photo looks like a drawing. To do that, go under the Enhance menu, under Adjust Color, and choose Hue/Saturation. When the dialog appears, drag the Saturation slider all the way to the left (as shown here) to remove the all color from the drawing. Click OK to apply this change.

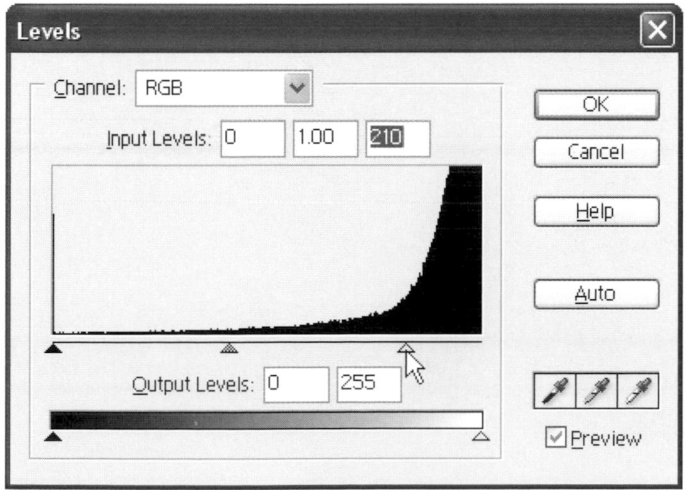

Step Five:

The Find Edges filter also usually creates a cluttered look by leaving thin lines and other artifacts throughout the image. To remove that cluttered look, press Control-L (Mac: Command-L) to bring up the Levels dialog box. When the dialog box appears, grab the top right Input Levels slider (the white one) and drag it to the left. As you do this, you'll see most of those faint lines disappear, leaving only the most well-defined lines. Look at the capture in the next step to see the results.

Continued

Step Six:

You can see in the example shown here the effects of using Levels to get rid of the excess lines; however, by lightening the image with Levels, the lines that remain may look a bit light (more gray instead of the nice thick black lines of a drawing). But you can fix that very easily (as you'll see in the next step).

Step Seven:

To thicken and darken these lines, make a duplicate of this layer by dragging it to the Create New Layer icon at the bottom of the Layers palette. Then, change the Blend Mode of this layer from Normal to Multiply (as shown here). This thickens and darkens the outlines of your line art.

Step Eight:

Now we'll bring some color back to our drawing. Remember the layer we duplicated in the second step, that I mentioned we'd use later? It's later now. Go to the Layers palette, and click on this layer to make it visible again.

Step Nine:
Now, change the Layer Blend Mode of this full-color layer from Normal to Color (as shown) to bring back some of the original color. The color will probably be too intense, so lower the Opacity of this layer to 50% (or as little as 20%, depending on the photo), to add just a hint of color. Last, choose Flatten Image from the Layers palette's More menu to flatten the layers and complete the effect. A Before and After is shown below.

Before: a full color photo

After: a drawing

Getting the Polaroid Look

This is a quick technique that lets you turn any photo into what looks like a Polaroid™ snapshot. This is an ideal effect to apply when you really want that "scrapbook" feel, or you're looking for that spontaneous "my-family-on-vacation" feel. Give this one a try—it's much, much easier than it looks.

Step One:

Open the photo you want to turn into a Polaroid. Press Control-A (Mac: Command-A) to put a selection around the entire image. Go under the Layers menu, under New, and choose Layer via Cut to remove the photo from the Background layer and copy it on its own separate layer above the background (as shown here).

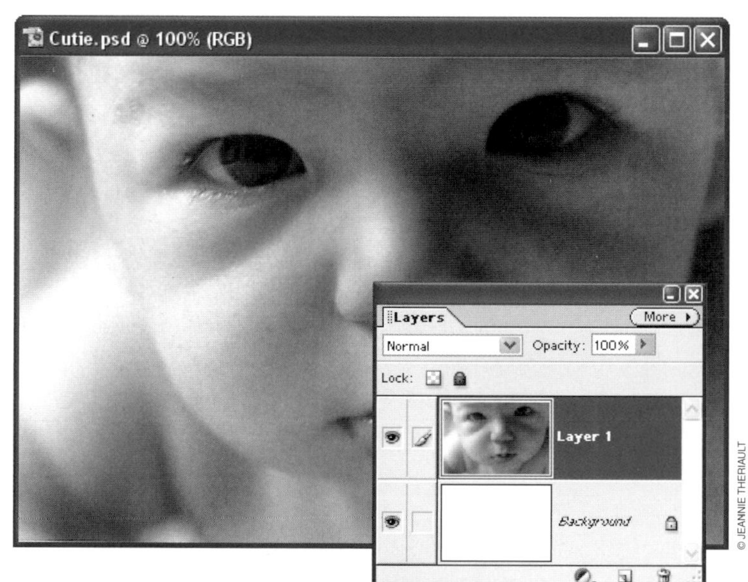

© JEANNIE THERIAULT

Step Two:

To create this effect, we need a little more working room, so to add some space around your photo, go under the Image menu, under Resize, and choose Canvas Size. When the Canvas Size dialog box appears, click the Relative checkbox, then add 2″ of space to both the Width and Height, then click OK (you'll see the results of adding the extra white space in the next step).

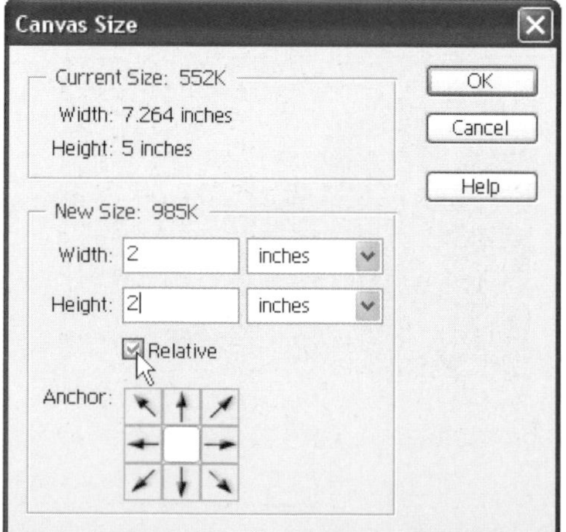

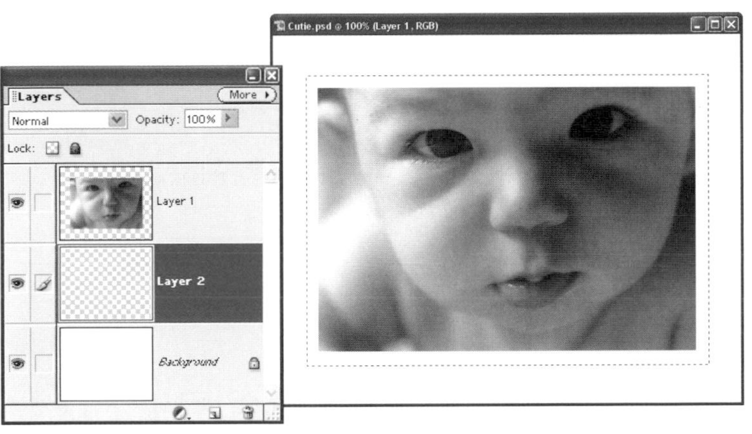

Step Three:
Create a new blank layer directly beneath your current layer by Control-clicking (Mac: Command-clicking) on the New Layer icon at the bottom of the Layers palette. Press the "M" key to switch to the Rectangular Marquee tool and on this layer draw a selection that is about ½" larger than your photo on all sides (as shown here) which will act as the border for your Polaroid image.

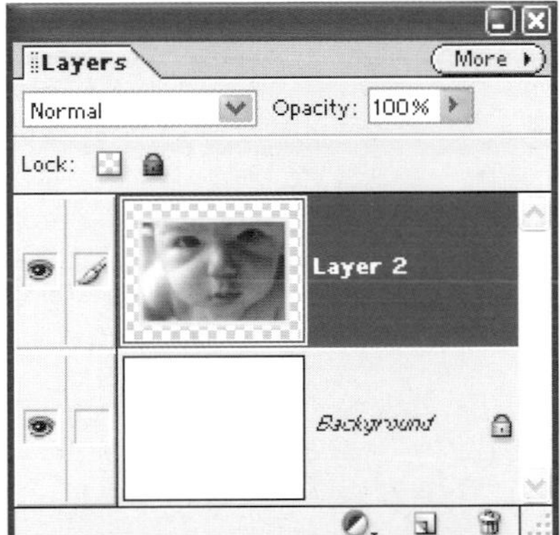

Step Four:
Choose a very light gray as your Foreground color (I used R=232, G=232, B=232), then fill your selection with this light gray by pressing Alt-Backspace (Mac: Option-Delete). Now you can deselect by pressing Control-D (Mac: Command-D). In the Layers palette, click on your top layer (your photo layer) then press Control-E (Mac: Command-E) to combine (merge) your photo with the gray rectangle layer below it, creating just one layer (as shown here).

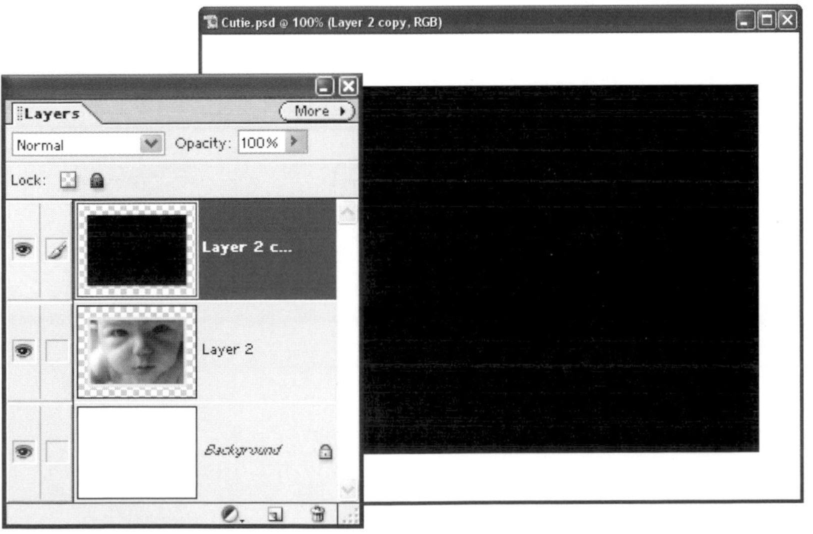

Step Five:
Make a duplicate of this merged layer by dragging it to the Create New Layer icon at the bottom of the Layers palette. Press the "D" key to set your Foreground color to black. Then, press Shift-Alt-Backspace (Mac: Shift-Option-Delete) to fill your merged layer with black (as shown here). Now, in the Layers palette, drag the black layer beneath your photo layer, so it's just below your photo layer. Now you're going to "bend" this black-filled layer.

Continued

Step Six:
Go under the Filter menu, under Distort, and choose Shear. When the Shear dialog box appears, click on the line at the center of the grid in the dialog box. This adds a center point to the grid. Click-and-drag this point to the left (as shown here). The bottom of the dialog box shows a preview of how your shear will look. When it looks like the preview shown here, click OK.

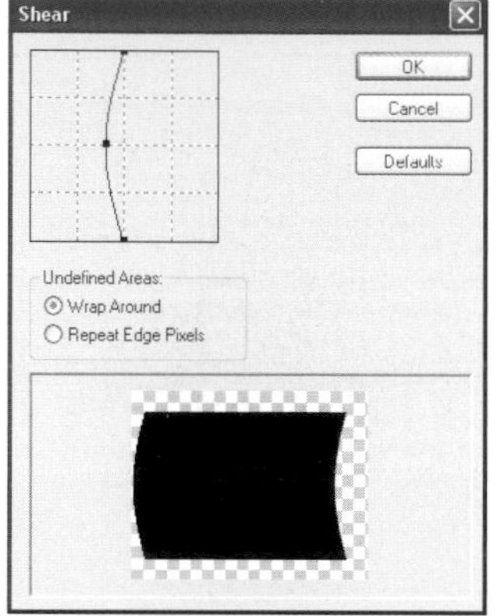

Step Seven:
Press the "V" key to switch to the Move tool. Then drag this black, sheared layer straight over to the right until the corners are peering out, giving the impression that the shadow is bent (as shown).

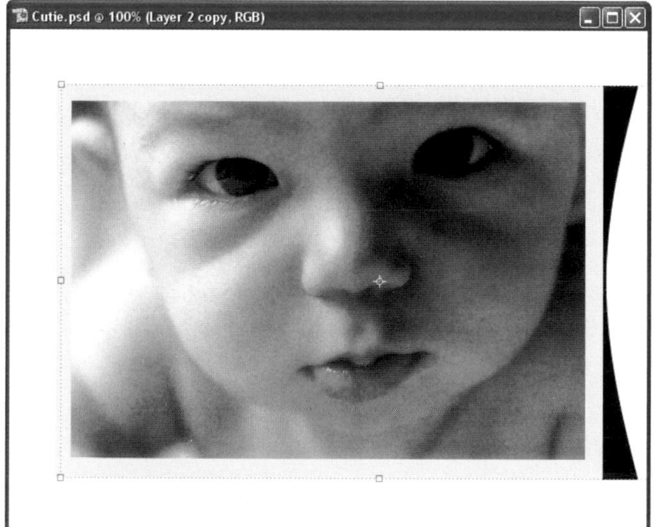

Step Eight:
To soften the edges of your shadow (and make them look, well…shadow-like), go under the Filter menu, under Blur, and choose Gaussian Blur. Enter a Radius of 6 and click OK (enter a Radius of 14 for high-res, 300-ppi images).

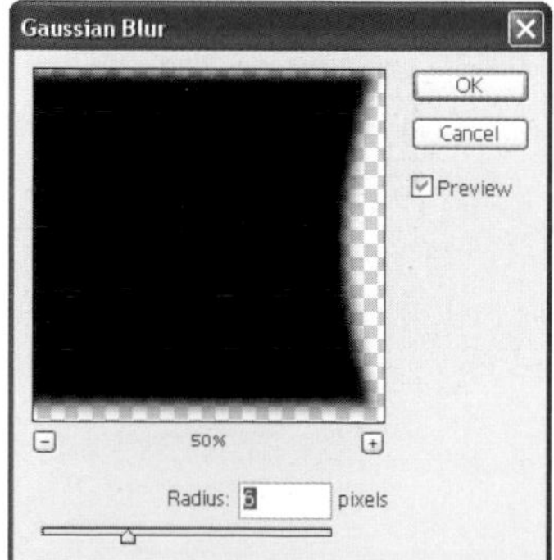

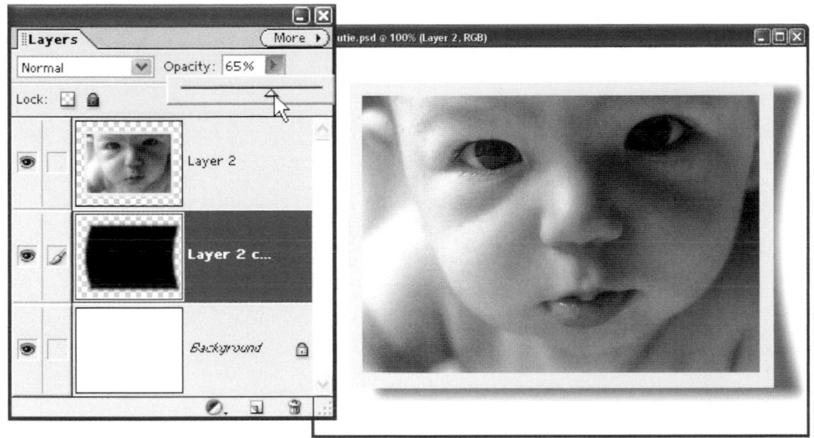

Step Nine:

Now that the shadow is soft, you'll need to lower its Opacity to make it appear more subtle. Go to the Layers palette and lower the Opacity setting to around 65%, as shown here. (You can go lower if you like—it's up to you.) Now that your shadow is finished, to make the effect look more realistic, you'll have to bend the edges of the photo itself.

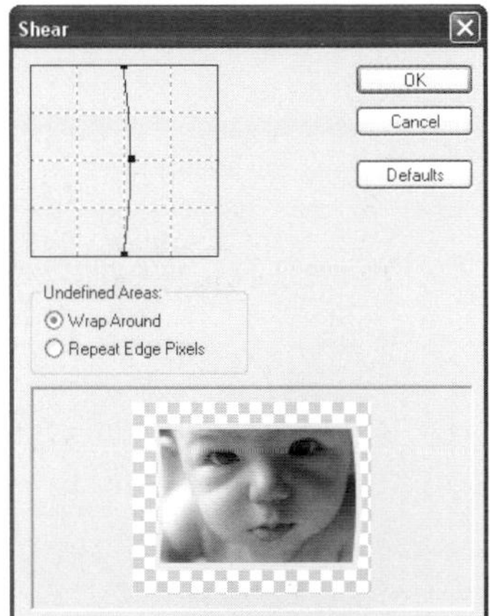

Step Ten:

In the Layers palette, click on your photo layer to make it active. Then, go under the Filter menu, under Distort, and choose Shear. When the Shear dialog appears, it will still have the last settings you applied in the grid. Click-and-drag the center point back to the center. Now, click-and-drag the top and bottom points (on the grid line) to the left, to bend the top and bottom edges of the image. When it looks like the capture shown here, click OK.

Step Eleven:

Last, merge the two layers into one by pressing Control-E (Mac: Command-E). Then, press Control-T (Mac: Command-T) to bring up the Free Transform bounding box. Move your cursor outside the bounding box, then click-and-drag upward to rotate the Polaroid, giving you the final effect (as shown here).

Photomerge

In theory, the Photomerge feature of Photoshop Elements will take a number of separate photos and automatically create a panorama. In reality, this is one "automatic" feature that actually works pretty well—if you're willing to do a little preparation up front and a bit of tweaking after the fact. When you're taking the photos, make sure that you include a slight overlap in each image and try to avoid including any moving objects. Also, use a tripod if you can and try to keep the exposure the same for each photograph. Before launching Photomerge, crop any unnecessary information to "help your cause." Then you're ready to roll...

Step One:

From the File menu, choose Create Photomerge. Choose the images you want to use in your panoramic image. If you have the images open when you open the Photomerge command, those images will appear in the dialog box. Otherwise, you'll have to browse to add the images.

TIP: Hold down the Shift key to add multiple images from the same folder in the Open dialog.

If you're lucky, once you click OK, your images will be placed into the Photomerge layout window and most of the work will already have been done for you. This assumes that Elements can determine where the overlap occurs.

If Elements cannot complete the automatic layout of your images, you'll see this warning dialog box, and you'll have to complete the layout manually.

At worst, all of the images you've selected will appear in the Lightbox at the top of the Photomerge dialog box and you'll have to add each image manually. Hopefully, you'll have at least partial success.

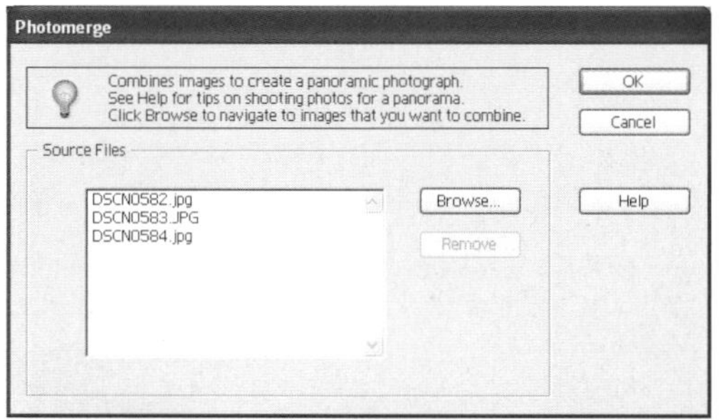

© DAVE CROSS

In this example, two of the three images were successfully added to the project while the remaining image is in the Lightbox area, ready to be dragged into the layout area.

Step Two:

Drag the remaining image into the layout window. In most cases, the Snap to Image checkbox should be checked, as this will usually help line up the images as you move the last image into place. As you drag an image, you'll be able to see both the image you're dragging and the underlying image. Focus on one or two key areas (or objects) that are common to both images and watch for a change from two overlapping objects into one object—that will indicate that your image is in the correct position.

TIP: Use the Navigator to zoom in on the area where to which you're dragging the image.

Continued

Step Three:

Experiment with the Composition Settings to get the best results. First, check the Advanced Blending box and then press the Preview button. Is there a more natural blend between the images with this option turned on? There may be, or you may choose to turn if back off again—that's why there's a Preview!

Next, compare the Settings for Normal and Perspective. If you can use the Normal setting, your overall image will be pretty much a rectangle that will only require a small amount of cropping. On the other hand, there may be some more obvious problems. (In this case, the photos were taken of a street that curves slightly, and in Normal setting, there are some mismatches in the street and sidewalk.)

Try the Perspective setting to see if any mismatches are corrected. As you can see, the three photos tend to match up a little better and the blend seems a little more natural. However, the extreme perspective means you'll have to do a little more cropping and/or cloning to get to a finished image.

If you determine that the Perspective setting improves the matching of the images, try using the Cylindrical Mapping setting under Composition Settings. Typically, this will reduce some of the "bow-tie" effect that you get with the Perspective setting. (Cylindrical Mapping is only available if the Perspective Setting has been used and can only be seen in Preview.)

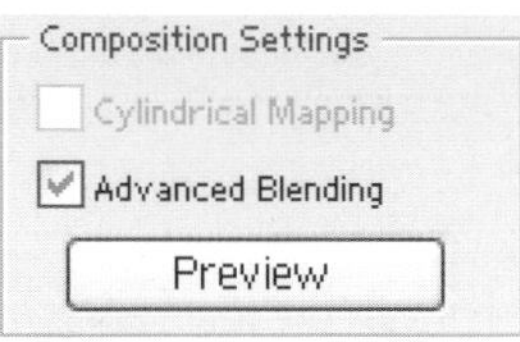

Step Four:
Once you're satisfied with the layout of your images, click OK to finalize the Photomerge. The result is a new document containing one layer called Photomerge, with transparency around the merged images.

Step Five:
To make the image rectangular you have two choices: crop the image or clone to fill in missing areas. (Actually you have a third choice which is do a little of both.) Ideally, you want to keep as much of the image as possible, so try to crop relatively close, and don't worry about small areas of transparency as you can use cloning methods to add in those missing areas.

Step Six:
Look for obvious problems such as differences in lighting or shading, or problems with mismatching areas. In our example, there are a couple of obvious problems: mismatching areas where the images overlap (upper) and obvious differences in shading between two images (lower) .

Mismatches can usually be fixed with the Clone Stamp tool. Clone small areas to help align and match up the details.

Continued

Step Seven:
Differences in shading can be addressed with a combination of adjusting the Levels and some cloning. Make a feathered selection of the area where the shading is obviously lighter than the rest of the image.

Then use the Levels command (Control-L [Mac: Command-L]) and move the middle gray triangle to the right to darken the midtones to match more closely with the darker shading. Click OK.

Deselect, then use the Clone Stamp tool with a soft-edged brush and an Opacity of around 50% in the Options Bar to touch up the areas where the shading still looks too obvious.

Here's a comparison between the original three photos (after cropping to prepare for Photomerge) and the finished product (below) after cropping, cloning to fix mismatches, and using Levels and cloning to fix problems with the shading between images.

Photographer Carol Freeman

Okay, I know you're thinking, "Hey, if this is a supposed to be a book for digital photographers, why are we restoring old damaged photos taken 50 years before digital cameras were invented?" Well, a secret loophole

Get Back
photo restoration techniques

in my book contract enables me, once in every book, to cover a topic that doesn't fall within the general purview of the book. For example, in *Photoshop 7 Down & Dirty Tricks*, (New Riders, 2002) I included a full chapter called "Underrated breakfast cereals." So when you're working your way through this chapter, keep thinking to yourself, "Hey, this could be another cereal chapter." Then you'll find not only does this chapter fit, but on some level it fits so well that it makes you want to want to fix yourself a huge bowl of Kellogg's® Smart Start™. Besides, there's another useful loophole: the theory that once a torn, washed-out, scratched photo of your great-grandfather is scanned, it then becomes a "digital" torn, washed-out, scratched photo of your great-grandfather. And once you open it in Elements, you'll be engulfed with a burning desire to repair that photo. If I hadn't included this chapter on how to repair and restore these old photos, then where would you be, Mr. "Hey this is supposed to be a book for digital photographers" frumpy-pants? Don't you feel just a little guilty? I thought so. Now put down your spoon and start restoring some photos. (Note: My publisher told me that if I found a way to work the phrase "burning desire" into the book, it would increase sales by as much as 7%. If that somewhat suggestive phrase makes you uncomfortable, feel free to mentally replace "burning desire" with "uncontrollable urge" even though its response rate is more along the lines of 3 to 4%.)

Repairing Washed Out Photos

If you've got an old photo that's washed out, lacking detail, and generally so light that it's about unusable, try this amazingly fast technique to quickly bring back detail and tone.

Step One:
Open the washed out photo.

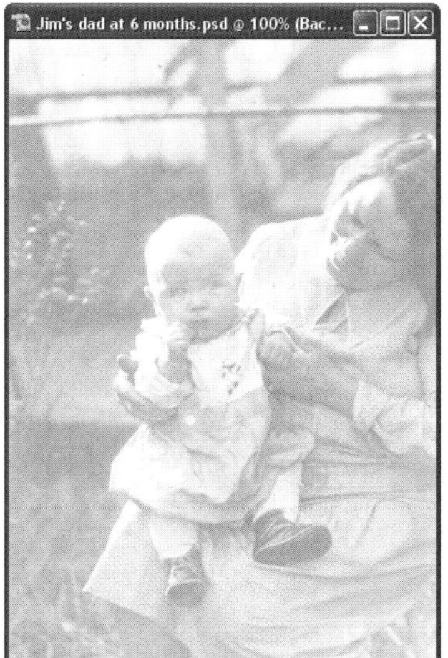

Step Two:
Duplicate the Background layer by dragging it to the Create New Layer icon at the bottom of the Layers palette. This creates a layer called "Background copy."

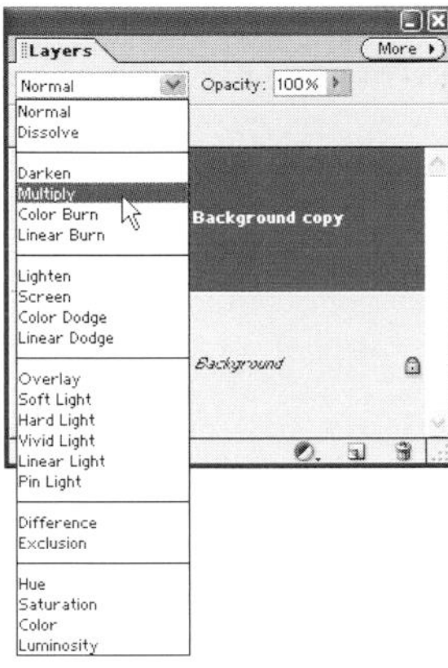

Step Three:
Change the Blend Mode of the Background copy layer by choosing Multiply from the pop-up menu at the top of the Layers palette. As the name implies, this has a "multiplier" effect that darkens the photo and brings back some of the tonal detail.

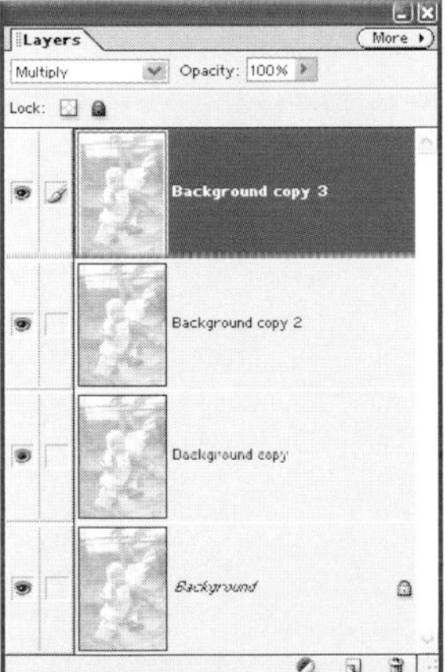

Step Four:
If the image is still too blown out, continue making copies of this duplicate layer in Multiply mode until the photo no longer looks washed out. If you add a layer and it looks a little too dark, then just lower the Opacity setting of this layer until it looks right.

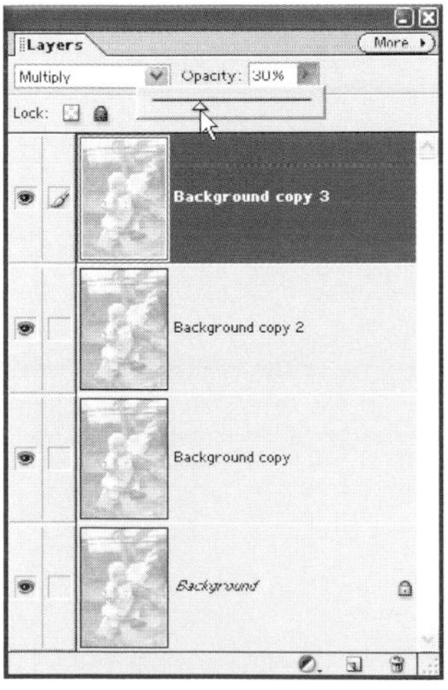

Step Five:
Now you may have a new problem—you've got a bunch of layers. The more layers you have, the larger your Elements file, and the larger your Elements file, the slower Elements goes, so there's no sense in having a bunch of extra layers. It just slows things down). So, once the photo looks good, go to the Layers palette, click the More button, and choose Flatten Image from the pop-down menu to flatten all those layers down into one Background layer.

Colorizing Black & White Photos

Once you've restored a photo, you might want to consider colorizing (hand tinting) the photo to bring added depth to it. This particular technique doesn't take a lot of Elements skills, it just takes a bit of patience, because colorizing a photo can take some time.

Step One:
Open the black-and-white photo you want to colorize.

Step Two:
To colorize a photo, your Elements image has to be in a color mode, so if your photo is in Grayscale mode (it will say "Gray" up in your document's Title Bar), you'll have to convert it to RGB mode by going under the Image menu, under Mode, and choosing RGB Color.

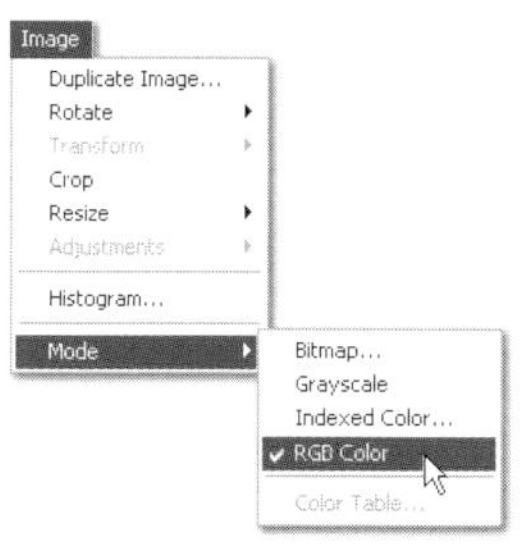

Step Three:
Use the Lasso tool to draw a selection around the first area within your photo that you want to colorize. Then go under the Select menu and choose Feather. When the Feather dialog appears, enter 1 pixel to soften the edge of your selection just a tiny bit, then click OK.

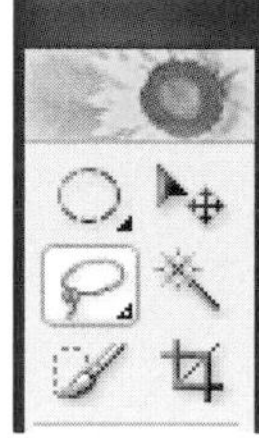

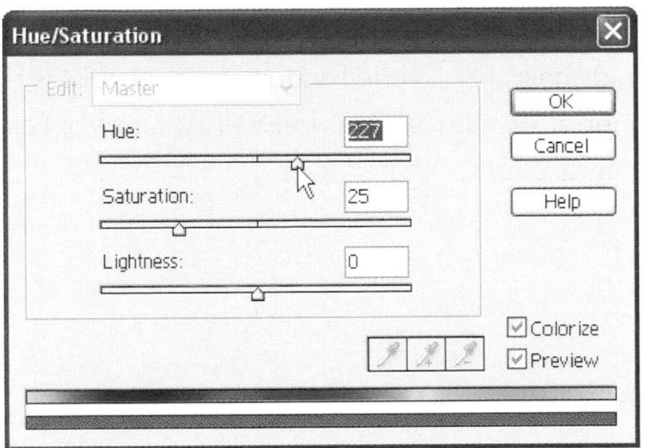

Step Four:
Go under the Enhance Menu, under Adjust Color, and choose Hue/Saturation. When the Hue/Saturation dialog box appears, click on the Colorize checkbox in the bottom right-hand corner of the dialog, then drag the Hue slider to the tint you'd like for this selected area.

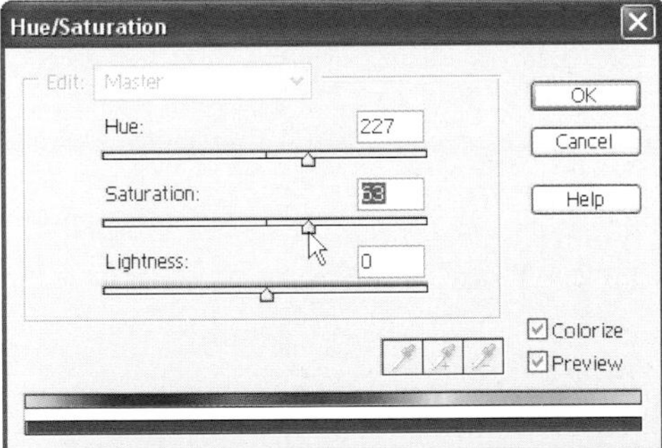

Step Five:
If the color looks too mild, drag the Saturation slider to the right. When it looks correct to you, click OK. Now you can deselect by pressing Control-D (Mac: Command-D).

Step Six:
You'll basically repeat this process to colorize the rest of the photo. Each time you select an area to be colorized, add a slight Feather, go to Hue/Saturation, click the Colorize checkbox, and choose your desired color using the Hue slider.

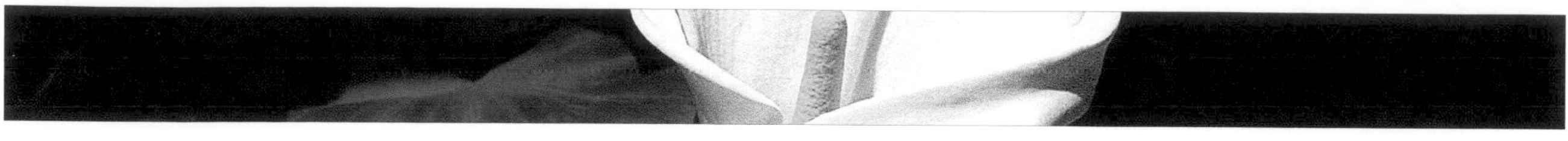

Removing Specks, Dust, and Scratches

If you've used Elements' Dust & Scratches filter, you've probably already learned how lame a filter it really is. That is, unless you use this cool workaround that takes it from a useless piece of fluff, to a...well...reasonably useful piece of fluff. This technique works brilliantly on background areas of your photos for removing these types of artifacts (that's "Elements-speak" for specks, dust, and other junk that winds up on your photos).

Step One:

Open the photo that need specks, dust, and scratches repaired. Duplicate the Background layer by dragging it to the Create New Layer icon at the bottom of the Layers palette. This creates a layer called Background copy.

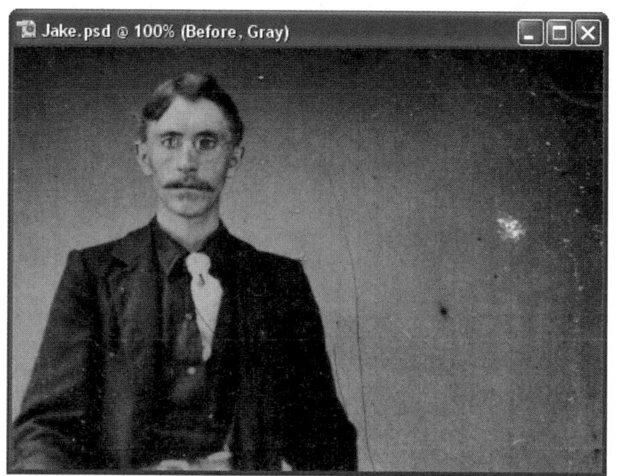

Step Two:

Go under the Filter menu, under Noise, and choose Dust & Scratches. When the Dust & Scratches dialog box appears, drag both sliders all the way to the left, then slowly drag the top one back to the right until the specks, dust, and scratches are no longer visible (most likely this will make your photo very blurry, but don't sweat it—make sure the specks are gone, no matter how blurry it looks, then click OK).

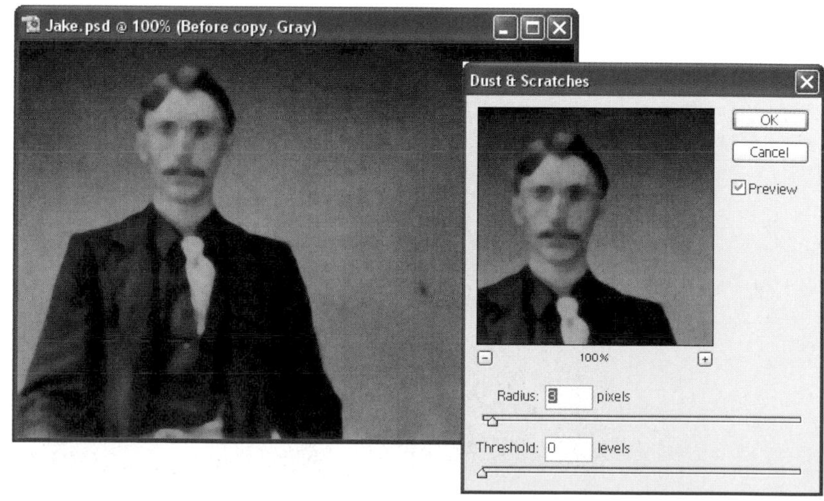

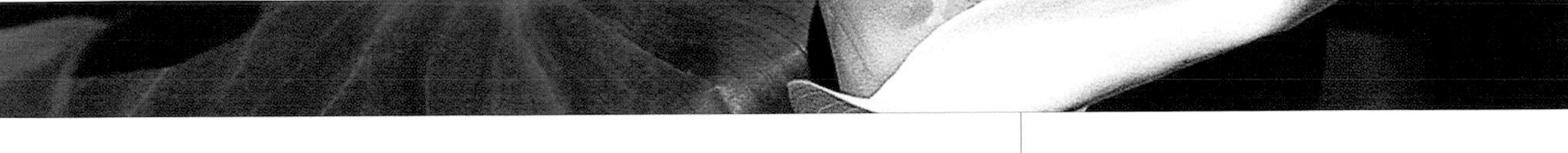

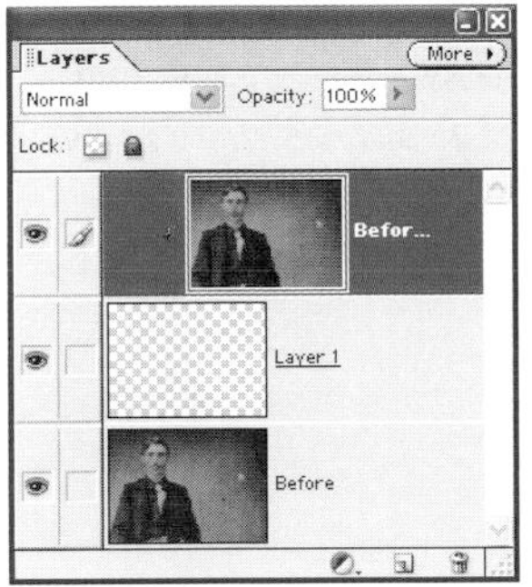

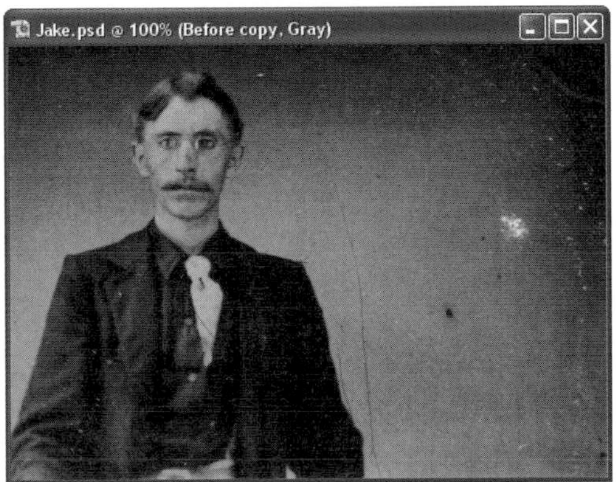

Step Three:

In the Layers palette, hold the Control key (Mac: Command key), and click on the Create New Layer icon to create a new blank layer beneath your current layer. Now, click back on the top layer, then press Control-G (Mac: Command-G) to Group your photo with the blank layer beneath it. Doing this hides the effect of the Dust & Scratches filter you applied earlier.

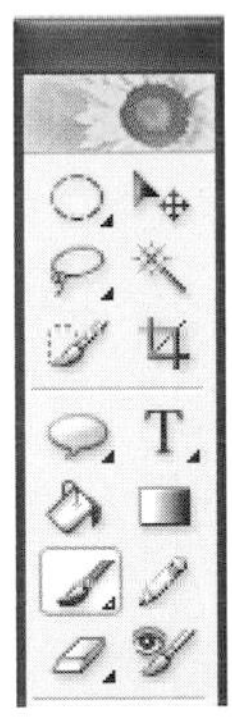

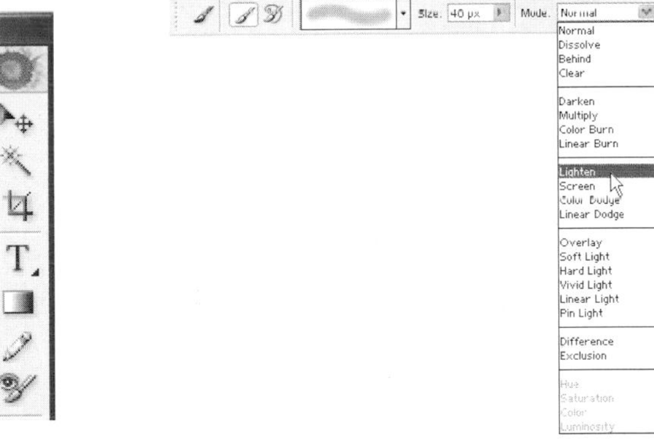

Step Four:

Press the letter "D" to set your Foreground color to black. Get the Brush tool from the Toolbox, then go up in the Options Bar and change the Blend Mode from Normal to Lighten. This changes the brush so that when you paint, it only affects the pixels that are darker than the area you're painting.

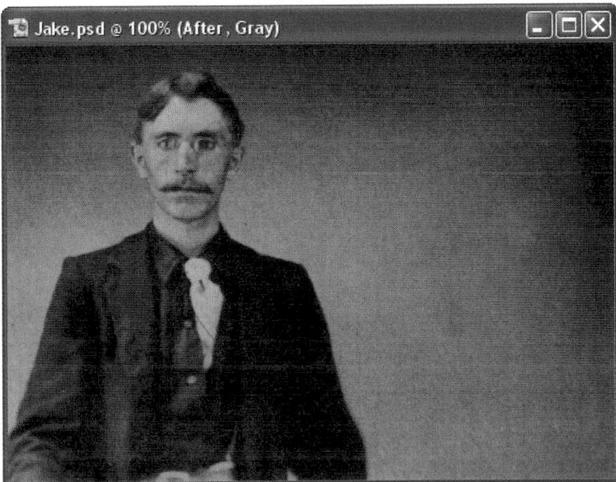

Step Five:

Click on the middle layer (you'll actually paint on this blank layer), then paint directly over the areas of your photo that have specks. As you paint, the specks and dust will disappear. Again, this technique works best on background areas, but it can also be useful for cleaning detailed areas. Just use a very small brush to minimize any blurring that may occur.

Repairing Damaged or Missing Parts

If you have an old photo with a serious rip, tear, stain, or other major anomaly, there's a reasonable chance that one of these little nasties could affect a part of your photo's main subject (for example, if it's a photo of a person, a stain could have a body part or facial feature covered, leaving you with quite a task). Here's how to repair missing or damaged parts, the easy way.

Step One:
Open the photo that contains a damaged feature (in this case, a missing eye and part of the face).

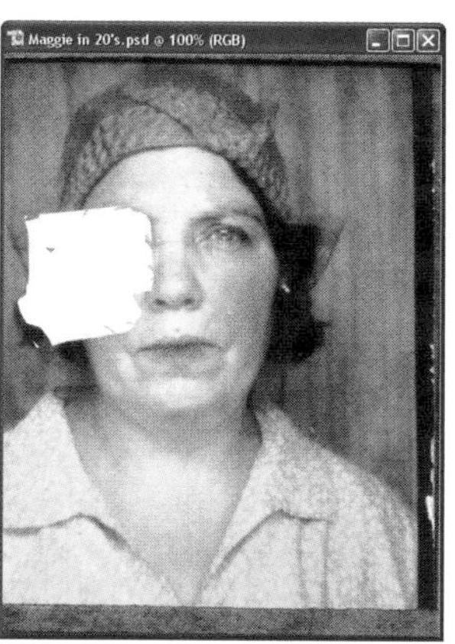

Step Two:
Use one of Elements' selection tools to select the undamaged part. In this example, I used the Lasso tool to make a selection around the left eye and cheek.

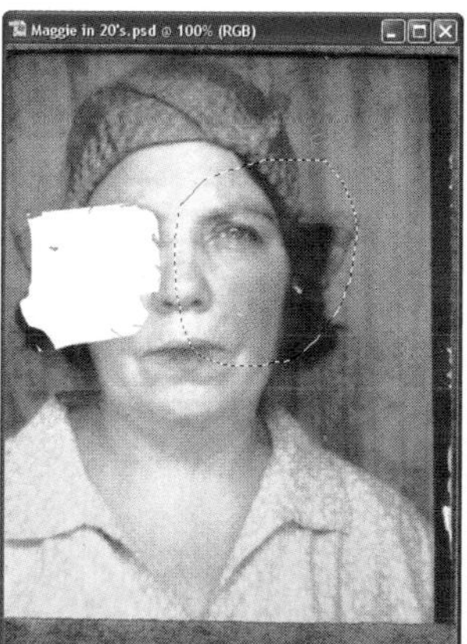

Step Three:
To keep from having a hard edge around the selected area, you'll need to apply a Feather to the edges of your selection. Go under the Select menu and choose Feather. When the dialog box appears, enter a Feather Radius. For low-res images use a 1- or 2-pixel Radius. For high-res, 300-ppi images, you can use as much as 4 or 5 pixels.

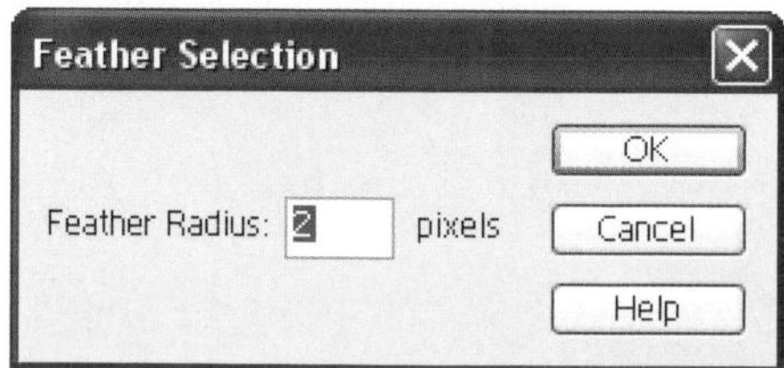

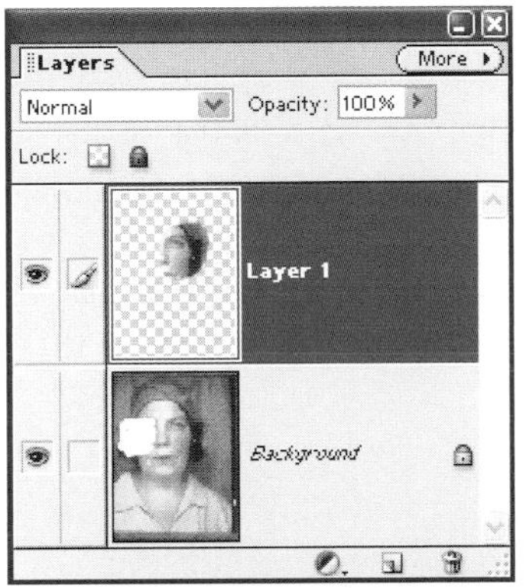

Step Four:

You'll need to duplicate the selection, so go under the Layer menu, under New, and choose Layer via Copy. This creates a new layer and copies your selected area to it.

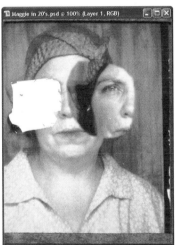

Step Five:

You can't just drag this patch over to fill the empty space because she'd wind up with two left eyes (leaving her looking slightly freakish). So, you'll need to flip the selection: Go under the Image menu, under Rotate, and choose Flip Layer Horizontal to turn your left eye and cheek into a right eye and cheek.

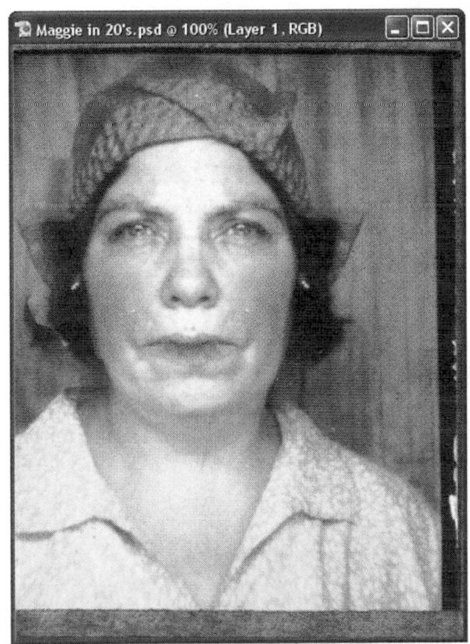

Step Six:

Now, switch to the Move tool and with the patch on its own layer, drag it over to where the empty space is. If you lower the Opacity of the patch layer to about 50%, it may help you to precisely position the patch because you'll be able to see some of the original features on the layer beneath it.

Repairing Rips and Tears

There are few things worse than rips, tears, or cracks from a photo being bent when it happens to old family photos you really care about. Here's a pair of simple techniques that let you hide these nasty rips by "covering them up."

Step One:

Open the photo with rips, tears, or bends. The photo shown here has cracks from being bent before it was scanned and opened in Elements.

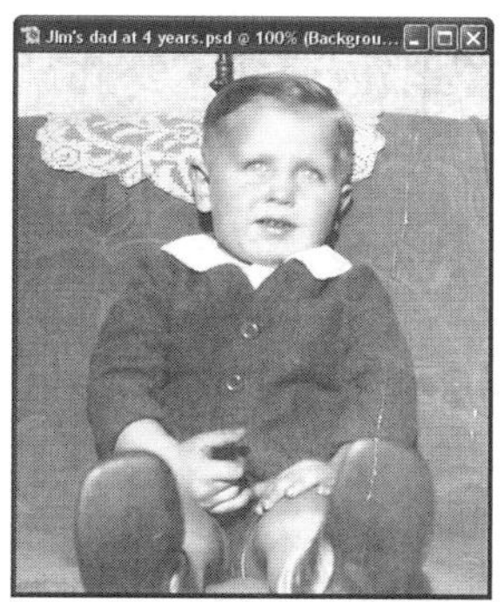

Step Two:

The plan is to clone over the cracks using non-cracked areas nearby. Start by getting the Clone Stamp tool from the Toolbox. Choose a medium to small, soft-edged brush from the Brush Picker in the Options Bar as shown.

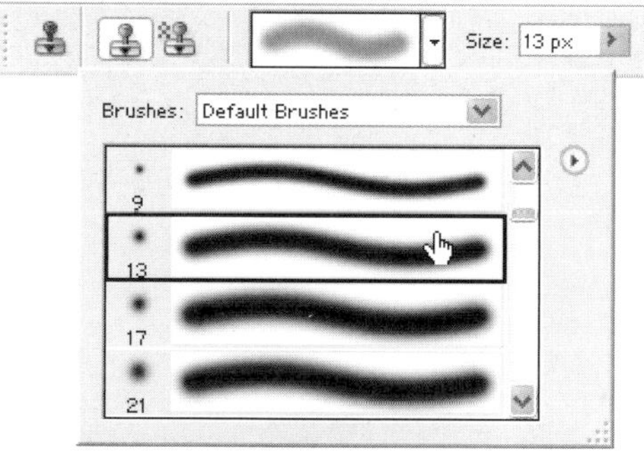

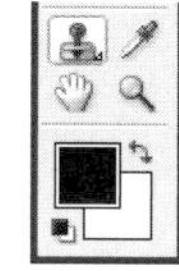

Step Three:

Hold the Alt key (Mac: Option key) and click in a "clean" area near the cracked area. (By clean, I mean Alt-/Option-click in an area that has no cracks or other visible problems. But to help ensure that your repair doesn't look obvious, it's important to click near the tear, and not too far away from it.)

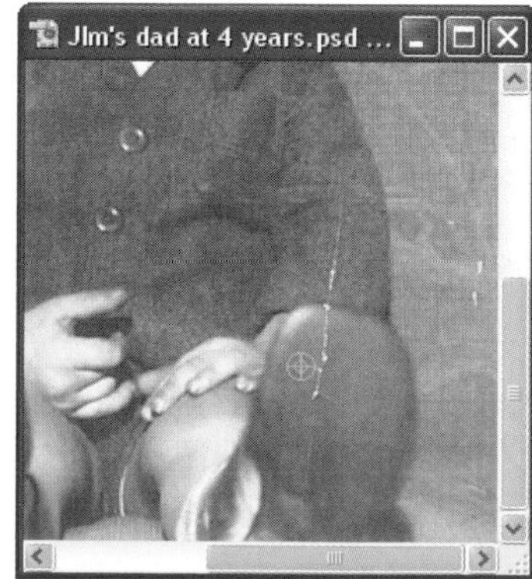

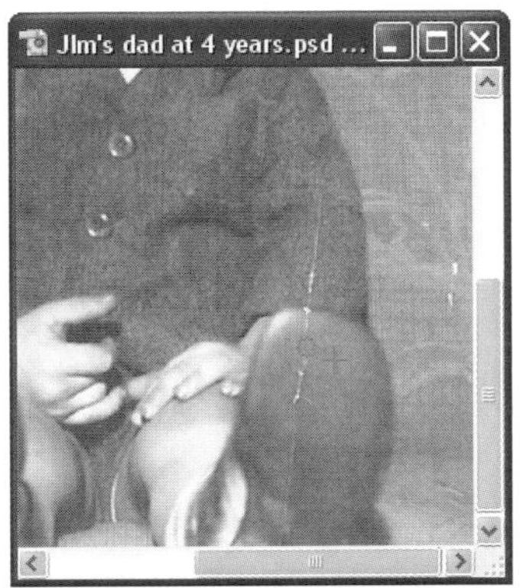

Step Four:
Now, move the Clone Stamp tool over the rip and begin painting (cloning) over the crack. As you paint, you'll see your brush cursor where you paint, and you'll also see a crosshair cursor at the same time, moving over the area you Alt-/Option-clicked on earlier. This lets you see the area you're cloning from (the crosshair) and the area you're cloning to (the brush cursor).

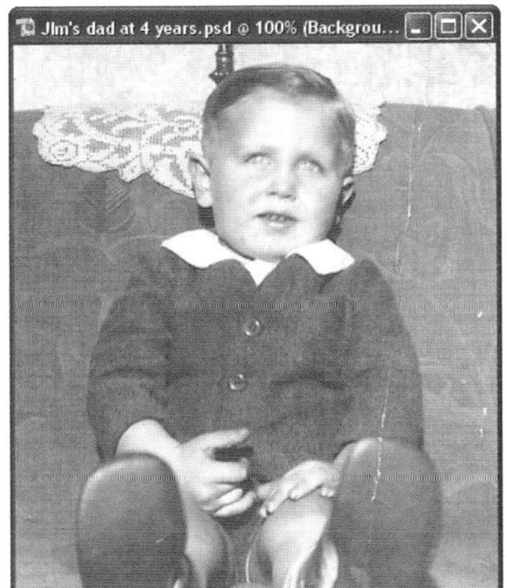

Before

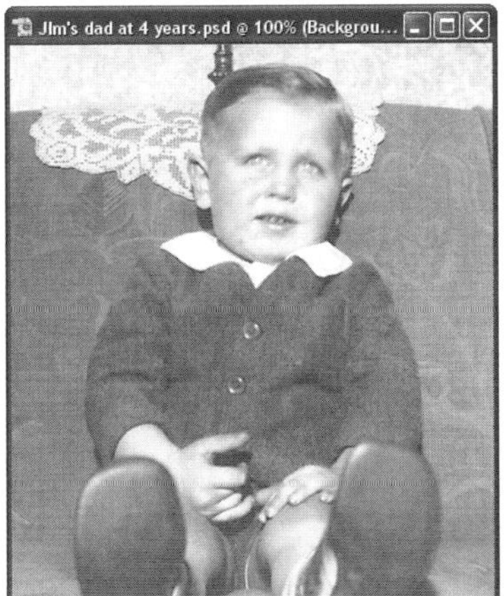

After

Step Five:
Now that you've learned "cloning," here's a tip that might help you hide the fact that you've been cloning. This tool seems to work best if, rather than painting, you Alt-/Option-click and then dab over the crack. Also, it will help "hide your retouch" if after you dab a little, you go and Alt-/Option-click in a slightly different area. This helps to keep your retouch looking more random. So when you come to the next crack, try this technique.

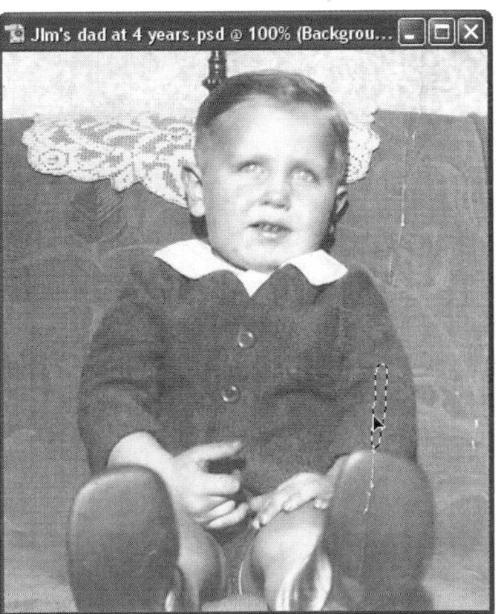

Alternate technique:
Another technique for hiding cracks and rips is to put a selection around a small part of the crack with the Lasso tool. While you still have the Lasso tool, click it inside the selected area, and drag the selection right beside the crack to a clean area. Then, go under the Select menu, choose Feather, and add a 2-pixel Feather. Next, hold Alt-Control (Mac: Option-Command), click inside the selected clean area, and drag a copy of that area over the rip, concealing it. Deselect by pressing Control-D (Mac: Command-D).

Photographer | Jim Patterson

You're about to learn some of the same sharpening techniques used by today's leading digital photographers and retouchers. Okay, I have to admit, not every technique in this chapter is a professional technique. For example,

Sharp Dressed Man

sharpening techniques

the first one, "Basic Sharpening," is clearly not a professional technique, although many professionals sharpen their images exactly as shown in that tutorial (applying the Unsharp Mask to the RGB composite—I'm not sure what that means, but it sounds good.) There's a word for these professionals—"lazy." But then one day, they think, "Geez, I'm kind of getting tired of all those color halos and other annoying artifacts that keep showing up in my sharpened photos," and they wish there was a way to apply more sharpening, and yet avoid these pitfalls. Then, they're looking for professional sharpening techniques that will avoid these problems—and the best of those techniques are in this chapter. But the pros are busy people, taking conference calls, getting pedicures, vacuuming their cats, etc., so they don't have time to do a series of complicated, time-consuming steps. So they create advanced functions that combine techniques. For some unexplainable sociological reason, when pros do this, it's not considered lazy. Instead, they're seen as "efficient, productive, and smart." Why? Because life ain't fair. How unfair is it? I'll give you an example. A number of leading professional photographers have worked for years to come up with these advanced sharpening techniques, which took tedious testing, experimentation, and research, and then you come along, buy this book, and suddenly you're using the same techniques they are, but you didn't even expend a bead of sweat. You know what that's called? Cool!

Basic Sharpening

After you've color corrected your photos and right before you save your file, you'll definitely want to sharpen your photos. I sharpen every digital camera photo, either to help bring back some of the original crispness that gets lost during the correction process, or to help fix a photo that's slightly out of focus. Either way, I haven't met a digital camera (or scanned) photo that I didn't think needed a little sharpening. Here's a basic technique for sharpening the entire photo.

Step One:

Open the photo that you want to sharpen. Because Elements displays your photo in different ways at different magnifications, it's absolutely critical that you view your photo at 100% when sharpening. To ensure that you're viewing at 100%, once your photo is open, double-click on the Zoom tool in the Toolbox, and your photo will jump to a 100% view (look up in the image window's Title Bar to see the actual percentage of zoom, circled at right).

© BRAND X PICTURES

Step Two:

Go under the Filter menu, under Sharpen, and choose Unsharp Mask. (If you're familiar with traditional darkroom techniques, you probably recognize the term "unsharp mask" from when you would make a blurred copy of the original photo and an "unsharp" version to use as a mask to create a new photo whose edges appeared sharper.) Of Elements' sharpening filters, Unsharp Mask is the undisputed first choice because it offers the most control over the sharpening process.

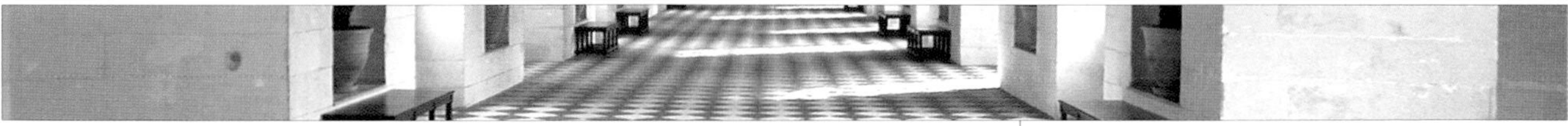

Step Three:

When the Unsharp Mask dialog box appears, you'll see three sliders. The Amount slider determines the amount of sharpening applied to the photo; the Radius slider determines how many pixels out from the edge the sharpening will affect; and the Threshold slider works the opposite of what you might think—the lower the number, the more intense the sharpening effect. Threshold determines how different a pixel must be from the surrounding area before it's considered an edge pixel and sharpened by the filter. So, what numbers do you put in it? I'll give you some great starting points on the following page, but for now, we'll just use these settings: Amount: 125%, Radius: 1, Threshold: 3. Click OK and the sharpening is applied to the photo. A Before and After is shown below.

Before sharpening

After sharpening

Continued

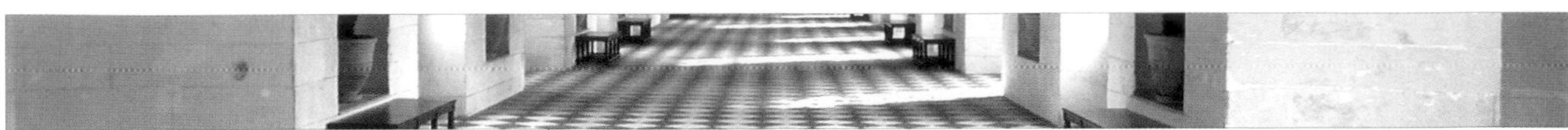

Sharpening Soft Subjects:
At right is an Unsharp Mask setting—Amount: 150%, Radius: 1, Threshold: 10—that works well for images where the subject is of a softer nature (e.g., flowers, puppies, people, rainbows, etc.). It's a subtle application of sharpening that is very well suited to these types of subjects.

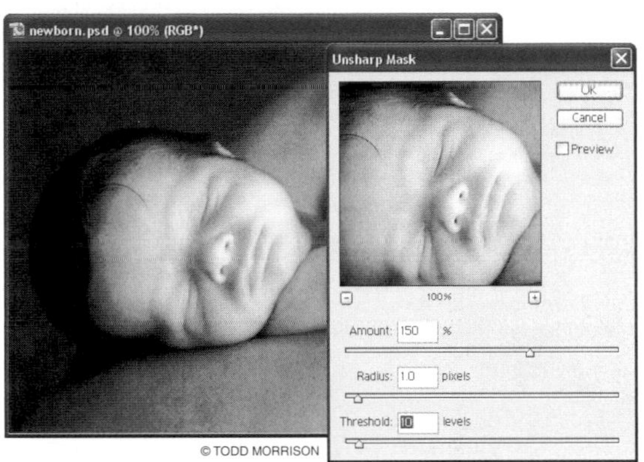

© TODD MORRISON

Sharpening Portraits:
If you're sharpening a close-up portrait (head and shoulders type of thing), try this setting—Amount: 75%, Radius: 2, Threshold: 3—which applies another form of subtle sharpening.

© TODD MORRISON

Moderate Sharpening:
This is a moderate amount of sharpening that works nicely on product shots, photos of home interiors and exteriors, and landscapes. If you're shooting along these lines, try applying this setting—Amount: 225%, Radius: .5, Threshold: 0—and see how you like it (my guess is—you will).

© BRAND X PICTURES

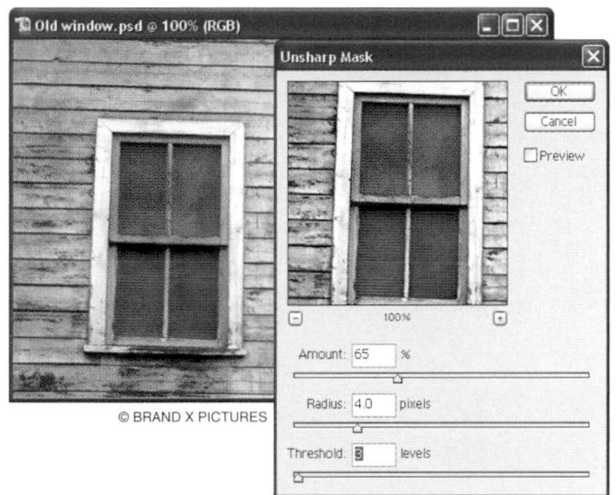

© BRAND X PICTURES

Maximum Sharpening:
I use these settings—Amount: 65%, Radius: 4, Threshold: 3—in only two situations: (1) The photo is visibly out of focus and it needs a heavy application of sharpening to try to bring it back into focus. (2) This high level of sharpening also works well where the photo contains lots of well-defined edges (e.g., buildings, coins, cars, machinery, etc.).

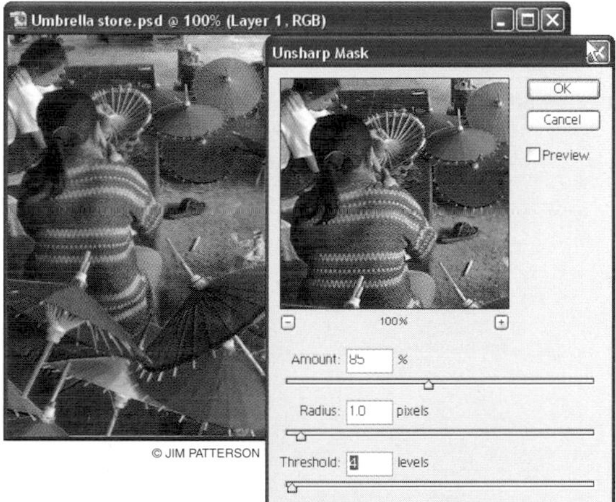

© JIM PATTERSON

All-Purpose Sharpening:
This is probably my all-around favorite sharpening setting—Amount: 85%, Radius: 1, Threshold: 4—and I use this one most of the time. It's not a "knock-you-over the-head" type of sharpening—maybe that's why I like it. It's subtle enough that you can apply it twice if your photo doesn't seem sharp enough the first time you run it, but once will usually do the trick.

© JIM PATTERSON

Web Sharpening:
I use this setting—Amount: 400%, Radius: 0.3, Threshold: 0—for Web graphics that look blurry. (When you drop the resolution from a high-res, 300-ppi photo down to 72 ppi for the Web, the photo often gets a bit blurry and soft.) If the effect seems too intense, try dropping the Amount to 200%. I also use this same setting (Amount 400%) on out-of-focus photos. It adds some noise, but I've seen it rescue photos that I would have otherwise thrown away.

Continued

Coming up with Your Own Settings:
If you want to experiment and come up with your own custom blend of sharpening, I'll give you some typical ranges for each adjustment so you can find your own sharpening "sweet spot."

Amount:
Typical ranges go anywhere from 50% to 150%. This isn't a rule that can't be broken, just a typical range for adjusting the Amount, where going below 50% won't have enough effect, and going above 150% might get you into sharpening trouble (depending on how you set the Radius and Threshold). You're fairly safe to stay under 150%.

Radius:
Most of the time, you'll use just 1 pixel, but you can go as high as (get ready)—2. You saw one setting I gave you earlier for extreme situations, where you can take the Radius as high as 4. I once heard a tale of a man in Cincinnati who used 5, but I'm not sure I believe it.

Threshold:
A pretty safe range for the Threshold setting is anywhere from 3 to around 20 (3 being the most intense, 20 being much more subtle. I know, shouldn't 3 be more subtle and 20 more intense? Don't get me started). If you really need to increase the intensity of your sharpening, you can lower the Threshold to 0, but keep a good eye on what you're doing (watch for noise appearing in your photo).

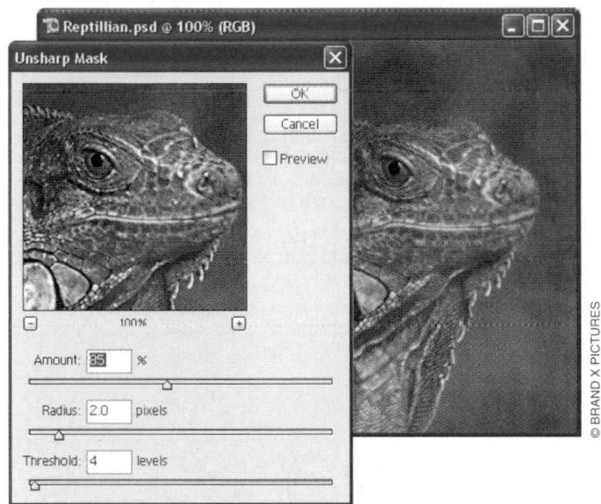

© BRAND X PICTURES

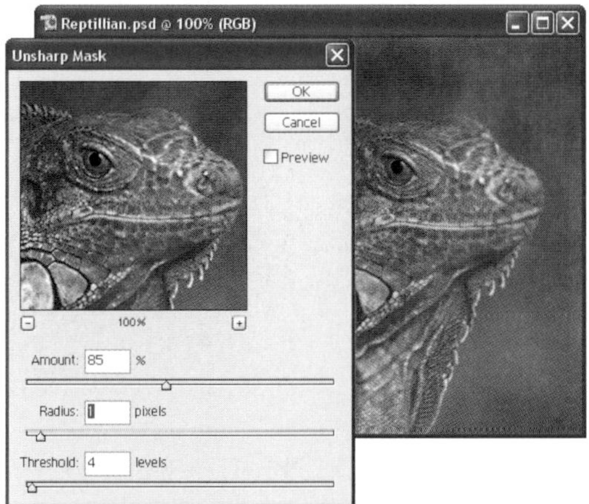

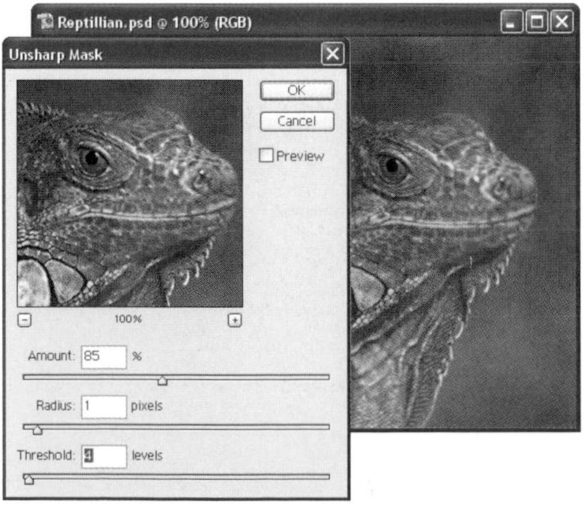

Luminosity Sharpening

Okay, you've already learned that sharpening totally rocks, but the more you use it, the more discerning you get about your sharpening (you basically become a sharpening snob), and at some point, you'll apply some heavy sharpening to an image and notice little color halos. You'll learn to hate these halos, and you'll go out of your way to get around them. In fact, you'll go so far as to use this next sharpening technique, which is fairly popular with pros shooting digital (at least with the sharpening snob crowd).

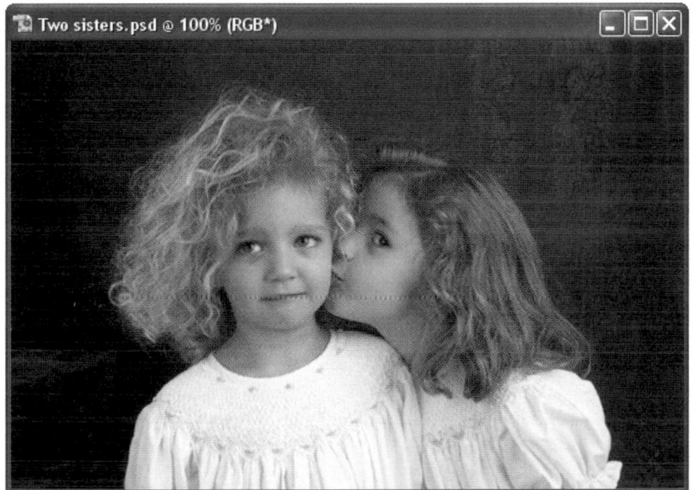

© TODD MORRISON

Step One:
Open a photo that needs some moderate to serious sharpening.

Step Two:
Duplicate the Background layer by going under the Layer menu, under New, and choosing Layer via Copy. This will duplicate the Background layer onto its own layer (Layer 1).

Continued

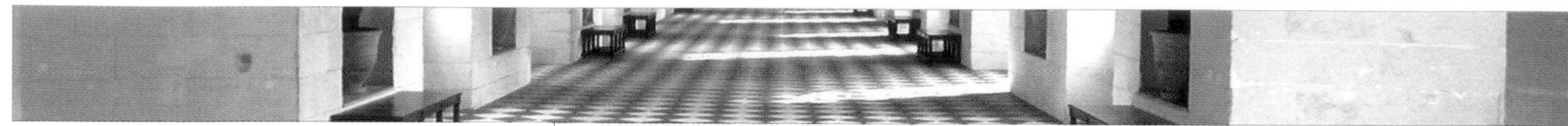

Step Three:
Go under the Filter menu, under Sharpen, and choose Unsharp Mask. After you've input your Unsharp Mask settings, click OK to apply the sharpening to the duplicate layer.

Note: If you're looking for some sample settings for different situations, look at the "Basic Sharpening" tutorial at the beginning of this chapter.

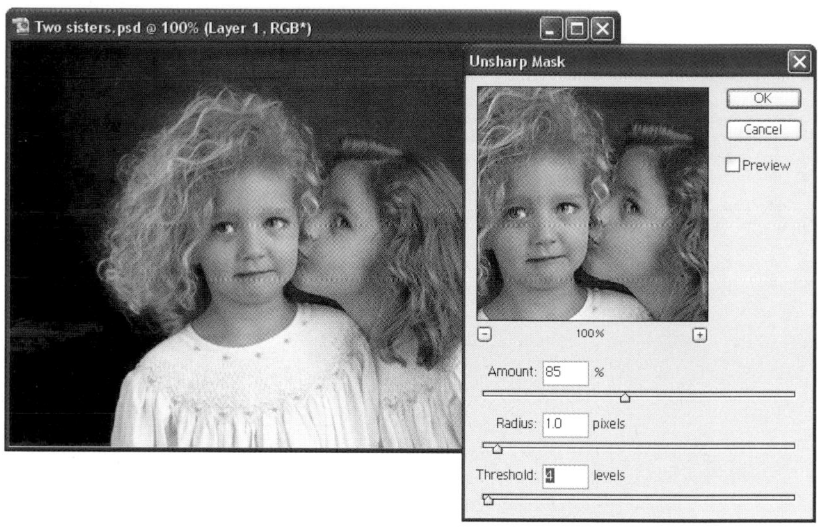

Step Four:
Go to the Layers palette and change the Blend Mode of this sharpened layer from Normal to Luminosity. By doing this, it applies the sharpening to just the luminosity (Lightness details) of the image, and not the color. This enables you to apply a higher amount of sharpening without getting unwanted halos that often appear when applying high levels of sharpening to color photos. You can now choose Flatten Image from the Layers palette's More pop-down menu to complete your Luminosity sharpening.

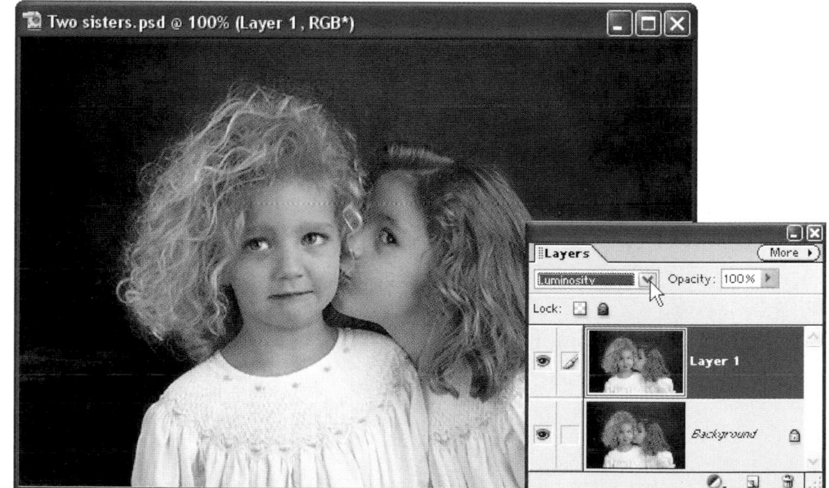

Edge Sharpening Technique

This is a sharpening technique that doesn't use the Unsharp Mask filter, but still leaves you with a lot of control over the sharpening, even after the sharpening is applied. It's ideal to use when you have an image that can really hold a lot of sharpening (a photo with a lot of edges), or one that really needs a lot of sharpening.

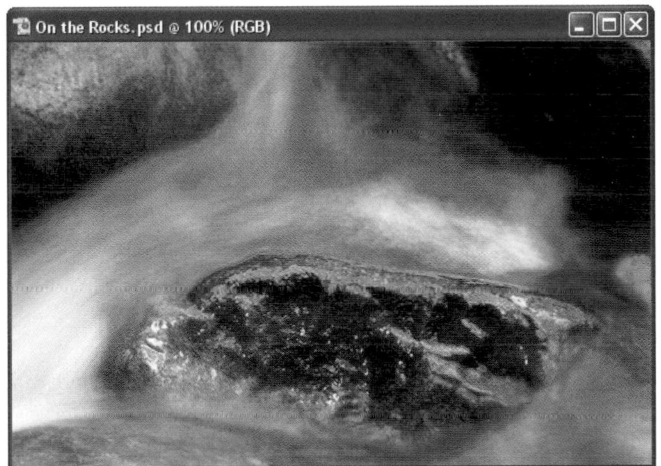

© BRAND X PICTURES

Step One:
Open a photo that needs edge sharpening.

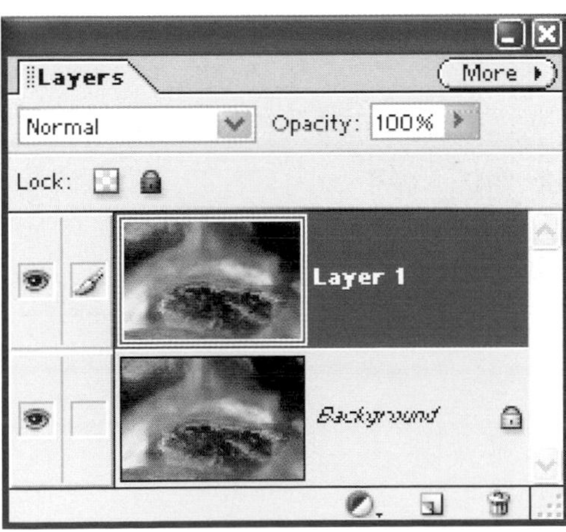

Step Two:
Duplicate the Background layer by going under the Layer menu, under New, and choosing Layer via Copy. This will duplicate the Background layer onto its own layer (Layer 1).

Continued

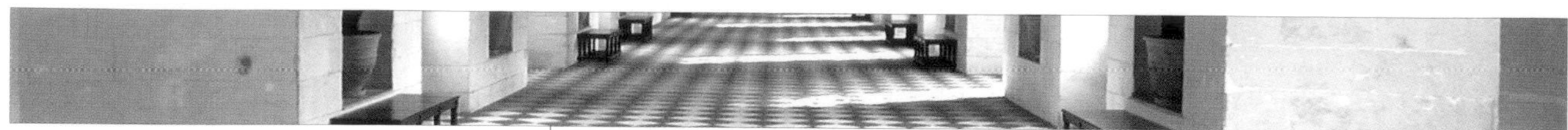

Step Three:
Go under the Filter menu, under Stylize, and choose Emboss. You're going to use the Emboss filter to accentuate the edges in the photo. You can leave the Angle and Amount settings at their defaults (135° and 100%) but if you want more intense sharpening, raise the Height amount from its default setting of 3 pixels to 5 or more pixels. Click OK to apply the filter, and your photo will turn gray, with neon-colored highlights along the edges.

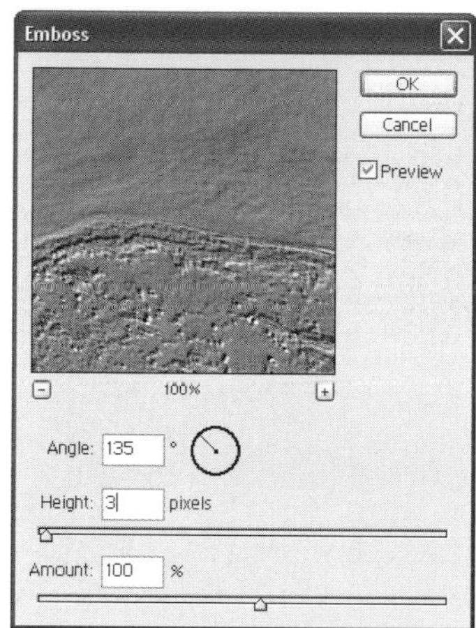

Step Four:
In the Layers palette, change the Blend Mode of this layer from Normal to Hard Light. This removes the gray color from the layer, but leaves the edges accentuated, making the entire photo appear much sharper.

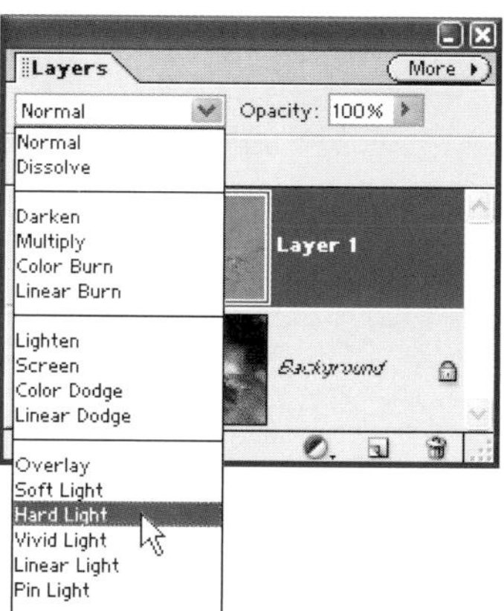

Step Five:
If the sharpening seems too intense, you can control the amount of the effect by simply lowering the Opacity of this layer in the Layers palette.

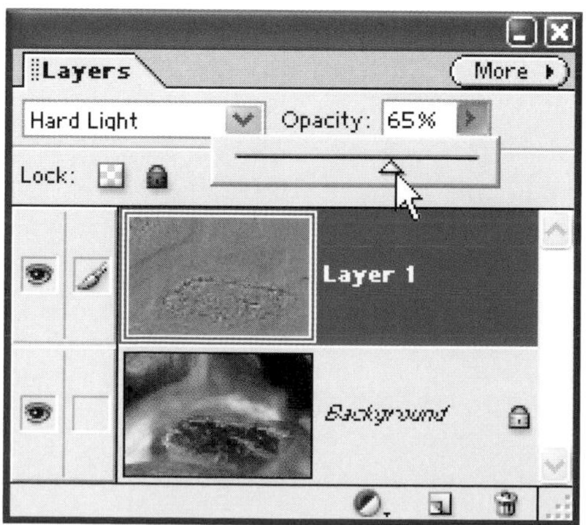

Here you can see your results.

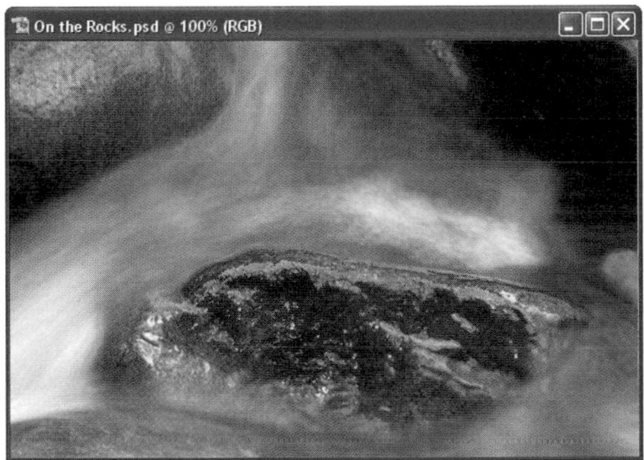

Before sharpening

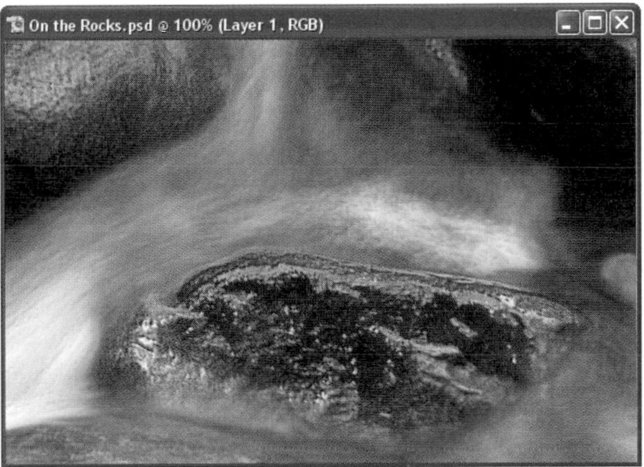

After sharpening

Sharpening with Layers to Avoid Color Shifts and Noise

This is another technique for avoiding noise and color shifts when sharpening, and this one also makes use of Layers and Blend Modes. The method shown here is a cross between a technique that I learned from Chicago-based retoucher, David Cuerdon, and one from Jim DiVitale, in one of his articles for *Photoshop User* magazine.

Step One:

Open the photo you want to sharpen using this technique. Duplicate the Background layer by going under the Layer menu, under New, and choosing Layer via Copy. This will duplicate the Background layer onto its own layer (Layer 1).

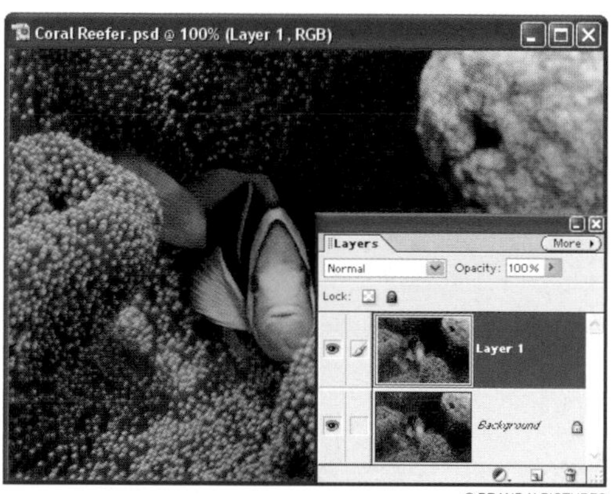

© BRAND X PICTURES

Step Two:

Change the Blend Mode of this duplicate layer to Luminosity (as shown).

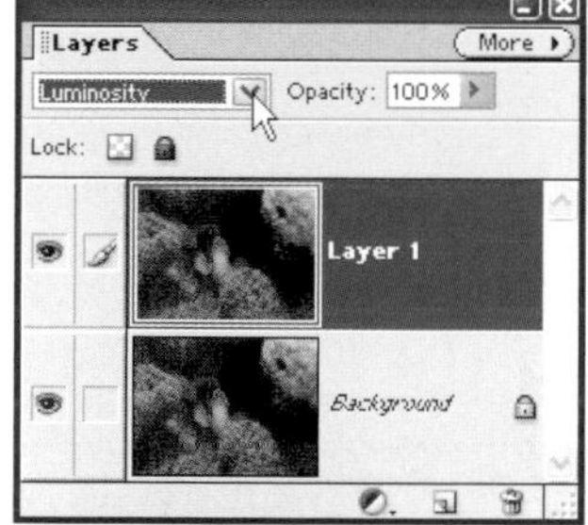

Step Three:

Apply the Unsharp Mask filter to this duplicate layer. (If you've read this far, you already know which settings to use, so have at it.)

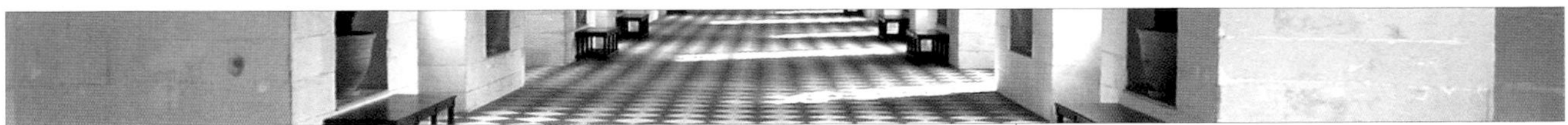

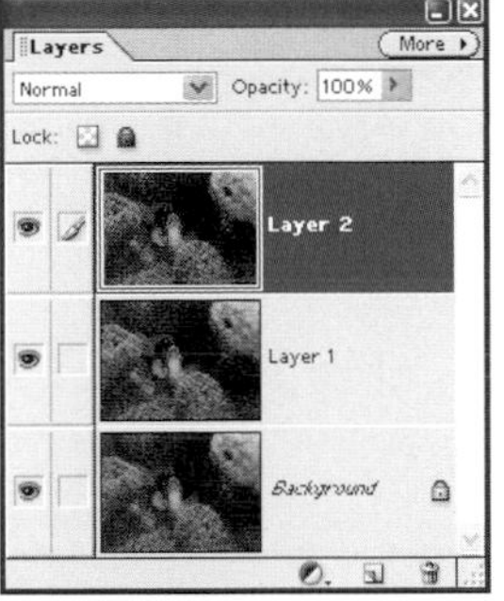

Step Four:

Now, duplicate this sharpened luminosity layer by going under the Layer menu, under New, and choosing Layer via Copy. This will duplicate the Background layer onto its own layer (Layer 2.)

Step Five:

Go under the Filter menu, under Blur, and choose Gaussian Blur. When the dialog box appears, enter 3 pixels to add a slight blur to the photo. If this setting doesn't make your photo look as blurry as the one shown here, increase the amount of blur until it does. This hides any halo, or noise, but obviously, it makes the photo really blurry.

Step Six:

To get rid of the blur on this layer, but keep the good effects from the blurring (getting rid of the noise and halos), change the Blend Mode of this blurred layer from Normal to Color. Zoom in on edge areas that would normally have halos or other color shifts and you'll notice the problems just aren't there. Now you can flatten the photo and move on. Note: In some cases this technique mutes some of the red in your photo. If you notice a drop-out in red, lower the Opacity of the blurred layer until the color is restored.

Photographer | Jeannie Theriault

Okay, you've sorted and categorized the photos from the shoot; you've backed up your digital negs to CD; and you've color corrected, tweaked, toned, sharpened, and otherwise messed with your photo until it

The Show Must Go On

showing it to your clients

is, in every sense of the word, a masterpiece. But now it's time to show it to the client. Hopefully, you'll get to show it to the client in person, so you can explain in detail the motivation behind collaging a 4x4 monster truck into an otherwise pristine wedding photo. (Answer: Because you can.) There's a good chance they'll see the photo first on your screen, so I included some cool tricks on how to make your presentation look its very best (after all, you want those huge 122″ tires to look good), and I even included some techniques on how to provide your own online proofing service using Photoshop Elements (in case your clients smell bad, and you don't want them coming back to your studio and stinkin' up the place). This is the last chapter in the book, so I want you to really sop up the techniques (like you're using a big ol' flaky biscuit) because once you're done with this chapter, once you've come this far, there's no turning back. At this point, some people will start to scour their studio, searching for that one last roll of traditional print film, probably knocking around at the bottom of some drawer (or hidden in the back of the refrigerator, behind some leftover Mu Shu Pork), so they can hold it up toward the light, smile, and begin laughing that hysterical laugh that only people truly on the edge can muster. These people are not Kodak shareholders.

Watermarking and Adding Copyright Info

This two-part technique is particularly important if you're putting your photos on the Web and want some level of copyright protection. In the first part of this technique, you'll add a see-through watermark, so you can post larger photos without fear of having someone download and print them; and secondly, you'll embed your personal copyright info so if your photos are used anywhere on the Web, your copyright info will go right along with the file.

Step One:

We're going to start by creating a template. Open a new document, in RGB mode, in your typical working resolution (72 ppi for low-res, 300 ppi for high-res, etc.). Click on the Foreground color swatch (at the bottom of the Toolbox) and choose a medium gray color in the Color Picker, then click OK. Now, press Alt-Backspace (Mac: Option-Delete) to fill the Background layer with your medium gray. Press the letter "D" to make your Foreground color black.

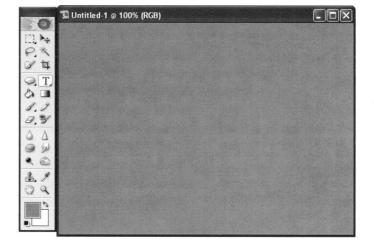

Step Two:

Get the Type tool and choose a font like Arial Bold or Helvetica Bold. In the Options Bar, click on the Center Text option. Hold the Alt key and type 0169 (Mac: Option-G) to create a copyright symbol. Then, press Enter (Mac: Return) to move your type cursor to the next line, and type in your name (or the name you want to have for the copyright on the photo). Hide the Background layer from view by going to the Layers palette and clicking on the Eye icon in the first column beside the Background layer.

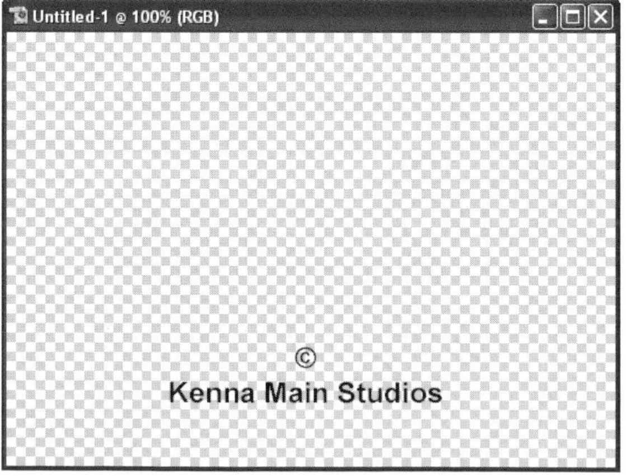

Step Three:
Highlight your name (but not the copyright symbol) and increase the size of your name to the size you'd like by using the Size pop-up menu up in the Options Bar. When it's at the right size, highlight the copyright symbol, and resize it upward until it's quite a bit larger than your name (as shown). In the example shown here, the type is 48 point and the copyright symbol is 200 point in size.

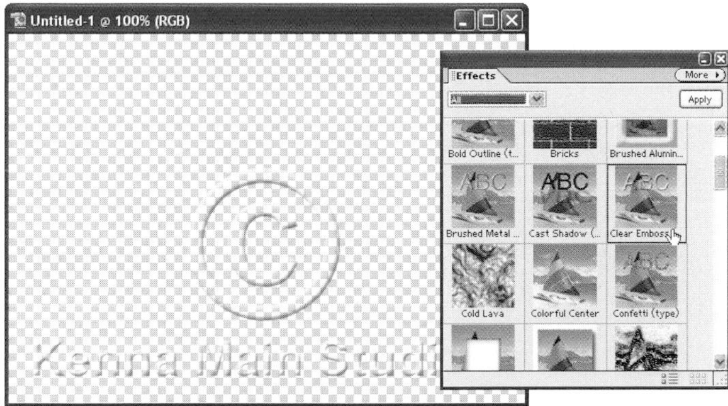

Step Four:
Go to the Effects palette (if it's not visible, go under the Window menu and choose Effects). Double-click on the effect named Clear Emboss. This applies a beveled effect, and makes the fill transparent.

Step Five:
Now you can make the Background layer visible again by going to the Layers palette and clicking in the first column where the Eye icon used to be. You can now see the Clear Emboss effect clearly (okay, that was pretty lame).

Continued

Step Six:
Open the photo you want to contain this transparent watermark.

© BRAND X PICTURES

Step Seven:
Make sure this photo, and the document with your embossed watermark, are both visible within Elements. Switch to the Move tool, then click-and-drag the large copyright symbol (in the embossed watermark document), and drop it onto your photo (you're dragging a layer between documents).

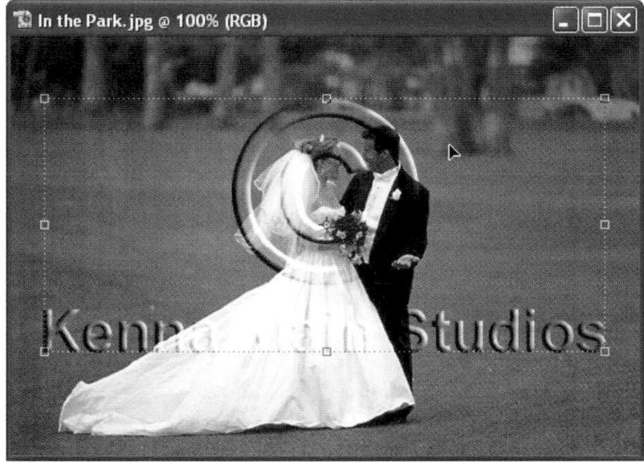

Step Eight:
Once the copyright symbol is in your new document, you can resize it as needed. Just press Control-T (Mac: Command-T) to bring up Free Transform and click-and-drag one of the corner adjustment points. Add the Shift key to resize it proportionately. Press Enter (Mac: Return) to complete your transformation. Use the Move tool if you need to reposition the symbol and text.

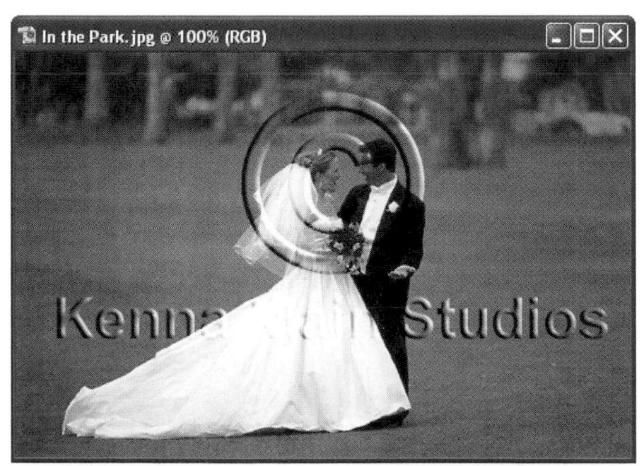

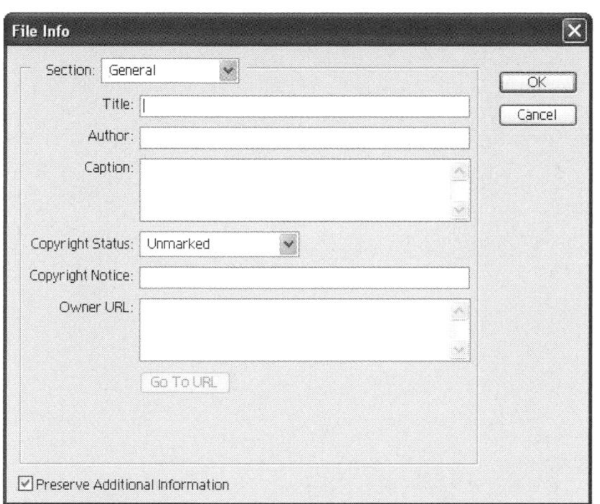

Step Nine:

Now for the second part—we'll embed your personal copyright info into the photo file itself. Go under the File menu and choose File Info to bring up the File Info dialog box (shown here). This is where you enter information that you want embedded into the file itself. This embedding of info is supported by all the major file formats on the Windows platform (such as TIFF, JPEG, EPS, PDF, and Photoshop's native file format) and it's supported by all Macintosh file formats.

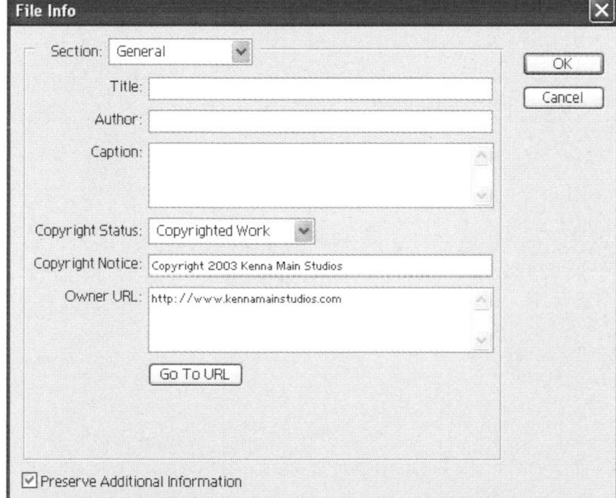

Step Ten:

In the File Info dialog, change the Copyright Status pop-up menu from Unmarked to Copyrighted Work (as shown). In the Copyright Notice field, enter your personal copyright info, and then under Owner URL enter your full Web address. That way, when someone opens your file in Elements, they can go to File Info, click the Go To URL button, and it will launch their browser and take them directly to your site.

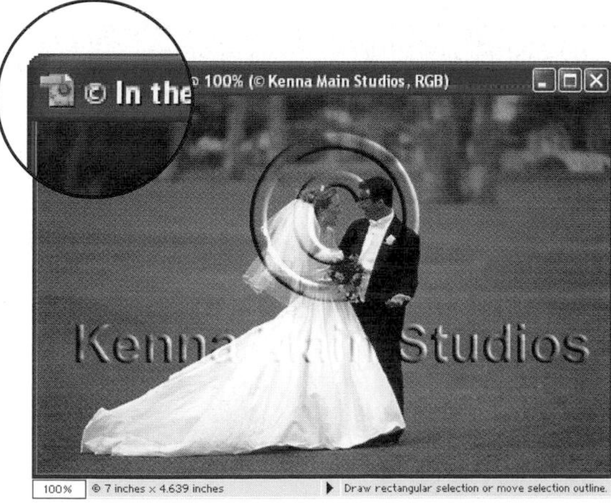

Step Eleven:

Click OK and the info is embedded into the file. Once copyright info has been added to a file, Elements automatically adds a copyright symbol before the file's name which appears in the photo's Title Bar (as shown here).

Putting Your Photos up on the Web

Elements has a built-in feature that not only automatically optimizes your photos for the Web, it actually builds a real HTML document for you, with small thumbnail images, links to large full-size proofs, e-mail contact back to you, and more. All you have to do is upload it to the Web and give your friends (or clients) the Web address for your new site. Here's how to make your own.

Step One:
Put all the photos you want to appear on your Web site into one folder.

Step Two:
Go under the File menu and choose Create Web Photo Gallery (as shown).

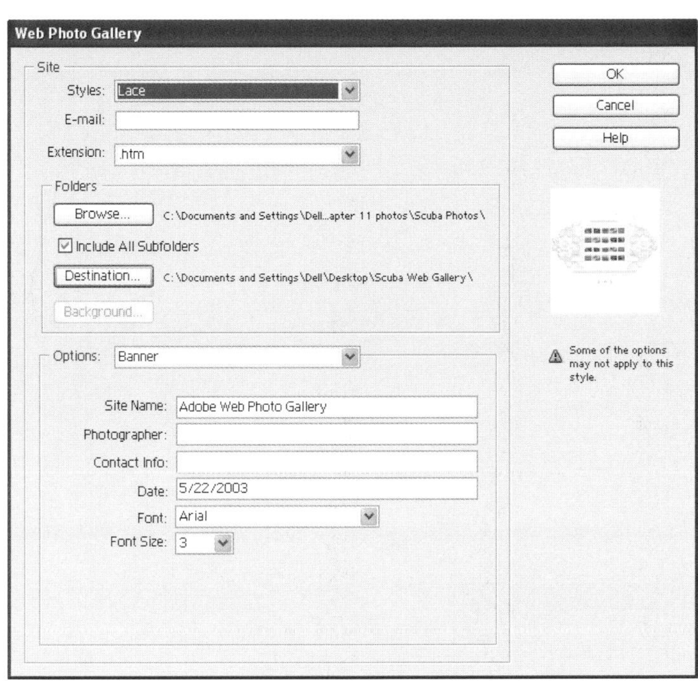

Step Three:

This brings up the Web Photo Gallery dialog. At the top is a pop-up list of Styles (presets) where you can choose from different Web page layouts. A thumbnail preview of each template appears in the far right column of the dialog (below the Help button) as you choose the different Styles. In this example, I chose Lace (as a silent tribute to the former WWF star), which creates a Web site that looks, well… "delicate." (My wife wouldn't let me use the term "wussy" which more adequately describes it.) It's perfect for photos of puppies, rainbows, fuzzy bunnies, missile systems, etc. Just below the Styles pop-up menu is a field for entering your e-mail address (which will appear prominently on your Web page), so people who visit your site can easily contact you (especially important if you're putting up client proofs).

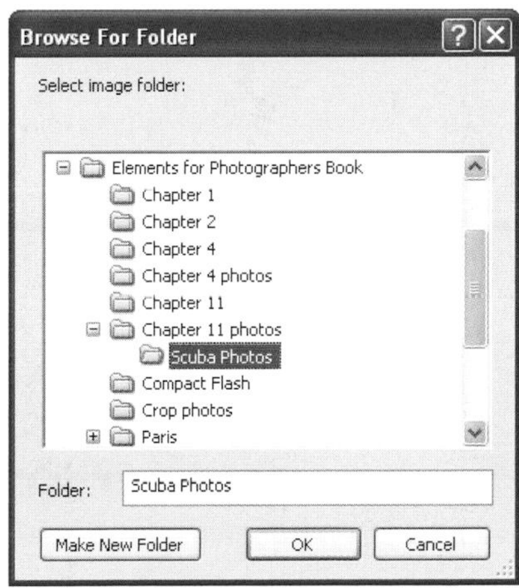

Step Four:

In the Folders section of the Web Gallery dialog, you specify the location of the folder of photos you want to put on the Web, and you determine which folder these Web-optimized images will reside in for uploading. When you click the Browse (Mac: Choose) button, a dialog appears prompting you to Select Image Folder (the folder full of photos). Locate the folder and click OK (Mac: Choose) as shown. When you click the Destination button, a dialog appears prompting you to select a destination location. Locate a folder that you want to save your Web files into and click OK (Mac: Choose).

Continued

Step Five:
In the Options section of the dialog, choose Banner from the pop-up menu to enter the headlines and subheads for the site (as shown here). Next, from the Options pop-up menu, choose Large Images (shown in the capture in Step Six).

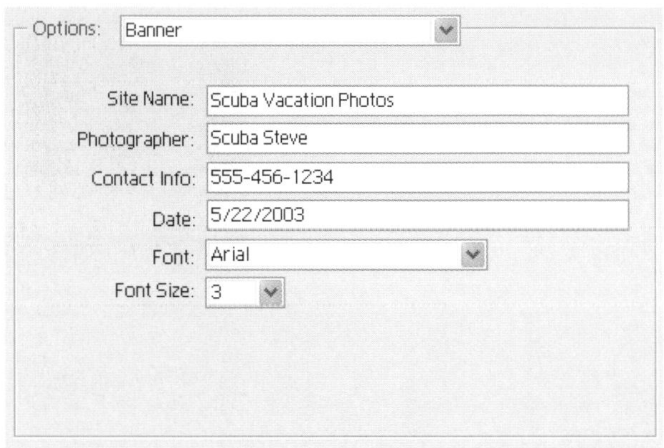

Step Six:
The Large Images Options area is where you choose the final size and quality of the full-size photos displayed on your Web page. You can also choose titles to appear under each photo in the Titles Use section. I recommend checking the Copyright Notice checkbox, which will display your copyright info under each photo.

Note: For this to work, you have to embed your copyright info in the photo first, by going under the File menu, choosing File Info, and entering your copyright text in the Copyright field. (See "Watermarking and Adding Copyright Info" at the beginning of this chapter.)

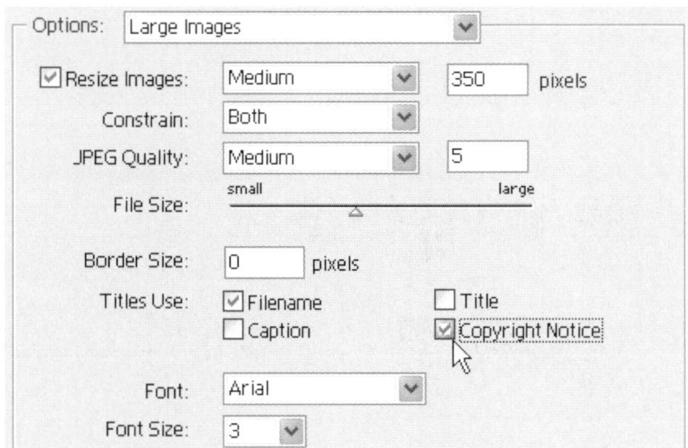

Step Seven:
Change the Options pop-up menu to Security, then in the Content pop-up menu choose Custom Text. This makes available the Custom Text field where you can enter text that will appear right across your large size photo. This is where you might add things like "Proof Copy," "Not for Printing," or "Not for Duplication." You can also specify the Font Size, Color, Opacity, and Position in this section.

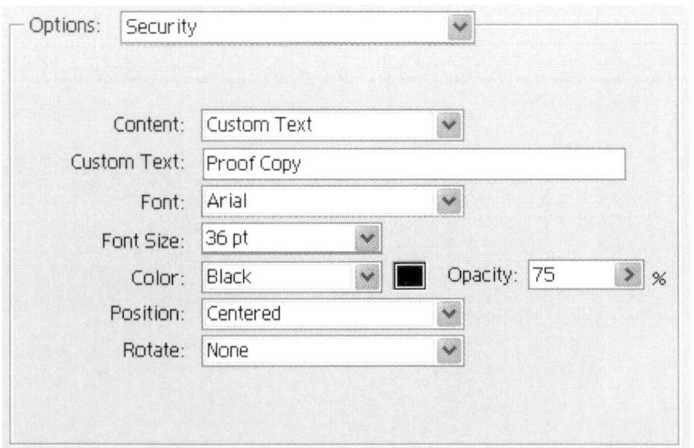

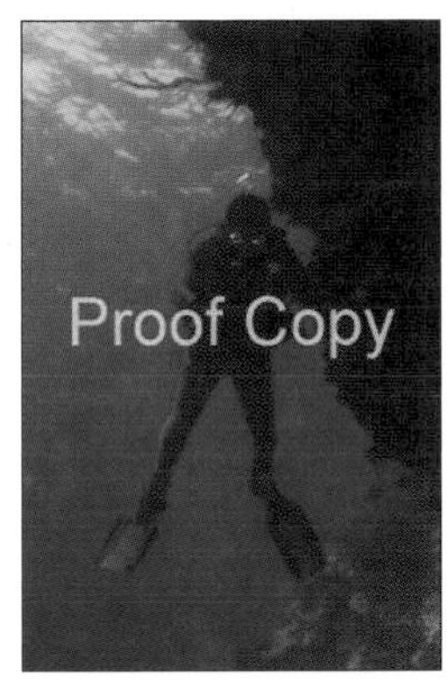

©BRAND X PICTURES

Step Eight:

When you add custom text, here's how that text will appear over your photo.

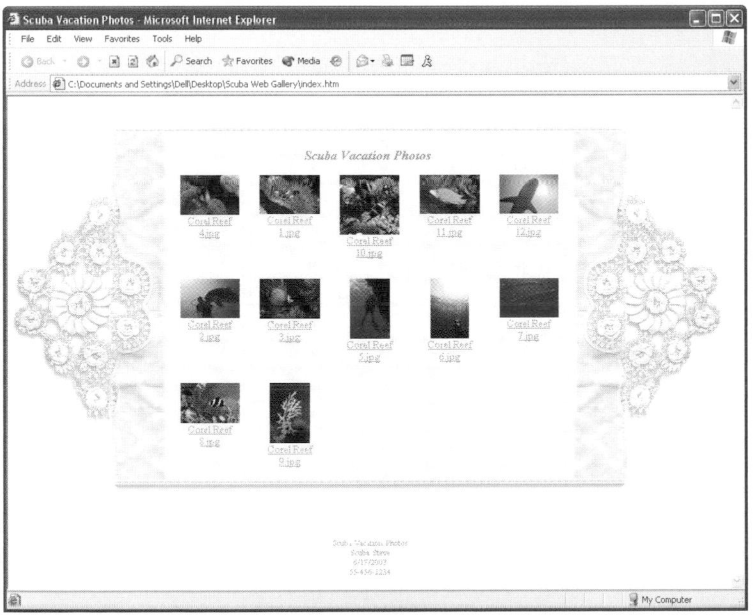

Step Nine:

Click OK and Elements will do its thing—resizing the photos, adding custom text, making thumbnails, etc. Then it will automatically launch your Web browser and display the HTML Web page it created for you. Here you can see the Site Name (which you entered in the Banner Options) centered at the top of the Web page. Your e-mail address appears with a live link at the bottom of the page (if your client clicks it, it will open their e-mail with your e-mail address already entered in the "To:" field). It displays a thumbnail of each photo that you can click on to view the full-size proof (with your custom text appearing over it) and the file's title (which is important so the client can tell you which photos they want). Below that is the Copyright info (taken from the embedded File Info for that photo), and at the bottom of the page is your phone number (so you can get dates).

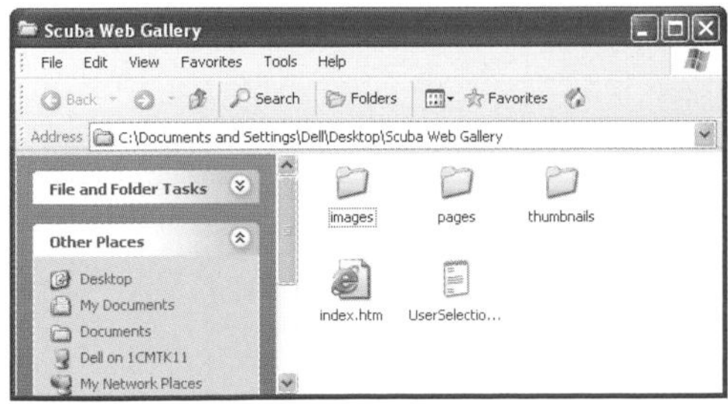

Step Ten:

Elements automatically creates all the files and folders you'll need (shown here) to put your Web Gallery up live on the Web, including your home page (index.htm), and puts them neatly in your destination folder ready for uploading.

Getting One 5"x7," Two 2.5" x 3.5"s, and Four Wallet Size on One Print

I've often joked that we're now one click away from becoming a "Sears Portrait Studio" since Adobe invented the "Picture Package" feature, which lets you gang-print common final sizes together on one sheet. With Picture Package, Elements does all the work for you. All you have to do is open the photo you want ganged and then Elements will take it from there; except for the manual cutting of the final print, which is actually beyond Elements' capabilities. So far.

Step One:

Open the photo you want to appear in a variety of sizes on one page, then go under the File menu, under Print Layouts, and choose Picture Package (the Picture Package dialog is shown here). At the top of the dialog, the Source block asks which photo you want to use as your Source photo. By default, if you have a photo open, it assumes that's the one you want to use (your Frontmost Document), but you can choose from the Use pop-up menu to use photos in a folder, or an individual file on your drive. By default, Picture Package chooses an 8x10 Page Size for you, but you can also choose either a 10x16 or 11x17 Page Size.

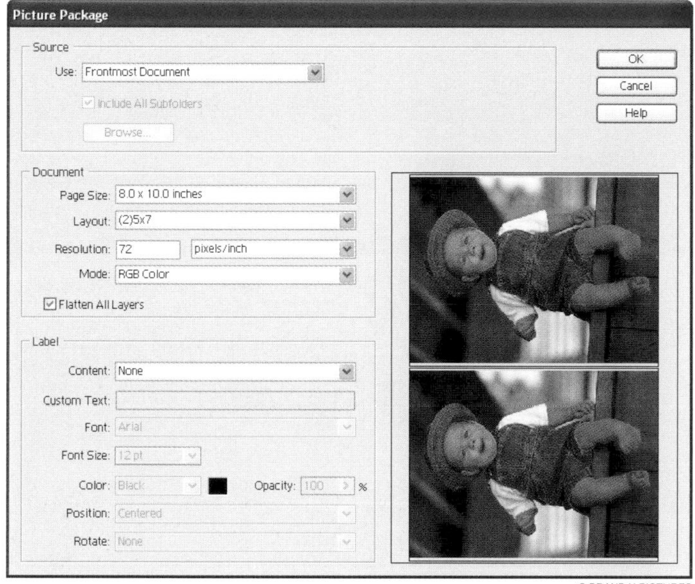

© BRAND X PICTURES

Step Two:

You choose the sizes and layout for your Picture Package from the Layout pop-up menu (shown here). In this example, I chose (1) 5x7 (2) 2.5x3.5 and (4) 2x2.5, but you can choose any combination you like.

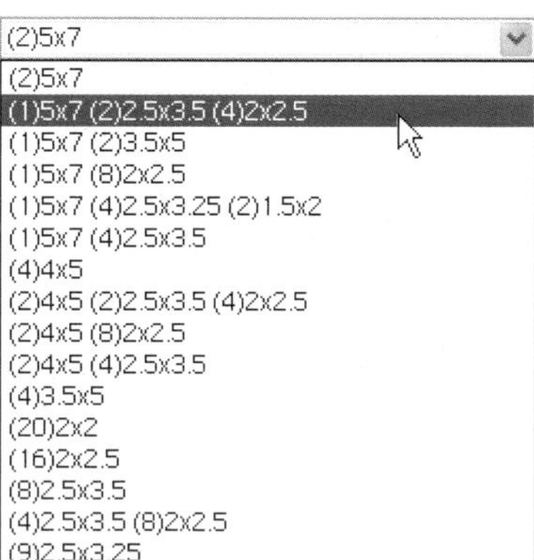

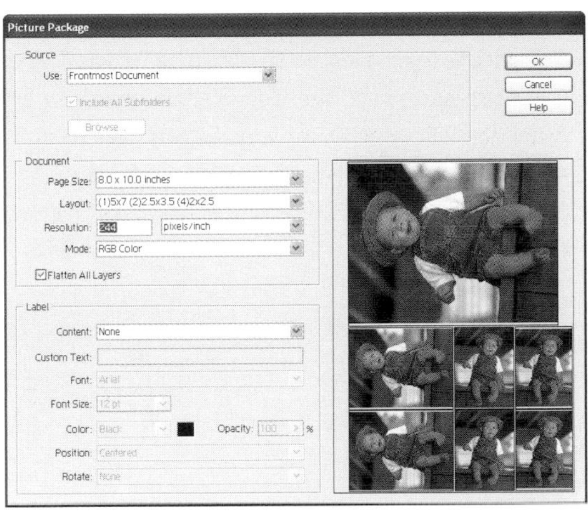

Step Three:

When you choose a layout, a large preview of the layout you've selected appears in the right column of the dialog. You can also choose the final output resolution you'd like in the Resolution field, and for the Color Mode you can choose either RGB (for full-color prints) or Grayscale (for B&W photos).

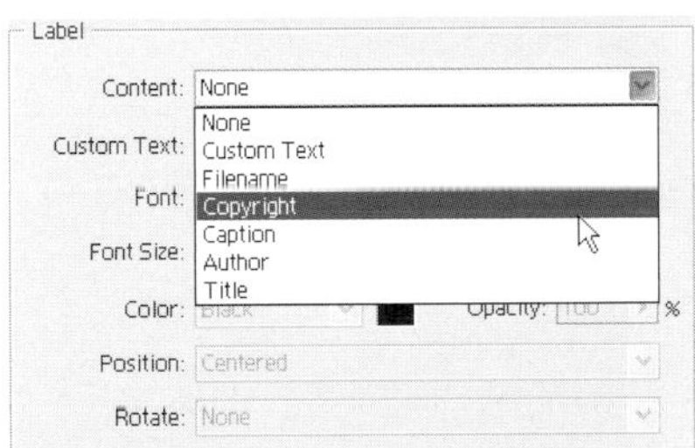

Step Four:

The bottom-left section of the dialog is for labeling your photos, but be forewarned—these labels appear printed right across your photos, so use these only if you're creating client proof sheets—not the final prints. Like the Web Photo Gallery, with the exception of adding your own custom text, this information is pulled from embedded info you enter in the File Info dialog, found under the File menu.

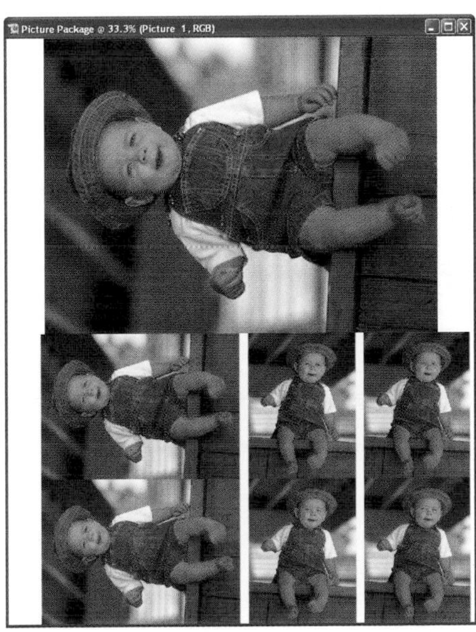

Step Five:

Click OK and Elements automatically resizes, rotates, and compiles your photos into one document (as shown). The one thing many photographers have complained about is that Picture Package doesn't offer you a way to add a white border around each photo in the package, but we've got a workaround for that in Step Six.

Continued

Step Six:

To have a white border appear around your photo in Picture Package, first you have to add it manually before you open Picture Package. So, start by pressing the letter "D" to set your Background color to white, then open your photo. Go under the Image menu, under Resize, and choose Canvas Size. Make sure the Relative box is checked and then enter the amount of white border you'd like in the Width and Height fields (I used 1/4 inch, but 1/2 inch works well too).

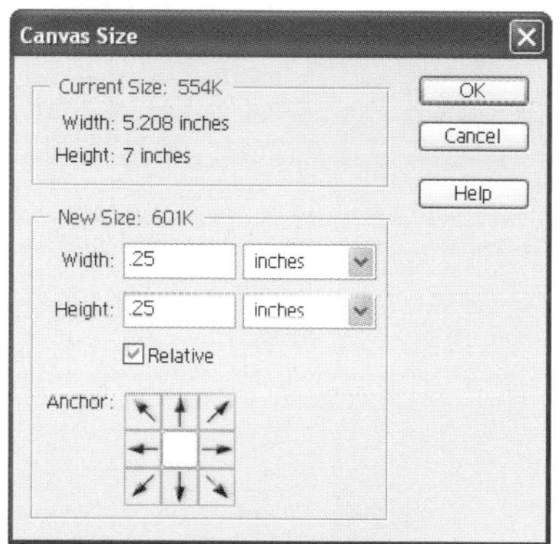

Step Seven:

When you click OK in the Canvas Size dialog, Elements adds a white border around your photo. Now you're ready to go under the File menu, under Print Layouts, and choose Picture Package.

Step Eight:

Here's how your final Picture Package output will look, with a border added around each photo (compare it with the Picture Package output on the previous page with no border). Remember, although the final print sizes will be correct (a 5x7 will still measure 5x7 including the border), adding this white border does make the photo itself a little bit smaller in order to compensate.

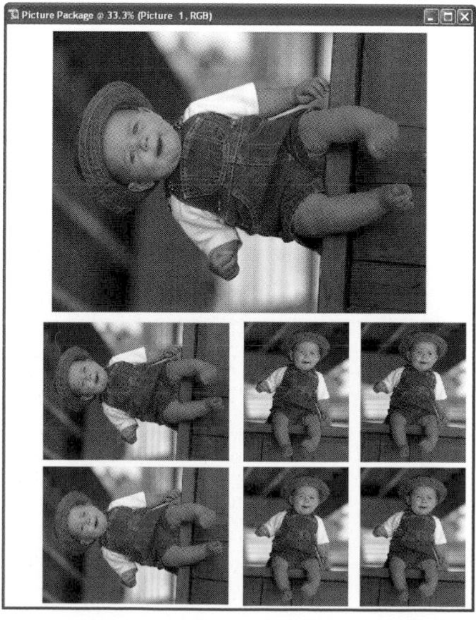

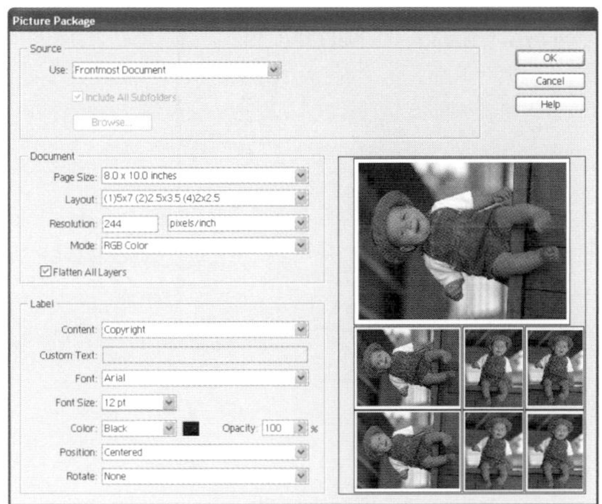

Step Nine:

Another feature of Picture Package is that you can have picture packages that use more than one photo. For example, to change one of the 2.5x3.5 prints to a different photo (while keeping the rest intact), just click on the preview of the image that you want to change to a different photo.

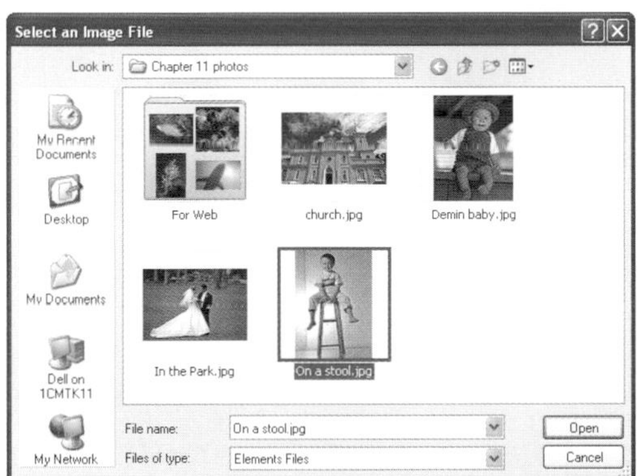

Step Ten:

When you click on this photo, a dialog will appear prompting you to Select an Image File. Navigate to the photo you want to appear here.

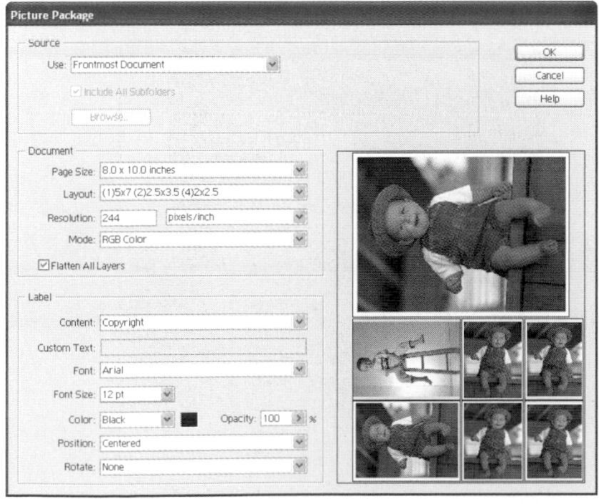

Step Eleven:

Click the Open button and that photo will now appear within your Picture Package (as shown here in the dialog's Preview column). You can replace any other photo (or all of the photos) using the same method.

How to E-Mail Photos

Believe it or not, this is one of those "most asked" questions, and I guess it's because there are no official guidelines for e-mailing photos. Perhaps there should be, because there are photographers who routinely send me high-res photos that either (a) get bounced back to them because of size restrictions, (b) take all day to download, or (c) never get here at all because "there are no official guidelines on how to e-mail photos." In the absence of such rules, consider these the "official unofficial rules."

Step One:

Open the photo in Elements that you want to e-mail. Go under the File menu and choose Attach to E-mail. If your photo is not already in JPEG format, you'll get the warning dialog shown here. I recommend pressing the Auto Convert button, which compresses the file in JPEG format (giving you a dramatically smaller file size—perfect for e-mailing), launches your e-mail application, and attaches the JPEG photo it just created to your e-mail. All you have to do is type in the recipient's e-mail address, and click Send.

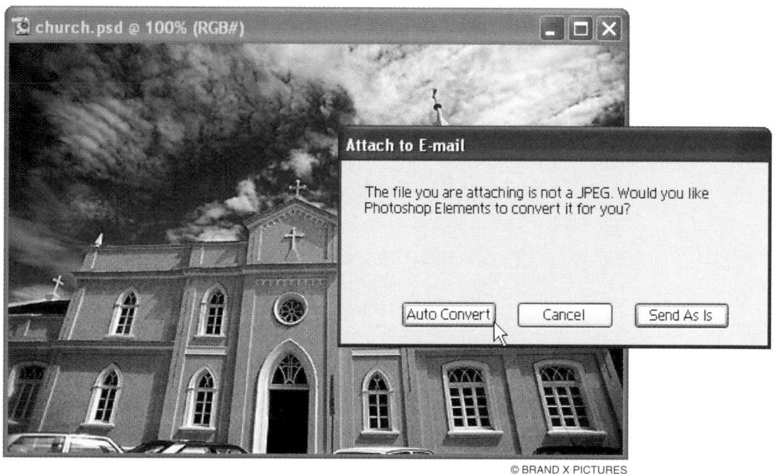

© BRAND X PICTURES

Step Two:

There's a downside to Auto Convert—it lowers your file's resolution (to make it smaller for e-mailing). That's fine if the recipient isn't going to print the photo at high resolution. But if you want to maintain the full resolution of the file, you'll want to choose Send As Is. But before you do that, I recommend saving the high resolution file as a JPEG anyway. That's because most e-mail applications support JPEG image files, and that means the person receiving your e-mail will have no trouble viewing the file, usually from right within their e-mail window. However, if you don't send your photo

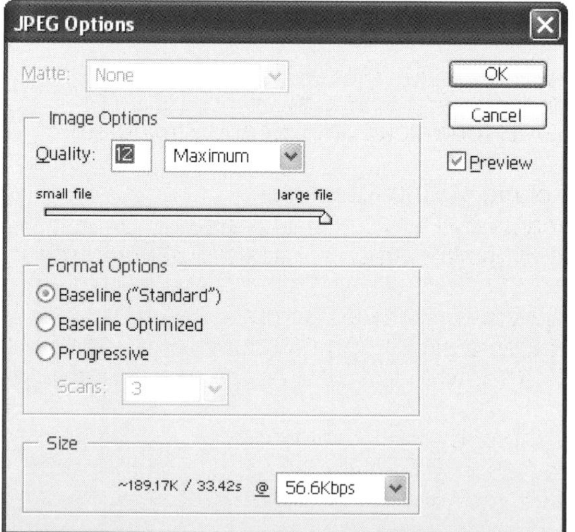

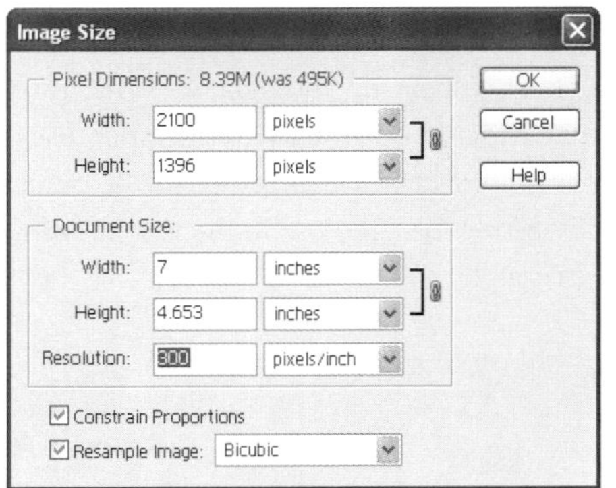

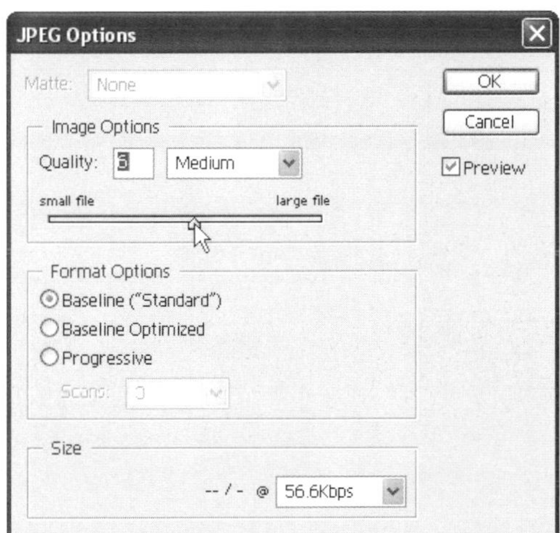

5x7 photo @ 300 Resolution
Saved as a JPEG with 12 Quality
= 2.2MB (download time: nearly 7 minutes)

5x7 photo @ 150 Resolution
Saved as a JPEG with 12 Quality
= 656K (download time: Less than 2 minutes)

5x7 photo @ 300 Resolution
Saved as a JPEG with 6 Quality
= 253K (download time: Less than 1 minute)

5x7 photo @ 150 Resolution
Saved as a JPEG with 6 Quality
= 100K (download time: 18 seconds)

as a JPEG but send it instead as a .PSD file (Elements' native format), the recipient will only be able to view the file if they have Photoshop Elements or Adobe Photoshop. So not only will saving the file as a JPEG reduce the file size (making for faster e-mailing and downloading times), it also makes the file more compatible with your e-mail recipients on both Windows and Mac platforms.

Step Three:

To save the file as a JPEG, go under the File menu and choose Save As. In the Save As dialog box, choose JPEG, then click OK. This brings up the JPEG Options dialog (shown here). This format compresses the file size, while maintaining a reasonable amount of quality. How much quality? That's up to you, because you choose the Quality setting in the JPEG Options dialog. Just remember the golden rule: the higher the quality, the larger the file size, and the longer it will take your client to download it.

Step Four:

Your goal is to e-mail your client a photo that is small in file size (so it downloads quickly), yet still looks as good as possible. (Remember, the faster the download, the lower the quality, so you have to be a little realistic and flexible with this.) The chart shown here gives you a breakdown of how large the file size and download time would be for a 5x7 saved with different resolutions and different amounts of JPEG compression. It's hard to beat that last one—with an 18-second download on a standard dial-up modem.

JIM PATTERSON

A writer/photographer for more than 50 years (yep, a half century), Jim now devotes most of his time to a pretty successful freelance travel writing and photography avocation. He writes the column for *Mac Design Magazine*, called "The Digital Camera," and also writes for *Photoshop User* magazine. Jim is part of the PhotoshopWorld "Instructor Dream Team" and he writes a weekly digital photography column for PlanetPhotoshop.com. He writes numerous reviews on digital cameras, including digital camera and ink-jet "shootouts" for both *Photoshop User* and *Mac Design* magazines. Jim is author of the novel *The Thirteen* and lives with his wife Betty in Largo, Florida

TODD MORRISON

Todd Morrison, a leader in the digital photography revolution, specializes in timeless portraits of infants and children. Todd's consulting company, Zero2Digital.com, offers training and support for portrait studios making the transition to a digital-capture environment. He's also the owner of Morrison Photography (www.morrisonphotography.com). Todd's experience includes commercial, editorial, stock and portrait photography as well as managing all aspects of a professional photo lab. Todd brings real-world experience and advanced Photoshop techniques to digital photographers. Clients include Epson America and Apple Computer. Todd also serves as a contributing writer for *Photoshop User* and *Digital Capture* magazines.

JEANNIE THERIAULT

Jeannie Theriault bought her first camera at a garage sale when she was in third grade. Special people and places have always inspired her work. After escaping the Chicago suburbs, she spent several years in Paris, taught college French and Spanish in Boston, and began alarming her husband by buying progressively more expensive camera equipment. A stint in Puerto Rico, punctuated by summers with friends in the Bahamas and Europe, moved her to begin exhibiting and selling her work. Her photographs will soon appear on greeting cards around the world. Jeannie lives in Jacksonville, Florida, with her husband and two sons.

CAROL FREEMAN

Carol Freeman is a gifted photographer who combines her graphic design and photographic skills with her love and appreciation for the natural world. She has been published in many publications including *The 2002 Audubon Wildflower Calendar, Kew Magazine, Nikon World Magazine*, and others. She is a Nikon-sposored photographer and a guest speaker for Fuji Photo Film USA, conducting seminars on the many intriguing and mystifying aspects of nature photography. Carol's work has won numerous awards, most recently the *Graphic Design USA* award and the Bronze Summit award for her *In Beauty, I Walk* 2002 calendar. Carol is happiest when she is out in nature looking for her next photograph. She can be reached at 847-404-8508.

NANCY ADAMSON

Nancy Adamson is a former chemist who began a career in computer and graphics support at the University of Virginia's Health Sciences Center. There she taught members of the scientific community to use Photoshop for biomedical and scientific imaging. More recently she provided computer and graphics support for the National Institutes of Health (NIH) National Human Genome Research Institute. At both institutions she contributed to publications in numerous papers and scientific journals. She lives in Bowie, Maryland, with her husband and one-year-old son. As an amateur photographer she spends time capturing as many digital images as possible of her toddler.

DAVID MOSER

Dave got his start in professional photography doing equestrian photography, and had his work published in numerous equestrian magazines. He then studied biomedical photography at RIT, before becoming a pioneer in Internet news delivery as one of the founders of Web portal MacCentral.com. Today Dave acts as Chief Operating Officer of KW Media Group, and Publisher of Nikon's *Capture User* magazine. Photography still remains an important part of his life where he now primarily shoots nature and concert shots, and his work appears in numerous Photoshop books.

INDEX

A

Add Noise 190
Adjustment Layer 86, 90–91. *See also* Levels; *See also* Threshold
  drag-and-drop 92
Ames, Kevin 134, 140
Attach to E-mail. *See* e-mail photos
Auto Color Correction. *See* Color Correcting

B

backdrop
  creating 188–191
Background layer 56, 58, 63, 65, 69, 71, 73, 75, 129, 131, 142, 153, 161
  duplicate 64, 66, 124, 128, 138, 148, 168, 170, 172, 182, 192, 208, 225, 227, 230
black-and-white
  colorizing 210–211
  converting from color 99–103
Blend Mode 55, 59, 63
  Color 59, 113, 135, 170, 179, 195, 231
  Darken 146
  Hard Light 228
  Lighten 119, 126, 129, 213
  Luminosity 226, 230
  Multiply 57, 141–142, 194, 209
  Overlay 131
  Screen 63
  Soft Light 133
body sculpting 156–165
  love handles 158–159
  slimming 156–157
    arms 164
    buttocks 160–162
    thighs 162–163
Brush tool 66, 68–69, 126, 131, 135, 139, 141, 170, 173
  Brush Picker 66, 69, 72, 126
  Opacity 126, 131, 133, 141
burn 130, 132–133
Burn tool 130

C

Canvas area 41–42
Canvas Size 196, 244
  Relative checkbox 196
Clone Stamp tool 118–119, 122–123, 129, 146–147, 153, 161, 163, 203–204, 216–217
  Opacity 129, 146, 204
  Options Bar 118, 122
collage 180–181
Color. *See* Blend Mode
  changing 174–175
color aliasing. *See* digital noise
Color Correcting 82–103. *See also* Levels
  Auto Color Correction 93
  flesh tones 94
  one area 96–98
Color Picker 74, 178, 188, 234
Color Settings 80
Color Stop. *See* Gradient Editor
Color Variations 187. *See also* collage
Colorize checkbox. *See* Hue/Saturation
colorizing. *See also* hair; *See also* black-and-white
CompactFlash 4
Contact Sheet 6–12
  font size 8-9
  Thumbnails 7
copy and paste 71
copyright info 234, 237
copyright symbol 234

Crop tool 157. *See also* cropping
add Canvas area 41–42
crop border 34–35
Options Bar 37–38
cropping 29, 34–39, 42, 47. *See also* Image menu
cancel crop 36
completing the crop 36
Crop tool 34, 37–39, 41–42, 47
specific size 37–38
with Rectangular Marquee tool 39–40
Cuerdon, David 148, 230

D

damaged photos 215. *See also* rips, tears, or cracks
repairing 214
Darken. *See* Blend Mode
delete image. *See* File Browser
DeLillo, Helene 160
depth of field 182–183
Digital negatives 4–6
digital noise 58–59
DiVitale, Jim 230
dodge 130, 132–133
Dodge tool 130
Dust & Scratches filter 212

E

e-mail photos 246–247
resolution 246
Easy CD Creator 5
Effects
Clear Emboss 235
Elliptical Marquee tool 107, 168, 184, 190. *See also* selections
Emboss filter 228
emphasizing with color 170–171
Enhance menu 65, 67, 72. *See also* Fill Flash; *See also* Hue/ Saturation; *See also* Levels; *See also* Color Correcting
enlarging images. *See* resizing images
Eraser tool 72, 149, 171, 173
EXIF data. *See* File Browser
eyebrows and eyelashes 140–143
Eyedropper tool
Sample Size 81
eyes. *See also* red eye
recoloring 70–72
removing dark circles 122–123
sharpening 138–139
whitening 136–137

F

facial retouching
hot spots 146–147
lessening freckles or facial acne 124
nose 152
removing blemishes 118–121
removing wrinkles 128–129
skin softening 148–149
transforming a frown into a smile 150–151
Feather Selection 61, 94, 108, 110, 120, 136, 144, 152, 160, 185, 210, 214, 217
File Browser 3–4, 12–27
Batch Rename 22–23
Browse for File 12
delete image 27
Details view 21
docking to the Palette Well 13
EXIF data 15–17, 20
Expanded View 20
meta data 15–17
navigate 15, 19, 23
Preview panel 15, 18–20, 26

rotate image 26–27
Shortcuts Bar 13
Sort By 20
thumbnail 8–10, 15, 18–21, 26–27
View By 19
File Info 237. *See also* copyright info
Fill Flash 63, 65–67
Fill with Overlay-neutral color (50% gray) 131
filters 107
Filter menu 58, 77, 107, 124, 138, 148, 150, 158. *See also* Liquify; *See also* Add Noise; *See also* Find Edges filter; *See also* Gaussian Blur; *See also* Motion Blur; *See also* Render Clouds; *See also* Shear filter; *See also* Dust & Scratches filter; *See also* Emboss filter; *See also* Unsharp Mask
Find Edges filter 193
flash 55–56, 60, 62–63, 65–68. *See also* Fill Flash
blown out subject 56–57
removing unwanted flash 60–62
Flatten Image 64, 102, 195, 209, 226
flesh tones. *See* Color Correcting
Flip Layer Horizontal 215
Foreground color 66, 68, 74, 98, 126, 132, 135, 141, 169, 171, 173, 183, 189–190, 197, 213, 234
Foreground Color Swatch 178
Free Transform 46, 75–76, 153, 156, 199, 236
Options Bar 46, 75, 157
reaching the handles 51
Full Color Management. *See* Color Settings

G

Gaussian Blur 124, 148, 169, 182, 190, 198, 231. *See also* digital noise
Gradient Editor 188–189
Gradient tool 181, 183, 188–189
Gradient Picker 183
Grayscale 99, 210
Grid. *See* straightening crooked images
Group. *See* layers

H

hair
colorizing 134
Hard Light. *See* Blend Mode
Hue/Saturation 72, 95–97, 100, 110, 134, 137, 145, 174–175, 186, 191, 193, 211

I

Image menu
Crop 39–40
Image Size. *See* resizing images
Straighten and Crop 43
Info palette 44
Inverse 185

J

JPEG Options 247

K

keystoning 74–77

L

Lasso tool 60, 71, 94, 109–110, 115, 120, 136, 140, 142, 144, 152, 160, 162, 210, 217
Layer menu
Layer via Copy 140, 162, 164, 168, 170, 172, 192, 196, 215, 225, 227, 230
Layer via Copy 140, 142, 152, 161
layers
create new layer below current layer 180, 182, 197
duplicate 197
fill with Foreground color 179, 197, 234

Group 125, 139, 141–142, 168, 173, 180, 182
hiding
Eye icon 71, 192, 234
merge 73
New Layer dialog 131
Opacity 149, 179, 199
Layers palette 125–126, 138–139, 141–142
Create New Layer icon 56–58, 63–66, 71, 125, 148
More button 64, 130
Flatten Image 64
Opacity 57, 64, 73
Levels 61, 65, 82, 89–91, 100–102, 169, 193, 204
Eyedropper tool 85, 87–88
Target Highlight Color 84
Target Midtone Color 84
Target Shadow Color 83
Lighten. *See* Blend Mode
Line tool 43–44, 75
Options Bar 75
Liquify 150–151, 158–159
Luminosity. *See* Blend Mode

M

Magic Wand tool 111, 176. *See also* selections
Options Bar 111
Magnetic Lasso tool 115
merge layers 73, 197, 199
meta data. *See* File Browser
montage. *See* collage
More button. *See* Layers palette
Motion Blur 172
motion effect 172–173
Move tool 51, 75, 161–162, 164, 180, 191, 198, 215, 236
Multiply. *See* Blend Mode

N

new documents 30
custom sizes 30
New Doc Sizes.txt 30
Preset Sizes 30, 33
resolution 33
nose. *See* facial retouching

O

Options Bar. *See* Crop tool; *See also* Free Transform
Overlay. *See* Blend Mode

P

Paste Into 177
photo into a sketch 192–195
photography filters 179
replicating 178
Photomerge 200–205
Advanced Blending 202
Composition Settings 202
Cylindrical Mapping 202
Lightbox 201
Navigator 201
Perspective 202
Photoshop User magazine 230
Picture Package 242–245
using more than one photo 245
Pinch filter 77
Polaroid™ effect 196–199
printing multiple images on one sheet. *See* Picture Package

R

Rectangular Marquee tool 39, 106–107, 111, 197. *See also* cropping; *See also* selections
red eye 68–70, 73
Red Eye Brush tool 68–69. *See also* red eye
Render Clouds 189
Resample Image. *See* resizing images
Reset Palette Locations 13
resizing images 48–53
  Image Size dialog 48, 50, 52
  increasing the size 52–53
  Resample Image 49–50
resolution 7, 15, 33, 38, 48–50. *See also* resizing images
RGB Color 210
rips, tears, or cracks
  repairing 216–217
Rotate Canvas. *See* straightening crooked images
rotate image. *See* File Browser
Roxio Toast Titanium 5

S

scratches. *See* specks, dust, and scratches
Screen. *See* Blend Mode
selections 60, 61, 106–115. *See also* Feather Selection; *See also* Elliptical Marquee tool; *See also* Lasso tool; *See also* Magic Wand tool; *See also* Magnetic Lasso tool; *See also* Rectangular Marquee tool; *See also* Selection Brush tool
  adding to 106
  constraining 107
  everything on a layer 113
  fill 197
  hide 61–62, 95
  saving 114. *See also* Select menu
Selection Brush tool 112
Select menu 61
  Save Selection 114
sepia tone effect 186–187
sharpening 220–231
  all-purpose 223
  edge sharpening 227
  Luminosity 225–226
  maximum 223
  moderate 222
  portraits 222
  soft subjects 222
  Unsharp Mask 138–139, 219–222, 226–227, 230
    Amount 138, 221–224, 228
    Radius 138, 214, 221–224
    Threshold 138, 221–224
  Web 223
  with layers 230–231
Shear filter 198–199
Shortcuts Bar 13
sky. *See also* Color Correcting: one area
  replacing 176–177
Smartcard 4
Soft Light. *See* Blend Mode
soft light vignette 168–169
specks, dust, and scratches 213
  repairing 212
straightening crooked images 43–44
  using a Grid 45–47
Straighten and Crop. *See* Image menu

T

tears. *See* rips, tears, or cracks
teeth
  whitening 144–145
Threshold 86–87
Type tool 234

U

underexposed photo 63–64
Unsharp Mask. *See also* sharpening

V

View menu 45, 47
vignette 184–185

W

Warp tool 150. *See also* Liquify
washed out photos 208–209
watermarking 234–236
Web Photo Gallery 238–241
Welcome Screen 12
wrinkles. *See* facial retouching

Z

Zoom tool 68, 70

Colophon

The book was produced by the authors and their design team using all Macintosh computers, including a Power Mac G4 733-MHz, a Power Mac G4 Dual Processor 1.25-GHz, a Power Mac G4 Dual Processor 500-MHz, a Power-Mac G4 400-MHz, and an iMac. We use LaCie, Sony, and Apple monitors.

Page layout was done using InDesign 2.0.2. Our graphics server is a Power Mac G3, with a 60-GB LaCie external-drive, and we burn our CDs to a TDK veloCD 32X CD-RW.

The headers for each technique are set in 20 point CronosMM700 Bold with the Horizontal Scaling set to 95%. Body copy is set using CronosMM408 Regular at 10 point on 13 leading, with the Horizontal Scaling set to 95%.

Screen captures were made with Snapz Pro X and were placed and sized within InDesign 2.0. The book was output at 150 line screen, and all in-house proofing was done using a Tektronix Phaser 7700 by Xerox.

Additional Resources

ScottKelbyBooks.com
For information on Scott's other books, visit his book site. For background info on Scott, visit www.scottkelby.com.

http://www.scottkelbybooks.com

National Association of Photoshop Professionals (NAPP)
The industry trade association for Adobe® Photoshop® users and the world's leading resource for Photoshop training, education, and news.

http://www.photoshopuser.com

KW Computer Training Videos
Scott Kelby is featured in a series of more than 20 Photoshop training videos, and DVDs, each on a particular Photoshop topic, available from KW Computer Training.Visit the Web site or call 813-433-5000 for orders or more information.

http://www.photoshopvideos.com

Photoshop Down & Dirty Tricks
Scott is also author of the best-selling book *Photoshop 7 Down & Dirty Tricks*, and the book's companion Web site has all the info on the book, which is available at bookstores around the country.

http://www.downanddirtytricks.com

Adobe Photoshop Seminar Tour
See Scott live at the Adobe Photoshop Seminar Tour, the nation's most popular Photoshop seminars. For upcoming tour dates and class schedules, visit the tour Web site.

http://www.photoshopseminars.com

PhotoshopWorld Conference & Expo
The convention for Adobe Photoshop users has now become the largest Photoshop-only event in the world. Scott Kelby is technical chair and education director for the event, as well as one of the instructors.

http://www.photoshopworld.com

PlanetPhotoshop.com
"The Ultimate Photoshop Site" features Photoshop news, tutorials, reviews, and articles posted daily. The site also contains the Web's most up-to-date resource on other Photoshop related Web sites and information.

http://www.planetphotoshop.com

Photoshop Hall of Fame
Created to honor and recognize those individuals whose contributions to the art and business of Adobe Photoshop have had a major impact on the application or the Photoshop community itself.

http://www.photoshophalloffame.com

Kelby's Notes
Now you can get the answers to the top 100 most-asked Photoshop questions with Kelby's Notes, the plug-in from Scott Kelby. Simply go to the How Do I? menu while in Photoshop, find your question, and the answer appears in an easy-to-read dialog box. Finally, help is just one click away.

http://www.kelbysnotes.com

Mac Design Magazine
Scott is Editor-in-Chief of Mac Design Magazine, "The Graphics Magazine for Macintosh Users." It's a tutorial-based print magazine with how-to columns on Photoshop, Illustrator, InDesign, Dreamweaver, GoLive, Flash, Final Cut Pro, and more. It's also packed with tips, tricks, and shortcuts for your favorite graphics applications.

http://www.macdesignonline.com

The Power of Layer Styles and Media Brushes in Elements 2

WHAT IS A LAYER STYLE?
A Style is a way to improve photos, type, or graphics — instantly! — by "overlaying" color, texture, -dimension, framing and a dozen other effects. All Layer Styles are originally created in the full version of Photoshop but are designed to work magnificently when applied in Elements 2.

WHAT IS A "WOW MEDIA BRUSH?"
Custom brushes, also originally created in Photoshop, can also be used in Elements 2 to imitate natural media effects like watercolors, pastel drawings and oil paintings – using colors "cloned" from your original photographs.

Simply stated, a Layer Style is a "look" that you can add to photos, type, or graphics instantly — simply by loading a Styles set from the Layer Styles palette and clicking on an specific Style **A.**

You may have run into a few especially nice sets of Layer Styles in your explorations of Elements – such as Wow Chrome, Wow Neon and Wow Plastic- which were created by Jack Davis and are built right into Adobe Photoshop Elements 2 as presets **B.**

To the right are a few of the highly sophisticated kinds of effects you can apply with the Styles from the ***Adobe Photoshop Elements One-Click Wow!*** CD-ROM (Adobe Press). To create such treatments *without* using Layer Styles could take a considerable amount of time, effort, extensive custom patterns and not a small amount of patience.

Layer Styles can create single-mouse-click photo enhancements such as tints **C** (Wow-Tint FX 06), soft-edged border treatments **D** (Wow-Edges 10), darkroom effects, duotone and antiquing treatments, paint and canvas textures, film grain and digital noise overlays, frames **E** (Wow-Frame 05), **F** (Wow-Frame 08), and even vignettes.

A

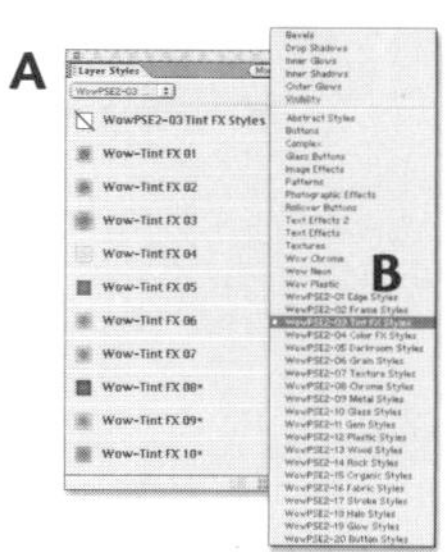

C

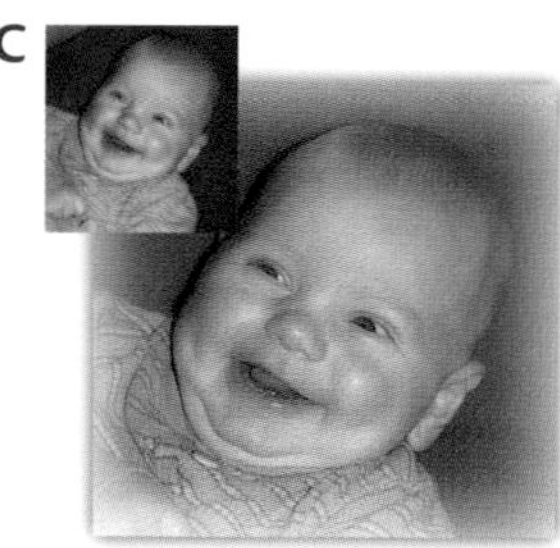

D

E

F

G

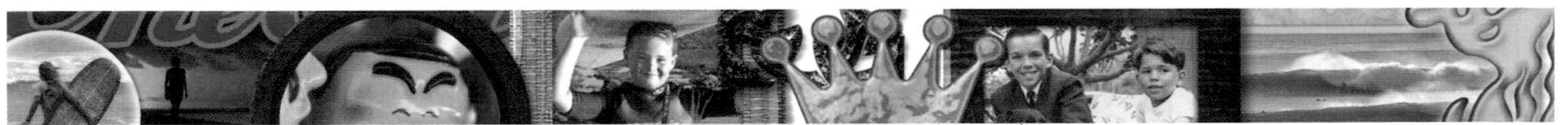

Styles can also be used to instantly unify a set of images, either to be used separately or as a collage **G** (Wow-Tint FX 02).

Elements can finally paint! By crafting custom brush tips, detailed settings and embedded paper and canvas textures **H** using the full version of Photoshop, and then optimizing them for use in Elements 2, One-Click Wow! has created a set of tools that for the first time allows Elements users to enjoy the pleasure of imitating natural art media on the computer.

There are dozens of custom natural-media One-Click Wow! Brushes for turning your photos into watercolors, oils, pastels, or other media **I**.

A Wow Style can also turn plain type or graphics into convincing material objects, such as polished chrome **J** (Wow-Chrome 15), woven mat **K** (Wow-Organics 05), mezzo tint etchings **L** (Wow-Halo 13), transparent blue plastic **M** (Wow-Plastics 08) or glowing tortoise shell **N** (Wow-Gems 16 and 19).

The Wow Presets on these pages are from the ***Adobe Photoshop Elements 2 One-Click Wow!*** book and CD-ROM by Jack Davis, and were created to be an indispensable companion to the Adobe Photoshop Elements program. For more information and sample Wow Styles (including the ones shown here) and Media Brushes see www.scottkelbybooks.com.

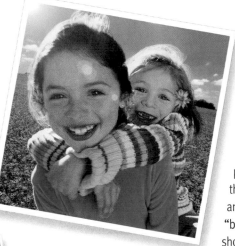

expert**TIPS**

[Scanning with Microtek ScanWizard™ Pro & Adobe® Photoshop® Elements]

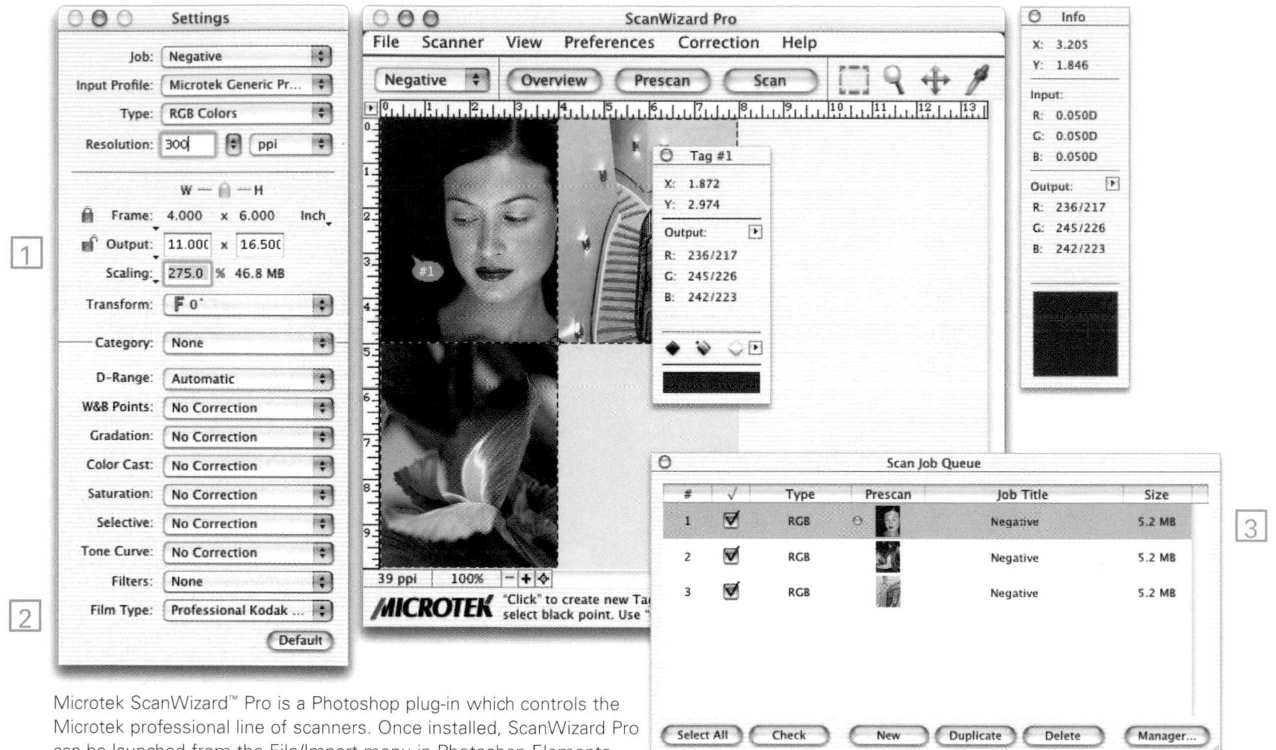

Microtek ScanWizard™ Pro is a Photoshop plug-in which controls the Microtek professional line of scanners. Once installed, ScanWizard Pro can be launched from the File/Import menu in Photoshop Elements.

1 work**BIGGER**
[scaling & resolution]

You've got a 4" x 6" original which you'd like to print on 11" x 17" paper at 300 dpi. Don't dig out the calculator, or worry about resolution settings. Leave the resolution at the desired end result, 300 dpi. Lock the frame and proportions by clicking on the lock icons. Then type your new width into the Output field; the correct height and scaling are automatically generated. The software will automatically scan the image at the appropriate optical resolution for the enlargement, resize it and deliver the correct file to Adobe Photoshop Elements. This saves calculation time as well as a File Size step in Photoshop Elements.

2 work**SMARTER**
[using film profiles]

Film types vary between manufacturers as well as brands. This means scans from the film will vary too. Using profiles in ScanWizard Pro for film scanning can dramatically increase the color accuracy of your image with literally no effort. Just choose your film type from the pull-down menu and continue scanning. The applied profile will automatically compensate for your specific film type and be embedded into the file. When the file is delivered to Adobe Photoshop Elements, you have an image which closely matches its original. Now you can use Elements to acheive other affects instead of dealing with color corrections.

3 work**FASTER**
[batch scanning]

Batch scanning is a great time-saver when you've got more than one image to scan. Place your originals on the scan bed, click the Overview button, and then marquee each of the images while holding down the Shift key. This will automatically create multiple jobs in the Scan Job Queue window. Each job represents a separate scanned file. When you have applied your desired settings to the images, click the Scan button. All of the images will then be scanned and sent to Adobe Photoshop Elements for further processing. You can even choose to simply scan them to file and open them in Elements at a later date.

ArtixScan 4000tf* ArtixScan 120tf*

ScanMaker 9800XL

ScanMaker 8700 Pro

ArtixScan 1800f

ArtixScan 2500f

www.microtekusa.com

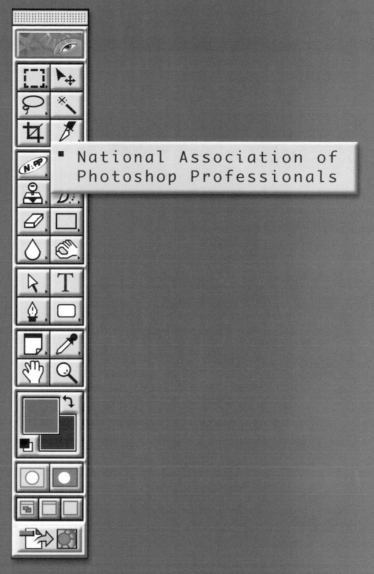

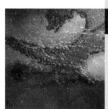

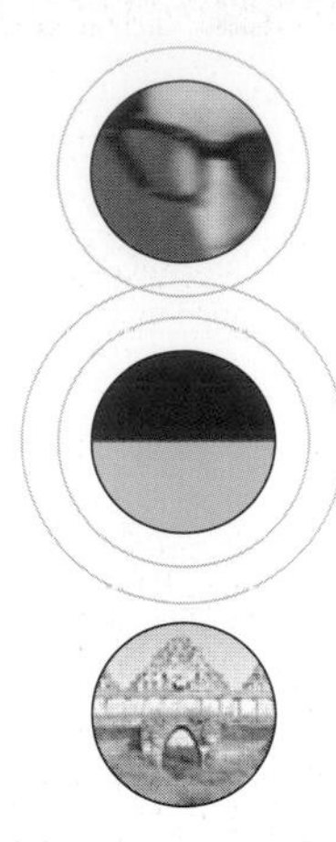
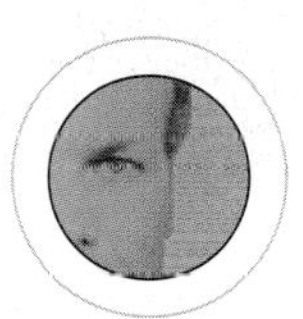

VOICES THAT MATTER

HOW TO CONTACT US

VISIT OUR WEB SITE

WWW.NEWRIDERS.COM

On our Web site you'll find information about our other books, authors, tables of contents, indexes, and book errata. You will also find information about book registration and how to purchase our books.

EMAIL US

Contact us at this address: **nrfeedback@newriders.com**

- If you have comments or questions about this book
- To report errors that you have found in this book
- If you have a book proposal to submit or are interested in writing for New Riders
- If you would like to have an author kit sent to you
- If you are an expert in a computer topic or technology and are interested in being a technical editor who reviews manuscripts for technical accuracy
- To find a distributor in your area, please contact our international department at this address. **nrmedia@newriders.com**
- For instructors from educational institutions who want to preview New Riders books for classroom use. Email should include your name, title, school, department, address, phone number, office days/hours, text in use, and enrollment, along with your request for desk/examination copies and/or additional information.
- For members of the media who are interested in reviewing copies of New Riders books. Send your name, mailing address, and email address, along with the name of the publication or Web site you work for.

BULK PURCHASES/CORPORATE SALES

The publisher offers discounts on this book when ordered in quantity for bulk purchases and special sales. For sales within the U.S., please contact: Corporate and Government Sales (800) 382-3419 or **corpsales@pearsontechgroup.com**. Outside of the U.S., please contact: International Sales (317) 581-3793 or **international@pearsontechgroup.com**.

WRITE TO US

New Riders Publishing
800 East 96th Street, 3rd Floor
Indianapolis, IN 46240

CALL US

Toll-free (800) 571-5840. Ask for New Riders.
If outside U.S. (317) 428-3000. Ask for New Riders.

FAX US

(317) 428-3280

WWW.NEWRIDERS.COM